Craig Claiborne's Favorites

SERIES II

Books by Craig Claiborne

The New York Times Cook Book
The New York Times Menu Cook Book
Craig Claiborne's Kitchen Primer
Cooking with Herbs and Spices
Classic French Cooking
WITH PIERRE FRANEY
The New York Times International Cook Book
The Chinese Cookbook
WITH VIRGINIA LEE
Craig Claiborne's Favorites Volume One

Craig Claiborne's Favorites from The New York Times

SERIES II

Times
BOOKS

We are indebted to a number of photographers and artists
whose work is reproduced in this book:
Bill Aller, pages 24, 31, 84, 161, 191, 196, 208, 214, 220, 228,
236, 244, 276, 309, 367, 373, 386, 408.
Karen Beckhardt, page 265.
Don Bierman, page 36.
Diana Bryan, page 63.
Nelson Bryant, page 46.
Michael Cook, page 79.
Culver Pictures Inc., page 131.
Tony Esparza, page 398.
Enrico Ferorelli, page 348.
Alice Golden, page 284.
James Hamilton, pages 55, 116, 118, 141, 252, 257, 296, 299.
J. Hnizdovsky, page 76.
André Kértesz, page 312.
Robert M. Klein, page 172.
Neil Libbert, page 377.
Carlos Llerena, page 272.
Gene Maggio, pages 21, 93, 134, 325.
James Mathews, page 330.
Jack Nisberg, pages 336, 357.
Noon, page 44.
Anne Raymo, page 304.
Richard Samperi, pages 168, 390.
George Stavrinos, page 109.
David Strick, pages 104, 111, 124.
George Tames, page 316.
Michel Tcherevkoff, page 271.
United Press International, page 88.
Alfred Wegener, pages 70, 404.

The Russell Baker article which appears on pages 357–359 is copyright © 1975 by
The New York Times Company. Reprinted by permission.

Published simultaneously in Canada by Optimum Publishing
Company Limited, 245 rue St-Jacques, Montreal, Quebec H2Y1M6.

Series editor: Ann Bramson
Design: Paul Hanson

Library of Congress Cataloging in Publication Data

Claiborne, Craig.
Craig Claiborne's Favorites from the New York times.

Includes index.
1. Cookery. I. Title: Favorites from the New York times.
TX715.C5743 1975   641.5   75-10599
ISBN: 0-517-324180

In memory of
Jeannette Edwards Rattray,
devoted friend, great author,
publisher of
The East Hampton Star

Contents

Foreword   13

January

Spaghetti in Foil   19
Indian Pudding   25
Chef Alfredo Viazzi   30
Cooking with Honey   35
Potatoes: Beyond Baked and Boiled   42
Cod: A Winter Gift from the Sea   45
Borscht, and Other Main Courses   50
Chef Tsung Ting Wang   54

February

Elegance, en Masse   63
Smoke Cookery   66
A Connecticut Cook   69
Pride of the Forest   75
Lessons from a Master   77
Persian Cookery   83
Stuffed Vegetables   88
Some Thoughts about Samp   91
Cooking as Therapy   92

March

The Barefoot Caterers of Malibu   103
Beans Any Old Time   108
Danny Kaye Cooks Chinese   110
Kitchen Help   115
Scandinavian Specialties   123
After the Easter Bunny   129
German Specialties   132

April

English Cookery   139
Sushi: Natural Wonder   144

The Dish Mother Used to Make *149*
Chef Jean Banchet *152*
A Passion for Chicken Wings *157*
Sausage Without Additives *160*
Admirably Stuffed *165*
Cooking Flatfish *168*
Chef Luigi Nanni *171*

May

Great Bird *179*
Russian Cookery *182*
A Well-Seasoned Liverwurst *187*
Sherry Wine Vinegar *189*
Southern Gumbo *193*
A Few Fine Cooks Revisited *196*
All Goulash *202*

June

Recipes for Lamb *207*
The Sausage Patty *212*
The Japanese Grill *214*
Chef Paul Bocuse *219*

July

A Summer Bounty *227*
The Fresh Coriander Leaf *232*
The Après-Honeymoon Cookbook *237*
The Golden Glories of Corn *243*
Cold Soups *249*
A Weekend with Diana Kennedy *251*

August

Spiked Pie *263*
Scrambled Stuffing *265*
Hot Summer, Hot Soup *269*
Seafood Trio *272*
A Summer Picnic *275*

September

Sorrel 283
Delectably Greek 288
Side Dish, Front and Center 291
Chef Wen Dah Tai 295
Pork as Caviar 303

October

Roadside Find 309
Egg Power 312
The Culinary Challenges of the South 315
Caterers' Choice 324
Vinegared 330
Chef Michel Guérard 333

November

Surprise à l'Anglaise 345
Beyond Lasagna 348
Dinner for Two in Paris 351
Tailgate Feast 361
The Bialy 364
Fennel: Crisp and Aromatic 366
No Turkey Thanksgiving 372
A Visit with Jane Grigson 375
Deviled 381

December

The Art of Preserved Goose 385
More Sausage, Homemade 390
For the Nostalgic: Salt-Rising Bread 392
Cold Weather Soups 394
From the Repertoire of Dinah Shore 397
Party Pâté 404
Chili con Carne 407

Sources for Foreign Ingredients 413
Index 417

Foreword

We are endlessly impressed with the subtle yet seemingly rapid increase in the sophistication of American taste. We can recall with utmost
clarity that 15 years ago—that was shortly after we joined *The New
York Times*—99 people out of 100 in this country would not have been
familiar with the word "zucchini." Back in those days, we used the generic term "green squash" when referring to the vegetable. Sometimes
we would elaborate and say "green or Italian squash." Little by little we
would refer to it as zucchini, explaining that this was green squash or
Italian squash. Today the country seems absolutely flooded with recipes calling for zucchini. There are even books dedicated solely to the
vegetable.

Similarly, Americans are knowledgeable with approximately four
kinds of pasta: spaghetti, lasagne, macaroni, of course, and perhaps ziti.
Linguine, which is now almost as common as lasagne, was all but unheard of less than two decades ago. With the recognition of linguine
came the formidable discovery of pesto genovese, that incomparable
sauce made with fresh basil and pine nuts. (Selfishly we rather deplore
that widespread popularity in that the cost of pine nuts has skyrocketed
within the last ten years and they are difficult to find at all when fresh
basil is in season.)

Harking back to the dark ages, which is to say, our childhood, there
was one exotic dish served throughout America, and that was curry.
Curried dishes, generally served with an assortment of garnishes, such
as chopped peanuts, grated coconut, fried onion rings, bacon bits, chutney, and so on, were really the bee's knees of that generation. As we
approached maturity, America suddenly discovered boeuf à la bourguignonne and coq au vin. Crème brûlée became a choice dessert. At approximately the same time, the delights of the shish kebab and steak tartare
became known, and Caesar salad became the national rage. Then came
quiche Lorraine, the making of which has become a national pastime,
and beef Wellington (for which we hold no high regard). Artichokes,
once considered the exotic, have become something of a commonplace;
shallots, once one of the rarest members of the onion family in America,
can now be found in thousands of supermarkets. We have had some
small hand, we hope, in introducing the public to the pleasures of imported mustards such as Dijon and Düsseldorf and weaning the public
away from "ball-park mustard" which we consider ideal for hot dogs
mid-game.

A correlative to all of this is the extraordinary proliferation of Japanese restaurants in America, particularly in metropolitan areas. Similarly, Chinese restaurants have become infinitely more sophisticated and have joined the French as part of the luxury class. Almost everyone we know seems to have discovered the joys of fresh coriander so widely employed in Chinese cooking, and in Mexican and Indian cookery as well.

One of the pleasures of writing a cooking column in the third quarter of the twentieth century is having an enthusiastic, responsive audience. In this day and age, we can discuss charcuterie or a chiffonade of lobster and feel confident we are not striking an indifferent chord. The time has literally arrived when Americans know no bounds when it's a question of taste and the ins and outs of international cookery. So, being that you know all about quiche Lorraine and beef burgundy (and who doesn't), we urge you to try your hand at some of the more unfamiliar recipes encased between these covers. Should you come upon a recipe for a pastry roll discovered in Vietnam or for such a basic and earnest dish as the Mexican stew called pozole, be adventurous. Try it. Remember that once quiche Lorraine was unfamiliar too.

Craig Claiborne's Favorites

SERIES II

January 1975

WE HAD A GOOD time last January on several counts. We discovered a fascinating method of cooking clams with spaghetti in foil or paper; we became involved in a most amusing imbroglio over Indian pudding; Alfredo Viazzi and his marvelous wife the actress Jane White came out to visit and cook Italian; we flew to Chicago to enlighten ourselves about bee-keeping, honey, and the uses thereof in cookery. And what a climax to a month: Chef T. T. Wang came to our kitchen to instruct in the making of some of our favorite Chinese dishes, chief among them, perhaps, his chicken soong. This is a seraphic first course that consists of marvelously flavored cubed chicken blended with pine nuts and served in a lettuce leaf so it can be eaten out of hand. We are frequently asked to name our favorite Chinese restaurants in Manhattan. Chef Wang's Shun Lee Palace would most certainly highlight that list, along with Uncle Tai's Hunan Yuan (see page 295), and Pearl's Chinese. Rarely a week goes by that we don't dine at one of the three.

Spaghetti in Foil

It was a come-on, of course, but uncommonly compelling. It was an advertisement of Alitalia airlines and it stated in part, "Unless you've been to the Trattoria di Ciccio in Amalfi, you don't know how spaghetti should taste. First, Ciccio makes a sauce with clams and olives. Next he boils some spaghetti. Then he puts both things into a paper bag, folds it shut and heats it in an oven. What comes out of that paper bag isn't just spaghetti with sauce on it. But spaghetti with sauce in it."

To our great regret we've never been to Amalfi and never dined with di Ciccio but with enough of a clue from Alitalia we've contrived what must be a fair approximation of his dish.

Interestingly enough, paper bag cooking, although never widespread in Europe, has a long and interesting history. In French it is called *en papillote*. In Italian it is *al cartoccio*.

We have in our possession a book by one Nicolas Soyer titled *Soyer's Paper-Bag Cookery*, published in New York in 1911. Mr. Soyer, the frontispiece notes, was the "late chef of the Brooks's Club in London," and his book embraces such fare as stewed eels and stuffed haddock, Irish stew and curried venison. There are listings for savory oysters and a salmis of duck.

The most famous—indeed the most celebrated—cooked-in-paper dish in America is the New Orleans specialty, pompano en papillote. In France, veal chops are occasionally cooked in paper. In both cases, and doubtlessly what di Ciccio in Italy employs, parchment paper is used to make the "bag" or casing.

In the dish we fabricated recently we used a double fold of heavy-duty aluminum foil and it worked admirably. Heavy freezer paper works well too, whereas parchment is far less available and has a tendency at times to burn in a very hot oven.

There is reason to believe that in the di Ciccio dish, whole baby clams are used. Baby clams are not allowed to be taken in American waters but chopped raw clams—littleneck or cherrystone—are excellent. It is possible to substitute canned clams with the canned juice and this, too, will work, although canned clams are canned clams are canned clams.

The technique for preparing the dish is quite simple and the results are infinitely superior to the traditional method of making spaghetti or linguine with white or "red" clam sauce. Cooked in foil (or parchment or heavy freezer paper), the pasta seems literally infused with the sauce.

Somehow, too, the clams seem more tender.

To prepare the dish, spaghetti or linguine is parboiled for exactly five minutes. It is quickly drained and emptied, along with sauce and the chopped clams, into a baking dish lined with heavy-duty aluminum foil or freezer paper. The foil or paper is sealed as hermetically as possible taking care that steam or liquid cannot escape as the mixture cooks. The dish is baked in a very hot oven for exactly ten minutes and it is ready to serve.

The pouch is opened either with scissors or the fingers, using a cloth to guard against burning. The spaghetti and sauce are distributed into one or more soup bowls and served immediately.

Up to a pound of spaghetti may be cooked in this method but smaller batches—either a half pound or a quarter pound—seem preferable. One of the recipes given here calls for a quarter pound of spaghetti, the other for a half pound. To increase the amount of spaghetti simply multiply all the other ingredients accordingly.

Imported pasta—widely available in Italian markets—does, to our way of thinking, work best in these recipes. In both recipes, linguine can be substituted for spaghetti.

Note: The sizes of clams vary considerably and so does the inner liquid they yield. It may be necessary to use more or fewer clams to produce the volumes indicated. Cherrystone clams can be used in place of littlenecks, but they may not be as tender.

Foil-Wrapped Spaghetti in Red Clam Sauce

1   cup tomato sauce (see recipe)
20   black olives, preferably imported Greek or Italian
24   to 30 littleneck clams, approximately (see note)
½   pound spaghetti

1. Preheat the oven to 500 degrees.

2. Prepare the tomato sauce and have it heated just to the point of boiling.

3. Remove the pits from the black olives and cut the olives in half. Add this to the tomato sauce. Bring to the boil and keep very hot while finishing the dish.

4. Line a baking dish with a double layer of heavy-duty aluminum foil, leaving the edges and ends free to be folded later into a package. Gently press the center of the foil to make a "well" for the spaghetti when it is cooked.

5. Open the clams and drain them, reserving both clams and their juice. There should be about a ½ cup of clams and at least ¾ cup of juice. Use only ¾ cup of juice. Heat the clam broth until nearly boiling. Chop the clams and set aside.

Left, top to bottom: (1) Open clams. (2) Line baking dish with foil. (3) Pour parboiled spaghetti into dish.

Right, top to bottom: (4) Add sauce and clams. (5) Seal foil securely. (6) Serve.

6. Drop the spaghetti into boiling salted water and stir until it becomes limp. Cook exactly 5 minutes; no longer.

7. Immediately drain the spaghetti into a colander and empty it into the center of the foil. Add the tomato sauce, clam broth, and clams. Quickly bring up the ends of the foil and seal securely all around, taking care that the sauce ·cannot leak and steam cannot escape at any point. Place the dish in the oven and bake exactly 10 minutes.

8. Remove the dish from the oven and, using a cloth and scissors, cut open the top of the foil. Transfer the spaghetti with the sauce to individual spaghetti bowls and serve immediately. Serve with freshly grated Parmesan cheese, if desired.

Yield: 2 main dish servings or 4 first course servings.

Note: This recipe may be doubled, but the baking time should be increased to about 12 minutes.

Tomato sauce

4   *cups red, ripe, fresh or canned peeled tomatoes, chopped or crushed*
2   *tablespoons olive oil*
1   *tablespoon chopped garlic, more or less to taste*
½   *cup finely chopped parsley Salt and freshly ground black pepper*
1   *teaspoon dried oregano*
1   *tablespoon dried basil*
¼   *teaspoon dried red pepper flakes, more or less to taste, optional*

1. Place the tomatoes in a saucepan and cook over moderate heat, stirring frequently, until the tomatoes are reduced to about 2 cups.

2. Heat the oil in a saucepan and add the garlic. Cook briefly without browning. Add the tomatoes, parsley, salt, pepper, oregano, basil, and pepper flakes. Cook, stirring, until thoroughly blended. Remove from the heat.

Yield: About 2 cups.

Note: This sauce will keep well stored tightly covered in the refrigerator. It can be frozen.

Foil-Wrapped Spaghetti in White Clam Sauce

12   *to 16 littleneck clams, approximately (see note)*
2   *tablespoons olive oil or equal amounts of oil and butter*
1   *clove garlic, finely minced*
½   *teaspoon dried thyme or oregano*
¼   *pound spaghetti (see note)*
2   *tablespoons finely chopped parsley*
¼   *teaspoon pepper flakes, more or less to taste, optional*
2   *teaspoons cognac Freshly ground black pepper*

1. Preheat the oven to 500 degrees.

2. Measure, chop and have at

hand all the ingredients necessary for this recipe before starting to cook.

3. Line a baking dish with a double layer of heavy-duty aluminum foil, leaving the edges and ends free to be folded later into a package. Gently press the center of the foil to make a "well" for the spaghetti.

4. Open the clams and drain them, reserving both clams and ½ cup of juice. Chop the clams and set aside.

5. In a small saucepan, heat the oil and add the garlic. Cook briefly without browning and add ½ cup of clam broth and thyme. Bring just to the boil but do not boil.

6. Drop the spaghetti into boiling salted water and stir until it becomes limp. Cook exactly 5 minutes; no longer.

7. Drain quickly into a colander and empty the spaghetti into the center of the foil. Sprinkle with parsley and pepper flakes and add the nearly boiling clam broth mixture and clams. Add the cognac and freshly ground pepper. Quickly bring up the ends of the foil and seal securely all around, taking care that the broth cannot leak and the steam cannot escape at any point. Place the dish in the oven and bake exactly 10 minutes.

8. Remove the dish from the oven and, using a cloth and scissors, cut open the top of the foil. Transfer the spaghetti with the sauce to 1 or 2 spaghetti bowls and serve immediately.

Yield: 1 main dish serving or 2 first course servings.

Note: This recipe may be doubled or quadrupled. If it is quadrupled the baking time must be increased to about 12 minutes.

Perhaps it is a misuse of the word, but we felt it a touch of serendipity when browsing through the pages of *The New York Times*, we discovered the airline ad extolling the ambrosial delights of a clam dish made by the chef of a small restaurant in Italy. The suggestion had particular appeal in that we live in what is to our mind the best clam country in America. The clams from the waters around Long Island are as fat, sweet, and tender as you're apt to find anywhere in the world.

For the nonexpert and would-be clam shucker there are two things to remember that enormously facilitate opening the bivalves. Clams are closed tightly because of the powerful (but delicious and tender) muscle that joins the two shells and keeps the shells well-seated. If the clams are well-chilled before they are to be opened, the muscle tends to relax. The clams can be chilled for several hours in the refrigerator or briefly (without freezing) in the freezer. It is also imperative that the clam knife be sharp to facilitate its insertion between the "jaws" of the clam. Avoid

Opening clams can be a tricky business. One hint: Chill them first, either in refrigerator for several hours or briefly in the freezer.

those guillotinelike clam-shucking gadgets. They mangle clams and are quite frankly an abomination.

Indian Pudding

WITH PIERRE FRANEY

If there was ever such a thing as a "classic" American dessert, it must be Indian pudding—much more valid than apple pie, which has a European heritage. We know of one recipe for Indian pudding, a variation of which is said to have been served in a New England family for nearly 200 years. It is that of Kathleen and Sam Scranton of Minneapolis. Their forebears started the custom of serving Indian pudding during the cold winter days in Connecticut. "Originally," Sam Scranton says, "it was served with hard sauce. Then Delmonico sauce became the family favorite." Delmonico sauce is an English custard flavored with vanilla.

Kathleen and Sam Scranton's Indian Pudding

5   cups milk
⅔   cup yellow cornmeal
    Salt
1   cup finely chopped beef suet
1   cup molasses
1   cup sugar
1   large egg
1   seedless orange
1   cup seedless raisins
½   cup dried currants
½   teaspoon ground cinnamon
½   teaspoon ground allspice
½   teaspoon ground cloves
½   teaspoon grated nutmeg
1   teaspoon baking powder

1. Preheat oven to 300 degrees.

2. Bring 4 cups of milk just to the boil and add it to the top of a double boiler. Gradually add the cornmeal, stirring constantly with a wire whisk. Stir in salt to taste and suet. Cook, stirring, about 20 minutes.

3. Stir in the molasses, sugar, and egg.

4. Trim off the stem end of the orange. Slice the orange thinly, then cut each slice—flesh, skin, juices and all—into very small cubes. Add the orange to the cornmeal mixture.

5. Finely chop or grind the raisins and add them. Add the currants and all the spices. Blend remaining cup of milk with baking powder and stir it in.

6. Generously butter a 2-quart crock or casserole, preferably made of stoneware. Pour in the mixture. Do not cover. Bake about 2 to 2½ hours. Serve warm with Delmonico sauce or vanilla ice cream.

Yield: 8 or more servings.

Delmonico sauce

5 egg yolks
⅔ cup sugar
2 cups milk
⅛ teaspoon salt
1 teaspoon vanilla extract

1. Place the yolks in a saucepan and add the sugar. Beat with a wire whisk until thick and lemon-colored.

2. Meanwhile, bring the milk almost but not quite to the boil.

3. Gradually add the milk to the yolk mixture, beating constantly. Use a wooden spoon and stir constantly, this way and that, making certain that the spoon touches all over the bottom of the saucepan. Cook, stirring, and add the salt and vanilla. Cook until the mixture has a custardlike consistency and coats the sides of the spoon. Do not let the sauce boil, or it will curdle.

4. Immediately remove the sauce from the stove, but continue stirring. Set the saucepan in a basin of cold water to reduce the temperature. Let the sauce cool to room temperature. Chill for an hour or longer.

Yield: 8 to 12 servings.

If Americans by and large cannot be called ardent epicures, there are, apparently, a dozen or so dishes about which they care passionately enough to take up their chef's knives and do battle.

These ire-arousing preparations include clam chowders, white and red; chili con carne; Boston baked beans; mint juleps; and, on the eastern tip of Long Island at least, clam pies.

We would have ranked Indian pudding relatively low on that list and we would have been mistaken, for rarely has any column elicited such a heated response as did this one.

"An emotional reaction seized me upon reading—and incredulously re-reading—the recipe for Indian pudding," Mrs. H. F. Fultz of Glen Ridge, New Jersey, wrote. It is "drastically twentieth century" and has "suffered more fanciful accretions over the years than the legends of some saints."

The basic recipe, she added, was "cornmeal, milk, molasses, with fresh-grated nutmeg, and a touch of ginger" in a buttered crockery bowl or deep granite pan.

"When Indian-meal was first combined with Barbados molasses and plentiful skimmed milk, white sugar was very expensive; it came in a loaf, was used for tea (lumps) and delicate recipes and would never have been wasted on an already sweet pudding."

In addition to which, the reader notes, "Possibly our not using raisins was an economy measure; the seeded black sultanas were expensive. Wasn't it about 1918 that the Thompson seedless came along? The milk and cornmeal cured (not curdled) together with the molasses. . . . Baking powder was unheard of, and unnecessary to boot." And so on.

Mary Willard Roe of Peterborough, New York, not only chastised us for that "ridiculous travesty," but added that Indian pudding was "invented" by poor country people who had cornmeal and molasses as staples of their diet.

"The recipe below may not be of antiquity—the tapioca is an effete nineteenth-century touch—but it is a lot closer to authenticity."

Indian Pudding

3 tablespoons cornmeal
3 tablespoons tapioca
½ cup molasses
¼ cup brown sugar
½ teaspoon salt

½ teaspoon ground cinnamon
½ teaspoon grated nutmeg
¼ teaspoon ground cloves
4 cups milk

Mix together and bake about 2 hours in a slow oven. Stir every half hour or so, oftener at the beginning.

"Fannie Farmer goes in for scalding the milk first, which is unnecessary. She also allows 2 eggs. My daughter used that recipe once, but forgot to stir it, so that she ended up with 2 perfect hard-boiled eggs in the middle of the pudding."

Ms. Roe's good-natured wrath was duly recorded in a subsequent column but far from staying the fray, it served to stimulate it.

A generous letter from Mrs. Lewis Cage of Rowayton, Connecticut, states, "I will mercifully withhold comments on the use of tapioca—and nonuse of eggs" in that last Indian pudding recipe. "Permit me to contribute something—even at this late date—to the Indian Pudding Controversy. Attached is a truly *excellent* recipe." The recipe is attributed to the Toll House Restaurant, Whitman, Massachusetts.

Baked Indian Pudding

3 cups milk
3 tablespoons yellow
  cornmeal

½ cup dark molasses
1 egg
½ cup sugar
1 tablespoon melted butter
½ teaspoon ground ginger
½ teaspoon cinnamon
  Salt

1. Preheat oven to 300 degrees.

2. Heat the milk in a saucepan and when it comes to the boil, gradually stir in the cornmeal, using a wire whisk. Cook, stirring constantly, until slightly thickened. Stir in the molasses.

3. Beat the egg in a large mixing bowl and add the sugar, butter, ginger, cinnamon, and salt to taste. Pour in the hot mixture, stirring rapidly. When thoroughly blended, pour the mixture into a greased baking dish. Bake 1 hour or until a knife inserted in the center comes out clean.

Yield: 6 servings.

We were also deluged with recipes that offered what is conceivably the most famous Indian pudding recipe in the world, that of the Durgin Park Restaurant in Boston:

Durgin Park's Indian Pudding

1 cup yellow cornmeal
½ cup black molasses
¼ cup sugar
¼ cup lard or butter
¼ teaspoon salt
¼ teaspoon baking soda
2 eggs, well beaten
6 cups hot milk

1. Preheat oven to 250 degrees.

2. Combine the cornmeal, molasses, sugar, butter, salt, soda, eggs, and half the milk in a mixing bowl. Stir with a wire whisk to blend well.

3. Stir in the remaining milk and pour into a well-greased baking dish, preferably a stone crock, and bake for 5 to 7 hours.

Yield: 8 to 12 servings.

One of the most fascinating pudding recipes came from Mrs. Ivy Dodd of Rockland, Maine. Mrs. Dodd is with the book division of Rockland's *Courier-Gazette*, which has published such books as *Maine Cookery—Then and Now* and *All-Maine Cooking*.

"Traditionally," Mrs. Dodd told us, "Indian pudding was composed solely of cornmeal, molasses, milk, and spices with no eggs, raisins or anything else added." She enclosed a recipe from a Mrs. Imogene Merrill, North Anson, Maine.

"Made according to tradition, the pudding when taken from the oven will quiver and be of a jellylike consistency. The old way that has never been improved upon was to bring a quart of milk to a boil in an iron kettle, and then to add to it about one scant cup of fine cornmeal with the left hand, holding the meal high and sifting it slowly through the fingers, stirring it constantly meanwhile with the right hand.

"When this has thickened and cooled a little, add ½ teaspoon of cinnamon and ½ pint of cold milk. Beat the whole mixture until smooth, then pour into a deep, well-buttered pudding dish.

"When it has baked nearly an hour (modern cooks might need to know about 300 degrees) pour over it a half pint of cold milk which must not be stirred but allowed to soak in gradually. Bake in a steady oven 3 to 4 hours, the longer the better. The New England housewife, in the days of the brick oven, baked hers in a stone pudding dish all night.

"In baking, if it should become too brown, cover the pudding with a thick plate. If it was desired to have the pudding extra rich, our forebears added 1 cupful of currants or raisins after the pudding had baked a few minutes. In this case, an additional ½ pint of milk was added. I have also added 2 well-beaten eggs, but oldtimers used no eggs.

"Note: When sweetening agents such as molasses and especially sugar were expensive and hard to come by, sweetener was added to taste after the pudding was cooked. Molasses could be poured over or sugar sprinkled on as might be available, if any. One-half cup of molasses could be added to this pudding with the cinnamon, if desired."

Chef Alfredo Viazzi

Julia Child has eaten and admired Alfredo's cooking. James Beard who, early on, had a stage career, is frequently with Alfredo and his wife, Jane White, the actress, discussing theater and dining on the likes of carpaccio alla veneto and macaroni shells with fresh sardine sauce. When Gael Greene entertained Paul Bocuse and three other of the finest and best-known chefs of France, she selected one of Alfredo's restaurants—and Alfredo did the cooking.

Alfredo Viazzi, a native of Savona, Italy, owns three of the most successful restaurants in New York, the Trattoria da Alfredo at 90 Bank Street, the Caffè da Alfredo at 17 Perry Street, and the Tavola Calda da Alfredo at 285 Bleecker Street, an Italian restaurant with take-out service modeled after similar type establishments in Rome, Venice, and Florence.

He came recently to our kitchen in East Hampton and demonstrated that he is not only a very fine cook but an engaging and enthusiastic food talker as well. While stirring four cheeses into a pot to blend with tagliarini, he told us that his liking and respect for food came about from two sources—his mother, who was a dreadful cook; and a humorist named Pittigrilli, who wrote for Italian newspapers in the 1930s.

"Pittigrilli created two characters, a man named Judge Pot and his friend named Jutta," Alfredo recalled. "She was a bareback rider in a circus. Together they traveled all over England, Italy, and France, drinking only the finest wines and eating only the finest food, and it seemed at the time to be the most enviable, desirable life in the world."

Alfredo shifted his attention to a kettle and added that his mother, thanks to his father, had a fantastic influence on his palate.

"My mother was—unashamedly—a shocking, abominable cook and yet she was always trying her hand at something in the kitchen," he said. "My father would come home each night and look at the table and say, 'Let's go out,' then he'd march us off to a marvelous old Tuscan trattoria on the waterfront in Savona."

Although Alfredo, 53 years old and the father of two married daughters by his first wife, is markedly and deservedly successful as a chef and restaurant owner, he came by his present métier late in life.

He came to America in 1946 and had an interesting if desultory series of experiences, few of which had anything to do with food in a professional sense.

He was a merchant seaman for seven years, wrote soap operas for

Italian radio, and published a best-selling paperback novel titled *The Cruel Dawn.* Eventually he managed a political club in Manhattan and in 1957 opened the restaurant Portofino, which is still in existence but which he sold in 1963 when he returned to Italy.

Two more things, vitally important in his life, happened at the Portofino. He learned to cook from a "fantastic" Italian chef named Gino Ratti, who returned to Italy 15 years ago.

At the Portofino, there was a small stage and there Alfredo staged plays on Monday evenings when the restaurant closed. A young actress named Jane White appeared in one of those plays and after a brief courtship they were married. Miss White is the daughter of the late Walter White, Executive Secretary of the National Association for the Advancement of Colored People. She recently starred in Ibsen's *Rosmersholm*

Alfredo Viazzi, one of the city's finest chefs and most successful restaurateurs. Assisting him is his wife, Jane White, the actress.

and was described in this newspaper as one of America's "finest classical actresses."

Mr. Viazzi is a veritable encyclopedia of pasta and pasta sauces. His several specialties include a sauce made of cream, butter, walnuts, pignoli, pesto genovese, and Parmesan cheese to be served over pansoti, a homemade, ravioli-type pasta stuffed with spinach and ricotta cheese; a cream, butter, Parmesan cheese, and fresh zucchini sauce served with rigatoni; green lasagne Bolognese made with layers of meat sauce, ricotta, Bechamel sauce, cheese, and mortadella; a salsa Corleone, named for a small town in Sicily, made with diced eggplant, anchovies, olive oil, parsley, and garlic to go with lingue di passeri; a fresh sardine sauce to go with linguine or spaghettini; and, perhaps the most famous of all, a blend of cream, butter, crumbled sausage, and mushrooms delicately flavored with tarragon and nutmeg to go with paglia et fieno—meaning straw and hay—a combination of white and green tagliarini.

Carpaccio alla Veneto
(A raw meat and mayonnaise appetizer)

1 pound boneless shell steak, trimmed of all fat and cut into 6 equal slices
1 cup salsa maionese, approximately (see recipe)

1. Using a flat mallet, pound each steak slice until it is quite thin, about ⅛-inch thick. Arrange the slices slightly overlapping on a large cold platter.

2. Serve the cold, raw meat with salsa maionese on the side, letting each guest serve himself. Traditionally the steak is served without seasoning and with the mayonnaise which also contains no salt. For those who wish it, salt may be served separately.

Yield: 6 servings.

Salsa maionese
(Mustard and tarragon mayonnaise)

3 egg yolks
1 teaspoon imported mustard, preferably Dijon or Düsseldorf
⅛ teaspoon white pepper
Juice of 1 lemon
1 tablespoon chopped fresh tarragon or 1 teaspoon dried
¾ cup olive oil

1. Combine the yolks, mustard, white pepper, and about 1 teaspoon of lemon juice in a mixing bowl. Add the tarragon. Beat with a wire whisk.

2. Continue to beat vigorously while gradually adding the oil. Beat in the remaining lemon juice. This should be a very thin mayonnaise and for carpaccio it is best left unsalted.

Yield: About 1 cup.

Mozzarella Fresca con Pomodoro e Acciughe
(Fresh mozzarella cheese with tomatoes and anchovies)

¾ to 1 pound fresh mozzarella cheese
12 slices red, ripe tomatoes
36 flat anchovy fillets
6 teaspoons dried oregano, more or less to taste
4 to 6 tablespoons olive oil
Freshly ground black pepper

1. Cut the mozzarella into 12 more or less equal slices and arrange them on a serving dish. Place 1 slice of tomato atop each. Garnish each serving with 3 flat anchovy fillets.

2. Sprinkle each serving with equal amounts of oregano and olive oil. Add a few turns of the peppermill and serve at room temperature.

Yield: 6 to 12 servings.

Tagliarini Verdi ai Quattro Formaggi
(Green tagliarini with four cheeses)

½ pound butter
¼ teaspoon freshly ground white pepper
¼ pound fontina cheese, cubed, available in Italian markets
¼ pound gorgonzola cheese, cubed, available in Italian markets
¼ pound bel paese cheese, cubed, generally available
¾ cup grated Parmesan cheese
1 cup heavy cream
1 pound green tagliarini or spaghetti
Salt

1. Melt the butter in a deep saucepan and add the pepper. Add the fontina, gorgonzola, and bel paese cheeses. Stir until the cheeses melt.

2. Stir in the Parmesan cheese and heavy cream.

3. Drop the tagliarini into salted boiling water and cook, stirring frequently, until tender, 7 to 12 minutes. Drain the tagliarini and toss in the cheese mixture.

Yield: 4 to 6 servings.

Scaloppine Bentivoglio
(Veal scallops with prosciutto and Marsala)

20 dried Italian mushrooms, available in Italian markets
¼ pound thinly sliced prosciutto or ham
12 thin slices veal, preferably from the leg, about 1 pound
2 tablespoons olive oil
12 tablespoons butter
2 teaspoons chopped fresh tarragon or 1 teaspoon dried
¼ cup finely chopped parsley
¾ cup Marsala wine
Salt and freshly ground black pepper

1. Place the mushrooms in a bowl and add hot water to cover. Let stand to soften. Drain and squeeze to extract excess moisture. Slice the mushrooms and set aside.

2. Stack the prosciutto slices and cut them into ¼-inch cubes. Set aside.

3. Pound the veal slices with a flat mallet to make them thinner.

4. Heat 1 tablespoon oil in each of two frying pans. When the oil is very hot without smoking, add the scaloppine in one layer. Cook over high heat about 30 seconds and turn. Cook about 1 minute.

5. Add the butter to another large skillet and when it is hot, transfer the scaloppine to the butter. Scatter the prosciutto over all. Add the tarragon and parsley. Add the mushrooms.

6. Cook over high heat about 30 seconds and add the Marsala. Cook over high heat about 4 minutes, adding salt and pepper to taste. When ready, the sauce should be buttery and clear. Transfer the veal pieces to 6 hot plates and spoon the sauce over.

Yield: 6 servings.

Later on in this volume (pages 348–350), we have another feature on Alfredo, again detailing his Merlinlike ways with pasta cookery. It has occurred to us that twice we have ignored one of the great strong points of Alfredo's cooking—his fresh vegetables, which are superb. If you should be in Manhattan, and expertly cooked (which is to say not overcooked) vegetables are your fancy, you might give Alfredo's a try.

Cooking with Honey

"In the Middle Ages," Sidney Gross told us over a glass of home-made bee-sting liqueur, "honeybees were used as agents of warfare. The combatants would catapult the hives over castle walls to rout the enemy."

Sidney Gross and his wife, Sue, are college teachers. He teaches philosophy; she teaches political science. They are also beekeepers who came by their hobby in a sentimental manner.

"One day we had an old house and there were bees in the chimney," Mrs. Gross said as she cut another slice of chocolate honey cake. "They made the most comforting sound in the world all summer long, and then one day they swarmed. Not a bee was left. Not one little hum. They'd flown to the branch of a neighbor's tree and a beekeeper came and took them away. Months later we bought him out."

It was a cold, wintry day in Cortland, Illinois, and the Grosses escorted us on a tour of their 54 hives which, they explained, need very little care in winter months. "Bees are hardly pets," Mr. Gross stated, "not like cats, dogs or an aquarium. You can walk off and leave them."

In answer to a question, Mr. Gross told us that the color of honey varies according to the season. "Early honey is from clover and is light in color; autumn honey is from flowers like asters and tends to be darker," Mr. Gross informed us. A preference for one or the other may correspond to a preference for light or dark chicken eggs, both of which have the same nutritional value.

Speaking of personal preferences, Mrs. Gross added that a lot of people will buy honey only in the comb. "This includes a lot of skeptics who think the processor may be adulterating his liquid honey with corn syrup," she said.

We asked the Grosses if they'd ever been stung. "Of course," they said. "There's a long-time superstition that a beekeeper and his bees have some sort of special rapport and that's nonsense. If you're nervous and jerk your hand quickly, you're almost certain to be stung."

Bees survive in very cold weather and exhibit very interesting behavior. "Through body movement bees keep the interior of their hives at around 96 degrees. All through the winter they move almost constantly in and out of a cluster, always with the queen in the center. They nourish themselves on honey and only fly outside when the outer temperature is 55 degrees and more."

One of the most discouraging things in beekeeping, the Grosses said,

Sidney and Sue Gross, experts on the honey bee.

is a time of swarming, a natural phenomenon that occurs when a hive is overcrowded. "Bees by instinct form new colonies and invariably with a queen in tow. They swarm around the queen and leave the hive in one big cloud. They fly around ten or fifteen minutes and settle on something—a tree branch generally—until they decide what they want to do. They look around for a natural home, of which a tree hollow seems the most natural," Mr. Gross said. When bees swarm, they generally leave the beekeeper with only about 20 percent of his erstwhile colony.

"So, you try to get them back," Mr. Gross said and sighed. "The key to that is the queen. If you can persuade her into a box or other container, the rest of the bees will follow. You fill the box with honey in the comb and if the queen falls for the lure, you stand back and wait ten minutes. With glee, of course. The neighbors are back there hiding and rooting for you. You're generally in somebody else's backyard, and they want to get both you and your bees off their premises as quickly as possible."

Curiously, when bees swarm year after year, they generally head for the same branch of the same tree used for an earlier escapade. And at the time of swarming, they are notably docile. "You can put your hand inside a swarm quite safely," Mr. Gross said. "You can wear gloves if you want to, but they only get in the way. But you've got to wear a veil. If a bee stings you in the eye, it's murder."

A queen bee, we were informed, is the only fertile female in a hive. Workers are infertile females while drones are fertile males, looked upon by the workers as "no-good, do-nothings whose sole purpose in life is the pleasure of reproduction." The workers' moment of glory comes in bitter cold when, acting as guards at the entrance of the hives, they allow the drones to escape for a little air and exercise, then staunchly refuse them ingress, letting them die from the cold without.

In good weather bees will fly as far as five miles from home, but they prefer a shorter distance—half a mile or so. They have a keen sense of reckoning, up to a point. "If you move a hive two feet after they have flown, they become disoriented," Mr. Gross noted.

Most people not conversant with beekeeping think of a hive as a comic-strip contraption resembling a stack of balloon tires of descending diameter, one on top of the other. That is, actually, the caricature of a skep, the hopelessly antiquated habitat for bees that was employed by ancient beekeepers. "It consisted," Mr. Gross told us, "of conical baskets woven from straw. In order to remove honey from a skep it was necessary to kill the bees and sometimes destroy the skep itself."

Modern hives consist of solid wooden boxes that resemble plain, functional bureau drawers, which can be stacked one atop the other. Each box can be fitted with frames which resemble small picture frames inset with thin sheets of pure beeswax.

"The way it works is this," Mr. Gross explained. "The workers fly out of the hive into the fields of clover, citrus groves, apple orchards, or whatever happens to be in flower in the neighborhood. The workers are quite specific about what they become involved in. Some collect pollen—you can sometimes look at a bee's legs and tell what kind of flower he's been into—and some collect nectar. The difference between nectar and honey is water. The nectar bees return to the hive and deposit the nectar in the cells of the beeswax frames. Then they evaporate the nectar by flapping their wings. When the nectar is reduced to 18 percent water, they cap the cells and that's honey. If the water content is more than 18 percent, the honey will tend to ferment and you get mead, but that's another story. Some people talk about 'organic' honey and that's nonsense. All honey is 'organic' in the sense that it is a natural and not manufactured product."

There are many sources for bees, the Grosses noted, including Sears and Montgomery Ward by mail order. You can buy the bees, one queen bee included in each order, and they arrive in wire cages. The Grosses started with two and one-half pounds of bees including a queen bee, and the estimate was that this was eight to ten thousand bees.

The accumulation of honey fluctuates wildly from year to year, depending on many factors, most having to do with the weather. In 1973, they produced a ton of honey from 25 hives. In 1974, they could account for only 250 pounds from twice the number of hives.

The Grosses have their fingers in a few other food pies not related to honey. Under the name Gross' Kitchen Harvest they publish numerous soundly written recipe booklets with such titles as "Bagels, Bagels, Bagels," "Fruit-Flavored Yogurt and More . . . ," "Holiday Baking," and "Sourdough Rye and Other Good Breads." The booklets, none more than 20 pages long, contain a good deal of food lore plus several well-tested recipes. The cost is $1.50 per copy and they may be obtained by writing Gross' Kitchen Harvest, Box 30, Cortland, Illinois 60112.

The recipes for the honey-chocolate cake and frosting were recently developed in Mrs. Gross's kitchen. The other recipes are from their booklet "The Honey Book."

Honey-Chocolate Cake

11 tablespoons butter
1¾ cups honey
½ cup cocoa
2 eggs
1 teaspoon vanilla extract
2½ cups sifted cake flour
1½ teaspoons baking soda
½ teaspoon salt
1 cup milk
    Honey frosting (see recipe)

1. Preheat the oven to 325 degrees.

2. Grease and flour 3 round 9-inch cake tins.

3. Cream the butter until soft. Beat the honey in gradually.

4. Add the cocoa and mix well. Beat in the eggs one at a time. Add the vanilla.

5. Sift together the dry ingredients. Add dry ingredients alternately with milk, beating constantly. Pour the batter into the prepared pans and bake 50 minutes, or until the cakes test done.

6. Turn the cake rounds onto racks to cool. Spread a little frosting between each layer and stack them. Frost the top and sides of the cake and serve cut in wedges.

Yield: 16 to 24 servings.

Honey frosting

1½ cups honey
2 egg whites
⅛ teaspoon salt
½ teaspoon vanilla extract
1 tablespoon cognac

1. Boil the honey over medium heat to the soft ball stage, 238 degrees on a candy thermometer.

2. Beat the egg whites and salt until stiff. Pour the hot honey into the egg whites in a thin stream, beating constantly. Add the vanilla and cognac. Beat the frosting until it is thick enough to spread.

Yield: Enough for one 9-inch 3-layer cake.

Honey Brownies

4 tablespoons butter
4 squares (ounces)
  unsweetened chocolate
4 eggs
½ teaspoon salt
1 cup sugar
1 cup honey
1 teaspoon vanilla extract
1 cup plus 2 tablespoons
  sifted flour
1 cup chopped nuts (pecans
  or walnuts)

1. Preheat the oven to 325 degrees.

2. Melt the butter and chocolate over low heat in a heavy saucepan.

3. Beat the eggs and salt in a mixing bowl until thick and pale yellow. Add the sugar and honey gradually, beating until the mixture is light in texture.

4. Add the melted chocolate and butter and vanilla. Stir in the flour. Add the nuts. Pour the mixture into a 9-inch square pan and bake for 45 to 60 minutes or until done. Cut in squares when cool.

Yield: About 16 brownies.

Honey-Pumpkin Pie

1 unbaked 9-inch pie shell
2 cups cooked pumpkin
1 cup canned evaporated
  milk
1 cup honey
¼ cup cognac

1 teaspoon finely chopped
  crystallized ginger
1 teaspoon ground cinnamon
¼ teaspoon ground allspice
½ teaspoon salt
3 eggs

1. Preheat the oven to 425 degrees.

2. Prepare the pie shell and set aside.

3. Beat the eggs and combine with the remaining ingredients. Pour into the pie shell. Bake the pie 15 minutes. Reduce the heat to 350 degrees and bake an additional 45 minutes or until a knife inserted in the custard comes out clean.

Yield: One 9-inch pie.

Bee-Sting Liqueur

2 cups honey
1 cup water
5 whole cloves
2 teaspoons chopped
  crystallized ginger
5 peppercorns
2 sticks cinnamon
8 whole allspice berries
1 1-inch piece vanilla bean
5 whole cardamom seeds,
  crushed
10 whole coriander seeds,
  bruised
1 strip fresh lemon peel
2 strips fresh orange peel
2½ cups (approximately) 190-
  proof pure grain alcohol,
  available in wine and
  spirits shops in some states

1. Combine the honey, water, spices, and lemon and orange peels in a saucepan and simmer 30 minutes.

2. Strain the mixture and measure it. Add an equal amount of grain alcohol. Blend and bottle. Store for a month or longer before using.

Yield: About 5 cups.

When this column appeared in an out-of-town newspaper with the headline, "Bee's Knees: This Is a Honey of a Cake," it elicited a response from Lorena Warnock of Wakefield, Quebec, who stated, "One of my friends has previously heard the expression 'bee's knees' and we have been trying to track down precisely what it refers to. When I saw that headline, I thought 'Eureka, at last!' but not once was it mentioned again."

The answer was, we thought, a cocktail. With the repeal of Prohibition in this country and even before that in such well-known watering places as the bar of the Savoy in London, bartenders were much given to the creation of new drinks, most of which were christened with fanciful if not to say coy names. In our 50-year-old *Savoy Cocktail Book*, whose recipes were compiled by Harry Craddock, the hotel barman, there are more than 200 pages of drinks that bear such appellations as Depth Charge, Maiden's Blush, Mah-Jongg, Sweet Patootie and White Cargo.

We tracked down the Bee's Knees cocktail in David A. Embury's *Fine Art of Mixing Drinks* (Doubleday, 1958, $5.95), to our mind the finest American bar book, although we find it of more interest as a historical reflection of certain aspects of the Charleston and 23 Skiddoo age, than as a guide to cocktail mixing.

In any event, we learned from Mr. Embury that a Bee's Knees cocktail is made with half an ounce of honey, one ounce of lemon juice, and four ounces of gin. These are shaken with cracked ice, strained and served to two thirsty parties.

But then we received a letter from Jeremy Davern of Park Avenue and Plattsburgh, New York, with a clipping of an article that appeared recently in a *McCall's* magazine interview with Prince Charles of England. "It is very difficult," the prince was quoted as saying, "not to become pompous and to think that you're the bee's knees and the best thing that ever happened."

"He used the term," Mr. Davern noted, "in ordinary conversation. Indeed, I have read the phrase occasionally in English novels . . . it was fairly commonplace slang, I believe, around 1910–1920. I wonder which came first the cocktail which you described or the slang which then became the name of a cocktail? None of this, of course, is very earthshaking but for trivia collectors it has a certain charm."

A friend named Barbara Scherer wrote from Washington to add that she would like to put up her "dukes on the bee's knees brouhaha."

"When I was young," she wrote, "our family lived in the summer on a farm near Mexico, Indiana. Every Fourth of July we had an absolutely smashing party of family and friends. Besides knockout fireworks we had two unchanging traditions. One was a case of twenty-four bottles of pop for the six of us children. The other was Bees' Knees for the adults.

"The Bees' Knees were made of equal parts of freshly squeezed orange and lemon juices, honey, and gin, garnished with fresh mint spears. When we children grew up and were allowed the Bees' Knees, we always figured our falling about so was due to the honey."

The definitive comment on the subject seems to have come from a cerebral and resourceful acquaintance, also from Washington, D.C., who notes that, "Besides being the name of a cocktail invented at the Savoy Hotel in London, 'the bee's knees' was a slang expression of the 1920s meaning something like 'super' or 'smashing.' According to H. L. Mencken's *The American Language*, the expression was coined by Tad Dorgan, the cartoonist, who also originated 'the cat's pajamas,' 'the snake's hips' and similar absurd superlatives."

Potatoes: Beyond Baked and Boiled

WITH PIERRE FRANEY

The potato that we call common, white or Irish (and its relative, the sweet potato) is one of the most versatile of vegetables, with a character that easily adapts itself to other foods and flavors. One small fraction of that versatility is reflected in the recipes on these pages.

Crumb Potatoes

2½ *pounds potatoes*
⅓ *cup peanut, vegetable, or corn oil*
5 *tablespoons butter*
Salt

1. Peel the potatoes and drop them into cold water. Remove them one at a time and cut a slice off all four sides plus a slice off each end. This will yield a potato with a boxlike shape. Reserve the outside slices for another purpose or discard them.

2. Cut the "boxes" into neat ¼-inch-lengthwise slices. Stack the slices, a few at a time, and cut the slices, lengthwise into ¼-inch-thick sticks.

3. Stack the sticks and cut them into ¼-inch cubes. Drop the cubes into cold water to prevent discoloration.

4. When ready to cook, drain the cubes into a colander. Run very hot, almost boiling water over them about 10 seconds. Drain well.

5. Heat the oil and 1 tablespoon butter in a large, shallow skillet. Add the potatoes and salt to taste. Cook, shaking the skillet and stirring the potatoes, about 7 to 8 minutes. Drain well. Wipe out the skillet.

6. Heat the remaining butter in the skillet and add the potatoes. Cook, shaking the skillet and stirring, 6 to 8 minutes longer or until the cubes are nicely browned and crisp. Drain and serve hot with salt.

Yield: 6 to 8 servings.

Caraway Potatoes

2 *pounds red, new, waxy potatoes*
Salt
4 *tablespoons butter*
1 *teaspoon caraway seeds*
Freshly ground black pepper

1. Rinse and drain the potatoes and put them in a small kettle or deep saucepan.

2. Cover with water and add salt to taste. Bring to the boil and simmer 20 minutes or until tender. Drain and, when cool enough to handle, peel.

3. Heat the butter in a heavy saucepan and add the potatoes. Sprinkle with caraway seeds, salt, and pepper. Cover and heat thoroughly.

Yield: 6 to 8 servings.

Rutabaga and Sweet-Potato Casserole

2 pounds rutabaga (yellow turnips)
¾ pounds sweet potatoes or carrots
Salt
3 tablespoons butter, at room temperature
Freshly ground black pepper
¼ teaspoon grated nutmeg
⅓ cup heavy cream

1. Preheat oven to 350 degrees.

2. Peel the rutabaga and sweet potatoes. Cut both in half, then into 2-inch chunks. If carrots are used, cut them into 2-inch lengths.

3. Place the rutabaga in a saucepan and the potatoes in another. Cover both with cold water and add salt. Bring to the boil and cook until tender. The potatoes

will require less cooking than the rutabaga. Drain well.

4. While hot, put the vegetables through a food mill into a mixing bowl. Stir in 2 tablespoons butter, salt and pepper to taste, nutmeg, and cream.

5. Spoon the mixture into a baking dish. Dot with remaining butter and bake 20 minutes. At the last minute run the dish under the broiler to glaze.

Yield: 4 to 6 servings.

Sautéed Potatoes

3 pounds fairly large potatoes
Salt
¼ cup peanut, vegetable, or corn oil
3 tablespoons butter
Freshly ground black pepper
1 teaspoon finely minced garlic
1 tablespoon chopped parsley

1. Rinse the potatoes and put them in a kettle. Add cold water to cover and salt. Simmer 30 to 45 minutes or until tender. Drain immediately.

2. Peel the potatoes. Cut each in half and cut each half into slices about ⅓ inch thick.

3. In a large, heavy skillet, heat the oil and butter. Add the potatoes, salt, and pepper. Cook, tossing and stirring with care, until the potatoes are golden brown, 15 to 20 minutes. Sprinkle

with garlic, toss, and spoon onto a hot dish. Serve sprinkled with chopped parsley.

Yield: 8 or more servings.

Straw Potatoes

4 *large Idaho potatoes*
    (about 1½ pounds)
    Oil for deep frying
    Salt

1. Peel the potatoes and drop them into cold water to cover.

2. Cut the potatoes into about ⅛-inch-thick slices with a knife or potato slicer. Stack the slices, a few at a time, and cut the potatoes into shreds about ⅛ inch thick (see note). Drop the shreds into cold water as they are prepared.

3. Drain the potatoes well into a colander.

4. Heat the oil to about 360 degrees in a cooker for deep frying. Add the potatoes, a few handfuls at a time, and cook them, stirring frequently, until they are crisp and golden brown. Drain on absorbent toweling and sprinkle with salt.

Yield: 8 servings.

Note: Specialty shops that deal in imported cooking utensils sometimes carry *mandolins*, a special French device for slicing and shredding. They have a special cutter for shredding potatoes for straw potatoes.

Cod: A Winter Gift from the Sea

Although Boston is celebrated as the home of the cod, that most delectable of winter fish is generally available—particularly at this time of the year—up and down the Eastern seaboard.

Gastronomically, cod belongs to that interesting group of foods distinguished by a more or less neutral flavor that complements naturally and to a fine degree a host of other flavors with which it is put in league. Just as a perfectly cooked potato can give unexpected luster to sour cream and chives (or sour cream and fresh caviar for that matter), so does poached cod seem to bring out the finest nuances of flavor in an assortment of sauces including mayonnaise, hollandaise, Mornay, and their derivatives. Cod has that splendid virtue of nonassertiveness that makes the palate revel in the things with which it is bedded or topped, including noodles, spinach, cheese, sauces, or simply plain melted butter with a touch of lemon.

This winter is not, according to fishermen, the greatest of all possible seasons for Atlantic cod, and yet the present haul, where taste and texture are concerned, is something to brag about.

. Some of the finest codfishing grounds in America are in the vicinity of Block Island and Montauk, off the eastern tip of Long Island, where most of the cod in the New York area originates. The bulk of the present harvest comes from draggers—commercial fishing vessels whose nets drag on or close to the ocean bottom—although those small boats with trawls are sometimes used.

A trawl—sometimes called a tub-o'-gear—consists of a round or square tub or bucket-shaped apparatus generally made of metal and containing a mass of coiled fishing line outfitted with approximately 1,000 hooks. The hooks are furnished with clams or other bait and are generally set early in the morning for a four- or five-hour period.

The lines are retrieved late in the evening and—with luck on good days—with a few four to seven pound cod in tow. Scrod, by the way, are nothing more than small cod, those weighing three pounds and under.

Although most of the cod sold today weighs from about four to seven pounds, the fish can actually grow to mammoth size. While the largest cod on record is said to have weighed more than 200 pounds, cod weighing more than 100 pounds are rare. *McClane's New Standard Fishing*

Encyclopedia observes that the cod is noted for the mass of eggs it can produce and adds that at least one 75-pound fish is known to have contained nine million eggs.

Fresh cod has seemingly endless uses in cooking. It can be cooked whole in court bouillon and served with an infinite number of oil, butter or cheese sauces; it can be cut into fillets or steaks and is suited to almost any preparation in the standard or classic repertoire. A few excellent uses are suggested herewith.

Cod Florentine

2½ cups Mornay sauce (see recipe, page 47)
2 pounds or 2 10-ounce packages fresh spinach
3½ tablespoons butter
1 tablespoon finely chopped shallots
   Salt and freshly ground black pepper
1¾ to 2 pounds skinless, boneless cod or striped bass fillets
½ cup dry white wine
3 tablespoons chopped onion
3 tablespoons grated Parmesan cheese

1. Preheat oven to 375 degrees.

2. Prepare the Mornay sauce and set aside.

3. If bulk spinach is used, pick it over well. Discard any tough stems. Wash the leaves thoroughly to rid them of all sand. Drop the spinach into boiling water to cover. Return to the boil and simmer about 2 minutes. Drain and run the spinach under cold running water. Squeeze the spinach between the hands to extract excess moisture.

4. Chop the spinach coarsely. Set aside.

5. Butter a baking dish with 2 tablespoons of butter. Sprinkle with shallots, salt, and pepper.

6. Cut the cod into 6 pieces of approximately the same weight. Arrange the pieces neatly over the baking dish. Sprinkle with salt and pepper and the wine. Cover with foil. Bring the wine to the boil on top of the stove, then put the dish in the oven. Bake 12 to 15 minutes or just until the fish flakes easily when tested with a fork.

7. Meanwhile, heat remaining 1½ tablespoons of butter in a skillet and add the onion. When it wilts, add the chopped spinach, salt, and pepper. Cook about 1 minute, no longer.

8. Spoon the spinach into an oval baking dish and smooth it over the bottom. Carefully transfer the baked cod pieces to the spinach, arranging them neatly over it. Cover and keep warm.

9. Pour the wine liquid from the baked fish into a saucepan and reduce it quickly over high heat to about ¼ cup. Add this to the Mornay sauce and stir. Bring to the boil.

10. Spoon the hot sauce over the fish, smoothing it to coat the fish evenly. Sprinkle with Parmesan cheese and bake, uncovered, until bubbling throughout and the fish is nicely browned on top.

Yield: 6 servings.

Gratin de Morue aux Nouilles

(Fresh cod with Mornay sauce and noodles)

1½ *pounds fresh skinless, boneless cod fillets*
½ *cup milk*
½ *bay leaf*
½ *small white onion stuck with 2 cloves*
⅛ *teaspoon cayenne*
Salt
10 *peppercorns*
2 *sprigs parsley*
¼ *pound fine noodles*

2 *tablespoons butter Freshly ground black pepper*
3 *cups Mornay sauce (see recipe)*
½ *cup grated Gruyère cheese*

1. Preheat oven to 500 degrees.

2. Place the cod in a saucepan and add water to cover, milk, bay leaf, onion, cayenne, salt, peppercorns, and parsley. The fish should be barely covered with liquid. Bring to the boil and simmer 1 minute. Remove from the heat and drain.

3. Cook the noodles in water about 2 to 3 minutes or until tender without being mushy. Drain quickly and run under cold running water. Return them to a saucepan and add the butter. Toss until coated with butter and sprinkle with salt and pepper.

4. Pour the noodles into an oval or other baking dish and arrange the fish over. Spoon the Mornay sauce over the fish and sprinkle with the cheese. Bake 10 to 15 minutes.

Yield: 4 servings.

Mornay sauce

2 *tablespoons butter*
3 *tablespoons flour*
1¾ *cups milk*
⅓ *cup heavy cream Salt and freshly ground pepper*
1 *cup grated Gruyère or Swiss cheese*
1 *egg yolk*
⅛ *teaspoon grated nutmeg*

1. Melt the butter in a saucepan and add the flour, stirring with a wire whisk. When blended, add the milk and cream, stirring rapidly with the whisk. Season with salt and pepper.

2. Add the cheese and let it melt. Bring to the boil.

3. Add the egg yolk, stirring rapidly with the whisk. Bring just to the boil and remove from the heat. Stir in the nutmeg.

Yield: About 3 cups.

Broiled Cod Fillets

2   cod fillets or codfish steaks
4   tablespoons butter
    Salt and freshly ground
    black pepper
½   cup fresh bread crumbs
½   teaspoon paprika

1. Preheat oven to 450 degrees.

2. Grease the bottom of a baking dish with 1 tablespoon of butter.

3. Arrange the fillets, skin side down, on the dish and sprinkle with salt and pepper.

4. Scatter the bread crumbs on a piece of wax paper. Hold a small sieve over the crumbs. Put the paprika through the sieve and blend paprika and crumbs. Sprinkle the fish fillets with the crumbs and melt and dribble the remaining 3 tablespoons butter over all. Broil about 6 inches from the heat until golden brown. Then bake 5 to 10 minutes.

Yield: 2 servings.

Poached Codfish

Court bouillon (see recipe)
1   4- or 5-pound codfish,
    cleaned weight

1. Prepare the court bouillon and let it cool.

2. The fish, preferably, should have the tail and head left on but with the gills removed. Wrap the fish in cheesecloth and tie with string. Place it in the court bouillon and bring to the boil. Cook 12 minutes and turn off the heat. There should be enough court bouillon to barely cover.

3. Let the fish remain in the court bouillon 15 minutes or so. Remove the fish. Remove the cheesecloth. Carefully scrape the skin from the fish. Serve the fish in portions with fresh mayonnaise or hollandaise.

Yield: 8 servings.

Court bouillon for
poaching fish

16   cups water
2   cups dry white wine
1   cup sliced carrots
1   cup sliced green part of
     leeks, firmly packed
1   cup chopped onion
1   cup chopped celery
¾   cup coarsely chopped
     parsley
1   bay leaf
⅛   teaspoon cayenne
3   sprigs fresh thyme or ½
     teaspoon dried
1   clove garlic, peeled
     Salt
12   black peppercorns

Combine all the ingredients in a fish poacher. Cover and bring to the boil. Simmer 20 minutes. Cool before using.

Yield: 4 to 4½ quarts.

Although this article deals exclusively with freshly caught cod, the same fish is the foundation for one of the great preserved fish of all times, salt cod. Salt cod is highly prized in Europe, particularly by the inhabitants of the Mediterranean countries. It goes by the name of bacalao in Spain and baccalà in Italy. The French term is morue. There is a mousse of salt cod in the south of France known as brandade de morue. A recipe for brandade, or salt cod mousse, appears on page 119.

Borscht, and Other Main Courses

WITH PIERRE FRANEY

Hot soup can serve admirably as mainstay of a midwinter meal—depending, of course, on the occasion. For a light lunch, a soup such as lentil or borscht might be served. For a meal of substance, a fish or gumbo type would be appropriate. Add a good loaf of bread, a wedge of cheese and a bottle of wine, and the meal is complete.

Lentil Soup

3   tablespoons butter
¼   pound slice of smoked ham, fat left on, cut into quarters
¼   cup coarsely chopped onion
½   pound dried lentils
5   cups fresh or canned chicken broth
2   cups water
½   bay leaf
1   sprig fresh thyme or ¼ teaspoon dried
     Salt and freshly ground black pepper

1. Heat 1 tablespoon of butter in a small kettle or deep saucepan and add the ham and onion. Cook briefly until onion wilts.

2. Add the lentils and 4 cups of the chicken broth. Add the remaining ingredients and simmer 30 to 40 minutes.

3. Remove ½ cup of the soup with lentils and set aside. Discard the bay leaf. Remove the ham pieces and set aside.

4. Put the soup through a food mill to eliminate the coarse lentil hulls. Return the soup to the stove and bring to the boil. Add the remaining cup of chicken broth and the reserved soup with lentils. Finely dice the ham and add it to the soup. Return the soup to the boil and swirl in the remaining butter.

Yield: 4 to 6 servings.

Borscht

2½   pounds meaty beef bones such as ribs or shin
1½   pounds beef neckbones or other soup bones
2   cups chopped celery
2   cups chopped carrots
1   large onion, stuck with 2 cloves
     Salt and freshly ground black pepper

2 sprigs fresh thyme or ½
   teaspoon dried
4 sprigs parsley
1 bay leaf
2 tablespoons butter
1 cup finely chopped onion
1 clove garlic, finely minced
1½ cups finely shredded
   cabbage
6 to 8 medium-size beets,
   about 1½ pounds, trimmed
   and peeled
2 cups cored, peeled,
   chopped tomatoes
¼ cup red wine vinegar
1 teaspoon sugar
   Boiled potatoes
   Sour cream

1. Combine the bones in a kettle and add cold water to cover. Bring to the boil and drain immediately. Chill the bones under cold running water. Put the bones in a clean kettle and add the chopped celery, chopped carrots, onion stuck with cloves, salt, pepper, thyme, parsley, and bay leaf. Add cold water to a depth of about 1 inch above the bones. Bring to the boil and simmer about 2 hours. Strain. Discard solids but reserve broth.

2. Heat the butter in a large, deep saucepan or a small kettle and add the finely chopped onion. Cook, stirring, until wilted and add the garlic and cabbage. Continue cooking, stirring the cabbage until it is wilted.

3. Grate or shred the beets and add them to the cabbage. Add the tomatoes, vinegar, sugar, salt, pepper, and 5 cups of the beef broth. Bring to the boil and simmer about 1 hour. Serve with boiled potatoes and sour cream

beaten lightly with salt to taste on the side.

Yield: 4 to 6 servings.

Note: Leftover beef broth can be frozen for future use.

Fish Soup

⅓ cup peanut, vegetable, or
   corn oil
1 clove garlic, chopped
1½ tablespoons loosely packed
   saffron
1 bay leaf
1 teaspoon dried thyme
1 teaspoon crushed anise or
   fennel seeds
2½ pounds very clean, well
   rinsed fish bones which
   may include the head if the
   gills are removed
   Salt
12 black peppercorns
⅓ cup flour
3½ cups dry white wine
8 cups water
   Tabasco to taste
4 live 1¼ pound lobsters
4 tablespoons cornstarch
2 pounds well-scrubbed
   mussels
36 littleneck clams, the
   smaller the better
2½ pounds skinless, boneless,
   white flesh, nonoily fish
   such as striped bass,
   blackfish, or flounder
1 cup heavy cream, optional
¼ cup Ricard, Pernod, or
   other anise-flavored
   liqueur
   Garlic toast (see recipe),
   optional

1. Heat the oil in a kettle and add the chopped garlic, saffron, bay leaf, thyme, anise seeds, fish bones, salt to taste, and peppercorns. Cook, stirring, about 10 minutes. Sprinkle with flour. Stir to coat the solids with flour.

2. Add 3 cups of the wine and the water, stirring vigorously. Bring to the boil, add Tabasco, and the whole lobsters. Cover and cook 15 minutes.

3. Remove the lobsters and let them cool. Continue cooking the soup. When the lobsters are cool enough to handle, dismember and split them. Remove the meat and cut into bite-size cubes. There should be about 2 cups.

4. Blend the cornstarch with the remaining ½ cup of wine and stir it into the soup. Cook 20 minutes longer.

5. Meanwhile, combine the mussels and clams in another kettle. Add 1 cup of the simmering soup. Cover and steam until the shellfish open (10 to 15 minutes). Remove shellfish, discard shells and add shellfish liquid to the soup. Set clams and mussels aside.

6. Cut the fish into 1-inch cubes. There should be about 5½ cups.

7. Add the fish to the soup and cook, stirring briefly and gently, about 4 to 5 minutes. Add the cream, if desired, and the reserved shellfish. Bring to the boil and add the Ricard. Garnish each serving with a slice of garlic toast.

Yield: 18 to 24 servings.

Garlic toast

Preheat the oven to 400 degrees. Rub a loaf of French bread liberally with a cut clove of garlic. Slice the loaf, brush the slices with olive oil and arrange the slices on a baking sheet. Bake until the slices are golden brown and crisp.

Chicken Gumbo

1 *3½–4-pound chicken, cut into serving pieces*
½ *cup flour*
   Salt and freshly ground black pepper
2 *tablespoons sweet paprika*
3 *tablespoons bacon fat*
4 *cups boiling chicken broth*
2 *tablespoons butter*
1 *cup finely chopped onions*
¾ *cup chopped green pepper*
3 *or 4 ears sweet corn or 1½ cups frozen corn kernels (do not use cream-style corn and do not defrost before using)*
2 *cups canned plum tomatoes*
¼ *cup uncooked rice*
½ *teaspoon hot red pepper flakes*
1 *10-ounce package frozen cut okra*

1. Dredge the chicken pieces in the flour seasoned with salt and pepper to taste and paprika. Shake the pieces to remove excess flour.

2. Heat the bacon fat in a large skillet and brown the chicken on all sides. As it is

browned, transfer the pieces to a deep saucepan or kettle. Add the chicken broth and cover. Cook 20 to 30 minutes or until chicken is tender.

3. Meanwhile, melt the butter in a saucepan and add the onion. Cook, stirring, until wilted and add the green pepper. Cook, stirring, about 2 minutes.

4. When the chicken has cooked for 20 minutes or until tender, add the pepper and onion mixture. Continue cooking about 10 minutes or until the chicken is tender. Remove the chicken pieces and let cool.

5. Drop the shucked corn into the boiling water to cover. When the water returns to the boil, cover and remove from the heat. Let stand 10 minutes. Drain and let cool. When cool enough to handle, cut the kernels from the cob. There should be about 1½ cups. Set it aside.

6. Core and peel the tomatoes and cut them into wedges. Add the tomatoes to the kettle.

7. Add the rice and hot pepper flakes. Simmer about 5 minutes, stirring frequently. Add the

okra and cook 10 minutes longer or until the rice is tender without being mushy.

8. Meanwhile, skin and bone the chicken pieces. Shred the chicken and add it to the kettle. Add the corn. Bring to the boil and serve very hot.

Yield: 6 to 8 servings.

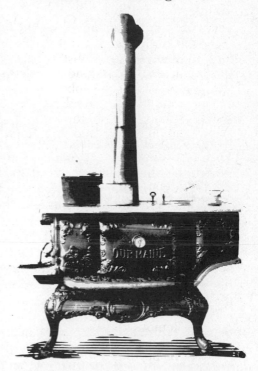

It seems even the darkest clouds can have silver linings.

We have heard in recent months that because of the depressed state of the American economy, hot soups are enjoying a new-found reputation. To our thinking, hot soups in the best of times or the worst of times are an absolute joy.

Chef Tsung Ting Wang

"If you wanted to become a chef back in the old days in China," Tsung Ting Wang said through an interpreter, "the most important attribute you could have was the ability to observe. When you were an apprentice—and I was placed in a Shanghai kitchen when I was 11 years old—the chefs never would tell you every trick in the trade. The principal duties were to keep the kitchen clean, make the chef's bed, and draw warm water for his bath. In less important matters you made the rice and warmed the wine. At the end of five years you would graduate to higher things."

Chef Wang (he prefers that name even though his family name is Tsung) is conceivably the most successful Chinese chef in the United States. He is an acting chef, stockholder, and major force in three of New York's best-known restaurants—the Shun Lee Palace at 155 East 55th Street; the Shun Lee Dynasty at 900 Second Avenue (at 48th Street), and the Hunam Restaurant at 845 Second Avenue (near 45th Street).

"In the traditional Chinese kitchen," he continued, "there were five principal stations—one for cooking, one for steaming, one for cutting, another for making pastry and, finally, one for making cold platters."

A great deal of his time, he told us, was spent as cutting chef and he added that back in the old days there were some chefs who did nothing but act as cutting chef—butchering, cutting, slicing, dicing, shredding the raw meat, and so on—for an entire lifetime.

"A cutting chef was one of the most important people in the kitchen because the size of a dice, slice or strip of meat before it is cooked is one of the essential refinements of the finest Chinese cookery. A good cutter knows within a fraction of an ounce—or the Chinese equivalent—precisely how much meat he will deliver with one slice of his cleaver."

Chef Wang, who can bone a fowl in five minutes or less, came to our kitchen to demonstrate his techniques and prepare a 12-course banquet that included among other things a sauté of duck feet and a soup served with one duck tongue embedded and steamed in one spoonful of fish mousse for each guest.

"These dishes," he elaborated, "are for formal ceremonial dinners and not for everyday dining." After all, one duck has only two feet and one tongue. These delicacies are arrived at by hoarding the duck feet and tongues over a period of time, although they can at times be purchased in butcher shops in Chinatown.

Chef Wang, who is 49 years old and the father of three children, continued from his first kitchen in Shanghai to Hong Kong to Japan where he was the chief chef to Ambassador Harrington Tung. Tokyo in those days was considered, along with the United States, the most important ambassadorial post for the Chiang Kai-shek regime, and his position as principal kitchen man was not come by easily. He was selected from the top 200 best-known chefs of the country.

When Ambassador Tung was appointed to Washington, D.C., chef Wang came with him. He left the position to join the Peking Restaurant—at one time perhaps the finest Chinese restaurant in the nation's capital. He came to New York where he worked as chef at two earlier, now defunct Shun Lee Restaurants, one at 23d Street and Lexington Avenue; the other at 91st and Broadway. During that period he was once summoned to Washington to preside over a banquet at Washington's Mayflower Hotel honoring John F. Kennedy.

The kitchen of the Shun Lee Dynasty, an almost immediate and important success among Manhattan's Chinese restaurants, opened under chef Wang's direction in 1965; the Shun Lee Palace, one of the town's best dining establishments, in 1971. The Hunam restaurant opened to excellent critical reviews in 1972.

As chef Wang proceeded to produce such excellent fare as a cold "phoenix bird" platter (the phoenix bird is a Chinese symbol of treasure, stemming from the legend that where the phoenix bird nests, there underlies good fortune or wealth), winter melon soup; abalone with fresh

Tsung Ting Wang, conceivably the most successful Chinese chef in the United States.

bamboo shoots; chicken soong made with diced chicken breast, stir-fried and served in cold lettuce leaves; plus perhaps the most delectable dish of all, Hunam-style lamb.

He told us that he is not a man of great appetite. Asked to elaborate on his own favorite foods, he stated that he gets maximum pleasure from the likes of such simple dishes as bean curd with spinach, fat pork with wine sauce, and whole carp with hot bean sauce.

He has a palate that is keen on spicy, Szechuan cookery, including eggplant with garlic sauce. He doesn't drink any kind of alcoholic beverage, is not at all attracted to Western cooking except perhaps an occasional steak, but he delights in Indian curries.

Until his recent success (and he still cooks numerous hours each week in the restaurants in which he holds shares, but most often at the Shun Lee Palace), he said that he had worked 14 hours a day and frequently seven days a week throughout most of his professional life. Now he takes one day off to relax, and he does turn his hand at times to cooking for his family. One of the dishes with great appeal for his family, particularly his son, is Chinese fried chicken. This consists of marinating the chicken in a mixture of salt, pepper, five spices powder (available in Chinatown), scallions, and wine. The chicken is dipped in a batter of flour and egg and deep fried.

The accompanying recipes include two appetizers recently prepared in our home kitchen by chef Wang—the pon pon chicken and tangy spicy shrimp.

Pon Pon Chicken

2 cups shredded, steamed, boiled, or gently simmered chicken
1 lettuce leaf
1 tablespoon chopped scallion
1 teaspoon or more chopped garlic
1½ teaspoons finely chopped-fresh ginger
3 tablespoons well-stirred sesame paste (available in bottles in Chinese and other Oriental groceries)
1½ tablespoons soy sauce, preferably dark soy sauce
1 tablespoon white vinegar, preferably rice vinegar
1 teaspoon sugar
1 teaspoon monosodium glutamate, optional
Salt
1 tablespoon chili paste with garlic
1 tablespoon sesame oil (available in bottles in Chinese and other Oriental groceries)

Place the chicken in the lettuce leaf on a serving dish. Blend the remaining ingredients and pour the sauce over the chicken.

Yield: 6 to 12 servings.

Tangy Spicy Shrimp

½ pound raw shrimp
1 cup finely chopped scallions
1 clove garlic, finely minced
1 teaspoon finely chopped fresh hot green or red chili pepper
1 teaspoon finely chopped fresh ginger
1 teaspoon shao hsing or dry sherry
  Salt
1 teaspoon monosodium glutamate, optional
½ teaspoon ground white pepper
1 teaspoon five spices powder (see note)
1 tablespoon or more chili paste with garlic (see note)
1 tablespoon hot oil (see note)
1½ teaspoons sesame oil

1. Shell and devein the shrimp. If the shrimp are large, cut them in half. Bring enough water to cover the shrimp to the boil. Add the shrimp and cook about 1 minute. Drain. Run under cold running water. Pat dry. Refrigerate.

2. Combine the remaining ingredients and pour over the shrimp. Serve cold.

Yield: 6 to 12 servings.

Note: Bottled chili paste with garlic and bottled hot oil are widely available in Chinese groceries. Five spices powder is a blend of ground anise, fennel, cloves, cinnamon, and Szechuan peppercorns. It is available in Chinese groceries.

Hunam Lamb

3 pounds lean leg of lamb
½ cup peanut oil
12 cloves garlic, crushed
12 hot dried red chili peppers
1 1-inch cube fresh ginger, thinly sliced
2 scallions, cut into 2-inch lengths
½ pound rock sugar (available in Chinese groceries and at times in supermarkets)
2 tablespoons chili paste with garlic (available in bottles in Chinese groceries)
¼ cup dark soy sauce (see note)
2 teaspoons salt
1 tablespoon monosodium glutamate, optional
2¼ cups (1½ bottles) beer

1. Cut the lamb into 2-inch cubes.

2. Bring to the boil enough water to cover the lamb. Add the lamb and cook about 3 minutes, stirring occasionally. Drain quickly and run under cold water until thoroughly chilled throughout. Drain.

3. Heat the oil in a wok or skillet and add the garlic. Cook about 10 seconds and add the chili pepper and ginger. Cook over high heat until garlic and chili peppers are dark brown. Add the scallions and cook, stirring, about 20 seconds. Add the lamb and cook, stirring, about 1 minute. Add the rock sugar, chili paste with garlic, soy sauce, salt, monosodium glutamate, and stir to

blend. Transfer the mixture to a casserole and pour in the beer.

4. Cover the casserole and cook until the lamb is tender, 45 minutes to an hour.

Yield: 6 to 12 servings.

Note: There are two kinds of soy sauce used in Chinese cookery. Thin or light soy is the most commonly found in supermarkets. Dark or heavy soy sauce, widely available in Chinese and other Oriental stores, has a greater viscosity.

Shrimp and Crab Meat Szechuan-Style

½ pound small raw shrimp, the smaller the better
1 egg white
2 tablespoons cornstarch
¼ pound cooked crab roe (see note)
¼ pound fresh crab meat, picked over to remove all trace of shell and cartilage
½ cup chopped scallion
2 teaspoons chopped garlic
¼ cup chopped fresh ginger
3 tablespoons chopped Chinese parsley, optional (see note)
4 hot dried red chili peppers, chopped
2 tablespoons shao hsing or dry sherry (see note)
4 teaspoons dark soy sauce(see note)
1 teaspoon sugar
¾ teaspoon ground white pepper
1 teaspoon monosodium glutamate, optional

1 tablespoon chili paste with garlic (see note)
1 tablespoon water
2 cups or more peanut, vegetable, or corn oil

1. Shell and devein the shrimp. Put the shrimp in a mixing bowl and add the egg white and 1 tablespoon of cornstarch. Blend well with the fingers. Refrigerate 30 minutes or longer.

2. Combine the crab roe and crab meat and set aside.

3. Combine the scallion, garlic, ginger, Chinese parsley, and dried red peppers. Set aside.

4. Combine the wine, dark soy sauce, sugar, white pepper, monosodium glutamate, and chili paste with garlic. Set aside.

5. Blend the remaining tablespoon of cornstarch and the water. Set aside.

6. Heat the oil in a wok or skillet. There must be enough oil to completely cover the shrimp when they are added. When the oil is hot but not smoking, add the shrimp and stir rapidly to separate them. Cook only about 30 seconds or just until the shrimp are separated. Drain quickly.

7. Return about 2 tablespoons of oil to the wok and add the scallion and garlic mixture. Cook, stirring, about 5 seconds and add the crab mixture. Cook, stirring, just until heated through, about 20 seconds, and add the shrimp. Add the wine and soy sauce mixture. Stir the cornstarch mixture until smooth and add it quickly. Stir rapidly about 30 seconds and spoon the mixture onto a hot serving platter.

Yield: 6 to 12 servings.

Note: Crab roe comes from the body of cooked female crabs. Twelve female crabs should supply enough crab roe and meat for this recipe. If crab roe is not available, increase the amount of crab meat to one-half pound. Shao hsing is the traditional wine used in Chinese cookery. It is available in wine shops in Chinese communities. Dry sherry is a thoroughly acceptable substitute. There are two kinds of soy sauce used in Chinese cookery. Their differences are detailed in the note in the preceding recipe. Bottled chili paste with garlic is widely available in Chinese and other Oriental stores. Chinese parsley (also called coriander, cilantro, and colantro) is available in Chinese and Spanish markets. A discussion of this intriguing herb appears on page 232.

Chicken Soong

(Cubed chicken in lettuce leaves)

1   *head iceberg lettuce*
1   *large, boned chicken breast, about 1 pound*
1   *egg white*
½   *teaspoon salt*
2   *tablespoons cornstarch*
2   *long green chilies, hot or mild*
10   *or 12 water chestnuts, canned or, preferably, fresh*
½   *cup finely diced celery*
3   *tablespoons finely diced carrots*
1   *teaspoon chopped fresh ginger*

2   *teaspoons or more finely chopped garlic*
3   *tablespoons finely chopped scallion*
2   *tablespoons shao hsing or dry sherry*
½   *tablespoon soy sauce*
½   *tablespoon chili paste with garlic*
1   *teaspoon sugar*
1   *teaspoon monosodium glutamate, optional*
1   *tablespoon water*
2   *cups peanut, vegetable, or corn oil*
½   *teaspoon sesame oil*

1. Core the lettuce and separate it into leaves. Pile on a platter and set aside.

2. Place the chicken breast on a flat surface and, holding a sharp kitchen knife almost parallel to the cutting surface, cut the breast into the thinnest possible slices. Stack the slices and cut into shreds. Cut the shreds into tiny cubes. There should be about 2 cups.

3. Place the chicken meat in a mixing bowl and add the egg white, salt, and 1 tablespoon cornstarch. Blend well with the fingers. Refrigerate 30 minutes longer.

4. Core the chilies. Split them in half and shred them. Cut the shreds into small cubes. There should be about ½ cup.

5. Slice the water chestnuts thinly. Cut the slices into small cubes. There should be about ½ cup.

6. Combine the chopped chilies, water chestnuts, celery, carrots, and ginger. Set aside.

7. In another bowl, combine the garlic and scallion and set aside.

8. Combine the wine, soy sauce, chili paste and garlic, sugar, monosodium glutamate, and set aside.

9. Combine the remaining 1 tablespoon of cornstarch and the water and stir to blend. Set aside.

10. Heat the peanut oil in a wok or skillet and when it is hot, add the chicken, stirring constantly to separate the cubes. Cook about 1½ minutes and drain. Set aside.

11. Return 2 tablespoons of the oil to the wok and add the celery and water chestnut mixture. Cook, stirring, about 30 seconds and add the scallion and garlic. Cook, stirring, about 10 seconds and add the chicken. Cook, stirring, about 30 seconds or until the chicken is piping hot. Add the wine and soy sauce mixture and the sesame oil. Stir the cornstarch mixture until smooth and add it quickly. Stir rapidly about 30 seconds and transfer to a hot platter.

12. Serve the chicken with the lettuce on the side. Let each guest help himself, adding a spoonful or so of the chicken mixture to a lettuce leaf, folding it before eating.

Yield: 6 to 12 servings.

February 1975

W<small>E'VE OFTEN BEEN</small> asked how, after two decades of writing about food, one can still find something "different" and hitherto unpublished to offer by way of recipes. We have stated often as a matter of pride that we rarely cook the same dish twice in our home kitchen other than the old standbys like spaghetti with tomato sauce, sauerkraut, chili con carne (our recipe appears on page 410), and other "necessities of life." Many of our recipes, as this book testifies, are borrowed from friends and new acquaintances, and once in a while we print recipes that are really sentimental recollections of our childhood in the South. In this month of February, we published a recipe for a dish that is as reminiscent of a southern background as cornbread and fried chicken. It is a recipe for a smoked southern sausage. This sausage was for many years prepared by a neighbor who a short while ago declared she was "too old" to make sausages any longer. Through one channel or another we were able to obtain a vague list of the traditional seasonings. A short while later, we were able to contrive a sausage that was identical to the one so fondly recalled.

Elegance, en Masse

WITH PIERRE FRANEY

Part of our national tradition is the American Gothic buffet for large groups: roast turkey, baked ham with potato salad, pickles, relishes, assorted cakes and pies. Certainly nothing is *wrong* with such a menu save its utter predictability. But with a fraction more effort (and no more cost, the price of chicken being what it is), it is possible to reach for elegance. Chicken in champagne—or perhaps a still dry white wine—sauce, for example. With rice and mushrooms, this menu could serve close to two dozen guests and neatly dispel the American Gothic image at the same time.

Chicken in Tarragon and Champagne Sauce

14 tablespoons butter
10 tablespoons flour
 6 cups rich chicken broth
⅓ cup coarsely chopped,
   loosely packed tarragon
   stems and leaves or 2
   tablespoons dried
 6 to 8 chickens, about 2½
   pounds each, cut into
   serving pieces
   Salt and freshly ground
   black pepper
 6 tablespoons finely minced
   shallots
 2 cups dry white champagne
   or a still dry white wine
 3 cups heavy cream
 2 tablespoons freshly
   chopped tarragon leaves or
   parsley

1. Heat 8 tablespoons of butter in a 2-quart (or larger) saucepan and add the flour, stirring with a whisk. Add the broth, continuing to stir vigorously. Simmer 10 minutes, stirring often, and add the ⅓ cup of chopped tarragon. Cook 45 minutes, stirring frequently.

2. Sprinkle the chicken with salt and pepper to taste.

3. In each of 2 skillets heat 3 tablespoons of butter and brown the chicken pieces on all sides. Cook, turning the pieces frequently, about 15 to 25 minutes, depending on the size of the pieces.

4. Remove the chicken and add equal amounts of chopped shallots to each skillet. Keep the chicken warm.

5. Add equal amounts of champagne to each skillet and cook over high heat, stirring, until the wine is almost totally reduced.

6. Combine the contents of both skillets.

7. Add the sauce to the skillet and cook, stirring, about 5 minutes. Add the cream and boil down over high heat, scraping the bottom of the skillet with the flat end of a pancake turner. Cook, stirring, about 5 minutes.

8. Put the sauce through a fine sieve, preferably a sieve known by French cooks as a *chinois*. Return the chicken pieces to one skillet. Pour the sauce over the chicken. Sprinkle with chopped tarragon and bring to the boil. Serve piping hot with baked rice.

Yield: 12 to 18 servings.

Rice with Mushrooms and Foie Gras

¾ pound mushrooms
 6 tablespoons butter
   Juice of 1 lemon
   Salt and freshly ground
   black pepper
⅓ cup finely chopped onion
 3 cups rice
4½ cups chicken broth
½ teaspoon dried thyme
 1 bay leaf
 2 sprigs parsley
 1 3⅓-ounce can foie gras,
   chilled

1. Preheat oven to 400 degrees.

2. Slice the mushrooms, then cut the slices into ½-inch cubes. There should be about 4 cups.

3. Heat 2 tablespoons of butter in a large skillet and add the mushrooms. Sprinkle with lemon juice, salt and pepper to taste. Cover and cook about 5 minutes.

4. Heat remaining 4 tablespoons of butter in a 6-to-8-cup casserole. Add the onion and cook, stirring, until it wilts. Add the rice and stir. Add the chicken broth, thyme, bay leaf, and parsley. Cover. Bring to the boil on top of the stove and place the casserole in the oven. Bake 17 minutes.

5. Stir the mushrooms into the rice. Cut the foie gras into small cubes and fold it in.

Yield: 12 to 18 servings.

We are frequently amused when we see the term "champagne sauce" on a menu. We are born skeptics and strongly suspect that most of the champagne sauces on most menus are really made with a still, dry white wine, rather than with champagne itself. Though we hasten to add that a first-rate still, dry white wine is a perfectly acceptable substitute for champagne as an ingredient, it seems a bit fraudulent to label a sauce "champagne" unless the real beverage has been used. In fact, the average palate would not know the difference.

Smoke Cookery

It is axiomatic that smoke "cookery" and the preservation of foods through smoking are almost as old as fire. It is also true that the original smoking process came about not to enhance the flavor of food but rather to make it last from one season to the next.

Primitive man was no fool, however. Early on he discovered that smoke not only extended the camp life of food but gave pleasure to the palate as well. Subsequently the flavor of smoked foods became an end in itself.

One of the best booklets (or books, for that matter) on smoking and smoke cookery is "The Nitty Gritty of Smoke Cooking," a giveaway that is included with a highly efficient and reasonably priced electric smoker manufactured by Luhr Jensen and Sons, Inc. The smokers are available from numerous sources including L. L. Bean, Inc., Freeport, Maine 04032, or from the Luhr Jensen factory, Post Office Box 297, Hood River, Oregon 97031 (in Canada it is 144 East Third Avenue, Vancouver, B.C.).

In the introduction to the booklet by Dan Stair, the author explains that there are three basic ways to smoke foods. The hottest and fastest is plain smoke cookery, which is "not much more than taking a backyard barbecue, putting a cover on it, sprinkling hardwood chips on the charcoals and then cooking the meat."

The second type is cold smoking whereby foods are cured at approximately 90 degrees for from several days to several weeks and, finally, hot smoking, in which the meat is entirely or partly cooked at temperatures ranging from about 100 degrees to 190 degrees. The latter also adds a highly desirable flavor.

The Jensen smoker will hold 20 pounds of meat or fish, operates on 1 cent of current per hour, measures 12 by 12 by 24 inches and comes with 1½ pounds of hickory chips. The cost is $29 postpaid.

Hickory Smoked Chicken or Game
(From Dan Stair)

1   *or more chickens or game birds such as pheasant, duck, quail, and grouse*

Melted butter

The brine

2   *quarts water*
½   *cup brown sugar*
4   *tablespoons ground black pepper*

1 *tablespoon onion powder*
1 *bay leaf*
¼ *cup lemon juice*

The presmoking mix

½ *cup brown sugar*
1 *tablespoon onion or garlic
  powder*
4 *tablespoons ground black
  pepper*

1. If the chicken or game birds are frozen, defrost them thoroughly.

2. Combine the ingredients for the brine in a stoneware or nonaluminum container. If there is not sufficient liquid to cover the bird or birds, double or triple the ingredients accordingly.

3. After the ingredients are thoroughly blended, immerse the chicken or other birds, using a weight to make sure no portion of the meat extends above the surface of the brine. Cure the fowl for 1 hour per pound.

4. Remove the bird or birds and rinse well under cold running water. Wipe dry inside and out and let stand in a cold, airy place 1 hour.

5. Suspend the fowl on the built-in meat bar of the smoker rack.

6. Meanwhile, preheat the smoker for 1 hour while the fowl dries.

7. Combine the presmoking mix ingredients and rub the fowl all over with the mix. Smoke 1½ hours per pound, following the instructions of the manufacturer. Brush the outside of the meat with butter every 90 minutes.

8. If the bird or birds are not thoroughly cooked, the cooking may be completed in the oven preheated to 300 degrees, taking care not to overcook.

Yield: 1 or more smoked birds.

Smoked Southern Sausage

3½ *pounds lean pork, cut into
   2-inch cubes*
2 *pounds solid pork fat, cut
   into 2-inch cubes*
2½ *tablespoons rubbed sage or
   more to taste*
4 *tablespoons sweet paprika
   Salt*
2 *teaspoons finely ground or
   cracked black pepper*
12 *dried hot red pepper pods
   or about 1 tablespoon
   ground*
10 *to 12 feet sausage casings
   (see note)*

1. Put the pork and pork fat into a large mixing bowl and add the sage, paprika, and salt.

2. If preground pepper is used, add it. Otherwise, grind the pepper, using a peppermill. Or grind it in a small, clean coffee grinder. Add it.

3. If preground hot red pepper is used, add it. Otherwise, grind the pepper in a small, clean coffee grinder. Add it.

4. Mix well with the hands, cover and let stand in the refrigerator overnight.

5. Put the mixture through a meat grinder fitted with the largest blade. Remove all the meat left in the grinder and clean the grinder blade.

6. Return the blade to the grinder and fit it, along with the special sausage attachment, to the mouth of the grinder.

7. Slide one prepared sausage casing onto the attachment and tie the end. Grind the meat, holding the casing to permit free entry of the filling into the casing. When about 16 inches of casing have been filled, pinch the casing at the end of the sausage attachment. Pull it out to leave about 4 inches of empty casing at that end. Tie that end. Tie both ends of the sausage together. Set aside. Continue making sausage in this manner until all the stuffing has been used.

8. Hang the sausages in a smoker and smoke according to the manufacturer's instructions.

Yield: 6 to 8 sausage rings, weighing ¾ to 1 pound each.

Note: Sausage casings are available in pork stores in metropolitan areas.

How to prepare sausage casings

Sausage casings are normally preserved in salt. When ready to use, put them in a basin of cold water and let stand. Drain and return to a basin of cold water. Lift up one end of a casing and blow into it. They will expand balloon-like. The reason for this is to determine if the casings have a hole in them. Discard casings with holes or cut the casings at the hole and use the partial casing.

It is a pity most people assume that the smoking of food is a highly elaborate and complex function which requires extensive and expensive equipment. This is wholly untrue. You can smoke in almost any confined area, even in an old oil drum, as long as it's equipped with a base for burning wood and a couple of racks. We ourselves own a standard smoker of the type described a few pages back.

The question frequently arises as to whether or not smoking is feasible in a small apartment, and the answer is yes, provided the apartment is equipped with a small terrace or other outside area. Some of the best home-smoked meats we've ever tasted have been cured on a small terrace outside a tenth floor apartment in lower Manhattan. Smoking is not recommended in highly confined interiors.

A Connecticut Cook

"When I first came to Wilton," Cecile Rivel said one morning recently, "it was a study in frustration. I'd always been a passionate cook and, after growing up in Manhattan, I was spoiled. Every time I needed a package of phyllo pastry or won ton skin or tarama, it meant a special trip to New York.

"So I opened this shop. I assumed there must be scores of other cooks in and around Fairfield County with the same yearnings, and this is the result."

The result she had in mind is the Culinary Arts boutique in the Gateway Shopping Center here. And an impressive result it is.

There are many fine pots-and-pans shops scattered around America today. There are also scores of fine stores that specialize in the finest imported foods. And excellent cooking schools to learn the world's cuisines. But if there is one single shop that embraces all these areas—plus a wall with 2,000 cookbooks for sale—it has not come within our purview.

Mrs. Rivel came from what might be called a 20-carat food background. Her father, Murray Bernstein, was founder and owner of Murray's Sturgeon Shop on Broadway near 89th Street until his retirement to Florida a few weeks ago (the store still prospers under new management). The family lived two blocks away and Mrs. Bernstein was known by her family and friends as a superlative Eastern European cook, noted for such delectable dishes as stuffed cabbage, mushroom and barley soup, and strudel.

The young woman spent two extended sessions at the Paris Cordon Bleu (and like many another knowledgeable and discriminating bec fin, she wasn't too impressed by the school; its reputation far outweighs its merits). She moved to Wilton, Connecticut, shortly after her marriage to Ardith Rivel, now a vice-president of the Benrus Watch Company in Ridgefield.

It is highly conceivable that a delight in fine food preparation will pass from one generation to the next. The Rivels are the parents of two boys, David, thirteen years old, and Brian, seven. David recently gave demonstrations in Japanese cooking before his junior high school class; Brian is an enthusiastic and adventurous cooky maker; both of them turn out homemade pasta with youthful panache.

Mrs. Rivel has a keen and discriminating eye for practical and yet off-beat items that would appeal to almost any cooking amateur (in the

Cecile Rivel, who solved a problem by opening her own store.

original sense, the word derived from the Latin amare, to love). Among
them is a highly purposeful English scale called a Weighmix that is furnished with two mixing bowls for ingredients. As each ingredient is
added (to choose a random example: flour, sugar, butter, raisins, currants
and so on for a fruitcake) the weight indicator can be zeroed so that the
next ingredient can be added without removing the preceding ingredient from the scale.

There is a fine new, imported spaghetti cooker with a perforated insert that permits draining by lifting up the insert rather than pouring
from the kettle.

The Culinary Arts boasts a veritable cornucopia of useful international gadgets—couscous steamers; woks; that splendid Rotor salad spin
drier from Switzerland that should be indispensable for rinsing and drying salad greens in apartments; paella pans; Belgian waffle makers; madeleine molds; French and German knives; and that most wondrous of
recently marketed gadgets, the Cuisinart Food Processor that blends,
grinds, slices, grates and does almost anything else essential to food
preparation except wash dishes.

The store also stocks a traditional selection of fine cookware of high
quality and broad uses, including omelet pans, soufflé dishes, crêpe
pans, pasta machines, wire whisks, first-rate Swiss copper cooking utensils lined with stainless steel (unlike tin-lined copper, the stainless steel
will presumably last forever), snail dishes, and special plates for mussels
and oysters.

The Culinary Arts management encourages the clientele to browse at leisure among the cookbooks. There is an open coffee bar, and on a recent morning numerous women were relaxing over cups of freshly brewed mocha, thumbing through books, and exchanging recipes. The store, incidentally, sells 12 varieties of special roast coffee—mocha, mocha java, Guatemalan, Colombian, Hawaiian kona and so on. Among the wares there is also an espresso-capuccino machine available for $199.95.

We were intrigued to learn from Mrs. Rivel that there has been a tremendous revival of interest in cake decorating during the past year. The shop has an extensive setup of cake decorating equipment including pastry tubes, pastry bags, cake pans ranging from single layers to wide-dimensioned, highstanding wedding cake pans.

Classes in international cooking are held at the shop in March, April, May, and June. Mrs. Rivel conducts classes inclined toward French techniques including hors d'oeuvre and such dishes as crêpes, hot soufflés, quiches, beignets, fish stews, and fish bonne femme. There are also classes in baking, Mediterranean cookery, Scandinavian, Mexican, Chinese, and Indonesian, the last of which it is said is most in vogue at the moment.

The Culinary Arts publishes a monthly newsletter that may be obtained without charge by writng The Culinary Arts, Gateway Shopping Center, Wilton, Connecticut 06897.

The receipes that follow are selected from those demonstrated at the Culinary Arts cooking school.

Brioches

¾ cup plus 1 tablespoon milk
½ pound (2 sticks) butter
5 cups flour
2 packages yeast
¼ cup sugar
2 teaspoons salt
5 eggs
1 egg yolk

1. Combine the ¾ cup milk and the butter in a saucepan and heat just until the butter melts, about 110 degrees. If the liquid becomes hotter, let it cool to that temperature.

2. In a mixing bowl, combine 2 cups of flour, yeast, sugar, and salt. Stir in the milk and butter mixture and 2 eggs.

3. Beat in 2 cups of flour and when thoroughly blended, beat in the remaining eggs and flour. The dough will be soft and shiny. Shape into a ball.

4. Butter lightly a clean mixing bowl and add the dough. Cover with plastic wrap and let stand in a warm place until dou-

ble in bulk, about 1½ hours. Punch the dough down. Cover and refrigerate overnight.

5. About 1½ hours before baking, punch the dough down once more and turn it onto a lightly floured surface. Divide the dough into approximately equal portions, each measuring about ¼ cup.

6. Nip off about ⅕ of each portion and set aside to be used as a top-knot. Roll the larger portion into a ball, using the palms of the hands. Place the ball into a greased brioche tin. Use a razor blade and cut a cross on top of the ball. Roll the nipped-off portion into a tear-drop shape. Arrange the tear-drop, pointed side down, in the middle of the cross. Continue shaping the remaining dough in a similar manner until all the portions are used. Cover the shaped brioches and let rise until almost double in bulk.

7. Preheat the oven to 400 degrees.

8. When the brioches are risen, blend the egg yolk with the remaining 1 tablespoon of milk. Use a pastry brush and brush the top of each brioche with the mixture. Bake 20 minutes.

Yield: 18 to 20 brioches.

Pissaladière

1   recipe for brioche dough (see recipe above)
6   tablespoons olive oil
2   onions, thinly sliced or chopped
1   clove garlic, finely minced
1   2-pound-3-ounce can peeled tomatoes, preferably imported
6   tablespoons tomato paste (omit this if the canned tomatoes already have tomato paste among the ingredients)
2   teaspoons oregano
2   teaspoons dried basil
    Salt and freshly ground pepper
½   cup grated Parmesan cheese
1   2-ounce can flat fillets of anchovy
10 pitted, quartered, imported black olives

1. Prepare the brioche dough but follow the recipe only up to and through the first rising.

2. Preheat the oven to 375 degrees.

3. Heat half the oil in a saucepan and add the onions and then cook, stirring, until wilted. Add the garlic, tomatoes, tomato paste, oregano, basil, salt, and pepper. Simmer, uncovered, 10 to 15 minutes, stirring occasionally, until the sauce is thickened.

4. Roll the brioche dough into a circle and fit it into a round 14-inch pizza pan. Using the fingers, build up the rim of the pastry.

5. Sprinkle the dough with ¼ cup grated Parmesan cheese. Spread the tomato mixture over it and sprinkle with the remaining cheese. Arrange the anchovies and black olives on top and dribble the remaining oil over all. Bake 20 to 30 minutes.

Yield: 6 servings.

Whole Wheat Orange Bread

2 cups water
4 tablespoons butter
4 cups white flour
1 package yeast
2 teaspoons salt
½ cup brown sugar
½ cup honey
1 egg
  Grated rind of 1 orange
2 cups whole wheat flour

1. Combine the water and butter in a saucepan and heat just until the butter melts or to a temperature of 110 degrees. If the liquid becomes hotter, let it cool to that temperature.

2. Combine 2 cups of the white flour, yeast, salt, and brown sugar in a mixing bowl. Add the water and butter mixture, honey, egg, and orange rind. Blend briskly and thoroughly and work in the remaining white flour and the whole wheat flour.

3. Turn the mixture onto a lightly floured board and knead until smooth and elastic. Shape into a ball.

4. Butter lightly a clean mixing bowl. Add the dough and turn it lightly to coat all sides.

5. Cover the bowl with plastic wrap. Let stand in a warm place until double in bulk.

6. Preheat the oven to 375 degrees.

7. Turn the dough out and knead it lightly. Cover and let rest for 5 to 10 minutes.

8. Shape the dough into 2 loaves. Arrange each loaf in a greased 1½-quart loaf pan (see note). Let rise again. Bake 45 minutes.

Yield: 2 loaves.

Note: If glass loaf pans are used, lower temperature to 350 degrees.

Chicken Ketjap

10 to 12 chicken thighs
   Salt and freshly ground pepper
½ teaspoon ground mace
4 tablespoons butter
1 large onion, finely chopped, about 3 cups
1 clove garlic, crushed
1 tablespoon lemon juice
1 tablespoon dark brown sugar
1½ teaspoons ground cumin (djinten) (see note)
1½ teaspoons ground coriander (ketumbar) (see note)
2 teaspoons bottled imported meat seasoning (bumboe sesate) (see note)
½ to 1 teaspoon imported hot chili paste (sambal oelek) (see note)
½ cup sweet soy sauce (ketjap manis) (see note)
2 ounces dried grated coconut (klapper) (see note)
1½ cups hot water

1. Preheat the oven to 325 degrees.

2. Skin the chicken thighs and place them in a bowl. Sprinkle

with salt, pepper, and mace and rub to coat well.

3. Heat the butter in a skillet and brown the chicken pieces lightly.

4. Meanwhile, combine the onion, garlic, lemon juice, sugar, cumin, coriander, meat seasoning, hot chili paste, and sweet soy sauce.

5. Transfer the chicken to a baking dish and place it in the oven.

6. Add the onion and spice mixture to the skillet. Cook, stirring, about 8 to 10 minutes.

7. Combine the grated coconut and water and let stand briefly, kneading with the hands. Squeeze the mixture through cheesecloth or a potato ricer. Add 1 cup of the coconut milk to the onion and spice mixture and stir to blend. Discard the coconut. Bring to the boil.

8. Pour the onion and spice mixture over the chicken and bake, uncovered, until the chicken is tender, 20 to 30 minutes. Turn the chicken pieces once as they cook. Serve with rice.

Yield: 5 to 6 servings.

Note: These are Indonesian names of the various spices available at outlets that sell imported spices.

Pride of the Forest

WITH PIERRE FRANEY

The traditional Black Forest cake, with its kirsch-scented chocolate layers and its tantalizing blend of sour and sweet cherries, is one of Germany's proudest contributions to the world's cookery. The version here is that of Albert Kumin, a leading pastry chef at the Culinary Institute of America, in Hyde Park, New York.

Black Forest Cake

1   10-inch chocolate
    spongecake (see recipe)
½   cup plus 1 tablespoon
    sugar
1   cup water
2   thin orange or lemon
    wedges
1   8-ounce can dark sweet
    pitted cherries (see note)
1   1-pound can sour cherries
⅓   cup kirschwasser
1   3-ounce (85-gram) bar of
    imported bittersweet
    chocolate
3   cups heavy cream
3   drops pure vanilla extract
    Scraped and/or grated
    chocolate for garnish

1. Prepare the spongecake and set aside.

2. Combine ½ cup of sugar and the water in a saucepan. Add the orange or lemon wedges and bring to the boil. Simmer about 3 minutes and let the syrup cool. Discard wedges.

3. Drain both cans of cherries separately and set cherries aside.

4. Combine the kirschwasser with ⅔ cup of the syrup. Set aside.

5. Place the chocolate in a saucepan and let it melt gradually in a warm place. When it is melted, gradually add 3 tablespoons of the remaining syrup, stirring.

6. Whip the cream and beat in the remaining tablespoon of sugar and the vanilla.

7. Fold 1½ cups of the whipped cream into the chocolate mixture. Set the remaining whipped cream aside.

8. Place the cake on a flat surface and, holding a long, sharp knife parallel to the bottom of the cake, slice the cake into thirds.

9. Place the bottom slice on a serving plate and brush with some of the syrup mixture. Add about half the chocolate mixture to the slice and smooth it over.

10. Cover with the top slice but place it bottom side up. Brush the slice with syrup and add the remaining chocolate mixture, smoothing it over. Using a pastry tube, pipe 3 rings of whipped cream around the cake. Pipe one ring in the center, another in the middle and the other around the rim. Arrange sour cherries in the center and between the middle and outer rings.

11. Top with the final slice of cake. Brush it with the remaining syrup. Add whipped cream to the top, but save enough cream to make 13 rosettes on top of the cake. Smooth the whipped cream around the top and sides of the cake. Use a No. 4 star pastry tube and pipe 12 rosettes, equally spaced, around the upper rim of the cake. Make one rosette in dead center. Garnish each rosette with one dark sweet pitted cherry. Garnish the top with scraped or grated chocolate. Hold in the refrigerator.

Yield: 10 servings.

Note: Fresh black bing cherries may be poached in syrup, pitted, and used in this recipe.

Chocolate spongecake

6 *eggs*
1 *cup sugar*
½ *cup plus 3 tablespoons flour*
4 *tablespoons cornstarch*
6 *tablespoons cocoa powder*
3 *tablespoons melted butter*

1. Preheat oven to 375 degrees.

2. Butter a round cake tin (ours measured 10 by 2 inches). Sprinkle the inside with flour and shake the flour around until the bottom and sides are well coated. Shake out any excess flour.

3. Put the eggs into the bowl of an electric mixer. Bring about 2 quarts of water to the boil in a casserole or other utensil large enough to hold the mixing bowl. Set the bowl in the water and beat vigorously while adding the sugar. Beat constantly about 5 minutes until the eggs are lukewarm.

4. Return the bowl to the electric mixer and continue beating on high speed until the mixture is thick, mousselike, and at room temperature. To test, run a spatula through the mass. If it is ready, the spatula will leave a track.

5. Meanwhile, combine the flour, cornstarch, and cocoa. Sift together two or three times. Fold the mixture into the batter, using a wooden spoon or spatula. Fold in the butter and pour the mixture into the prepared pan. Bake about 25 to 30 minutes or until the cake pulls away from the pan. Turn the cake out onto a rack to cool.

Yield: 1 spongecake.

Lessons from a Master

The incident was real but it followed a plot line nearly as old as stagecraft itself: an aspiring young actor waiting in the wings; a star performer suddenly indisposed; a virtuoso turn by the youth; thundering applause and shouts of bravo bravo.

A couple of summers ago, David Liederman, then a 23-year-old native of Princeton, New Jersey, found himself somewhat miraculously doing a brief stint as a vegetable-peeler, pot-washer, and chief-observer in one of the most prestigious kitchens in the world, that of the Troisgros Restaurant in Roanne, France.

Over a period of days he had been allowed to throw a few things into the stock pot and make a sauce or two and had once helped the pastry chef make macaroons and sherbet. With his notably keen sense of perception, he knew the Troisgros menu by heart.

"It was five minutes after two in the afternoon one day in summer," he recounted recently. "There was an almost inviolate rule in that kitchen. At precisely 2 o'clock it shut down and everybody on the staff scattered no matter who was in the dining room.

"On this particular day I was allowed to leave when suddenly there was this awful yelling and screaming in the dining room. It was a man from Connecticut and his wife who had just arrived from Paris in their BMW. He was yelling at Guérard, the maître d'hôtel, that he had driven all that distance to eat at Troisgros and if he wasn't fed he would not be responsible for the dire things that would happen to the premises and the staff.

"Guérard came running into the kitchen, took one look at me and said, 'You're on.' I grabbed a 12-year-old kitchen boy who had come back for his coat and said, 'You do it,' but he was having nothing to do with it!" Within an hour the man and his wife had dined on salmon with sorrel sauce, sautéed beef with marrow in a sauce bordelaise, dauphine potatoes, and fresh wild strawberry sherbet.

"It was no big deal," David stated modestly. The bases for the sauces were already made. It simply meant cooking the fish and meat and knowing what to add to the bases. At the end of the meal the Connecticut man dispatched his compliments to the chef.

When David packed to leave the restaurant a week or so later, Jean Troisgros looked at him and winked. "Good show," he said.

David Liederman's association with the restaurant has an interesting history. He grew up in a home where he was served carefully prepared but conventional food by his mother, Adele Adlerstein, a director of counseling for Rutgers University in Newark, whom he describes as "a typical American cook—chicken and pot roast."

In high school, David was an all-state athlete, "very much into football and lacrosse." And he was recruited to play lacrosse at Denison University in Ohio. His father is a "board chairman of several companies," his stepfather a psychologist and computer scientist.

The turning point for David came when he was 20 years old and traveled to Europe. During a stay in Lyon he looked up all the restaurants in the area in the Guide Michelin and settled on the Troisgros in Roanne because it seemed the least expensive. "Dining there," he reflects, "was fantastic, a sort of spiritual revolution. I'd never tasted food like that." He stayed a few days and was largely ignored by the staff. He met one of the Troisgros frères, Pierre, who wasn't particularly impressed.

At that time he didn't know there was another brother named Jean who would play a large role in his future. David returned to America, "turned on to the whole cooking thing—I started buying all the cookbooks I could get my hands on." He put aside his collection of stamps and coins and started collecting copper pots and wines. "And giving dinner parties. Lots of them."

The following year he returned to France, this time expressly to visit the Troisgros dining room again and once in a while he made his presence known in the kitchen.

"Late one evening," he said, "I was seated at the bar having a drink and this big man with a beard comes over. I didn't know who he was. 'Tennis?' he said. I said 'Yes' and the next afternoon we went to the courts. He spoke very little English. We played for a couple of hours and he said, 'Basketball?' I said 'Sure.' We played until six o'clock and he introduced himself. It was Jean Troisgros. He took me back to the kitchen with him and threw me a bunch of asparagus to clean. I was so nervous I broke more than I scraped.

"The next morning at six A.M. he took me around to all the purveyors in town—sausage makers, hog butchers, cream suppliers, bakers, and so on. He walks around that town like a god. So I fell into a routine—shopping in the morning, watching in the kitchen throughout lunch, tennis, basketball, a swim, and back for the evening meal. Then we'd pass out from exhaustion."

One of his fondest memories of the Troisgros Restaurant is a lunch shared with five of the titans of French gastronomy, the Troisgros brothers, the Haeberlin brothers of the distinguished Auberge de l'Ill in Illhäusern (Alsace) and Paul Bocuse of Lyon. They sat at table playing the game "I'm a better chef than you."

Since his return to New York last year Mr. Liederman has been

working toward his law degree at Brooklyn Law School as well as studying toward a restaurant degree at New York City Community College.
Incidentally he has the highest regard for the Community College. It is,
he states, a great value for anyone interested in cooking professionally. It
is a fantastic bargain with first-rate training in classic French cooking.

Although Mr. Liederman intends to pursue a career in law on graduation, his ultimate aim is to open his own restaurant with himself in-
stalled as chief chef.

David will return to the Troisgros for a third stint in late July following his bar examination. This time his stay will be extended and more
serious in the sense that he will participate as a full-time apprentice
rather than as a casual participant. He will receive $25 a week plus room
and board for his 16 hours a day.

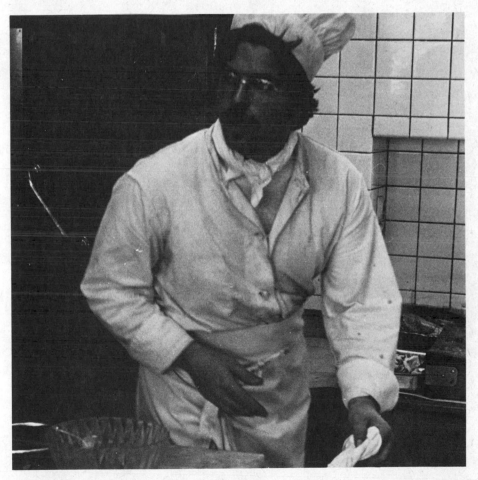

David Liederman, in the kitchen of the Troisgros.

Duck with Green Peppercorn Sauce

½   cup condensed duck stock
     (see recipe)
6   tablespoons crème fraîche
     (see recipe)
1   4–5-pound fresh duck
     Salt and white pepper
2   teaspoons water-packed
     green peppercorns (see
     note)

1. Prepare the duck stock and the crème fraîche at least one day in advance.

2. Bone the duck carefully, working the knife around the breast bones and thigh bones to keep the meat as nearly intact and in one piece as possible. Save the duck carcass to make soup or another batch of duck stock. Do not cut the fat covering the breast meat and thighs, but discard all remaining excess duck fat except 1 tablespoon to be used in the duck stock recipe.

3. Cut the boned duck into 4 pieces as follows: 2 breast halves and 2 completely boned thighs. Carefully and neatly trim around the breast pieces and the thighs to remove all peripheral fat. Sprinkle the pieces on all sides with salt and pepper.

4. Use a heavy skillet and when it is hot, add the duck pieces fat side down. Cook until the skin starts to become crisp and the meat immediately adjacent to the fat starts to lose its reddish color, about 3 minutes.

5. Turn the duck pieces and cook about 2 minutes on the other side. The outside should be nicely browned but the inside of the flesh preferably should remain rare. Tastes vary, however, so cook it like steak to any desired degree of doneness.

6. Transfer the duck pieces to a warm platter and let rest briefly while preparing the sauce. Add the duck stock to a small, heavy saucepan and bring to the boil. Add the crème fraîche and stir until thoroughly blended and smooth. Bring to the boil. Crush the peppercorns and stir them in. Strain through a sieve, if desired, or leave the sauce unstrained.

7. Using a sharp knife, cut the duck pieces on the diagonal into ¼-inch-thick slices. Arrange them overlapping on 4 or 6 warm plates. Spoon the hot sauce over each serving and serve.

Yield: 4 to 6 servings.

Note: Green peppercorns packed in water are available at specialty food shops.

Condensed duck stock

1   duck carcass including the
     heart and gizzard (the liver
     may be used for another
     purpose)
4   to 6 carrots, about 1 pound
2   leeks, well trimmed and
     washed
4   to 6 onions, about 1 pound
2   ribs celery
6   parsley sprigs
1   bay leaf
¼   teaspoon dried thyme
1   clove garlic, unpeeled and
     left whole

1 *tablespoon duck fat,*
   chopped
5 *quarts water*

1. Chop the duck carcass into 2-inch pieces. Set aside.

2. Coarsely chop the carrots, leeks, onions, and celery. Set aside.

3. Tie the parsley, bay leaf, thyme, and garlic in a cheesecloth bag.

4. Brown the pieces of duck carcass and the chopped vegetables with the duck fat in a heavy skillet or kettle. It is not necessary to add additional fat. When well browned, add the water and cheesecloth bag. Do not add salt and pepper. Bring to the boil and simmer, skimming the surface as necessary, about 4 hours. Strain. Discard the solids.

5. Add the stock to a saucepan and cook it down to 1½ cups.

Yield: 1 to 1½ cups.

Note: Leftover duck stock can be frozen. Duck stock will keep for several days if refrigerated.

Crème Fraîche
(A thickened fresh cream)

1 *cup heavy cream*
1 *teaspoon buttermilk*

Pour the cream into a jar or mixing bowl. Add the buttermilk and stir. Cover tightly with plastic wrap and let stand in a slightly warm place 12 to 14 hours or even longer or until the cream is about twice as thick as ordinary heavy cream. Refrigerate and use as desired in cooking, on fresh fruits, fruit pies, and so on. Keep closely covered.

Yield: About 1 cup.

Striped Bass with Tomato Vinaigrette Sauce

2 *quarts water*
2 *tablespoons white wine*
   vinegar
½ *cup dry white wine*
1 *cup sliced onions*
½ *cup sliced carrots*
1 *teaspoon crushed black*
   peppercorns
1 *large bay leaf*
6 *parsley sprigs*
2 *teaspoons salt*
1 *3–4-pound striped bass,*
   cleaned and with gills
   removed but preferably
   with the head and tail left
   on
1 *pound seaweed (obtained*
   from fish markets that deal
   in lobsters or taken fresh
   from the water), enough to
   cover the fish
¾ *cup tomato vinaigrette*
   sauce (see recipe)

1. Combine the water, vinegar, wine, onions, carrots, peppercorns, bay leaf, parsley sprigs, and salt. Bring to the boil. Stir and let cool. This is a court bouillon.

2. Pour the court bouillon into a fish poacher. Wrap the bass in cheesecloth and tie it at both ends. Place the fish in the poacher and cover with seaweed. Cover

with a lid. Bring to the boil and simmer gently 15 to 20 minutes. Turn off the heat and let the fish remain in the court bouillon 10 minutes longer.

3. Discard the seaweed and lift the fish from the poacher. Discard the cheesecloth and arrange the fish on a platter. Remove the skin with a knife and serve the tomato vinaigrette sauce on the side.

Yield: 6 to 8 servings

Tomato vinaigrette sauce

2 *tablespoons wine vinegar*

Salt
½ *teaspoon freshly ground black pepper*
2 *tablespoons chopped Italian (flat-leaf) parsley*
½ *cup imported olive oil*
1 *cup peeled, seeded, chopped tomatoes*

In a mixing bowl, combine wine vinegar, salt to taste, pepper, and parsley. Gradually add the olive oil, stirring rapidly with a wire whisk. Add tomatoes and stir to blend. Serve.

Yield: About 1¾ cups.

Note: Leftover sauce can be stored for a day in the refrigerator.

Persian Cookery

To listen to Jennifer Manocherian tell it, Persian cooking is the ultimate answer to that consummate question, how to cook for company, turn off the heat, and greet the guests, anxiety-free, nonchalant, insouciant, and full of the assurance that the food with only a touch of heat will be ready to serve an hour, two hours or an even more protracted time later.

Mrs. Manocherian, who cooks three meals a day for her family of six including herself, contends that Iranian food is the easiest food in the world to cook.

"In America, if someone drops by at the last moment, it's panic time. You know there is only food for four or however many guests are on hand—four lamb chops, four Idahos and so on. In Iran, you always add a little more meat or a few more vegetables to the pot and there's enough for everyone." The innate thing about Persian cooking is that all cooked foods—roasts or whatever—are served well done.

Mrs. Manocherian has a rather solid background in cooking. Born Jennifer Robbins, she is the daughter of Ann Roe Robbins, who for many years directed one of the best cooking schools in Manhattan, until it closed in 1971.

Mrs. Robbins gave her lessons and the family lived in one of the oldest apartment buildings in Manhattan, one of those old Rosemary's Baby-type places on Central Park West. It was in that building that Miss Robbins met her Iranian husband, Fraydun (better known as Fred) Manocherian, a real estate executive, who also lived there. "I had a Siamese cat who strayed out of the apartment one morning, and I was exploring all those corridors and stairwells when Fred and I bumped into each other," Mrs. Manocherian said.

Mr. Manocherian, who had been born in Teheran, came to this country in 1946 when he was 14 years old and came from a family where fine food was a tradition. His mother excelled at Persian cookery.

"Fred and I spent one summer there. Only one, unfortunately," Mrs. Manocherian said. "Flying makes me nervous. Fred's mother taught me everything I know, just as she taught all of her daughters-in-law." Mrs. Manocherian has one sister-in-law who comes to New York fairly often, laden with plastic bags filled with dried Iranian spices.

One of the many fine recipes sampled recently in the young woman's home (the Manocherian children range in age from one year to fifteen) was an excellent roast lamb with yogurt, the meat having been marinated for many hours in yogurt with seasonings. There was, in addition, a fine Persian "omelet" made with eggs and spinach and known as coocoo; an admirable eggplant and yogurt appetizer, improved with the addition of fried onions before serving; and that superb rice with dill cooked on potato slices that become crisp and tender on the bottom.

"Everything eaten in Persia," she stated with only slight exaggeration, "is either cooked with yogurt or eaten with yogurt." One reason, she contends, is that "yogurt is the greatest tenderizer in the world."

Mrs. Manocherian is a stockholder and works in the public relations field for the New York Health Clubs. She has also edited a spiral bound 130-page and very interesting cookbook called *The Betty Quaker Cookbook*, sales of which benefit the Quaker Ridge School Parents and Teachers Association in Scarsdale.

The book, which contains many of her own recipes, is available by sending $3.50 in check or money order to her in care of the school on Weaver Street, Scarsdale. The health club food bars, incidentally, offer her special Persian salad made with yogurt, cucumbers, and raisins on the menu.

"In America," says Jennifer Manocherian, "if someone drops by at the last moment, it's panic time. In Iran, you add a little more to the pot and there's enough for everyone."

Coocoo
(A Persian spinach "omelet")

2   *10-ounce packages frozen chopped spinach*
½   *cup finely chopped onion (1 large onion)*
1 . *cup finely chopped leeks (1 large or 2 small bunches) or green onions*
1½ *cups finely chopped parsley*
8   *tablespoons butter*
8   *eggs*
    Salt
2   *tablespoons peanut, vegetable, or corn oil*
1   *cup yogurt*

1. Let the spinach stand at room temperature until thoroughly defrosted.

2. Combine the spinach, onion, leeks or green onions and parsley.

3. Melt 6 tablespoons of butter in a large, heavy skillet and add the vegetable mixture. Cook over medium heat, stirring often, until thoroughly cooked, about ½ hour. The vegetables will become dark green. Remove from the heat and cool.

4. Beat the eggs in a large mixing bowl and add the vegetable mixture. Add salt to taste.

5. Melt the remaining butter and the oil in the large, heavy skillet and pour in the egg mixture. Cover and cook over medium heat until the egg is set and the bottom is nicely browned, 20 to 30 minutes. To test the bottom, lift the edge of the "omelet" up gently with a spatula.

6. Cut the "omelet" into quarters with a sharp knife and turn over each quarter in the skillet to brown the other side. Brown the second side without covering. Serve warm cut in wedges like a pie with yogurt on the side.

Yield: 8 servings.

Masto Badenjohn
(Eggplant and yogurt appetizer)

1   *eggplant, about 1 pound*
1   *teaspoon finely minced onion*
1   *teaspoon lemon juice or more to taste*
1   *cup plain yogurt*
    Salt
3   *tablespoons butter*
1   *large onion, cut into thin, lengthwise slices, about 2 cups*
    Middle Eastern bread or French bread

1. Preheat the oven to 350 degrees. Place the eggplant on a sheet of aluminum foil in the oven and bake about 1 hour or until the vegetable is thoroughly tender inside and the skin almost collapsed. Let cool

2. Cut the eggplant in half and scrape the insides into a mixing bowl. Discard the skin. Mash the flesh with a fork and add the minced onion, lemon juice, yogurt, and salt. Blend well and chill.

3. When ready to serve, heat the butter in a skillet and add the onion slices and cook, stirring often, until soft and nicely browned. Spoon the onions over the eggplant dip. Serve with bread.

Yield: 8 to 12 servings.

Masto Khiar

(Persian yogurt salad)

1   *cup plain yogurt*
1   *small onion, grated*
1   *small or ½ large cucumber, peeled and diced*
¼   *cup raisins*
    Salt
¼   *cup loosely packed fresh mint leaves, if available*

Spoon the yogurt into a mixing bowl and add the remaining ingredients. Blend well and chill.

Yield: About 2 cups.

Leg of Lamb Persian-Style

1   *6–7-pound leg of lamb*
1   *cup plain yogurt*
¼   *cup olive oil*
½   *cup grated onion*
    Salt and freshly ground black pepper

1. Place the lamb in a large plastic bag and add the yogurt, olive oil, onion, salt and pepper to taste. Seal tightly and, using the hands, maneuver the marinade all over the meat. Refrigerate overnight or leave at room temperature for several hours. Leave the lamb in the bag but turn it oc-

casionally to redistribute the marinade.

2. Preheat the oven to 500 degrees.

3. Remove the lamb from the bag and place it in a roasting pan large enough to hold it amply. Pour and squeeze the marinade over the meat and bake, uncovered, until the meat is very brown on top, 30 to 40 minutes. As the meat bakes add ½ cup or so of water to the roasting pan to prevent sticking. There should be about ⅛ to ¼ inch of liquid on the bottom of the pan at all times. When the meat is brown on top, turn it and bake about 15 minutes on that side. Cover tightly with the lid and reduce the heat to 375 degrees. Bake from 1 to 1½ hours, or until almost fork tender. Serve with the natural pan juices, skimmed of most of the fat.

Yield: 8 to 12 servings.

Rice with Dill Persian-Style

2   *cups long-grain rice*
¼   *cup salt*
1   *10-ounce package frozen baby lima beans*
12 *tablespoons butter*
2   *tablespoons water*
1   *or 2 Idaho potatoes*
1¾ *cups chopped fresh dill leaves (1 large bunch, tough stalks discarded)*

1. Several hours before cooking the rice, wash it and rinse through several times. Place it in a mixing bowl and add cold water to a depth of about 1 inch above the top of the rice. Add the salt and let stand until about 1½ hours before cooking.

2. Drain the water into a large, heavy kettle. Add about 3 more quarts of water and bring to a vigorous boil. Add the drained rice and lima beans. Bring back to a boil and cook about 5 to 7 minutes, testing the grains frequently for state of doneness. The grains are ready when they are tender on the outside but have a tiny hard core in the center. Drain immediately or the rice will overcook.

3. Meanwhile, melt the butter with the 2 tablespoons water in a saucepan. Set aside.

4. Similarly, as the rice cooks, peel the potato or potatoes and cut into ¼-inch slices. There should be enough slices to cover the bottom of the same heavy kettle when the slices are placed snugly together without overlapping and in one layer.

5. Pour enough melted butter into the kettle to barely cover the bottom and arrange the potatoes over it. Spoon about ¼ of the rice over the potatoes and add about ¼ of the dill. Carefully stir the rice with a spoon to blend in the dill.

Do not disturb the potatoes at any point until the dish is fully cooked. Continue adding rice and dill layers, stirring to blend after each addition. Shape the rice-dill mixture into a coneshaped mound. Pour the remaining butter evenly over the rice. Place the kettle on the heat and cook over medium heat for 5 minutes or until steam comes through the center. Cover with a heavy bath towel folded so that it fits the top of the pot. Cover this with the lid and place a weight over the lid so that no steam can escape as the rice cooks. Reduce the heat and cook 45 minutes to 1 hour.

6. When ready to serve, spoon the rice onto a large platter and garnish with the potato slices, bottom side up. The bottoms should be golden brown and crisp. Test the potatoes before removing. If the potatoes haven't browned, uncover and cook over medium heat for a few minutes until browned. If the rice is not sufficiently tender, add a few tablespoons of boiling water to the kettle and cook another 15 minutes. This rice can be cooked ahead of time and reheated by pouring a little boiling water over the rice and steaming 15 minutes longer.

Yield: 8 servings.

Stuffed Vegetables

WITH PIERRE FRANEY

There is every reason to presume that the first stuffed vegetable came about through some fortuitous deployment of a leftover food, such as a roast. Chances are that the result was so eminently delectable that the stuffing became an end in itself, as in the case of a French version of peppers stuffed with pork and flavored with tarragon. For want of a leftover meat, the stuffed eggplant Sicilian-style might send one out to the supermarket for fresh ground meat.

Tarragon and Pork-Stuffed Peppers

   4   large green peppers
       Salt and freshly ground
       black pepper
   1   pound leftover roast pork
   ¼   pound fresh mushrooms,
       rinsed and drained.
   6   tablespoons butter
   1½ cups finely chopped onion
   2   cloves garlic, finely minced
   2   sprigs fresh thyme, finely
       chopped, or ½ teaspoon
       dried
   ½   bay leaf, finely chopped
       (this can be done in a
       small, clean coffee grinder)
   2   tablespoons finely chopped
       parsley
   1   tablespoon finely chopped
       fresh tarragon or 1
       teaspoon dried, crushed
   1   cup cooked rice
   2   eggs
   ½   cup pine nuts, optional
   ¼   cup fresh bread crumbs
   ¼   cup grated Parmesan
       cheese

Edward Weston still life.

   2   cups peeled tomatoes,
       preferably Italian plum
       tomatoes if canned ones
       are used
   ½   cup chicken broth

1. Split the peppers in half lengthwise. Sprinkle inside with salt and pepper.

2. Put the meat through a meat grinder fitted with a coarse blade, or chop it finely. There should be about 4 cups. Put the meat in a mixing bowl.

3. Put the mushrooms through the grinder and set aside.

4. Melt 1 tablespoon butter in a skillet or saucepan and add the mushrooms, 1 cup of onion and half the garlic. Cook, stirring, until the mushrooms give up their liquid. Cook until most of the liquid evaporates. Add the thyme, bay leaf, parsley, and tarragon.

5. Add the mushroom mixture to the pork. Add the rice, eggs, salt and pepper to taste, and the pine nuts. Blend well.

6. Stuff the pepper halves with the mixture and sprinkle with bread crumbs and cheese.

7. With 3 tablespoons butter, grease a flameproof baking dish large enough to hold the peppers. Add the remaining ½ cup of onion and garlic and sprinkle with salt and pepper. Arrange the peppers in the dish.

8. Blend the tomatoes in an electric blender and pour them around the peppers. Add the chicken broth. Sprinkle salt and pepper over all. Melt remaining 2 tablespoons of butter and dribble it over the peppers.

9. Preheat oven to 350 degrees.

10. Bring the dish to the boil on top of the stove, then place it in the oven. Bake 45 minutes. Serve the peppers with the natural tomato sauce in the pan.

Yield: 8 servings.

Sicilian-Style Stuffed Eggplant

1   *eggplant, 1–1½ pounds*
    Salt
2   *cups chopped, peeled, seeded, and juiced fresh tomatoes or drained Italian plum tomatoes*
6   *tablespoons olive oil, approximately*
1   *cup chopped onion*
1   *teaspoon dried oregano, crushed*
    Freshly ground black pepper
6   *to 8 thin slices salami*
⅓   *pound ground beef*
⅓   *pound ground lean pork*
1   *egg, lightly beaten*
3   *tablespoons heavy cream*
⅓   *cup toasted bread crumbs*
½   *cup grated Parmesan cheese*
1   *clove garlic, finely chopped*
¼   *cup finely chopped parsley*
¼   *teaspoon freshly grated nutmeg*

1. Trim off and discard the stem of the eggplant. Cut off a thin slice lengthwise from opposite sides of the eggplant and discard. Cut the eggplant lengthwise into 4 slices of equal thickness. Sprinkle the slices, top and bottom, with salt. Place the slices on a rack and let stand.

2. Preheat oven to 400 degrees.

3. Heat a tablespoon of olive oil in a wide saucepan and add the onion. Cook, stirring, until wilted. Add the chopped tomatoes and oregano and cook, stirring

frequently. Add salt and pepper to taste. Cook about 10 minutes and set aside.

4. Rinse the eggplant slices and pat them dry. Heat a little of the remaining oil in a skillet and when it is very hot add the eggplant slices. Cook to brown on one side, adding a little more oil at a time as necessary to prevent burning or sticking. Turn the slices and brown on the other side, adding more oil as necessary. Drain the slices when they are ready.

5. Stack the salami and slice finely. Cut the strips into fine dice. Add the salami to a mixing bowl. Add the beef and pork, egg, cream, bread crumbs, half the cheese, the garlic, parsley, and nutmeg. Blend well with the fingers.

6. Divide the meat mixture into 3 equal parts. Shape each part into a flat oval of approximately the same shape as the eggplant slices. Brown the ovals on both sides in a little olive oil.

7. Make a double-decker "sandwich" with the eggplant slices, filling between slices with the ovals of meat. Tie with string if necessary to keep the "sandwich" intact.

8. Spoon a little of the tomato sauce over the bottom of a deep dish large enough to hold the stuffed eggplant. Add the stacked eggplant and cover with the remaining sauce. Cover tightly with aluminum foil and a lid. Place in the oven and bake 1 hour and 15 minutes. Serve with the remaining Parmesan cheese.

Yield: 4 servings.

It is one of the major clichés of our life that if someone gave us a fillet of beef we would grind it up to make hamburgers. It is quite obvious we have a passion for ground meat dishes of almost any sort. It might be ground chicken, pork, beef, or lamb. But we are convinced some of the most ambrosial dishes on earth are those involving ground meat for stuffing purposes. You'll find a host of such recipes in this book.

Some Thoughts about Samp

Samp is a coarse hominy made from kernels of dried corn. Although many of today's residents on the eastern end of Long Island may not know it, it is as typical of the region—if not more so—than clam pies. Many tales are told by long-time residents of the area, including the legend that whaling vessels plying the bay waters offshore even in the thickest fog or darkest night could tell from the sound of samp-pounding how close in-shore they were.

We recently heard from Mary Mooney Getoff of Southold, who sent us a copy of her mimeographed booklet titled "Samp." It is chock full of samp lore and includes several good-sounding recipes for complete meals made with the hominy.

For those who have access to it, here is a one-dish meal using samp, chicken, and tomatoes. Samp, incidentally, is derived from the Narragansett word nasaump meaning corn mush. Dried samp is available in Bridgehampton at IGA on Main Street; in Southold at Gifts, Goodies and Gadgets and The Health Hut; Catenals in Southampton; and in Shelter Island at George's Market, Route 114.

Mrs. Getoff's 11-page booklet may be obtained postage-paid by sending a check or money order for $1 to Mary M. Getoff, Waterview Drive, Southold, New York 11971.

Chicken and Tomato Samp

1 cup samp, preferably
  yellow samp
4 cups stewed tomatoes with
  their liquid
3 cups chicken broth
1 2-pound chicken, cut into
  serving pieces
  Salt and freshly ground
  black pepper

1. Soak the samp overnight in water to cover.

2. Combine the tomatoes and broth in a kettle and bring to the boil.

3. Add the chicken. Drain the samp and add it. Add salt and pepper to taste.

4. Cover the kettle and let simmer 1 to 2 hours, testing the samp and cooking until it is chewy or soft, depending on taste. Serve in soup dishes.

Yield: 4 to 5 servings.

Cooking as Therapy

A note recently from a favorite correspondent Feinschmecker informed us he'd just dined in the home of a Dr. Louis Parrish, a physician and friend "who has taught many of his friends about herb cookery.

"Dr. Parrish is from the South, Louisiana specifically, and is a fantastic southern cook with several creole specialties to his credit," our friend assured us. "His true forte, however, is pleasant dishes and things made with leftovers. The thing is, his leftovers just don't taste like leftovers."

The latter thought was enough to send us scudding to Dr. Parrish's stylish apartment on the East Side one cold late afternoon, and we arrived just as the doctor was in the midst of preparing a salad dressing for the evening greens. He held a bottle containing a nicely perfumed vinegar with an assortment of herbs—some familiar, some not so familiar—tangled inside.

"What is it?" we asked, sniffing the bottle cap. "Amalgamansett," he replied with a straight face. "Amalgamansett?" we asked and he laughed.

"It's a friend's joke," he said. "Last summer I spent a few weeks in the Hamptons tending the herb garden of an acquaintance who lives in Amagansett. It was overrun with things like basil and dill, lovage, rosemary, savory, tarragon, and thyme, so before he closed the house, I bottled enough vinegar with a blend of herbs for several friends as well as myself. Thus Amalgamansett."

We commented on the fact that he was still wearing a buttoned shirt and tie and looked uncomfortably formal, to which he replied that it was a characteristic circumstance.

"To me," he said, "cooking is the greatest therapy on earth. It gratifies my senses as much as eating. I spend a long day listening and talking to patients and when I get home at night, the first thing I do is rush to the kitchen.

"I never bother to get comfortable until the meal is laid out. I chop the vegetables, slice the meat, get out the pots and pans and when everything is ready to be cooked, I get into something comfortable and relax. Someday I'll do a book on the therapeutic value of cooking."

The doctor withdrew the undevoured portion of a cold roast chicken and the remains of a cold rare roast beef from the refrigerator and tore away the flesh of the bird, cut the meat into very thin slices. The chicken would go into a Louisiana gumbo; the beef into a quick sauté of leftover meat with soy sauce and ginger.

"It's true," he commented, "I'm a great champion of leftovers and almost invariably I cook in larger quantities than I'll serve at one meal, just to have leftovers. I sometimes think I prefer foods second time around.

"I'm not a competitive cook and probably—indeed, do—improvise because I don't like being compared. I know a lot of people who get involved in very complicated things like crêpes and omelets and soufflés—a lot of them, I think, are people who basically *enjoy* having failures.

"I tend to avoid these overwrought dishes. I probably couldn't do an expensive steak very well, but I have a passion for making my own fritters, using almost anything in the refrigerator that can be finely chopped."

The fritter recipe came about during his navy days when he was stationed in Nashville, Tennessee. "I used to go to a luncheonette frequented by warehouse workers and sailors. It was a seedy sort of a place, but they made the best fritters in the world, crisp and brown on the outside, soft as polenta within."

Dr. Louis Parrish, who cooks more food than he needs just to have leftovers.

Dr. Parrish, who is a general practitioner and psychiatrist and is in the process of writing a book for Reader's Digest Press on the change of life in men and women, told us that he has a constantly simmering stock pot into which he throws all bones, leftover vegetables, scraps of meat and vegetables, as well as the leftover liquids from simmering meats and vegetables.

He added that he frequently buys bean sprouts to use in soups and salads and as a vegetable, not only because they are nourishing and taste good but because they are "incredibly inexpensive" and, properly refrigerated in a plastic bag, last a long time.

Dr. Parrish has an interesting formula for roasting an eye round of beef. He preheats his oven to 500 degrees or the highest heat it can achieve, salts and peppers the meat, places it on a rack in a pan, and puts it in the oven. He lets it roast four to five minutes for each pound, turns off the oven heat and lets the roast rest in the oven without opening the door from one and one-half to two hours. The result is a marvelous rare and tender roast with the juices well distributed.

"I slice what I need for the first meal and after it is in the refrigerator it is still nice and rare and can be reheated or sliced and cooked with other seasonings."

He recently used leftover garlic sausage and the chicken in a southern dish of red beans and rice; leftover cooked sweetbreads and week-old bean sprouts in a delicious soup (see bean sprout and shrimp soup) several chopped leftover foods in his fritters and the beef in a ginger sauce.

Bean Sprout and Shrimp Soup

2 *cups chicken broth*
1 *cup fresh bean sprouts*
½ *cup loosely packed watercress leaves and stems*
1 *teaspoon butter*
½ *cup chopped cooked shrimp (or leftover sweetbreads)*
1 *teaspoon curry powder*
½ *cup heavy cream*

1. Bring the chicken broth to a boil in a saucepan. Add the bean sprouts and watercress and simmer about 5 minutes.

2. Meanwhile, heat the butter in a small saucepan and add the chopped shrimp. Sprinkle with the curry powder and cook briefly until thoroughly hot. Add the curry and shrimp mixture to the soup. Pour the mixture into the container of an electric blender and blend until smooth.

3. Return the mixture to a saucepan and add the cream. Bring to the boil and serve.

Yield: About 4 servings.

Red Beans and Rice

2 cups dried red or kidney beans
1½ cups thinly sliced Polish (garlic) sausage
1½ cups thinly sliced leeks
1½ cups chopped fennel bulb, if available
½ teaspoon dried thyme
Salt to taste
1 small dried hot red pepper, crushed
1 tablespoon vinegar
1 cup rice
2¼ cups chicken broth
½ cup finely chopped parsley
½ teaspoon lemon juice
½ teaspoon salt
1 cup diced, cooked chicken
Chopped green pepper, optional

1. Soak the beans overnight in cold water to cover.

2. Drain the beans and add enough cold water to cover to a depth of 1 inch above the top of the beans. Add the sausage, leeks, fennel, thyme, salt, pepper, and vinegar. Cover and cook until beans are done and most of the liquid has been absorbed. Add more liquid as necessary or uncover to reduce the amount of liquid

3. Meanwhile, combine the rice with the broth, parsley, lemon juice, salt, and chicken. Cover and bring to the boil. Cook until all the liquid is absorbed, 12 to 14 minutes.

4. Combine the rice and beans and serve hot garnished with chopped green peppers.

Yield: 6 to 8 servings.

Cornmeal Fritters with Leftovers

1 cup yellow cornmeal
¼ cup flour
½ teaspoon baking powder
½ teaspoon salt
½ teaspoon freshly ground black pepper
⅛ teaspoon cayenne
1¼ cup boiling broth such as pork or chicken
¾ cup finely diced cooked meat and/or chopped vegetables (see note)
Oil
Hot pepper jelly (see recipe), optional

1. In a mixing bowl, combine the cornmeal, flour, baking powder, salt, pepper, and cayenne. Add the boiling broth gradually, stirring constantly. Stir in the meat and/or vegetables.

2. Heat just enough oil on a griddle or in a black iron skillet to prevent the fritters from sticking. Drop the batter by spoonfuls onto the griddle and cook, turning as the fritters are browned on one side, like pancakes. Cook until browned on the second side and serve, if desired, with hot pepper jelly.

Yield: 12 to 20 fritters, depending on size.

Note: Vegetables such as chopped celery, green onions, green peppers, etc. can be used.

Hot pepper jelly

1   cup red or green peppers, cored and ground with the seeds
½   cup long, hot, red or green peppers, cored and ground (*see note*)
6½ cups sugar
1½ cups white vinegar
¼   teaspoon salt
1   6-ounce bottle fruit pectin (*Certo*)
     Red or green food coloring

1. Combine the green peppers, hot peppers, sugar, vinegar and salt in a saucepan. Simmer about 10 minutes, stirring occasionally.

2. Strain or not as desired and return it to the saucepan. If strained, the solids are good as a relish. Pour in the pectin and bring to the boil. Stir in the food coloring. Pour into sterilized half-pint jars and seal with paraffin. Store in a cool place.

Yield: 8 to 10 half-pint jars.

Note: If long, hot peppers are not available, drained tinned jalapeño peppers, available in many supermarkets, may be substituted according to taste.

Ginger Beef

½   pound leftover rare roast beef, cut into thin strips
¼   cup soy sauce
1   teaspoon finely minced garlic
1   to 2 teaspoons grated or finely chopped ginger root
1   teaspoon peanut, vegetable, or corn oil

1. Place the meat in a mixing bowl and add the soy sauce, garlic, and ginger. Cover and let stand several hours.

2. Heat the oil in a wok or skillet and cook the meat, stirring, over high heat about 10 seconds. Turn off the heat and continue stirring about 30 seconds longer. Serve with rice.

Yield: 2 servings.

Lazy Man's Eye Round Roast

1   3½–8-pound eye round of beef roast
     Salt and freshly ground black pepper

1. Preheat oven to 500 degrees or its maximum setting.

2. Sprinkle the roast with salt and pepper. Outfit a shallow roasting pan with a rack and place the beef on it. Place the beef in the oven and bake exactly 5 minutes a pound. At the end of that time do not open the oven door. Let the roast remain in the oven from 1½ (for a small roast) to 2 (for a large roast) hours. The meat will be nicely browned on the outside and juicy within. If the meat seems too cool when removed from the oven, reheat it briefly in a hot oven before slicing.

Yield: 4 to 16 servings.

Louisiana Gumbo

⅓ cup plus 1 tablespoon lard,
  vegetable oil, or bacon fat
10 tablespoons flour
½ cup chopped onion
1 cup chopped green pepper
1 cup chopped celery
1 10-ounce package sliced
  frozen okra
  Salt and freshly ground
  black pepper
3½ cups boiling chicken broth
¼ pound Polish (garlic)
  sausage cut into ½-inch
  slices
¼ cup water
1 hot red pepper, crushed
¾ cup peeled, cooked shrimp,
  cut into ½-inch pieces
1½ cups shredded cooked
  chicken, white or dark
  meat
  Gumbo-filé powder,
  optional

1. Use a Dutch oven, preferably made of cast iron. Add ⅓ cup fat and the flour. Stir constantly with a wooden spoon until the flour is uniformly brown, 15 minutes or longer. The flour should achieve a dark caramel or light chocolate color, but care must be taken not to burn the flour or it will take on a bitter taste. Cook slowly and stir constantly.

2. Add the onion and cook about 2 minutes, stirring. Add the green pepper and celery and cook, stirring occasionally, about 15 minutes.

3. Meanwhile, heat the remaining tablespoon of fat and add the okra. Cook, stirring, about 15 minutes and sprinkle with salt and pepper. Add this to the dutch oven. Add the broth.

4. Simmer the Polish sausage in the water about 3 minutes. Drain. Add this to the dutch oven. Add the remaining ingredients except filé powder and stir. Simmer 15 minutes. Serve hot with rice and filé powder on the side.

Yield: 4 to 6 servings.

We have known for years that one of the most popular and talked about recipes ever to appear in *The New York Times* was printed in the July 28, 1966 issue. The headline stated "Ann Seranne's Recipe for a Perfect Roast: Put It in the Oven and Relax."

We had forgotten just how popular that column was until we printed Dr. Parrish's technique for roasting an eye round of beef and received dozens of indignant letters from readers presuming we had some sort of memory loss and had forgotten the Seranne technique.

By no means. We hasten to state that Ann Seranne is not only a friend of many years' standing, a first-rate cookbook author, but one of the finest and most imaginative cooks we've ever known in America or abroad.

For the benefit of those who may not have encountered her recipe for the "relaxed" method of cooking a rib roast of beef, we offer it once more, with some updating. We spoke to Ann by phone a few weeks ago, and she told us her technique today is even simpler (or easier to remember) than the one we printed nearly ten years ago.

The rib roast, she noted again, must be at room temperature. It should be salted and peppered on the outside and, if desired, dredged lightly all over in flour. It is placed fat side up, on a rack in a roasting pan. It is then placed in an oven that has been preheated to 500 degrees or the highest oven temperature.

It is then baked for exactly 15 minutes *for each rib*. The oven is then turned off and the roast is allowed to rest in the oven—the oven door should not be opened—until the oven is lukewarm, about two hours. The roast will have a crunchy brown outside and will still have an internal heat suitable for serving as long as four hours. The yield is two servings per rib.

And now to Dr. Parrish's formula. Although it is, indeed, similar in technique, his recipe is not for a rib roast of beef but rather for eye round which is, to use a phrase, another kettle of fish. His cooking time for that boneless meat is five minutes per pound in a 500-degree oven, then one and one-half hours of resting time. The roast comes out crunchy brown on the exterior and decidedly rare but delicious within.

Regarding Dr. Parrish's roast meat formula, John Ciolino of Palisades Park, New Jersey, wrote, "I believe that roasting meat at any temperature less than the usual 325 or 350 F (which is essentially what the good doctor does by turning the oven off) is bound to improve the results. My recipe for medium-rare roast beef is as follows:

"For a six-pound first-cut rib of beef (thawed but at refrigerator temperature), preheat the oven to its hottest temperature. Dry the meat thoroughly and pepper lightly. Place in a shallow pan with quartered onions and put in oven. Roast for four to five minutes per pound or until slightly browned. Shut off oven and open the oven door for five minutes. Turn the oven back on and set at 200 F; close oven door. Roast for four and one-half to five hours until meat thermometer reaches the desired temperature (about 145 F).

"I also follow almost the same recipe for loin of pork except I set the oven temperature to 225 F."

Morris Mendelson, a professor of finance at the Wharton School, University of Pennsylvania, wrote of a roasting technique "based on the principal that prevents a bag full of water from catching fire if held over a flame. Prepare the roast for the oven according to taste. Preheat the oven to at least 350 degrees. Place the roast on a rack in the preheated oven and roast for an hour. Turn the heat control, at the end of the hour, to temperature you want the inside of the meat to have when done. I have a General Electric stove and I turn it down as far as it will go. That is beyond the calibration, and my guess is that it goes down to approximately 145 or 150 degrees. I leave the meat at that temperature all day.

If you put the meat in in the morning, you can serve it at any time from, shall we say 5 P.M. on and the meat will stay at exactly the same degree of doneness. The object in cooking it at high heat at the beginning is to kill bacteria and to brown the meat on the outside. This method of cooking does permit the use of cheaper cuts because of the long slow cooking involved."

We also had a letter from Bill Slattery of Jamestown, Rhode Island, who offered us his preferred recipe for roast leg of lamb. "Heavily salt the room-temperature leg of lamb, sliver a garlic clove and insert the slivers in the holes you have cut to varying depths and scattered randomly about the leg and put it into an oven preheated to 500 degrees. The leg comes out 45 minutes later and you may begin carving it 20 minutes later.

"The advantage to this method is that you are able to offer your guests well, medium or rare lamb. The disadvantage is that your house fills up with smoke."

"I forgot to add that the cooking time and temperature remains the same for any size leg of lamb."

March 1975

OR A FEW SCORE years we had assumed that almost anything out of California was made of celluloid and plastic. We scoffed at the notion that there were people out there who cooked and entertained with exceeding care and excelling taste. In truth, it was becoming progressively difficult to reconcile our prejudices with the information that was drifting east. For years we had heard of Danny Kaye's expertise in the Chinese field. When we heard that Mary Martin's grandchild, Heidi Hagman, was an outstanding international cook and part-time caterer at the grand age of 17, we decided to enplane for the West Coast with little further ado. Besides, it was March and it was cold in New York.

To our utter astonishment, the talents of both subjects wildly exceeded our expectations. Danny regaled us with a banquet prepared by his own hands that would have pleased the palate of the Dowager Empress. Heidi Hagman and a friend devastated us with a menu that was a marvel of imagination and good taste.

The Barefoot Caterers of Malibu

It was shortly after noon on a piercingly bright sunny day. California champagne flowed with spigotlike generosity into the glasses of guests on the brick and concrete patio attached to the home of Burgess Meredith and his wife, Caja. Carroll O'Connor, Archie Bunker himself, was there with his wife, Nancy. So were Charles Lloyd, the great jazz musician, and Robert Mondavi, proprietor of the distinguished vineyard that bears his name. Brenda Forbes, the actress, arrived and explained that Ingrid Bergman, who had promised to be there, couldn't make it. And Mary Martin was detained in Palm Springs, but her son, Larry Hagman, the actor, was there.

As the time for dining approached, Robert Balzer, the California wine expert and author, was about to toast something or other, when two supersylphs soared onto the terrace, barefoot and robed in high-neck, turn-of-the-century peasant dresses. They were Heidi Hagman and Jonine Bernstein, both 17 years old, the Barefoot Caterers of Malibu.

In and out of the kitchen they came, bearing aloft for the delectation and delight of the assembled guests, such international delicacies as homemade gravlax, the Swedish salt-and-sugar-cured fresh salmon with mustard sauce; spanakopitta or Greek spinach pie; a seductively seasoned dish of mushroom- and cheese-stuffed zucchini halves; breasts of chicken flavored with white wine and lemon; a gossamer jelly roll dessert, and assorted imported cheese.

And for openers, so to speak, the young ladies offered guests that superb Swiss creation, raclette made with half a wheel of Bagnes cheese (a special and not easily obtainable melting Swiss cheese traditional for raclette), melted and scraped a little at a time and served with good French bread and hot boiled potatoes.

Heidi Hagman is the daughter of Larry Hagman and the granddaughter of Mary Martin. Jonine Bernstein is the daughter of Calvin Bernstein, a successful West Coast filmmaker. The two of them will celebrate their first year of catering this coming Easter.

We had arrived at the Hagman kitchen earlier that morning to watch the preliminaries for the feast. The Hagman home is also on the beach and adjacent to the Meredith home. Heidi was in the midst of slicing the gravlax and preparing the lemon chicken; Jonine was steaming spinach

for the spanakopitta and assembling the ingredients for the stuffed zucchini. To our amazement, there wasn't a parent to act as guiding hand or
give cooking advice.

The young women explained that they were both juniors at a private
high school in North Hollywood, that they had always had an interest in
cooking and that their food background, while related, was dissimilar.

We asked Miss Hagman if she had learned to cook from her celebrated grandmother, Mary Martin. She giggled, "She's been the actress
all her life and never had to cook a day in her life. Sometimes Jonine and
I send her CARE packages to Palm Springs, casseroles and fruit pies and
quiches and things like that. She also sent us the lemons from her own
lemon grove for the chicken."

Heidi said she had first baked a pie when she was three or four years
old and so small she had to ask her mother to light the oven. Her mother
and her mother's sisters are Swedish and all of them are first-rate cooks.
Much of her cooking, Heidi added, stems from the teaching of one aunt
in particular, Berit Axellson, called Bebe. It was Bebe, she told us, who
taught her to make the gravlax.

Jonine's mother is well known among her friends as an outstanding
cook and played a large role in developing Jonine's interests.

"And Jonine goes to restaurants a lot with her parents," Heidi ex-

*Heidi Hagman, one of the 17-year-old
partners in the Barefoot Caterers.*

*Jonine Bernstein prepares some food for
party.*

plained, "and gets all these great ideas for a lot of the foreign dishes we prepare."

The Barefoot Caterers generally exhibit their skills for weekend and holiday functions.

Last New Year's they catered a "sausage and chili party." Their fees depend on several factors, including "how much the food costs, how long it takes to prepare, and who the people are." By that they mean they are apt to charge less for a charity function.

Preston, Heidi's 12-year-old brother, raced barefoot through the kitchen and we asked if he ever cooked. "Yeah," he answered dead pan. "Hamburgers, french fries, hot dogs. Things like that."

Neither Heidi nor Jonine knows how long they will continue in the catering field. They have diversified interests including art and music as well as food. Heidi, in addition to catering on weekends and holidays, taught art at an elementary school all last summer.

Information about the catering services of the Barefoot Caterers can be obtained by sending a stamped self-addressed envelope to the Barefoot Caterers, 23730 Malibu Colony, Malibu, California 90265.

Here are several specialties from the Barefoot Caterers. The spinach pie is adapted from Eva Zane's excellent book, *Great Cooking for the Gods*.

Mushroom and Cheese-Stuffed Zucchini

14 small zucchini, each about
    6 inches in length
¾ cup olive oil
1½ cups chopped onions
1½ cups finely diced
    fresh mushrooms
3 cloves garlic, finely minced
1 cup cream cheese
3 eggs
2 cups grated Parmesan
    cheese
2 cups finely chopped
    parsley
    Salt and freshly ground
    black pepper
4 hot chilies, chopped,
    optional

1. Preheat the oven to 350 degrees.

2. Cut the zucchini in half lengthwise. Using a melon ball cutter or a spoon, scoop out the flesh of each zucchini half, leaving a shell about ¼-inch thick. Set the zucchini halves aside. Chop the pulp and set aside.

3. Heat the oil and add the onions. Cook, stirring often, until onions are wilted. Add the mushrooms and garlic. Cover and cook until mushrooms give up their juices. Add chopped zucchini pulp. Cook over high heat, uncovered, stirring, until the liquid evaporates. Add the cream cheese, eggs, 1½ cups of Parmesan cheese, parsley, salt, pepper, and hot chilies. Cook, stirring often, about 10 minutes. Let cool.

4. Stuff the zucchini shells with equal parts of the mixture. Sprinkle with the remaining ½ cup Parmesan. Arrange in a baking dish and bake 10 minutes or until piping hot. Run under the broiler to brown briefly.

Yield: 14 to 28 servings.

Gravlax

(Salt- and sugar-cured salmon)

> 2   *bunches fresh dill*
> 1   *3½–4-pound section of fresh salmon, preferably cut from the center of the fish*
> ¼   *cup kosher salt*
> ¼   *cup sugar*
> 1   *teaspoon coarsely ground white peppercorns Mustard-dill sauce (see recipe)*

1. Cut off and discard any very tough stems from the dill. Rinse the dill and pat it dry.

2. Bone the salmon section or have it boned. There should be two fillets of equal size and weight. Do not rinse the fish but pat it dry with paper toweling.

3. Combine the salt, sugar, and pepper. Rub this mixture into the pink flesh of the salmon.

4. Spread ⅓ of the dill over the bottom of a flat dish. Add one of the salmon pieces, skin side down. Cover this with another third of the dill. Add the remaining piece of salmon, placing it sandwich-fashion over the dill, skin side up. Cover with the remaining dill and place a plate on top. Add a sizable weight and let stand in a very cool place or in the refrigerator for 48 hours. Turn the "sandwich" every 12 hours, always covering with the plate and weighting it down. Serve thinly sliced on the bias like smoked salmon. Serve with mustard-dill sauce.

Yield: 12 to 20 servings.

Mustard-dill sauce

> ½   *cup Dijon, Düsseldorf, or dark prepared mustard*
> 2   *teaspoons dry mustard*
> 6   *tablespoons sugar*
> ¼   *cup white vinegar*
> ⅔   *cup vegetable oil*
> ½   *cup chopped fresh dill Salt*

1. Combine the prepared mustard, dry mustard and sugar in a mixing bowl.

2. Using a wire whisk, stir in the vinegar. Gradually add the oil, stirring rapidly with the whisk. Add the dill and salt. Taste and correct the flavors by gradually adding more sugar, vinegar, or salt.

Yield: About 1½ cups

Spanakopitta

(Greek-style spinach pie)

> 3   *pounds fresh spinach*
> ¾   *cup olive oil, approximately*
> 2   *bunches scallions, trimmed and chopped*

¼ cup chopped parsley
½ pound feta cheese,
   crumbled
6 eggs, lightly beaten
   Salt and freshly ground
   black pepper
½ pound or 10 sheets phyllo
   pastry (see note)

1. Preheat the oven to 350 degrees.

2. Pick over the spinach to remove and discard all blemished leaves and tough stems. Rinse the spinach in several changes of cold water to remove all traces of sand. Steam the spinach briefly over boiling water just until the leaves are wilted. Let cool. Chop the spinach coarsely.

3. Heat 1 tablespoon of oil in a skillet and add the scallions. Cook, stirring, until the onions are wilted.

4. In a mixing bowl, combine the spinach, scallions, parsley, cheese, eggs, salt and pepper to taste. Add 1 tablespoon of oil and blend thoroughly.

5. Select a baking pan measuring approximately 13-by-9 inches. Or use a round pan of similar size. Cover the pan with one layer of phyllo pastry, letting the edges of the pastry hang over the sides. Brush the pastry generously with oil. Continue adding 4 more layers, brushing each layer with oil as it is added. Spoon the spinach mixture into the center and smooth it over. Cover with another layer of phyllo, brush with oil and continue adding 4 more layers, brushing oil between each layer. Use a sharp knife or scissors to trim off the overhanging edges of pastry. Bake the pie for 40 to 50 minutes or until it is piping hot throughout and golden brown on top.

Yield: 18 or more servings.

Note: Phyllo pastry is available in most specialty food shops and stores specializing in Greek foods.

Beans Any Old Time

WITH PIERRE FRANEY

Considering their versatility, it would seem that dried beans are put to limited use in most American homes. Oh, they're used for baked beans, of course, and most people feel deprived without red beans in their chili con carne, but beans' uses go much farther afield. They are delectable when cooked and put through a food mill, with a little cream to smooth them, and they make splendid soups when seasoned with herbs. The recipe on this page for a hearty meal-type soup made with beans and lamb shanks comes from a friend and good cook, Hazel De Marco.

Hazel DeMarco's Bean and Lamb-Shank Soup

1   *pound dried lima beans*
1¼   *to 1½ pounds lamb shank*
2   *tablespoons butter,*
     approximately
     Salt
1   *clove garlic, crushed*
4   *cups chicken broth*
4   *cups water*
¾   *cup finely chopped onion*
¾   *cup finely diced carrots*
½   *cup finely chopped celery*

1. Place the beans in a mixing bowl and add cold water to cover about 2 inches above the beans. Soak overnight.

2. Brown the lamb shank on all sides in a heavy kettle. If there is any fat on the shank, it is not necessary to add more fat to the kettle. Otherwise, brown the shank in 1 tablespoon of butter just so it doesn't stick.

3. Pour off any fat that may have accumulated in the kettle.

4. Drain the beans and add them to the kettle, along with salt to taste, the garlic, chicken broth, and water. Cook, partially covered, about 1½ hours. Stir occasionally.

5. Add the vegetables and cook 30 minutes longer, stirring occasionally.

6. Remove the shank and take the meat from the bone. Cut the meat into small pieces and return it to the soup. Swirl in 2 tablespoons of butter and serve piping hot.

Yield: 6 to 8 servings.

Bean Soup with Sage

½   pound dried beans such as
     jumbo marrow, baby lima,
     or pea beans
¼   pound salt pork, cut into
     ½-inch cubes
2   cups chopped onion,
     about ½ pound
3   cloves garlic, finely
     chopped
10 cups water
     Salt
1   or 2 smoked pork butts or
     ham hocks
2   cups chopped tomatoes
1   tablespoon sage or to taste
¼   cup heavy cream
2   tablespoons butter

1. Soak the beans overnight in cold water to cover about 2 inches above the beans.

2. Cook the salt pork pieces in a kettle until rendered of fat. Add the onion and garlic and cook until the onion is wilted.

3. Drain the beans and add them to the kettle. Add the water, salt to taste, pork butts or ham hocks, tomatoes, and sage. Cover and cook about 2 hours or until beans are tender. Remove the pieces of salt pork. Crush half the beans with the back of a wooden spoon. This will help thicken the soup. Add the cream and swirl in the butter. Bring just to the boil and serve hot.

Yield: 8 to 12 servings.

Danny Kaye
Cooks Chinese

There were eight guests at table. Danny Kaye was at the stove with volcanolike, billowing smoke ascending from one of his three professional woks, as he stirred a dish of cubed beef with onions, Chinese-style.

"The trouble with Danny's cooking," Olive Behrendt was saying, "it spoils you forever for going to restaurants. You could eat in this home every night for a month and never be served the same dish twice." Mrs. Behrendt, president of the Los Angeles Philharmonic and a frequent guest at Danny Kaye's table, added that Luciano Pavarotti had recently dined there and agreed that the multitalented Mr. Kaye makes perhaps the best fegato alla veneziana, or calf's liver Venetian-style, in the world.

For years we had heard of Mr. Kaye's prowess as a chef, particularly in the province of Chinese cooking, and tended to regard it with at least a touch of skepticism. One more touch of Hollywood, we mused.

But if we came into the man's kitchen to scoff, we stayed to stare with open-mouthed awe as he proceeded to bone a chicken or two with surgical skill and, at the moment of cooking, wield his cleaver, wok scoops, and wok spoons with maestrolike dexterity.

Danny Kaye, who is 62 years old, was born in Brooklyn of Russian parents, and his father did most of the cooking. "He cooked very simple dishes," Danny recalled. "Great soups like borscht and schav, and Russian stews. He got so much joy out of raw ingredients, and I think I inherited that."

Danny's abiding interest in Chinese cooking came about when he traveled to Shanghai in 1934 with a group of American entertainers. "Every day they'd spend their off hours in search of bargains—shoes, suits, trinkets." On his first day there, he recounted, he was taken to a Chinese restaurant by friends, and it was something like getting religion. He was taken into the kitchen.

"It was overwhelming; 180 degrees in contrast to anything I'd ever experienced in the Western world. I was absolutely riveted by the heat, the flames and the technical speed of the chefs." He knew from the beginning he had to become involved. Some years later he met Johnny Kan who owned one of the best-known restaurants in San Francisco's Chinatown. "Johnny and I became friends and for weeks he let me stand around his kitchen and watch. Eventually they let me do a little chopping and a few of the simpler dishes."

When you write of Danny Kaye's cooking, there is an inherent temptation to drift into superlatives. He has what is undoubtedly the finest Chinese kitchen of any private home in America and as far as we know the world. He has cooked for many of the world's notables. His guests in government circles have included Henry Kissinger; in the arts, Luciano Pavarotti, the singer; Beverly Sills, the soprano; Jascha Heifetz and Itzhak Perlman, the violinists, and Zubin Mehta, the conductor.

And who else would cook for those peripatetic wizards of the French kitchen, Paul Bocuse of the restaurant that bears his name in Lyon; Roger Vergé, the celebrated chef-patron of the Hostellerie du Moulin de Mougins; and Jean Troisgros of Frères Troisgros restaurant in Roanne?

Within the past six weeks he has had them in his home to dine on an eight-course Chinese banquet—cucumber soup, beef with onion rings, "banjo" duck, deep-fried squab, sweet and sour deep-fried scallops, stir-fried shrimp with oysters. And there was an Italian feast—fettucine with pesto, the fegato alla veneziana, chicken cacciatore. The chefs, we have it on the best authority, gluttonized; Danny Kaye took it all in professional stride, unfazed in the midst of that mass, prodigious talent.

The Kaye kitchen consists primarily of a 10-foot stainless steel, professional Chinese battery of stoves, custom-made by Robert Yick, a San Francisco designer and perhaps the best-known fabricator of Chinese

With the help of Ming Lo Chin, Danny Kaye prepares a meal at a professional Chinese range in his home.

cooking equipment in America. The range consists of three wok ranges fired by enormous jets of gas, the controls of which can be operated by a lever at knee height.

There are easily accessible refrigerator drawers across from the stove and a professional oven for roasting duck next to it. It has been rumored that most of the ingredients used by Danny Kaye when he cooks are prepared by a team of Chinese souschefs, which is patently untrue. He has one kitchen helper, Ming Lo Chin, a joyous, good-natured woman in her mid-50s.

When Danny Kaye entertains, he never sits at table until after the end of the meal. He presides over the woks, preparing one course at a time, each of which is served in succession on a lazy susan permanently placed in the middle of his round table, situated to one side of his Chinese kitchen. The ventilating system is silent and a marvel of efficiency. There are no fumes.

The gentleman does all of his own shopping, most of it in Chinatown in Los Angeles, about a 15- or 20-minute drive along the freeway from his home. Among his "permanent" ingredients can be counted a gallon of thin licorice root and anise-flavored sauce that he has had on hand for 11 years. As the sauce is used—as a dip for squab before roasting, for example—the ingredients such as soy sauce and wine are replenished. It is brought to the boil every 10 days to keep it in good condition.

Danny Kaye has one wall decoration in his kitchen that bears a special significance. It is a hand-painted black calligraphy drawing that says simply in Chinese, "Danny Kaye, skilled hands." It was given to him by one of the chefs after his early days in the Johnny Kan kitchen.

Here is a small sampler of the Danny Kaye repertory.

Stir-Fry Oysters and Shrimp

1 cup raw oysters
¼ cup flour
½ pound raw shrimp, shelled and deveined
2 tablespoons peanut, vegetable, or corn oil
1 2-inch piece fresh ginger, peeled and cut into fine shreds
5 scallions, trimmed and cut into 2-inch lengths
1 teaspoon light soy sauce
¼ teaspoon sesame oil
Salt and freshly ground black pepper
1½ tablespoons cornstarch
1½ tablespoons water

1. Place the oysters in a bowl and add the flour and water to cover. Stir the oysters in the liquid. Drain well and run under several changes of cold water. Drain well. The flour will both cleanse and plump the oysters. They must be rinsed well before draining.

2. Drop the oysters into barely simmering water. Turn off the heat. Let stand 1 minute and drain. Set aside. Repeat with the shrimp.

3. Heat the oil in a wok or skillet over high heat. Add the ginger, scallions and cook, stirring, about 5 seconds. Add the oysters and shrimp and stir rapidly. Cook about 15 seconds. Add the soy sauce, sesame oil, salt and pepper to taste, stirring constantly.

4. Blend the cornstarch with water and stir it into the dish. Cook 15 seconds, stirring quickly, and serve.

Yield: 8 servings.

Batter-Fried Scallops

2 cups whole bay scallops or ocean scallops, quartered
Flour for dredging
½ cup flour
½ cup cornstarch
1 egg white
1 tablespoon peanut, vegetable, or corn oil
1 tablespoon white vinegar
1 teaspoon baking soda
½ cup or more water
Peanut, vegetable, or corn oil for deep frying
2½ cups sweet and sour sauce (see recipe)

1. If desired, rinse and drain the scallops well.

2. In a mixing bowl, combine the flour, cornstarch, egg white, 1 tablespoon oil, vinegar, and baking soda. Mix well.

3. Gradually add the water, stirring constantly with a wire whisk. Add enough water to make a thick pancakelike batter.

4. Dredge the scallops in flour.

5. Heat the oil almost to smoking and, if desired, test one scallop by dipping it in the batter and frying to determine if the batter is too thick. If so, stir in a little more water.

6. Add the scallops to the batter and quickly drop them one at a time into the hot oil. Deep fry, stirring and turning with a strainer, making sure that the scallops do not stick together. Remove and drain well. Pour onto a serving dish. Pour over the heated sweet and sour sauce and serve.

Yield: 8 servings.

Sweet and sour sauce

1 cup sugar
¾ cup white vinegar
½ cup plus 3 tablespoons water
¾ cup pineapple juice
1½ tablespoons cornstarch
½ teaspoon red food coloring

1. Combine the sugar, vinegar, ½ cup water, and pineapple juice in a saucepan. Bring to the boil and simmer, stirring, until sugar dissolves.

2. Blend the cornstarch with the remaining water and stir into the sauce. Stir in food coloring.

Yield: About 2½ cups.

Lion's Head

8   dried black mushrooms
1¼   pounds ground pork
20   water chestnuts, finely
     diced
1   teaspoon finely minced
     fresh ginger
3   scallions, chopped
1   teaspoon finely minced
     garlic
     Grated rind of 1 orange
¼   teaspoon sesame oil
1   tablespoon dry sherry or
     shao hsing Chinese wine
1   tablespoon light soy sauce
1   teaspoon salt
1   tablespoon cornstarch
     Peanut, vegetable, or corn
     oil for deep frying
     Steamed spinach or
     broccoli, optional

1. Place the mushrooms in a mixing bowl and add hot water to cover. Let stand 20 minutes or longer until softened.

2. Place the pork in a mixing bowl. Drain the mushrooms and squeeze dry. Chop them. Add them to the pork.

3. Add the water chestnuts, ginger, scallions, garlic, grated orange rind, sesame oil, the wine, soy sauce, salt, and cornstarch. Mix well and shape into 8 to 12 balls. Set aside.

4. Heat the oil for deep frying and add the meat balls. Deep fry until crisp and golden on the outside. Drain well. Place the meat balls in a steamer and steam 20 to 25 minutes. Serve on a bed of spinach or broccoli.

Yield: 8 servings.

Crazy Chicken

1½   cups skinned, boned
     chicken cut into ½-inch
     cubes
1   egg white
4   tablespoons peanut,
     vegetable, or corn oil
1   tablespoon cornstarch
½   cup thinly sliced water
     chestnuts
10   lychee nuts, cut into
     quarters
1   tablespoon dry sherry wine
     or shao hsing Chinese wine
1   tablespoon light soy sauce
½   to 1 teaspoon sambal oelek
     (see note)
     Salt
½   teaspoon sugar
½   cup crushed roasted peanuts

1. Combine the chicken, egg white, 1 tablespoon oil, and cornstarch. Mix well with the fingers. Refrigerate 30 minutes.

2. Heat the remaining 3 tablespoons oil in a wok or skillet and add the chicken, stirring rapidly just to separate the pieces. Drain chicken, reserving oil.

3. Return 2 tablespoons of the oil to the wok. Add the chicken and stir quickly about 30 seconds. Add the water chestnuts and lychees and stir to blend. Add the wine, soy, sambal oelek, salt, and sugar, stirring and tossing quickly. Add the peanuts, toss quickly and serve.

Yield: 8 servings.

Note: Sambal oelek is a hot chili seasoning from Indonesia. It is sold where Indonesian products are available.

Kitchen Help

WITH PIERRE FRANEY

It has been labeled, and not without justice, the twentieth-century French Revolution. It is the equivalent of an electric blender, electric mixer, meat grinder, food sieve, potato ricer and chef's knife rolled into one. Its invention, in the minds of serious cooks, ranks with that of the printing press, cotton gin, steamboat, paper clips, Kleenex, wastebaskets, contour sheets, and disposable diapers. It has, in many minds, rendered the electric blender a hopeless antique, and we are willing at any time to relegate our old faithful to the Smithsonian.

The new mechanical Merlin is a French import known in this country as the Cuisinart Food Processor. It is a multifaceted marvel that has, as the saying goes, more uses than money. It blends, slices, grinds, grates, and purees, or, as one kitchen enthusiast put it, "does everything except sweep floors, wash dishes, and talk back." And it is expensive. At last quote it was selling at Bloomingdale's, Gimbels East, Hammacher Schlemmer, Macy's and other fine stores from coast to coast for approximately $190.

The Cuisinart appliance bears the name Magi-Mix in France, where it is infinitely less well known than in the United States. Thereby hangs a small but interesting tale. An acquaintance of ours—a dedicated cook—on a recent trip to Paris had been splendidly entertained, and, thinking to reward and surprise his hostess with a substantial gift which he knew she didn't have, he bought her a food processor, which he delivered forthwith to her kitchen. He also proceeded to show her the intricate tricks it performs. "This is great," she exclaimed. "Is it made in America?"

Numerous reasons for the Cuisinart's obscurity in France have been volunteered by various people who are familiar with (1) the food processor, (2) the French, and (3) what might be called "The French Food Establishment," which is to say those who write about and propagandize the pleasures of cooking and dining well.

"The French are just getting to the point," one of them said, "where they are willing to invest in something more mechanical in the kitchen than an electric hand beater. I have lots of friends with servants who refuse to install an electric dishwasher. As everywhere else, the age of the servant is on its way out in France. Five years ago almost anybody with slightly above average means could afford the cheap kitchen labor offered them in the form of Spanish and Portuguese cooks, mostly female.

But that's coming to an end. Until now the French have simply not thought in terms of kitchen aids but in terms of kitchen help."

"The French Food Establishment," another observer states, "simply isn't interested in informing the public about fine kitchen equipment. Perhaps they have never tried it themselves. And that goes for Christian Millau and Henri Gault, the well-known restaurant-guide and magazine publishers, as well as Robert Courtine, the restaurant and food critic of *Le Monde*. They are writing to élitist audiences, most of whom they assume to have servants. New applicances are frequently featured in the popular homemaking publications, but it isn't the same thing."

The food processor is made by the 15-year-old and much respected firm of Robot Coupe, principally known among professional chefs for the larger models of the food processor. Robot Coupe is located in the Burgundy region, about 250 miles south of Paris, in Montceau-les-Mines, a town known mostly for its Roman ruins and an early Gothic church. The president of the company is a man named Pierre Verdun, who delights in telling of the time he arrived anonymously at the celebrated Troisgros restaurant in Roanne a few years ago. When one of the chef-owners discovered his presence, he approached Mr. Verdun, shook his hand warmly and paid him the following tribute: "Without you, M. Verdun, this establishment could not exist." There is many a chef in America who could echo the sentiment, for Mr. Verdun's products are literally like having an extra set of hands around the premises.

A catalogue of the things of which the food processor is capable reads like a manual of cooking techniques. On the simplest level it purees vegetables in seconds, and it may well bring one of the glories of God—pureed potatoes—back into fashion. Or better yet, pureed celery root and potatoes. It makes soups and bisques that are silken. It shreds vegetables and cheese in seconds (one friend of ours turned 50 pounds of cabbage into the base for sauerkraut, one of the most tedious of things to do, in what could be reckoned in minutes). For Chinese cooking buffs it is a godsend—making shrimp paste, for example, or chopping those two ever-constant ingredients that go into woks, garlic and ginger. It also grinds fresh horseradish for cocktail sauces and "grates" bread crumbs quicker than you can scramble eggs. It slices vegetables (carrots, cucumbers, and so on) with a twist of the wrist and a slight downward pressure on the object. The size of the slice depends on the pressure exerted; the texture of grated foods—coarse or fine—depends on the length of time they are processed.

The processor makes a devastatingly good guacamole, following the version of Diana Kennedy (author of *Cuisines of Mexico*), which includes grinding together one-quarter of an onion, a serrano chili pepper, and fresh coriander before adding avocado, salt, tomato, and a touch of lime. It also solves the problem of ground pork, the problem being that many butchers will not grind it if their store is equipped with only one grinder—a health regulation. Otherwise, the butcher has to clean the machine before using it for the meats. The food processor "grinds" quite masterfully. One of the most extraordinary things the food processor can do is grind to a fine puree fish such as salmon, pike, or sole for such dishes as mousse of fish or pike quenelles. In other days it was necessary to pound the fish fine, then laboriously press it through a hair sieve. Fish can be pureed in seconds to the most gossamer texture conceivable.

The Cuisinart Food Processor is purely and simply a multipurpose machine with a sound-free, sturdily constructed motor, housed in a heavy, handsomely designed plastic base. The base is surmounted by a clear plastic cylinder encircling a spindle that can be outfitted with any of four attachments, including two double-bladed knives (one of stainless steel and the other of plastic) and two stainless-steel disks (one for slicing, one for shredding). Actually the stainless-steel knife can be used for all blending procedures, such as pureeing soups, preparing mousses, "chopping" meats, "grinding" nuts, blending cheese dips, and so on. The plastic blade is nonessential, although it can be used in making sauces such as mayonnaise. The slicing disk is for slicing foods such as

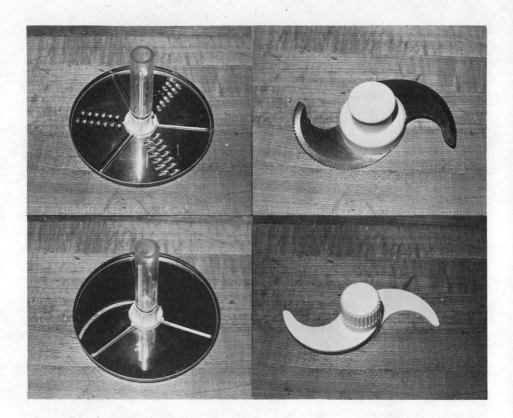

cucumbers, carrots, and so on; the shredder is for shredding cabbage and other vegetables. The machine's lid has a funnel through which the various foods are introduced for processing by pressing down on a solid plastic "pusher."

The food processor is engineered to be fail-safe. The motor can be activated only when the top of the cylinder is fastened in place and locked in by hand with a counterclockwise motion. Getting a hand inside the funnel while the blades are in motion could only be an act of premeditation and derangement.

The machine has a few limitations. It cannot whip cream, beat eggs, or dice or chop foods into uniform pieces. There are times (dicing vegetables for salade russe, for example) when such uniformity is desirable to please the eye. Although it cannot shape potatoes for french fries, it will grate them for potato pancakes.

The food processor can accommodate two or three times the volume of a standard electric blender, and it is miraculously easy to clean. Now if they will only teach it to sweep floors. . . .

Here is a sampling of dishes recently contrived using the Cuisinart Food Processor.

Brandade de Morue
(Salt cod mousse)

1 *pound boneless, skinless salt cod, cut into 4 or 5 pieces*
3 *or 4 Idaho potatoes, 1 pound*
½ *cup heavy cream*
½ *cup milk*
1½ *cups olive and/or peanut oil*
3 *or 4 large cloves garlic, peeled*
 Cayenne
 Freshly ground black pepper

1. Place the cod in a dish and add cold water to cover. Let stand several hours, changing the water often.

2. Preheat oven to 400 degrees. Place the potatoes in the oven and bake until tender, 45 minutes or longer.

3. Meanwhile, add the cream and milk to one saucepan, the oil to another. Heat them over low heat until piping hot, but do not let the liquids either boil or smoke.

4. Drain the cod and put it in a saucepan. Add cold water to cover and bring to the boil.

5. Equip the container of a food processor with a steel blade and add the garlic. Blend until fine. Drain the cod and add it.

6. Cut the hot potatoes in half and scoop out the flesh. Add the hot potato flesh to the garlic and cod. Start to blend and immediately start adding the oil pouring it into the feed tube of the cover. Add the hot cream while blending. Add the cayenne and black pepper to taste and when blended stop the motor. Serve lukewarm or at room temperature with fried-toast croutons or French bread. Chopped truffles are also frequently scattered over the dish both for color and flavor, but they are optional.

Yield: About 5 cups.

French Nut Pie

Sweet pastry for one 10-inch pie made a day in advance (see recipe)
2 *cups whole pecans and/or walnuts*
¼ *cup honey*
¾ *cup light brown sugar*
½ *cup granulated sugar*
2 *tablespoons butter*
½ *cup heavy cream*

1. Preheat oven to 425 degrees.

2. Roll the pastry to about ¼ inch thickness. Line a 10-inch pie tin with dough. Scraps of leftover dough may be used for cookies or smaller pies.

3. Prick the bottom of the pie shell and line it with wax paper. Pour a cup or so of dried beans in to prevent the dough from swelling as it bakes. Bake 15 minutes or longer, until the rim of the dough is nicely browned and the bottom is cooked. Let cool.

4. Put the nuts into the container of a food processor and chop them coarsely by blending (with the stainless-steel blade) for only a few seconds. Do not over-blend or the nuts will become too fine. Set aside.

5. Combine the honey, brown sugar, granulated sugar, and butter in a saucepan. Boil exactly 33 minutes, no less or longer. Add the nuts and cream and remove from the heat. Let cool.

6. Remove the dried beans and wax paper from the pie shell. Add the cooled nut filling and smooth it over. Let stand in a cool place until the filling sets (it will not become hard). If desired, spread with lightly sweetened whipped cream, flavored with rum or cognac, and serve.

Yield: 8 to 12 servings.

Sweet pie pastry

 12 tablespoons (1½ sticks) butter
 ⅓ cup plus 4 teaspoons sugar
 ¼ teaspoon vanilla extract
 1 egg
 1¾ cups flour
 ½ teaspoon baking powder

1. Empty the butter into the container of a food processor and blend (with the stainless-steel blade) until manageable and soft. Add the sugar, vanilla, and egg. Blend well. If necessary while blending, stop the motor and scrape the sides with a rubber spatula. Blend thoroughly.

2. Sift together the flour and baking powder and add it to the butter mixture. Continue blend-

ing, stirring down as necessary with the spatula. When thoroughly blended scrape the mixture into a mixing bowl, cover with plastic wrap and chill overnight. This dough may be frozen. It is excellent for making cutout cookies and tart shells.

Yield: Enough pastry for one 10-inch pie.

Mousse of Shrimp with Sauce Joinville

 1½ pounds raw shrimp, shelled and deveined
     Salt and freshly ground black pepper
 ¼ teaspoon cayenne
 ¼ teaspoon grated nutmeg
 2 eggs
 2½ cups heavy cream
 3 cups sauce Joinville (see recipe)

1. Preheat oven to 375 degrees.

2. In the container of a food processor, combine the shrimp, salt, pepper, cayenne, and nutmeg. Blend about 30 seconds, stopping the motor and stirring down with a rubber spatula if and as necessary.

3. Add the eggs and blend, stopping the motor and stirring down as necessary, about 20 seconds or until the mousse mixture is smooth. Add the cream slowly while blending. Blend about 30 seconds. To taste for seasoning, drop a small spoonful of the mixture into a small saucepan with boiling water. Cook briefly and taste. Add more salt, pepper, nutmeg, or cayenne if desired.

4. Generously butter a round, 6-cup ring mold and spoon the mixture into it. Cover with a buttered round of wax paper cut to fit over the top of the mousse. Place the mold in a basin of water and bring to a boil on top of the stove.

5. Bake 30 to 40 minutes. To test for doneness, insert a long needle into the center of the mousse. If it comes out clean, the mousse is done. Do not overbake.

6. Unmold the mousse onto a round serving platter. If any liquid seeps from the mousse, drain it off. Dribble some of the sauce Joinville over and around the mousse and serve the remainder on the side.

Yield: 8 to 12 servings.

Sauce Joinville

8 tablespoons butter
4 tablespoons flour
2 cups fish stock (see recipe, page 156)
1 cup heavy cream
Salt and freshly ground black pepper
1 egg yolk
½ pound fresh mushrooms
½ pound raw shrimp, shelled and deveined
3 tablespoons finely chopped shallots
¼ cup dry white wine
Juice of ½ lemon

1. Melt 3 tablespoons of butter in a saucepan and add the flour, stirring with a wire whisk.
When blended, add the fish stock, stirring rapidly with the whisk. When blended and smooth, continue to cook, stirring frequently, about 20 minutes. Add the cream, stirring. Add salt and pepper.

2. Bring to the boil and add the yolk, stirring rapidly with the whisk. Swirl in 4 tablespoons of butter. Remove from the heat.

3. Meanwhile, as the sauce is being made, thinly slice the mushrooms and cut the shrimp into ½-inch cubes.

4. Heat a tablespoon of butter in a saucepan and add the shallots. Stir briefly and add the mushrooms. Cook about 5 minutes, until wilted and limp. Add the shrimp, salt, and pepper. Cook, stirring occasionally, about 1 minute and add the wine. Cook, stirring occasionally, about 5 minutes. Add the sauce, stirring. Add salt to taste and bring just to the boil. Add the lemon juice and serve.

Yield: About 3 cups.

Vichy Carrots

1½ pounds carrots, trimmed and scraped
Salt and freshly ground black pepper
1 teaspoon sugar
¼ cup water
4 tablespoons butter
Chopped parsley

1. Equip a food processor with the slicing blade. Slice the carrots. There should be about 4 cups. Put them in a skillet and add salt and pepper to taste, sugar, water (Vichy water if you want to be authentic), and butter.

2. Cover with a round of buttered wax paper and cook over moderately high heat, shaking the skillet occasionally. Cook about 10 minutes, until carrots are tender, the liquid has disappeared and they are lightly glazed. Take care they do not burn. Serve sprinkled with chopped parsley.

Yield: 6 servings.

Mousseline of Chicken Livers

¾ cup pure chicken fat (see note)
1 cup thinly sliced onions
½ pound lean veal, cut into ½-inch cubes
   Salt and freshly ground black pepper
¼ teaspoon grated nutmeg
1 teaspoon chopped garlic
½ bay leaf
2 sprigs fresh thyme or ½ teaspoon dried
1 pound picked-over raw chicken livers
3 tablespoons cognac
¼ cup heavy cream
¼ cup chopped pistachios
   Buttered toast or French bread

1. Melt chicken fat in a skillet and add the onions. Cook, stirring, and when wilted, add the veal,

salt, pepper, and nutmeg. Cook about 2 minutes, stirring, and add the garlic, bay leaf, thyme, and chicken livers. Cook, stirring occasionally, about 5 minutes.

2. Remove the thyme sprigs, if used, and bay leaf and add the cognac. Pour the mixture into the container of a food processor and blend to a puree. Spoon the mixture into a mixing bowl.

3. Whip the cream until stiff and fold it into the chicken liver mixture with a rubber spatula. Spoon the mixture into a mold and smooth it over. Chill well.

4. Serve sprinkled with pistachios, if desired, directly from the mold with buttered toast. Or, if desired, use 2 soup spoons to shape the mixture into oval "eggs." To do this, dip one of the spoons into hot water, then scoop up a portion of the mousseline. Dip the other spoon in water and run it inside the first spoon and around the mousseline to shape the egg. Spoon portions onto plates and sprinkle each serving with pistachio nuts. Serve with buttered toast.

Yield: 10 to 16 servings.

Note: Rendered chicken fat may be purchased in some supermarkets, but it is easy to prepare. Simply cook scraps of chicken fat in a skillet over moderate heat until rendered. Drain. This mousseline may be made firm and unmolded if one envelope of softened unflavored gelatin is added to the hot chicken-liver mixture as it is being blended. In that case, reduce the heavy cream by half.

Scandinavian Specialties

One of the great vogues in American dining for the last couple of decades has been the combination of beef with lobster, broiled and generally served on skewers.

It goes by such whimsical names as surf and turf, or beef and reef, and Ken Hansen, one of the country's most distinguished restaurateurs, is persuaded that the concept of serving meat with seafood is of Swedish origin. It has to do, he contends, with the frequent midnight dalliances of King Oskar II of Sweden, who reigned from 1872 to 1907 and covertly frequented the Operakelleren Restaurant in Stockholm with many of his nation's great beauties.

According to Mr. Hansen, the monarch was particularly fond of veal, crayfish, and asparagus tips, and the restaurant's maître d'hôtel created a dish for the royal palate combining all three items, their flavors linked with a sauce béarnaise.

Mr. Hansen, who owns the Scandia Restaurant here, further states that he was the first to introduce the dish, subsequently named veal Oscar, to this country. It is frequently seen on the menus of luxury restaurants on the West Coast.

Mr. Hansen is a man of legends, and his restaurant in one sense is a legend unto itself. It is almost without question the only semiluxury restaurant in the United States—perhaps the world—that serves from 22,000 to 24,000 customers a month, a place whose patronage to this day has been almost unmoved by thoughts or talk of recession and depression.

The gentleman has been host on numerous occasions to Scandinavian royalty, including the King and Queen of Denmark (plus almost all Hollywood royalty). His menu is almost exclusively Scandinavia-oriented from its fresh cured gravlax and herring dishes to an assortment of 40 Danish sandwiches. Small wonder that he was knighted 14 years ago by King Frederick IX of Denmark for being a good Danish ambassador.

Among other things, Mr. Hansen, who celebrated his 70th birthday last February 22, is a man of understated humor, dedication to his profession and a knowledgeable booster of California wines. He is also seemingly indefatigable and blessed with a sturdy, uncommonly handsome Scandinavian face, macho-Danish without cliché.

A native of Copenhagen, Mr. Hansen was 14 years old when he shipped on as a kitchen apprentice with the Scandinavian-American lines. In 1921 he came to the United States and worked in numerous well-known establishments throughout the country, ending up in Los Angeles in 1929, where he was engaged to prepare hors d'oeuvre at the Brown Derby Restaurant.

"At that time," he stated, "the Brown Derby wanted to go fancy and open a French kitchen. After all, they'd been known for years for their hamburgers and chilies and then as a place for steaks and chops."

The French kitchen backfired, he recalled, with the old customers complaining loudly that they didn't want caviar on their eggs or fancy terrines and liver. pâtés. By 1936 Mr. Hansen was chef at the Bit of Sweden, another enormously successful enterprise well-patronized by the rich and famous. It was the restaurant that introduced smorgasbord to the Hollywood colony, and all went well until he bought the place with a partner. They disagreed, and a big-time split, filled with recriminations, ensued.

Mr. Hansen then opened his own place, the Scandia, about a block away ("as close as possible, so my partner could watch the lines"). The partner, Mr. Hansen recalls with ill-disguised delight, went broke. The Scandia opened in its present site, 9040 Sunset Boulevard, in 1958. It

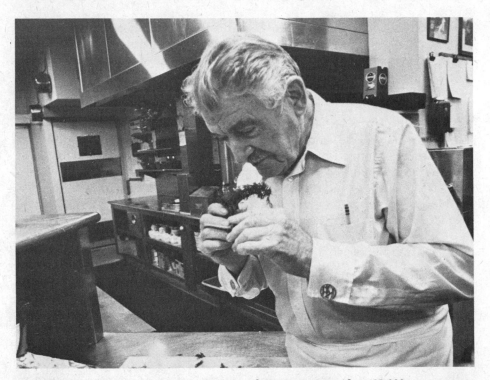

Ken Hansen, whose restaurant in Los Angeles serves more than 22,000 customers a month, laments the hustle and bustle attached to eating out today.

has no connection with the restaurant of the same name in New York.

"Our place," he said, "is very democratic. We've tried to educate the masses to eat good food, but now it's a real Frankenstein. They stream in here, nothing but hustle and bustle, and a lot of our old clientele from old Hollywood are unhappy that they can't be alone and exclusive somewhere in a corner."

The restaurant's menus are extensive and each day there is a blackboard menu with specialties of the day written on it. The Scandia is an enormous restaurant with a seating capacity for 275 customers. If there is a "most popular" day, it is Sunday, when a complete family lunch is priced at $5.25; and a special duck dinner priced at $8.50.

Although there is no smorgasbord, per se, customers may order a complete smorgasbord to be served at table. The several courses include herring, smoked salmon or gravlax, assorted seafood, liver pâtés with salads, cold meats, hot fricaddeler (a sort of Scandinavian meat ball) with red cabbage and cheese. The cost is $9.50 per person.

Swedish Lamb and Dill Stew

2 pounds lean, boneless lamb
  Salt
1 bunch fresh dill
2 bay leaves
10 peppercorns
2 sprigs fresh thyme or 1
  teaspoon dried
3 sprigs parsley
1 onion, finely chopped
6 tablespoons butter
3 tablespoons flour
5 tablespoons white vinegar
2 tablespoons sugar
  Freshly ground black
  pepper
  A few drops of Tabasco
¼ teaspoon monosodium
  glutamate, optional
½ cup heavy cream
1 egg yolk
  Rice pilaf blended with
  freshly cooked green peas,
  optional

1. Cut the lamb into 2-inch squares. Place the meat in a kettle and add cold water to barely cover. Bring to the boil and immediately drain the meat and run cold water over the meat until it is thoroughly chilled and the water runs clear. Drain. Return the meat to a clean kettle and add cold water to cover to about 1 inch above the top of the meat. Add salt to taste.

2. Rinse the dill well and pat it dry. Cut off the tough bottom stems. Reserve the feathery leaves for later.

3. Combine the dill stems, bay leaves, peppercorns, thyme and parsley in a square of cheesecloth. Tie this with string and add it to the lamb. Add the onion. When the liquid boils, lower heat and simmer the meat until thoroughly tender, 45 minutes to 1 hour.

4. Drain and reserve the cooking liquid. Discard the cheese-

cloth bag with the herbs. Keep the meat warm.

5. In a saucepan, melt 3 tablespoons of the butter and add the flour. Stir with a wire whisk. Add the reserved cooking liquid, stirring constantly over low heat until thickened and smooth. Let simmer.

6. Combine the vinegar and sugar in a small saucepan and cook until slightly syrupy.

7. Return the meat to the thickened broth and add the vinegar syrup. Add salt and pepper to taste, Tabasco, monosodium glutamate. Chop the reserved dill leaves and add all but about 2 tablespoons to the meat.

8. Beat the cream with the egg yolk. Remove the meat from the heat and stir in the egg and cream mixture. Swirl in the remaining 3 tablespoons butter and serve hot with the rice and peas. Serve sprinkled with the reserved chopped dill.

Yield: 4 to 6 servings.

Scandinavian Stuffed Cabbage

½ cup raw rice
1½ cups milk
1 3-pound head of cabbage
½ pound ground lean veal or beef
½ pound ground lean pork (or substitute an equal amount of veal or beef)
2 tablespoons grated onion
1 egg, lightly beaten
2 tablespoons flour

Salt and freshly ground black pepper
⅛ teaspoon grated nutmeg
¼ teaspoon ground allspice
7 tablespoons melted butter
½ teaspoon paprika
2 tablespoons dark molasses
1 cup fresh or canned beef broth
Whipped potatoes, optional
Lingonberries or cranberries, optional

1. Preheat oven to 400 degrees.

2. Combine the rice with 1 cup of milk in a saucepan. Cover and bring to the boil over low heat, preferably on an asbestos mat or Flame-Tamer. The heat must be low as the rice cooks or it will tend to overflow. Cook the rice about 15 to 20 minutes or until tender and the milk absorbed. Remove from the heat, uncover and let cool, fluffing the rice with a fork.

3. Meanwhile, bring enough water to the boil to cover the whole cabbage when it is added.

4. Using a sharp paring or boning knife, cut away the center core of the cabbage. A melon ball cutter can also facilitate this. Drop the cabbage into the boiling water and cook, turning occasionally in the water, until the center is tender, about 10 minutes. The leaves must be able to be easily separated and removed whole without tearing them. Remove the cabbage and drain it coreside down.

5. Place the meats in a mixing bowl and add the rice (add only half the rice for a less starchy dish), grated onion, egg, 1 tablespoon flour, salt, pepper, nutmeg, allspice, and the remaining ½ cup of milk. Blend thoroughly.

6. When cool enough to handle, separate the cabbage leaves, using 10 to 12 of the large outer leaves as a base for the stuffing. Arrange these leaves on a flat surface, curve side up. Use a sharp knife and cut away the tough center vein of each leaf. Overlap the cut portion and add equal portions of the filling to each leaf. Cover the filling with smaller center leaves, center vein removed. Roll the leaves to enclose the filling, tucking in the edges neatly.

7. Pour about 2 tablespoons of melted butter over the bottom of a baking dish measuring about 8 by 14 by 2 inches. As the cabbage rolls are prepared, arrange them in the dish close together.

8. Sprinkle with salt, pepper, and paprika. Pour all but 1 tablespoon of butter over the cabbage rolls. Pour the molasses in a thin, even stream over the cabbage rolls and add the cup of beef broth. Cover with foil and place in the oven. Let bake until the liquid around the cabbage rolls is cooking rapidly. Reduce the oven heat to 350 degrees. Bake 30 minutes. Remove the foil and turn the cabbage rolls in the cooking liquid. Cover with foil and bake about 15 minutes longer. Remove the foil and bake 15 minutes longer.

9. Pour the pan liquid into a saucepan and bring to the boil. Cover the cabbage rolls and keep warm.

10. Reduce the liquid to about 1 cup. Combine remaining 1 tablespoon of butter with remaining 1 tablespoon of flour and blend well. Add this, stirring constantly, to the sauce. Cook, stirring, until the sauce is thickened and smooth. Spoon the sauce over the cabbage rolls. Serve with whipped potatoes and lingonberries or cranberries.

Yield: 5 to 6 servings.

Fish Stuffed with Sauerkraut

1   4–5-pound white fish such as striped bass or baquata, a West Coast fish
10   tablespoons butter
    Salt and freshly ground black pepper
2   tablespoons chopped shallots
3   or 4 cups cooked sauerkraut
2   cups dry white wine
    Juice of 1 lemon
2   bay leaves
10   peppercorns
20   sprigs fresh dill, rinsed and patted dry
¼   cup white vinegar
4   tablespoons sugar
2   tablespoons flour
½   cup heavy cream
1   egg yolk

1. Preheat oven to 375 degrees.

2. To prepare this dish properly, the fish must be boned, opening up the body from the stomach and working to the backbone. This can be done by any

professional fish man. The head can be removed.

3. Butter a metal baking dish large enough to hold the fish with 2 tablespoons of butter. Sprinkle with salt, pepper, and shallots. Place the fish in the dish and open up the center. Sprinkle with salt and pepper and brush with 2 tablespoons of melted butter. Scatter the sauerkraut inside the fish, making about a 1-inch layer. Fold the fish over to enclose the stuffing and skewer the opening.

4. Dot the top of the fish with 4 tablespoons of butter. Sprinkle with salt and pepper. Pour over it 1½ cups of white wine and the lemon juice. Surround the fish with bay leaves, peppercorns, and dill. Cover closely with foil. Bring the cooking liquid to a boil on top of the stove. Place the fish in the oven and bake 45 minutes to an hour or until the fish flakes easily and is not dry.

5. Pour off the cooking liquid from the fish into a saucepan. Bring to the boil and cook rapidly to reduce slightly, about 5 minutes.

6. Meanwhile, combine the remaining ½ cup of wine, vinegar, and sugar. Cook, stirring, until slightly syrupy and reduced by half.

7. Blend 2 tablespoons of butter with the flour and add this gradually to the sauce, stirring rapidly with a whisk. Stir in the syrup. Blend the cream and egg yolk and add it, off heat, to the sauce, stirring rapidly.

8. Serve the fish sliced with the sauce spooned over it.

Yield: 4 to 6 servings.

After the Easter Bunny

WITH PIERRE FRANEY

It is in no sense an exaggeration to state that within the next few days Americans will be off on what could be called the annual hard-cooked egg binge. It is the season when the nation's kettle runneth over, so to speak, with what they used to laughingly refer to in the American South as hard-cooked chicken fruit. Now is the best of times, it would seem, to decide what to do with all those eggs once they have served their lawn-rolling function. Truth of the matter is, hard-cooked eggs can be transformed into numerous delectable luncheon dishes, including one called eggs Chimay in which the eggs are stuffed with mushrooms, covered with Mornay sauce and baked. A recipe for that dish (plus recipes for a complete menu) is included here.

Chicken and Tomato Broth with Sour Cream and Herbs

3   cups rich chicken broth
    (see note)
3   cups tomato juice
    A touch of Tabasco
    Salt and freshly ground
    black pepper
    Juice of ½ lemon or more
    to taste
½   cup chopped parsley (see
    note)
½   cup chopped scallions
¼   cup chopped, canned (or
    fresh) mild green chilies,
    optional
    Other chopped herbs if
    desired (see note)
1   cup sour cream
    Parmesan toast (see recipe)

1. Combine the chicken broth and tomato juice in a saucepan and bring to the boil. Add the Tabasco, salt and pepper to taste, and lemon juice. Bring to a simmer without boiling.

2. Spoon equal amounts of parsley, scallions, green chilies, and other herbs, if desired, into the bottom of each of 6 to 8 soup bowls. Pour equal portions of the soup into each bowl.

3. Beat the sour cream with salt to taste and spoon equal portions of sour cream atop each serving. Serve immediately with Parmesan toast (see recipe).

Yield: 6 to 8 servings.

Note: A rich chicken broth is easily made by combining the bony parts of chicken, such as backs, necks, and wings, with water to cover about 1 inch above the pieces, adding salt to taste and simmering to the desired richness of flavor. Vegetables such as chopped celery, carrots, leeks, an onion stuck with cloves, peppercorns, and parsley sprigs may also be added with the water. Although they will improve the flavor of the broth, they are not essential. Chopped Chinese parsley, which is really fresh coriander, is excellent in this dish. Other herbs that might be added include dill and a touch of celery leaf.

Parmesan toast

¼ pound butter at room temperature
¾ cup freshly grated Parmesan cheese
⅛ teaspoon Tabasco, optional
12 very thin slices bread, preferably protein bread

1. Preheat oven to 450 degrees.

2. Place the butter in a mixing bowl and work it with a plastic spatula or wire whisk until it is smooth and spreadable.

3. Add the cheese and Tabasco and beat until thoroughly blended. Spread equal portions of the butter on one side of each slice of bread. Arrange the slices, buttered side up, on a baking sheet. Bake 10 minutes or until the bread is golden. The bread should brown on both sides without turning. Watch carefully to guard against burning or overbrowning. Let cool and cut each slice into two rectangles or triangles.

Yield: 6 to 12 servings.

Stuffed Eggs in the Style of Princess Chimay

8 hard-cooked eggs
½ pound fresh mushrooms
1 tablespoon butter
1 tablespoon finely chopped onion
1 tablespoon finely chopped shallots
   Salt and freshly ground black pepper
2 tablespoons finely chopped parsley
3 tablespoons heavy cream
3 cups hot Mornay sauce (see recipe, page 47)
¼ cup grated Parmesan cheese

1. Preheat oven to 500 degrees.

2. Peel the eggs and split them in half. Put the yolks through a fine sieve into a mixing bowl. Set the whites aside.

3. Finely chop the mushrooms or put them through a food processor or the fine blade of a meat grinder.

4. Empty the mushrooms into a square of cheesecloth or a clean napkin and squeeze to extract most of the moisture. The remaining pulp should measure about ¾ cup.

5. Heat the butter in a skillet and add the onion and shallots. Cook, stirring, until wilted and add the mushroom pulp. Cook, stirring, until the mushroom mixture is "dry" without browning. Let cool.

or until the eggs are piping hot throughout and nicely browned on top.

Yield: 8 servings.

Grapefruit and Lemon Ice

2 cups sugar
2 cups water
  Grated rind of 1 grapefruit
4 cups fresh, unsweetened grapefruit juice (4 or 5 grapefruits)
⅓ cup lemon juice

1. Combine the sugar and water in a saucepan and bring to the boil, stirring until sugar is dissolved. Boil 5 minutes and add the grated rind. Remove from the heat and let cool.

2. Combine the syrup, grapefruit juice, and lemon juice in the container of an electric ice-cream maker. Freeze according to the manufacturer's instructions. Scoop out the grapefruit ice into a mixing bowl, packing it down. Cover with plastic wrap and place in the freezer until ready to use.

Yield: 2 quarts (12 to 14 servings).

Note: This ice is delectable when served with sweetened grapefruit sections steeped in a little vodka as a garnish.

6. Add the mushroom mixture to the egg yolks. Add salt and pepper to taste, parsley, and cream. Blend well with a spoon.

7. Use a pastry bag outfitted with a large star tube (No. 4) and pipe the mixture into the cavities of the whites or spoon the mixture into the cavities. Spoon some of the Mornay sauce over the bottom of a baking dish (we used an 8-by-14-inch oval dish) and arrange the eggs, stuffed side up, over the dish. Spoon the remaining sauce over the eggs. Sprinkle with cheese and bake 10 to 15 minutes

German Specialties

—A lengthy note from our friendly, far-ranging correspondent Feinschmecker, that gentleman of impeccable taste and appetite, informed us that the finest German cooking he's found in any home on the East Coast was that of Christina Drechsler of New Canaan.

"Her herring salad is *wunderbar*," he said, "her lentil soup is *koestlich*, her Koenigsberger klopse are *himnalisch* and her rote grütze—a compote of berries with heavy cream—*ausgezeichnet*."

We telephoned Mrs. Drechsler, who invited us to a gathering of eight people one midweek evening, and when we arrived one late afternoon, she was in the midst of breaking up the carcass of a roast goose removed from her freezer. It was destined for a kettle of lentil soup.

"The goose is left over from some holiday we celebrated at the end of last year," she said. "I always save carcasses for soups and goose is especially good for lentil soup. The bones of roast duck or turkey would work. Chicken wouldn't be too good, I think; not enough body."

Mrs. Drechsler told us that everyone knows her as Dixie, originally Dicksie, a German nickname for a chubby child, which she was in her early youth, which she definitely isn't in her stylish maturity. Her husband, Guenther, is a steel executive with offices in Manhattan, and they are the parents of two children, 8 and 6 years old.

Mrs. Drechsler told us that she had always puttered around the kitchen, and that although her family had servants in Hamburg, the city of her birth, her mother did most of the cooking at her father's insistence.

Oddly enough, she told us, although she is reasonably well known for her German specialties, most of her in-depth knowledge of food came about during a two-year stay in London when she was an au pair girl for a London family. "I acted as governess for the children and cooked for the family each evening," she explained. "The lady of the house was an extraordinary cook who taught me many of the basics I'd never learned at home." Mornings, in London, she spent at school learning English.

"After that I traveled a lot, working for various German firms, five and a half years in Mexico and a year in Spain. I came to New York ten years ago and met my husband here."

One of the things that impressed her most on arrival was the quality of the foods—particularly the meat and sausage products and imported German delicacies she found in the Yorkville area of Manhattan on 86th Street between Second and Lexington Avenues and vicinity.

On the evening in question, Mrs. Drechsler prepared her excellent and much-praised herring salad, which she told us is North German; a rich lentil soup, at once robust and delicate, and a rouladen, the well-known meat rolls. Both the soup and meat rolls are standard fare throughout Germany. Mrs. Drechsler's specialties are of such excellence, a dessert might have seemed an anticlimax, but not so. Her rote grütze made with berries and a black currant beverage is an incredibly delicate and refreshing sweet nectar.

One of the chief characteristics of many German dishes is a smoked flavor, generally achieved by the addition of double-smoked bacon, which is available in the meat markets of Yorkville. That flavor is distinctly present in the rouladen. It may be a bit too prevalent for the average American taste, and the milder ordinary breakfast bacon may be substituted.

Rouladen
(German-style meat rolls)

12 slices top round, about 3 pounds, each slice measuring about 4 by 11 inches and each slice weighing about ¼ pound
    Salt and freshly ground black pepper
1   tablespoon or more dried marjoram
¼   cup or more prepared mustard, preferably imported mustard such as Dijon or Düsseldorf
½   pound bacon, preferably slab bacon, unsliced (see note)
3   cups finely chopped onions
½   cup finely chopped parsley
½   cup finely chopped chives, approximately
12 small imported sour pickles (cornichons) or use ½-inch strips of dill pickles
8   tablespoons butter, approximately
1½ cups thinly sliced carrots
1¼ cups dry red wine
1   cup fresh or canned beef broth
1   teaspoon flour
2   teaspoons water
1   cup heavy cream
    Freshly cooked spaetzle (see recipe)

1. Place the meat on a flat surface and pat dry.

2. Sprinkle meat on one side with salt and pepper. Sprinkle with equal amounts of marjoram and spread top to bottom and side to side with mustard.

3. Remove the rind from the bacon and cut the bacon into ¼-inch cubes. There should be about 2½ cups. Set ½ cup bacon aside for later use. Combine the 2 cups of bacon, 2 cups of chopped onion, parsley, and chives. Sprinkle the meat with equal portions of this mixture, leaving a clear margin of about ½ inch around the edges of each slice. Place 1 pickle about 1 inch from the bottom of each slice and start rolling the meat from the bottom up, folding the sides toward the center as you

roll. Use a skewer to keep the roll intact.

4. Heat 2 tablespoons butter in a saucepan and add the carrots, remaining 1 cup onions, and reserved ½ cup bacon. Cook, stirring, until vegetables are lightly browned, about 10 minutes. Remove the vegetables and bacon with a slotted spoon. Set aside.

5. Heat the remaining 6 tablespoons butter in one or two heavy skillets large enough to hold the meat rolls. Add the meat rolls to the skillet or skillets and cook, turning to brown on all sides. Scrape the bottom of the pan as necessary to loosen any brown particles that stick to it. When the rolls are well browned, remove them and keep warm. Add the wine and beef broth, stirring to dissolve the brown particles. Blend the flour and water and stir it in. Return the meat rolls and any liquid that has accumulated around them to the skillet. Add the reserved vegetables and bacon. Cover. Cook, turning the rolls occasionally. Cook 1 hour.

6. Remove the meat rolls and keep them warm. Pour and spoon the sauce into the container of an electric blender or food processor. It may be necessary to do this in two steps. Blend until smooth and return the sauce to the skillet. Add the cream, stir and bring to the boil. Add the meat rolls, cover and simmer 15 minutes longer over low heat. Serve with freshly cooked spaetzle.

Yield: 12 servings.

Note: For the sake of authentic German taste, Mrs. Drechsler stressed that the bacon used in

Some steps in preparing the rouladen, from the top: Doling out mustard, adding bacon mixture, rolling the meat, using skewer to keep roll intact. Below: Ready for the skillet.

this recipe should be double-smoked. Double-smoked bacon is available in German food shops.

Spaetzle

2   8¾-ounce packages prepared spaetzle
4   tablespoons butter
¼   cup sour cream
2   tablespoons grated Parmesan cheese

1. Cook the spaetzle according to package directions and drain.

2. In a saucepan, melt the butter and stir in the sour cream. Do not boil but blend well. Stir in the cheese. Add the spaetzle and stir until blended.

Yield: 8 to 12 servings.

Herring Salad

5   "new" waxy potatoes
    Salt
1   celery root (also called knob celery and celeriac) (see note)
2   cups Bismarck herring (available in jars), drained and cut into ½-inch cubes
3   cups cooked beets cut into ¼-inch cubes
2   cups dill pickles cut into ½-inch cubes
4   apples, peeled and cut into ½-inch cubes, about 2½ cups
2   tablespoons chopped fresh dill
1   cup mayonnaise, preferably freshly made

6   hard-cooked eggs
    Chopped parsley for garnish

1. Do not peel the potatoes. Put them in a saucepan and add water to cover and salt to taste. Bring to the boil and simmer until tender. Do not overcook or they become mushy. Drain and let cool. Peel the potatoes and cut them into ½-inch cubes. There should be 1½ cups. Set aside.

2. Meanwhile, peel the celery root and cut it in half or quarter it. Drop into cold water and add salt to taste. Bring to the boil and simmer until tender without being mushy. Cut into ½-inch cubes. There should be 2 cups. Set aside.

3. Combine in a mixing bowl the potatoes, celery root, herring, beets, pickles, apples, and dill. Add the mayonnaise and toss to blend well. Add a bit more mayonnaise, if desired.

4. Peel the eggs. Chop 4 of them and add to the bowl. Toss gently, just enough to blend. Spoon the salad into a serving dish. Slice the remaining eggs and garnish the top of the salad. Sprinkle with chopped parsley and serve cold.

Yield: 12 or more servings.

Note: Mrs. Drechsler serves herring salad with small, buttered pumpernickle finger sandwiches. If celery root is not available, cut enough stalk celery into small dice to make 2 cups. Drop into boiling salted water and cook about 10 seconds. Drain and chill quickly under running cold water. Drain well.

Rote Grütze

(A fruit and berry compote)

1 *1-pint-7-ounce bottle imported black currant beverage, about 3 cups (see note)*
1 *pint (2 cups) frozen raspberries or when available, use 2½ cups fresh*
1 *pint (2 cups) frozen blackberries or when available, use 2½ cups fresh*
2 *cups canned, undrained sour (tart) cherries, available in many supermarkets*
1 *2-inch piece vanilla bean or 1 teaspoon pure vanilla extract*
   Peeled rind of ½ lemon
   Juice of 1 lemon
½ *to 1 cup sugar or more to taste*
½ *cup cornstarch*
½ *cup water*
   Chilled heavy cream or whipped cream

1. Pour the black currant beverage into a large saucepan and add the raspberries, blackberries, cherries, with their liquid. Split the vanilla bean in half and scrape the seeds into the mixture. Add the bean itself.

2. Add the lemon rind, lemon juice, and sugar according to taste. Bring to the boil and stir until the sugar is thoroughly dissolved.

3. Blend the cornstarch and water and add it to the saucepan gradually, stirring constantly. Cook until thickened. Let cool. Remove the lemon rind and vanilla bean. Chill thoroughly. This compote should be served very cold. Serve with heavy cream or whipped cream.

Yield: 12 servings.

Note: Imported black currant beverage is available in German food shops.

One of the things which in retrospect impressed us most in our meeting with Mrs. Drechsler was a dish that honestly dates back to our first efforts in front of a stove. We still have in our possession an old worn cookbook given to us shortly after graduation from college which contains a recipe for which we gained a certain celebrity in our younger days. The dish bears the unwieldy title of Koenigsberger klopse, and it was for many years an enormous favorite at the Saturday night suppers we prided ourselves upon. Koenigsberger klopse are, in effect, a sort of German meatball cooked in a liquid with capers. We hadn't thought of the dish for nearly 30 years when Christina made them for us, and it was then that we realized for the first time how inept and amateurish our original efforts had been. Space limitations kept Mrs. Drechsler's recipe for Koenigsberger klopse from appearing in this article, but if you turn to page 197, you'll find it there.

April 1975

WE WERE REMINDED, in perusing the pieces which appeared on the food page during the month of April, that there are certain minor facets of almost any article which for one reason or another do not appear in print. The sort of things we have in mind are pertinent to an interview with a foreign friend—John Tovy, a highly enthusiastic young chef and proprietor of a hotel in England's Lake District—and to a column we wrote about sushi, a dish on which we dote.

To start with John Tovy, it was with some delight that he recounted for us the tenderness and wonder he felt for his American clientele. John does not have a large staff and, when his one bartender leaves his station at ten o'clock each evening, he advises his guests, mostly American, to help themselves at the bar. He reported that each morning he would arrive at the bar to find all the glasses washed and neatly replaced in their cabinets. There would also be a flurry of IOUs and explanatory notes, written on cocktail napkins and the like, with notations such as, "I drank half a bottle of tonic water," "I used two limes," "I helped myself to the tomato juice," and so on—each note dutifully signed by the client involved. John much admired such meticulous accounting and over a gin-and-tonic wondered aloud if it were pure and simple goodness or a lack of worldliness; whatever it was, he hoped it remained a national characteristic.

The aside that was left unmentioned in the column about sushi regards the steep price of addiction to this fine dish. Sushi, of course, is composed of various kinds of raw fish wrapped around or centered on a delicate pad of cooked rice lightly flavored with vinegar. Most of what we know about sushi and that other great raw fish specialty of Japan, sashimi, we learned on trips to Osaka. On occasion, when in Osaka, which is an industrial town, we have been taken to a restaurant which has been described to us as perhaps the greatest raw fish restaurant in all of Japan. It is called Fukki-zushi and it happens to be also one of the most expensive restaurants in the world. As we recall, a typical lunch for one costs in the vicinity of sixty dollars. It was at Fukki-zushi that we were introduced to a Japanese industrialist who told us he has dined there at least once every day of his life. As is customary with many Japanese businessmen, he charges his meals. Legend has it that the cost of lunch for one solid year totals approximately $10,000. If you can afford the freight, and would like to sample some of the best maguro, kappa maki, norimaki, and su zu ki, among other things, Fukki-zushi is located at

Nipponbashi-itchomé, Minamiku, Osaka. (Tell the taxi driver it's behind Kamata-Tokkyo-Jimusho at Nipponichi.) The telephone number is 06 (Osaka) 632-0865. If you are interested in lunch, we advise getting there shortly after 11 o'clock in the morning as a place at the sushi bar is one of the most sought after things in Osaka.

English Cookery

When we learned that John Tovey, proprietor of an English hotel, was en route to Manhattan we invited him to visit our kitchen, if for no other reason than because of an article we'd read some time back in *The London Times*. It was written by Margaret Costa, one of England's most admired food writers, who stated unequivocally that "John Tovey is the best British pastry cook I know."

We greeted the young man shortly after his arrival from South Africa, where he had taken a crew of four cooks from his hotel to demonstrate cooking and to stage "a festival of English country cooking," in a few hotels in Rhodesia. "The festival was great fun," he stated, "but not without exasperations. The hotels spent a good deal of time and money to convert their dining rooms into a 'stately homes of England' idea— fireplace, harpist, that sort of thing, very elegant—but the management was mortified at some of my food costs. They thought 14 pounds of butter and 12 pints of cream for 60 people was outrageous and all they cared about was a balance sheet. I've never costed a meal in my life. Quite frankly, I'm not interested in making money. I'd rather make less money and pay less tax." A somewhat novel and interesting point of view, we thought, and we asked how he had entered the hotel field.

"To tell the truth," he recalled, "it happened a few years ago when I was destitute. But not destitute through cooking. I'd lost all my money in the theater, the complete disaster, about 15 years ago. I had my own repertory company at Her Majesty's Theater, Barrow-in-Furness in Lancashire. And I mean all my money."

He added that since childhood he'd always been intrigued with cooking and since food seemed somehow related to hotel keeping, he became a hotel manager. He was general manager at various times for three hotels.

"Five years ago I chucked it all," he continued, "and bought a house in the Lake District with the simple idea of taking in guests and offering bed and breakfast. It's called Miller Howe, howe being a Cumberland word for hill, so the name really means Miller Hill. The windows open onto Lake Windermere and in the early spring the fields are blanketed with daffodils and hydrangeas. One travel writer has described it as having one of the dozen or so most spectacular views in all of Europe." Miller Howe prospered from the beginning and now has a clientele from all over the world that includes country folk and gentry, London bankers and many, many Americans.

By what training had he come to be billed by an established authority as "the best pastry cook in all of England?" It was not, he said, through any formal instruction: his pastry-making is homestyle. "I learned almost everything I know about cooking from a grandmother who raised me," he said. "When I was born my parents were Colonial Office stationed in India and they left me back in England. My grandmother had gone into service in a private home at the age of thirteen. She worked for a wealthy vegetable importer and his wife, and her cooking was mostly North Country. She was very good at roasts, super at desserts."

Although his original intention four years ago when he opened his own hotel was to offer only bed and breakfast, he almost immediately offered his guests a "set" dinner with no choice. Today there are five choices. His lakeland breakfast alone is a mammoth affair that includes such things as bacon, eggs, sausages, mushrooms, fried apples, grilled tomatoes, black pudding, and bubble and squeak.

Bubble and squeak?

"The dish was conceived as something to be served in England on Mondays, the traditional wash day," Mr. Tovey explained. "The meal on Monday consists of cold beef with leftover vegetables and potatoes and a fried egg on top and after you eat it you bubble and squeak." More serious dinner fare in the gentleman's kitchen includes various kinds of quiches, of which a shrimp and almond is most popular; local trout; local game; and many, many English pastries and desserts.

Before departing, Mr. Tovey told us an engaging story about the parsimonious nature of one of his grandfathers. "He was a cagey old Yorkshire man," he said, "and once a week my grandmother made roast beef with Yorkshire pudding. 'Children,' grandpa would say, 'who eats the most pud gets the most meat.' Naturally we filled up on the pud and had no appetite for anything else."

Shrimp and Almond Quiche

1   recipe for savory pastry, at room temperature (see recipe)
½   pound raw shrimp, shelled and deveined
¼   cup chopped toasted almonds
1   cup heavy cream
2   tablespoons bottled clam broth
2   eggs plus 1 egg yolk, lightly beaten
⅛   teaspoon grated nutmeg
    Salt

1. Preheat oven to 325 degrees.

2. Roll out the pastry to fit a 9- or 10-inch pie dish, preferably a tin dish with a removable bottom.

Trim the sides and flute the pastry, if desired. Line the pastry with a round of aluminum foil and add about 2 cups of dried peas or beans to keep it flat. Bake 30 minutes.

3. Remove the pastry from oven and remove the foil. The beans may be saved for another baking.

4. Increase oven heat to 400 degrees.

5. Combine the remaining ingredients and pour the mixture into the pie shell. Bake 35 to 45 minutes or until the custard is set. Let the quiche stand at room temperature for at least 5 minutes before cutting.

Yield: 6 to 8 servings.

Savory pastry

2 *cups flour*
1 *tablespoon confectioners' sugar*
  Salt
10 *tablespoons butter, at room temperature*
1 *egg*

1. Sift the flour, sugar, and salt into a mixing bowl.

2. Put the butter onto a flat surface, preferably marble, and make a well in the center. Add the egg to the well. Using the fingers, pat and work the butter and egg together until they look like scrambled eggs.

3. Smooth the mixture out with a spatula. Sprinkle all the flour mixture over this. Using the spatula, chop the flour into the

John Tovey

butter mixture, chopping left to right and top to bottom, always pushing the mixture to the center. Continue until the pastry is well blended and all the flour is coated with butter. Gather the dough into a ball, wrap in foil, and refrigerate.

Yield: Enough pastry for a single 9- or 10-inch crust.

Tarragon Cream Sauce

2 *eggs*
½ *cup sugar*
½ *cup tarragon vinegar*
  Salt, optional
½ *cup heavy cream, stiffly beaten, optional*

1. Place the eggs and sugar in the top of a double boiler and, preferably, using a portable electric beater, beat the eggs until they are thick and lemon colored.

2. Gradually beat in the vinegar. Continue beating until piping hot. Add salt, if desired. The sauce may be served at this point or, if desired, fold in the heavy cream. Serve over steamed vegetables.

Yield: About 2½ cups.

Pork Chops in Mustard-Cream Sauce

6   *loin pork chops, each about 1 inch thick*
½   *cup dry white wine*
¾   *cup flour*
    Salt and freshly ground black pepper
¼   *cup peanut, vegetable, or corn oil*
1   *teaspoon finely chopped dried thyme or sage*
2   *tablespoons butter*
4   *cloves garlic, peeled and split in half*
2   *cups heavy cream*
1   *tablespoon powdered mustard*
2   *tablespoons tomato puree*
½   *cup thinly slivered cornichons (French sour pickles, available in bottles in specialty food shops)*
    Watercress for garnish

1. Preheat oven to 300 degrees.

2. Place the chops in a baking dish or other container and pour the wine over them. Let stand an hour or so.

3. Remove the chops and pat dry. Dredge them lightly in a mixture of flour, salt, and pepper.

4. Heat the oil in a large skillet and brown the chops on both sides, about 4 minutes to a side.

5. Transfer the chops to a heavy casserole or Dutch oven and sprinkle with salt and pepper, and thyme or sage.

6. Melt the butter in a saucepan and add the garlic. Stir without browning and pour on top of the chops. Place the chops in the oven and cover. Bake 1½ hours, basting frequently.

7. Meanwhile, pour the cream into a saucepan and boil, uncovered, until reduced to ⅔ cup. Combine the mustard and tomato puree in a mixing bowl and beat with a whisk. Gradually add the reduced cream, beating well. Spoon the sauce over the chops and reduce the oven heat to 250 degrees. Cover and bake 30 minutes longer. Garnish with the slivered cornichons and watercress.

Yield: 6 servings.

Farmhouse Pastry
(Sweet pastry for fruit tarts)

3   *cups flour*
1   *cup cornstarch*
1   *tablespoon baking powder*
½   *teaspoon salt*
¾   *pound butter, at room temperature*
    Grated rind of 1 lemon
1   *cup granulated sugar*
2   *egg yolks*

1. Sift together the flour, cornstarch, baking powder, and salt into a bowl.

2. Cut in the softened butter by running cupped hands through the flour and butter and lifting up the ingredients without rubbing. Let the ingredients drop back into the bowl. Continue this lifting and dropping motion until all the mixture is crumbled or looks crumbled. Add the grated lemon rind and sugar. Mix as delicately as possible, using the fingers.

3. Lightly beat the yolks and sprinkle them zigzag fashion in a thin stream over the ingredients. Do not stir. Hold the mixing bowl between the hands and slightly away from you. Shake it to toss the pastry inside as if panning for gold. Larger and larger crumbs will form as the ingredients are tossed.

4. When well blended, place the bowl on a flat surface. Use the hands to gather the pastry together, working gently and shaping the dough quickly into a ball. Place the ball in a plastic bag and refrigerate for an hour or so. Before rolling the pastry, remove it from the refrigerator and let it return to room temperature.

Yield: Enough pastry for two 8-inch pies or one large 12-inch pie.

Miller Howe Carrot Soup with Coriander

¼ pound butter
1½ cups finely chopped onion
½ cup dry white wine or dry sherry
6 cups (2 pounds) finely diced carrots
2 teaspoons ground coriander
2 cups rich chicken broth
2 cups milk or cream
Salt and freshly ground black pepper
1 cup toasted croutons
Chopped parsley

1. Melt the butter in a heavy saucepan and add the onion. Cook, stirring often, until onion is golden brown.

2. Add the wine and carrots. Sprinkle with coriander and stir. Cover closely with a round of wax paper. Cook over very low heat about 1 hour, taking care that the carrots do not stick or burn.

3. Add the chicken broth and simmer 20 minutes. Add the milk or cream, salt and pepper to taste. Bring to the boil and serve garnished with toasted croutons and parsley.

Yield: 6 servings.

Sushi: Natural Wonder

WITH PIERRE FRANEY

To the uninitiated palate, sushi—raw fish served on rice—is one of the gastronomic curiosities of the world. Some people, even those who dote on raw oysters and clams, find the thought of eating raw fish in any form bizarre.

To those who enjoy sushi, however, it is one of the natural gastronomic wonders, in or out of its native Japan, and to call sushi an appetizer—as many people do—is not to understand the nature of the dish. Of course, it may be served in small portions at the beginning of a meal, but to dig into the subject like a native you must sit at a sushi bar pointing with glee and uncontrollable gluttony at the scores of pieces of fish and seafood on view behind the glass of an immaculately polished display case.

In Japan there is a good deal of interesting folklore surrounding the dish. Legend has it beginning 2,000 years ago near Tokyo with an emperor who dined on fish that was just beginning to ferment. Tokyo to this day is considered the sushi capital of the world (although the finest sushi house we've ever stumbled on anywhere is the Fukki-zushi in the Minami district in Osaka).

For want of written records it is impossible to determine the exact date when sushi was created, but the greatest likelihood, according to food authorities in Japan, is that it probably started in China in a different form. It is theorized that, originally, raw fish was packed between layers of rice and left until the fish started to take on a slightly fermented, sour taste. Then it was eaten with a new-found relish. This technique was probably imported to Japan, where eventually the present custom of serving nothing but the freshest of fish on a hand-shaped pad of vinegar-flavored rice came into being. There are said to be still in existence in Japan a few rare places where fish is lightly fermented between rice layers as in the original manner.

The kinds of fish and shellfish that can be eaten raw as sushi are practically endless. It is true that tuna, one of the favorite fish used for sushi, is seasonal, but any very fresh and edible ocean fish or shellfish can be used. Sea bass, striped bass, and fresh mackerel are all excellent. Salmon roe, sometimes called red caviar and available in jars 12 months a year, is delicious as a topping for seaweed-wrapped sushi rice. Thinly sliced raw clams, even the large chowder clams sliced razor thin along the meaty section, are delectable. Sea urchins, that delicacy so prized in

Mediterranean regions, offer an incredibly good roe best eaten raw. The important thing is that each morsel to be served should be of the freshest quality and sliced bite-size before using. Here are the basic techniques for making sushi.

Charts like this one hang in many Japanese restaurants to show the kinds of sushi that can be ordered.

Sushi Rice

3   cups rice (about 1½ pounds), preferably Japanese or Italian (such as Avorio), available in Japanese and Italian markets

1   piece dried kelp (seaweed) about 3 inches square (see note)

1½   teaspoons mirin (sweet sake), available in Japanese markets

½   cup sushi vinegar (see recipe)

1. Place the rice in a kettle and add cold water to cover. Stir rapidly with the hands and drain. Return the rice to the kettle and wash again, stirring. Drain. Repeat once more. Drain finally in a sieve and let stand 1 hour.

2. Measure the rice once more. It should measure about 3½ to 4 cups. Put it in a saucepan. Add an equal quantity of cold water. Add the kelp and bring to the boil. As soon as the water boils remove and discard the kelp. Cover the saucepan and cook the rice over high heat (the lid may rock from the steam) about 6 minutes or until the rice is tender. Sprinkle with the mirin and cover with a cloth, then with the lid. Let stand 20 minutes.

3. Empty the piping hot rice into a bowl, preferably wide and made of wood, and gradually add the vinegar, turning the rice with a wooden spoon so that the vinegar is evenly distributed. Traditionally the rice should be fanned to cool it quickly as the vinegar is stirred in. Smooth the rice into a thin layer and let stand until thoroughly cooled.

Yield: About 6 cups.

Note: Kelp is called kombu in Japanese and is available at Japanese markets.

Sushi vinegar

1   *cup rice vinegar, available in some supermarkets and in most Japanese groceries*
1¼   *cups sugar*
¼   *cup salt*
      Pinch of monosodium glutamate, optional

Combine all the ingredients in a saucepan and heat, stirring, until the sugar is dissolved. Remove from the heat.

Yield: About 1½ cups.

Sushi dip

Sushi is traditionally served with a small saucer or bowl of light soy sauce with wasabi (Japanese horseradish) on the side. The wasabi is added to the soy sauce as desired.

Fish Fillets for Making Sushi

Although tuna (see note) is the most basic, traditional fish for making sushi, it is by no means the sum of it. Almost any fresh-caught, firm-fleshed, saltwater fish may be used, including sea bass, striped bass, mackerel, and so on.

The fillets must be free of bones and skin. Place a slab of the fish on a cutting board and, using a very sharp slicing knife, cut the fillet, preferably on the bias, into ¼-inch-thick slices. Shape according to directions below.

Note: In Japan considerable importance is placed on the cut of tuna used for sushi. The quality ranges from akami or zuke, which is very lean tuna, to chutoro, which is medium fat, to otoro, which is the fattest of all. Most connoisseurs, it is said, prefer the otoro, or fattest, quality.

Large clams for sushi

Open the clams and remove the body. Cut away any digestive organs, leaving the firm, meaty muscle of the shellfish. Cut the muscle into thin slices and add salt. Massage well and rinse under cold running water. These slices may be butterflied to make them larger. Score the slices gently with a knife without cutting through the meat.

Shrimp for sushi

Although raw shrimp are a great delicacy in Japan, they are not recommended to be served as sushi in this country unless they are purchased live and out of pure waters. The vast majority of shrimp sold in America have been frozen. In Japan the shrimp are known as odori, or dancing shrimp, because of their jumping motions just before they are prepared for sushi. The raw tails are shelled and butterflied and eaten. The upper carcass is liberally salted, grilled over charcoal, and eaten hot.

How to Shape Plain Sushi

Prepare the fish or seafood and the rice to be used in making sushi. Follow the recipe for sushi rice carefully. Have ready a small bowl of prepared wasabi and a small bowl of cold water to which has been added a teaspoon of rice vinegar.

Take a thin slice of fish fillet or a piece of seafood in one hand (the left hand usually). Dip the index finger of the other hand into the wasabi and smear a little of it into the center of the fish. Wet the palm and fingers with the vinegar water and take up about 1½ tablespoons of sushi rice. Shape it into a ball, using one hand. Apply it to the wasabi-smeared fish and shape it into an oval so that it just fits the fish. Serve with sushi dip (see recipe).

Seaweed-Wrapped Sushi (Doté)

There are several ways of wrapping foods in seaweed to be served as sushi. One of the most common is to shape about 1½ tablespoons of sushi rice into an oval, apply a dab of wasabi to the top and encircle the rice with a rectangle of laver or nori (seaweed; see directions for preparing below), leaving an open space at the top for other small ingredients such as tiny scallops, slivers of raw fish, salmon roe, sea-urchin roe, and so on. At times a sprinkle of lemon juice is added.

Another common technique is to place a rectangle of seaweed flat on a rectangular shaping mat made with thin bamboo reeds. This device is called a makisushi and is available where Japanese cooking utensils are sold. Put 2 or 3 tablespoons of sushi rice in the center and, using the fingers, spread it out neatly over the seaweed but leave a margin top and bottom. Add a dab of wasabi to the center, left to right, and add a thin

strip of tuna or other fish or seafood across the center. Add a strip
of cucumber if desired. Or use
strips of broiled eel and Japanese
pickles in place of the tuna and
cucumber.

Fold the bamboo mat over in
such a manner that the filling is
enclosed in seaweed. Cut the
sushi roll into sections of any desired length and serve with sushi
dip on the side.

Dried seaweed (laver or nori) for sushi

To prepare the seaweed for
sushi, pass it quickly on both
sides over heat such as a gas flame
or a hot grill. Cut it to any desired
size, and shape around sushi rice
plus other ingredients. As noted,
the name for sushi fish wrapped in
seaweed is doté. It means an em-
bankment.

One of those questions that seems to persist on our frequent en-
counters with readers is, "How can you be so involved with food and yet
maintain a reasonable build?" There are several secrets we could name,
including the morning use of a bathroom scale, a daily adherence to
small portions, and moderation in most things. However, despite our
good intentions, the bathroom scale occasionally gives us cause for
alarm. It is then that we really appreciate sushi. Although sushi is made
with rice, it is a great vehicle for maintaining a stable weight and is enormously gratifying to the appetite.

The Dish Mother Used to Make

Recently, we were interviewed on a radio program, and when the subject veered around to childhood foods, we described in some detail the dish that had given us most pleasure in early youth and adolescence and still gives us comfort as we approach senility.

It was a family creation known as chicken spaghetti. It consisted of spaghetti or spaghettini and sometimes vermicelli baked in a casserole, layered with a tomato and cream sauce, a meat sauce, boneless chicken, and two kinds of grated cheese.

It was almost always served when large numbers were invited for special occasions.

Subsequent to the program we received numerous requests for the recipe and discovered with some astonishment that we had somehow never had occasion to use it in a story. The recipe follows.

My Mother's Chicken Spaghetti

1   3½-pound chicken with giblets
    Chicken broth to cover (see note)
    Salt
3   cups canned tomatoes, preferably Italian peeled tomatoes
7   tablespoons butter
3   tablespoons flour
½   cup heavy cream
⅛   teaspoon grated nutmeg
    Freshly ground black pepper
½   pound fresh mushrooms (see note)
2   cups finely chopped onions
1½ cups finely chopped celery
1½ cups chopped green pepper
1   tablespoon or more finely minced garlic
¼   pound ground beef
¼   pound ground pork
1   bay leaf
½   teaspoon hot red pepper flakes, optional
1   pound spaghetti or spaghettini
½   pound Cheddar cheese, grated, about 2 to 2½ cups
    Grated Parmesan cheese

1. One of the stipulations in the original recipe for this dish is that the spaghetti including all the ingredients be combined at least 4 hours before baking.

2. Place the chicken with neck, gizzard, heart, and liver in a

kettle and add chicken broth to cover and salt to taste. Bring to the boil and simmer until the chicken is tender without being dry, 35 to 45 minutes. Let cool.

3. Remove the chicken and take the meat from the bones. Shred the meat, cover and set aside. Return the skin and bones to the kettle and cook the stock down 30 minutes or longer. There should be 4 to 6 cups of broth. Strain and reserve the broth. Discard the skin and bones.

4. Meanwhile, put the tomatoes in a saucepan and cook down to half the original volume, stirring. There should be 1½ cups.

5. Melt 3 tablespoons of butter in a saucepan and add the flour, stirring to blend with a wire whisk. When blended and smooth, add 1 cup of the reserved hot broth and the cream, stirring rapidly with the whisk. When thickened and smooth add the nutmeg, salt and pepper to taste. Continue cooking, stirring occasionally, about 10 minutes. Set aside.

6. If the mushrooms are very small or button mushrooms, leave them whole. Otherwise, cut them in half or quarter them. Heat 1 tablespoon of butter in a small skillet and add the mushrooms. Cook, shaking the skillet occasionally and stirring the mushrooms until they are golden brown. Set aside.

7. Heat 3 tablespoons of butter in a deep skillet and add the onion. Cook, stirring, until wilted. Add the celery and green pepper and cook, stirring, about 5 minutes. Do not overcook. The vegetables should remain crisp-tender.

8. Add the garlic, beef, and pork and cook, stirring and chopping down with the edge of a large metal spoon to break up the meat. Cook just until the meat loses its red color. Add the bay leaf and red pepper flakes. Add the tomatoes and the white sauce made with the chicken broth. Add the mushrooms.

9. Cook the spaghetti or spaghettini in boiling salted water until it is just tender. Do not overcook. Remember that it will cook again when blended with the chicken and meat sauce. Drain the spaghetti and run under cold running water.

10. Spoon enough of the meat sauce over the bottom of a 5- or 6-quart casserole to cover it lightly. Add about ⅓ of the spaghetti. Add about ⅓ of the shredded chicken, a layer of meat sauce, a layer of grated Cheddar cheese, and another layer of spaghetti. Continue making layers, ending with a layer of spaghetti topped with a thin layer of meat sauce and grated Cheddar cheese.

11. Pour in up to 2 cups of the reserved chicken broth or enough to almost but not quite cover the top layer of spaghetti. Cover and let the spaghetti stand for 4 hours or longer. If the liquid is absorbed as the dish stands, add a little more chicken broth. Remember that when this dish is baked and served, the sauce will be just a bit soupy rather than thick and clinging.

12. When ready to bake preheat the oven to 350 degrees.

13. Place the spaghetti casse-

role on top of the stove and bring it just to the boil. Cover and place it in the oven. Bake 15 minutes and uncover. Bake 15 minutes longer or until the casserole is hot and bubbling throughout and starting to brown on top. Serve immediately with grated Parmesan cheese on the side.

Yield: 12 or more servings.

Note: A rich chicken broth is easily made by combining the bony parts of the chicken such as backs, necks, and wings with water to cover a depth of about 1 inch above the pieces, adding salt to taste and simmering to the desired richness of flavor.

Vegetables such as chopped celery, carrots, leeks, an onion stuck with cloves, peppercorns, and parsley sprigs may also be added with the water, and although they will improve the flavor of the broth, they are not essential. If fresh mushrooms are not available, as they frequently weren't when this recipe was prepared some 50 years ago, use drained canned button mushrooms.

Chef Jean Banchet

To a provincial New Yorker, the discovery of an excelling French restaurant in Chicago might seem a distinct and provocative cultural happening. To discover a restaurant of outstanding merit in a small and otherwise undistinguished village approximately 40 miles north of the Windy City's Loop comes as cosmic revelation. But Le Français restaurant here would rank on almost any count with the finest French restaurants in America. In some areas it all but outdistances any but those on the top rung of the gastronomic ladder.

Le Français is the culinary offspring of Jean Banchet, a 34-year-old Burgundian whom we had known only by reputation through the plaudits of several French chefs in Manhattan. We had been told that he is a young man of exceptional talent, imagination and industry, and over a bottle of Taittinger champagne in his Chicago apartment, he informed us that he had not been born to the métier, although he was born in the Burgundy town of Roanne, best celebrated as the home of the lavishly praised and must discussed Troisgros restaurant.

"My mother was a good cook, yes, but in my very earliest years I never thought of becoming a chef. I met the Troisgros brothers, Pierre and Jean, and they were kind to me. At some point I started reading the magazines for chefs and everything started to crystallize when I was 14 or 15.

"There was no room for me in the Troisgros kitchen, so I got a job next door at the Terminus, which also had a good kitchen but not as famous. After my apprenticeship there, the Troisgros brothers helped place me in the Fernand Point establishment, the Pyramide restaurant in Vienne. Both the Troisgros had apprenticed there and were very close to the family."

His first station abroad was in London as executive chef of the Sporting Club, a "big casino" in Knightsbridge. Two things of uncommon direction happened to his life there. He met and married his wife, Doris, a native of Germany who was also working in a restaurant, and he met an executive of the Playboy Club of Lake Geneva, Wisconsin. He was persuaded to come to this country as chef of that establishment. After almost four years of working in the Chicago vicinity he had one consuming desire: to own his own restaurant.

"I saw too many things in the places I worked. Too many short cuts, too much emphasis on cost accounting. I started putting my money on the side, and when the moment came, my wife and I scouted all over including Chicago. She was convinced that the people who dine in French restaurants live in the suburbs."

Chef Banchet had invited us to join him at his restaurant the next day to inspect the place and watch him cook. After an hour's drive we arrived in a fairly nondescript setting, a neat, white frame house on a small road with a good deal of traffic passing by.

"This house," he told us, "is 50 years old. It had been a roadside inn for 25 years with a succession of owners." He completely revamped the kitchen with new equipment. The present dining room is small, with only 18 tables and seating capacity for 60. It is a handsome, modestly decorated place, with fresh flowers and old copper. Le Français has been a success since it opened its doors about two years ago.

"In the beginning we had a bad time trying to honor reservations, because people were starting to book weeks in advance, and a lot of them would fail to show after telephoning two or three weeks earlier. Now we won't take a reservation more than a week in advance."

One reason for Mr. Banchet's outstanding and deserved success is his intense dedication to his work. Although the Banchets have an apartment in Chicago they live in a small home near the restaurant. He is generally at his stove by 8:30 A.M., making mousses, soups, desserts, and other basics before the hordes arrive at 6 P.M.

He is enormously innovative, and the clientele dines on some of the most memorable inventions of the "new wave" of French chefs, which includes the Troisgros brothers and Paul Bocuse, all of whom are friends.

One of his most popular dishes is a Troisgros creation, now celebrated wherever serious eaters gather, the salmon with sorrel sauce. Or the marvelous cold salmon in pastry dish created by Bocuse. Or some of his own "new" creations such as a fantastic lobster tail, smeared with lobster mousse and baked in puff pastry (a variation and vast improvement over beef Wellington) served with a tarragon and Pernod sauce. On the day of our visit he prepared another elegant dish he had conceived a day or so before, a quiche of sweetbreads with mushrooms and spinach.

Although Mr. Banchet's virtuosity is laudably apparent in the major things—the pâtés, mousses, galantines, and in such innovations as lobster tails baked in pastry—there are occasional lapses on lesser levels.

The rice that accompanied one dish was overcooked, the meringues for the floating island imperfectly shaped and the coffee seemed noticeably weak. Many of the dishes at Le Français are overly garnished with parsley and/or lemon, giving the individual servings a burdened look and diminishing the appeal both to the eye and appetite.

Mr. Banchet states that he will serve any dish in the French literature, new or old, if ordered six days in advance and for a minimum of four people. One thing, he declares with undisguised satisfaction, he would never serve banal French cooking and never has.

Mrs. Banchet, who acts as hostess, states that the average dinner check is from about $10 to $20. Main courses at midday are priced about $4 to $6.95; evenings from about $8.50 to $10.50. The telephone number is (312) 541-7470, and the exact address is 269 South Milwaukee Avenue. The restaurant is closed Mondays, holidays, and the month of January.

Quiche of Sweetbreads and Mushrooms

1   *small pair sweetbreads, about ¾ pound*
    Salt and freshly ground black pepper
½   *pound fresh mushrooms, sliced, about 2½ cups*
½   *pound fresh spinach, trimmed and rinsed well*
6   *tablespoons butter*
4   *eggs*
1½ *plus ⅓ cups heavy cream*
⅛   *teaspoon grated nutmeg*
¼   *cup dry white wine Enough pastry for 6 individual pies or 1 large 10-inch pie*

1. Soak the sweetbreads for several hours in cold water to cover. Drain.

2. Place the sweetbreads in a large saucepan and add cold water to cover. Bring to the boil and simmer 5 minutes. Drain immediately, run under cold water and let cool. Chill well.

3. Place the sweetbreads in a dish large enough to hold them and cover with a weight. Weight them down at least 6 hours and refrigerate.

4. Preheat the oven to 450 degrees.

5. Trim off the outside membranes and veins from the sweetbreads. Cut the sweetbreads into 1-inch cubes. Sprinkle with salt and pepper and set aside.

6. Sprinkle the mushrooms with salt and pepper and set aside.

7. Drop the spinach into boiling salted water. Simmer 1 minute. Drain and run under cold water. Squeeze to extract most of the moisture. Chop coarsely and sprinkle with salt and pepper and set aside.

8. Heat 2 tablespoons of butter in each of 3 skillets. Cook the sweetbreads, stirring and tossing in one skillet, about 5 minutes. Set aside. Cook the spinach in another skillet, about 2 minutes, stirring and tossing. Set aside.

9. Beat together the eggs and 1½ cups cream. Season with salt, pepper, and nutmeg.

10. Cook the mushrooms in the third skillet, about 3 minutes, stirring and tossing. Add the sweetbreads and any pan juices to the mushrooms. Cook together, stirring, about 1 minute. Scoop out the sweetbread mixture and set aside. Add the wine to that skillet and cook until almost totally reduced. Add the remaining ⅓ cup of heavy cream and cook, stirring, about 1 minute. Add this to the egg and cream mixture.

11. Line 6 individual, disposable, aluminum pie pans or one 10-inch pie pan with the pastry.

12. Add equal amounts of the spinach to the bottoms of each of the individual pie shells or the larger pie shell. Cover the shells or larger shell with equal portions of the sweetbread mixture. Pour in the egg mixture.

13. Chef Banchet places the pies on a baking sheet and bakes them on an oven rack placed on the floor of the oven. Bake the individual pies 20 minutes or the larger pie 30 minutes. Reduce the heat to 350 degrees and bake 10 to 15 minutes longer.

Yield: 6 individual pies or one 10-inch pie.

Saumon à l'Oseille

(Salmon with sorrel sauce)

1   3–3½-*pound boned,*
    skinned salmon or striped
    bass fillets
¼   *cup chopped shallots*
4   *cups fish stock (see recipe)*
1½ *cups dry vermouth*
1   *cup dry white wine*
2¼ *cups heavy cream*
    Salt and freshly ground
    black pepper
3   *tablespoons fish glaze (see*
    note), optional
¼   *pound fresh sorrel or*
    spinach, stems removed
4   *egg yolks*
2   *tablespoons butter*
    Juice of ½ lemon
    Flour for dredging
½   *cup clarified butter (see*
    recipe)

1. Cut the fish on the bias like smoked salmon into ¼-inch-thick slices. Flatten gently with a flat mallet. Refrigerate.

2. In a deep skillet, combine the shallots, fish stock, vermouth, and white wine. Cook over high heat about 40 to 45 minutes until the liquid is reduced to about ½ cup.

3. Add 2 cups cream, salt and pepper to taste. Bring to the boil and stir in the fish glaze, if used. Cook over high heat about 2 minutes.

4. Cut the sorrel or spinach into very fine shreds (chiffonade). Add the sorrel or spinach to the cream mixture and bring to the boil. Beat the yolks with the remaining cream. Remove the sauce from the heat and stir in the yolk and cream mixture. Swirl in the 2 tablespoons butter. Season with lemon juice.

5. Keep the sauce hot but do not boil or it will curdle.

6. Dredge the fish slices lightly in flour seasoned with salt and pepper.

7. Heat the clarified butter in one or two large skillets. When it is very hot but not smoking, add the fish slices. Cook about 1 minute on one side until golden brown. Turn and cook about 1 minute on the other. Serve the fish with the sauce spooned over.

Yield: 4 to 6 servings.

Note: Fish glaze is a long-simmered reduction of fish stock. The stock is cooked many hours until it becomes a thick gelatinous, lightly brown mass, like thick, smooth caramel. It is a classic foundation glaze in French kitchens.

Fish stock

2½ pounds fish bones (may include head of fish with gills removed)
2 cups coarsely chopped celery
2 cups thinly sliced onions
1 whole clove garlic, unpeeled, sliced in half
2 cups chopped, well-washed green part of leeks
3 sprigs fresh thyme
1 bay leaf
2 quarts water
½ bottle dry white wine
¼ teaspoon peppercorns
Salt

Combine all the ingredients in a large pot. Bring to a boil and simmer about 20 minutes. Strain.

Yield: 8 to 10 cups

Note: Leftover stock may be frozen.

Clarified butter

To clarify butter, place the butter in a heatproof glass measuring cup and let it melt slowly in a 200-degree oven. Do not stir the butter. Pour off the clear, golden liquid on top, leaving the white milky substance at the bottom. The clear liquid is clarified butter.

Coupe Normande
(Vanilla ice cream with apples and Calvados)

4 firm cooking apples
4 tablespoons butter
½ cup sugar
¼ cup Calvados or applejack
6 servings vanilla ice cream

1. Core and peel the apples. Cut them into quarters and cut the quarters into slices. There should be about 4 cups.

2. Heat the butter in a heavy skillet and add the apples. Cook, stirring gently and tossing, about 6 to 10 minutes. The slices should remain firm and not become mushy. Add the sugar and cook 2 minutes, stirring and tossing gently. Sprinkle with the Calvados and ignite it. Serve hot or warm over ice cream.

Yield: 6 servings.

To our great regret, six weeks after the preceding article on Jean Banchet and his restaurant Le Français appeared, the restaurant burned to the ground. The owner/chef has told us recently that with good luck the restaurant will be completely rebuilt and in full operation by the middle of 1976. In the interim, or so we are advised as this book goes to press, M. Banchet is serving as consultant to the kitchen of the new Ritz Carlton Hotel on Michigan Avenue in Chicago. We wish his construction team godspeed.

A Passion for Chicken Wings

WITH PIERRE FRANEY

We have always treasured the writing of Janet Flanner, who for many years has written a frequent letter from Paris, signed Genêt, for *The New Yorker*. We were delighted to read in an interview recently that she shares our passion for chicken wings. First off, she declared that she is not a gourmet but a gourmand (infinitely preferable in our books). "My favorite dish is chicken wings," she declared. "It's the most refined part of the creature." We can only add bravo and contribute two refined uses for that part of the creature. One is for curried chicken wings, the other for chicken wings chasseur made with tomatoes and mushrooms.

Curried Chicken Wings

4   pounds chicken wings (18 to 24)
3   tablespoons curry powder
¾   cup finely chopped onion
1   tablespoon finely minced garlic
2   apples, cored, peeled, and cut into small cubes (about 2 cups)
1   banana, peeled and cut into small cubes
1½ cups water
1   cup plain yogurt
1   cup drained tomatoes
1   bay leaf
    Salt and freshly ground black pepper

1. Cut off and discard the small wing tips of the chicken wings. Leave the main wing bone and second wing bone attached and intact.

2. Heat a large, heavy skillet and, without adding fat, add the chicken wings. Cook, stirring often, to brown. The chicken will brown in its own natural fat. When lightly browned, sprinkle the pieces with curry powder and stir. Cook, stirring often, about 10 minutes.

3. Add the onion, garlic, apples, and banana. Stir and add the water, yogurt, tomatoes, bay leaf, and salt and pepper to taste. Cover and cook about 45 minutes to 1 hour.

Yield: 6 to 8 servings.

Chicken Wings Chasseur

4   pounds chicken wings (18
    to 24)
    Salt and freshly ground
    black pepper
½   pound thinly sliced
    mushrooms
4   tablespoons chopped onion
2   tablespoons chopped
    shallots, optional
1   teaspoon minced garlic
¼   cup flour
1   cup dry white wine
1½ cups tomatoes
1   cup chicken broth
1   tablespoon dried tarragon

1. Cut off and discard the small wing tips of the chicken wings. Leave the main wing bone and second wing bone attached and intact.

2. Sprinkle the chicken wings with salt and pepper to taste.

3. Heat a large, heavy skillet and, without adding fat, add the chicken wings. Cook, stirring often, to brown. The chicken will brown in its own natural fat. When lightly browned, add the mushrooms, onion, shallots, and garlic. Cook, stirring occasionally, 5 minutes.

4. Sprinkle with flour and stir to coat the pieces of chicken and mushrooms.

5. Add the wine, tomatoes, chicken broth, and tarragon. Add salt and pepper to taste. Cover and cook 35 to 40 minutes or until chicken wings are thoroughly tender.

Yield: 6 to 8 servings.

Subsequent to this column, we received a letter from Blanch Finley of Manhattan, who stated that she was "prompted to write after seeing the recipes, for I, too, am an ardent devotee of chicken wings, have known Janet Flanner over a number of years, and never miss her Paris letter in *The New Yorker.*"

"I am sending you a recipe I am fond of," she went on, "and have been using for some years, hot for a meal or cold for a snack with drinks."

Oven-Baked Chicken Wings with Honey

3   pounds chicken wings
    Salt and freshly ground
    black pepper
2   tablespoons vegetable oil
½   cup soy sauce
2   tablespoons tomato
    ketchup
1   cup honey
½   clove garlic, chopped

1. Preheat oven to 375 degrees.

2. Cut off and discard wing tips of chicken wings. Cut the remaining wings in two parts and

sprinkle with salt and pepper.

3. Combine remaining ingredients and pour over chicken wings in a greased baking dish. Bake for 1 hour until well done

and sauce is caramelized. If chicken starts to burn, reduce heat.

Yield: 6 servings.

In the same mail we received a communication from Libby Hillman, who runs a well-known cooking school in New Hyde Park, Long Island. She enclosed one of her favorite chicken wing recipes, which she attributed to one of our longtime friends, Dr. Calvin Lee, chancellor at the University of Maryland. It appeared, she states, in his book *Chinese Cooking for American Kitchens* (G. P. Putnam).

We spoke to Dr. Lee, who told us that that work is now out of print, but he is the author with his wife of a forthcoming and extensive book on regional Chinese cooking.

Here is Mrs. Hillman's favorite chicken wing dish.

Chicken Wings in Oyster Sauce

8   *chicken wings*
3   *scallions*
4   *thin slices fresh ginger root*
4   *tablespoons oyster sauce*
1   *teaspoon light soy sauce*
1   *tablespoon dry sherry*
2   *teaspoons cornstarch*
2   *tablespoons water*
1   *teaspoon sugar*
    Freshly ground black pepper
½   *cup chicken broth*
2   *tablespoons oil*
½   *teaspoon salt*
    Chinese bead molasses

1. Cut each wing into 3 pieces and set aside.

2. Cut green part of scallions into 1-inch pieces and shred white part into 1-inch shreds. Set aside.

3. Smash the ginger and set aside.

4. Mix the oyster sauce, soy sauce, and sherry together and set aside.

5. Mix the cornstarch with water. Add sugar and a dash of pepper and set aside.

6. Heat chicken broth and keep hot.

7. Using highest flame, heat a wok or frying pan until very hot. Add oil, salt, and ginger and stir fry until ginger turns brown. Add the chicken wings and stir fry until brown.

8. Add oyster sauce mixture and stir until wings are completely coated. Add hot chicken broth, cover, and turn flame down to simmer. Cook 10 minutes.

9. Uncover, add a few drops bead molasses until you get a rich brown color. Turn flame to high and add cornstarch mixture and scallions. Stir until thick and serve.

Yield: 4 servings.

Sausage Without Additives

We first heard of Faicco's pork store in Greenwich Village about 20 years ago.

"Have you ever seen New York's only lady butcher?" James Beard asked. "Her name is Ann Faicco," he said, "and the shop is at 260 Bleecker Street."

We shortly made her acquaintance and found her to be a diminutive, smiling, pleasant-faced woman, then in her late twenties. She was wearing the uniform of the trade, a white almost spotless butcher's coat, and working side by side with her brother, Edward, and her late brother, Tom, who died in 1959.

Many times over the years we have stopped by the shop for dried sausages, cervelat, and caul-wrapped liver with bay leaf. When we recently learned that the store is celebrating its 75th anniversary we made a special visit to learn for the first time the origins of the place.

It began, Ann told us, with a tiny piece of wood, a splinter that her grandfather discovered in an order of sausage. "My grandfather, Eduardo Faicco, came to this country from Naples in the late 1880s. You can still find his name in a Dun and Bradstreet listing of 1890. He was in a livery and carting business, horse and buggy really. He dealt in things like bananas and watermelons, which he delivered, according to legend, over the old plank roads in Jersey. He was a tall man, and my brother resembles him. Eddie has his nose.

"My family tells the story that in the year 1900, my grandfather went to a sausage shop near his home and placed an order. When he got home, he found that splinter in one of the sausage links. He was furious. He went back to the shop and told the owner, and an argument followed. My grandfather walked out, telling the man he knew nothing about sausage-making in the first place, that he planned to open his own shop and run him out of business. Which, they say, he did. He opened that year on Elizabeth Street on the Lower East Side. Then he moved to an open basement establishment on Thompson Street. Our shop existed at 152 for 40 years, and we opened here in 1951.

Ann Faicco explains that she is not a butcher in the serious sense. She started to work at the store after high school. ("My first job was to learn to make fegatini, that's the calf's liver wrapped in caul fat with a bay leaf. That was the absolute bottom of the ladder. When you learn to make those, you progress to cutting spareribs or pork chops. I shudder to think of all the chops I messed up when I was young.")

The Faiccos view with pleasure and some astonishment what they see as a serious trend in their clientele. Within recent years a tremendous number of young people, they observed, have turned to serious cooking. Until five years ago the bulk of their customers were middle-aged and older. Today, the preponderance of their clientele seems to be in their early thirties, late twenties or younger.

The Faiccos distribute on occasion their family recipes to customers who ask for them. Ann gives frequent advice to customers on how to cook their favorite dishes—the meat braciole or the skin braciole, which, she explains, are stuffed rolls of meat or pork skin lightly filled with garlic, pepper, salt, parsley, and grated Romano cheese. Or the long, thin coils of cervelat seasoned with provolone cheese. Or the sweet (Neapolitan style) or hot (Abbruzzi style) salamis, which are made and dried on the premises. The Faiccos also make a dry sausage and bridle at the thought that it is peperoni. "That," they explain, "sounds like something mass-produced by large meat packers." There are no additives in their homemade merchandise, they protest, "not even water."

Ann explains that she and her brother dine on spaghetti with the tomato sauce she refers to as "gravy." It is the recipe of her mother and presumably her mother before her. The Faiccos add that their shop is a "two-man" operation. They work 12 hours a day preparing all of the sausages and so on. Ed Faicco reflected recently somewhat wistfully on the days when sausages were 32 cents a pound, spareribs 15 cents a pound and pig's feet 8 cents a pound. He predicts that the high cost of meat will persist to his dismay for the rest of anyone's lifetime. With that discouraging note, here is a sampling of the Faicco family recipes.

Edward Faicco and his sister Ann

Ann Faicco's Spaghetti Sauce

2   *links hot Italian sausage*
4   *links sweet Italian sausage (see note)*
1   *ready-to-cook braciole, about ¾ pound (see note)*
1   *pound spareribs, cut into 3- or 4-inch squares, or 1 pound boneless pork, left whole*
1   *2-pound-3-ounce can tomatoes, preferably Italian peeled tomatoes*
1   *6-ounce can tomato paste*
¾   *cup water*
½   *cup finely chopped onion*
2   *cloves garlic, finely minced*
    Salt and freshly ground black pepper
½   *teaspoon hot red pepper flakes, more or less to taste*
2   *teaspoons dried oregano*
1   *pound pasta such as ziti, fusilli, shells, rigatoni, linguine, or spaghetti, preferably imported*
½   *cup grated cheese, preferably Romano*

1. In a large, heavy skillet, brown the sausages. When they start to give up their fat, add the braciole and spareribs. Cook until all the meats are well browned on all sides.

2. Meanwhile, strain the tomatoes and add them to a kettle large enough to hold the meats. Add the tomato paste. Rinse the can out with the water and add the water.

3. Transfer the meats to the kettle and pour off all but 2 table-spoons of fat from the skillet. Add the onion and cook until transparent. Add the garlic and brown lightly. Add this to the kettle. Add the salt, pepper, pepper flakes, and oregano. Partly cover. Cook, stirring often from the bottom to prevent sticking and burning, for a total of 2½ hours, skimming the surface as necessary to remove fat and scum.

4. Cook the pasta to the desired degree of doneness. Drain the pasta and return it to the pot. Add a little sauce and ½ cup cheese. Toss lightly to coat.

5. Place the meat on a platter. Spoon a cup or so of sauce on the bottom of a hot, deep serving dish. Add the pasta and spoon a little more sauce on top. Serve the remaining sauce on the side. Serve, if desired, with additional grated cheese.

Yield: 6 to 10 servings.

Note: All sweet sausages may be used in this recipe. Leftover sauce will keep for several days in the refrigerator and may be frozen. Skin braciole can be substituted for regular braciole.

Signor Faicco's Pork Stew

4   *links sweet or hot Italian sausage*
2   *pounds pork neck bones (see note), cut into 3- or 4-inch pieces*
2   *shoulder pork chops, each cut into thirds*

1 *1-pound-1-ounce can whole tomatoes, preferably Italian peeled tomatoes*
1 *cup water*
4 *carrots, thinly sliced*
  Salt and freshly ground black pepper
5 *potatoes, about 1½ pounds, peeled and cut into 1½-inch cubes*
2 *onions, about ½ pound, thinly sliced*
½ *teaspoon dried basil*
½ *teaspoon dried oregano*

1. Cook the sausages in a heavy casserole or Dutch oven. When they start to give up their fat, add the neck bones and pork chops. Cook, stirring and turning, to brown well.

2. Add the tomatoes, water, carrots, salt and pepper to taste and cook 45 minutes. Add the remaining ingredients and cook another 45 minutes, or until all the meats are tender.

Yield: 4 to 6 servings.

Note: Pork chops, boneless pork, or spareribs, all cut into 2- or 3-inch cubes, may be substituted for the neck bones.

Pork Cutlets Parmigiana

1½ *pounds cooked, breaded pork cutlets (see recipe)*
1½ *cups tomato sauce*
4 *thin slices mozzarella cheese*
  Grated Romano or Parmesan cheese

1. Preheat oven to 400 degrees.

2. Prepare the pork cutlets. Spoon a little sauce over the bottom of a flat baking dish. Add the cutlets in one layer. Spoon more tomato sauce on top and cover with mozzarella cheese and the remaining sauce. Sprinkle with Romano or Parmesan cheese and bake until piping hot and the cheese is melted.

Yield: 4 servings.

Breaded Pork Cutlets

1½ *pounds boneless pork cutlets, about 8 slices*
  Salt and freshly ground black pepper
2 *eggs*
3 *tablespoons milk*
2 *cups fresh bread crumbs*
  Olive oil
  Lemon wedges

1. Season the pork cutlets with salt and pepper.

2. Beat the eggs with the milk and add salt and pepper to taste. Coat the pork cutlets with egg and dip in bread crumbs. Place the cutlets on a flat surface and tap lightly with the flat side of a heavy knife to help crumbs adhere.

3. Heat about ¼ inch oil in a heavy skillet and cook the pork cutlets until golden brown on all sides and cooked through. Serve with lemon wedges or use in recipe for pork cutlets parmigiana.

Yield: 4 servings.

Pizza Rustica
(A cheese and sausage pie)

Pasta frolla (see recipe)
1 pound torma cheese or
  mozzarella cheese
1 pound sopressata or
  Sicilian salami
¼ pound prosciutto or baked
  ham
1½ pounds hot or sweet
  semidry sausage
8 large eggs, approximately
1½ pounds ricotta cheese
2 tablespoons chopped
  parsley

1. The quantities of this recipe are designed for a rectangular
baking dish measuring 12 by 18
by 2 inches. Prepare the pastry
and line the pan. Chill. Save all
scraps of pastry.

2. Preheat the oven to 350 degrees.

3. Cut the torma cheese, sopressata, prosciutto, and semidry
sausage into ¼-inch cubes.

4. Combine the eggs, ricotta,
and parsley and beat well. Do not
add salt. If mixture is very dry,
add 1 or 2 more eggs. Stir in the
cubed meat and cheese. Pour the
mixture into the prepared dish.
Roll out the scraps of pastry and
cut into strips. Make a lattice pattern on top of the pie. Bake
1 hour.

Yield: 12 or more servings.

Pasta frolla

3 cups flour
1 teaspoon salt
¾ cup pure pork lard,
  available in pork stores
1 cup cold milk,
  approximately

Sift together the flour and salt
into a bowl. Cut the lard into the
flour until lard looks like pastina.
The smaller the pieces, the flakier
the crust. Add the milk until all
flour can be gathered into a ball.

Yield: Enough pastry for 1
large or 2 small pies.

Admirably Stuffed

WITH PIERRE FRANEY

Shrimp, oranges and anchovies
Sauce vinaigrette with rosemary
Pasta
Rollatini di vitello al pomodoro
Pears and Gorgonzola cheese

Soave
Valpolicella

Italian cooks have known for years that while veal may be the most expensive meat on the market, it is possible to make a very few slices go an admirably long way by stuffing them. There are as many Italian methods for stuffing veal as there are beans in a kettle of minestrone, but one of the best is offered here. The filling is made with a base of bread crumbs and prosciutto (or other ham), parsley, nutmeg, garlic, basil, and oregano. To round out a menu there is also an excellent Italian shrimp appetizer made with oranges and anchovies.

Shrimp, Oranges, and Anchovies

24 *raw shrimp in the shell*
6 *whole allspice berries*
  Salt
2 *small onions, preferably the red-skin variety*
3 *or 4 seedless navel oranges*
8 *flat anchovy fillets*
½ *cup sauce vinaigrette with rosemary (see recipe)*

Black olives, preferably imported Greek olives

1. Put the shrimp in a saucepan and add the allspice and salt to taste. Add cold water to barely cover and bring to the boil. Turn off the heat and let the shrimp stand until they are room temperature. Drain, shell, and devein. Set aside.

2. Peel and cut the onions into ¼-inch-thick slices. Place them in a small bowl and pour boiling

water over them. Stir for about 15 seconds and drain immediately. Drop them into a small bowl containing cold water and a few ice cubes. When thoroughly chilled, drain and set aside.

3. Peel the oranges and slice them. Arrange an equal number of slices on 4 salad plates. Arrange the shrimp on the oranges and scatter onion rings over each serving. Garnish each with 2 anchovy fillets. Spoon the sauce vinaigrette with rosemary over each serving and add the black olives. Serve immediately.

Yield: 4 servings.

Sauce vinaigrette with rosemary

2 teaspoons imported mustard, preferably Dijon or Düsseldorf (do not use the domestic ball-park variety)
   Salt and freshly ground black pepper
½ teaspoon chopped garlic
4 teaspoons red wine vinegar
½ cup peanut, vegetable, or corn oil
1 teaspoon chopped fresh rosemary or half the amount dried

1. Place the mustard in a small mixing bowl and add salt and pepper to taste, garlic, and vinegar.

2. Use a wire whisk and gradually add the oil, stirring vigorously with the whisk. Stir in the rosemary and serve.

Yield: About ½ cup.

Rollatini di Vitello al Pomodoro
(Veal rolls with tomato sauce)

¼   pound prosciutto or other ham
⅓   cup fine, soft bread crumbs
½   cup grated Parmesan cheese
4   tablespoons finely chopped parsley
½   teaspoon grated nutmeg
2   eggs
1   teaspoon dried oregano
2   tablespoons chopped fresh basil or ½ teaspoon dried
¼   cup heavy cream
1½ teaspoons chopped garlic
    Salt and freshly ground black pepper
12 thin slices of veal (scaloppine), preferably cut from the leg
1   tablespoon butter
3   tablespoons finely chopped onion
½   cup dry white wine
2   cups drained canned peeled tomatoes, preferably imported
    Spaghetti or other pasta

1. Chop the prosciutto finely. Combine it in a mixing bowl with the bread crumbs, cheese, parsley, nutmeg, eggs, oregano, basil, heavy cream, 1 teaspoon garlic, and salt and pepper to taste. Blend well.

2. Pound the pieces of veal lightly without breaking the meat. Spoon equal portions of the stuffing onto each slice and smooth it over the meat with a spatula. Roll and tie with string.

3. Heat the butter in a heavy skillet and brown the meat on all sides, about 10 minutes. Remove the meat rolls and add the onion and remaining garlic to the skillet. Cook, stirring, about 3 minutes and add the wine. Stir to dissolve the brown particles that cling to the bottom and sides of the skillet.

Add the tomatoes, salt and pepper to taste and bring to the boil. Return the meat rolls and cover. Cook about 45 minutes. Serve with spaghetti or other pasta and more grated Parmesan cheese.

Yield: 6 servings.

We remember once, years ago, taking a trip with one of *The New York Times'* veteran photographers, Ernest Sisto, to an assignment somewhere in Connecticut. Ernie, who is of Italian descent, loves to talk about food and we have known over the years that there are certain dishes for which he has an incurable craving. One of these is mussels. Ernie calls them "black mussels," and it suddenly occurs to us that we've never thought to ask Ernie what other kind of mussels there might be on earth.

In any event, he asked if we'd ever tried an Italian appetizer which seemed at the time an unlikely combination of foods and flavors. The dish, he told, was composed of orange sections, onion rings, anchovies, oil and vinegar, black olives, and lots of black pepper. It is one of those dishes we thought about often but only got around to trying a couple of years ago. It was, as he had assured us it would be, astonishingly good. Sometime later, we added our own embellishment: cooked shrimp. We are not all that certain that the dish was vastly improved by such substitution but it certainly didn't hurt. The recipe for the appetizer appears a page back. We cordially recommend you give it a try. It is a great dish for a buffet.

Cooking Flatfish

WITH PIERRE FRANEY

There is no fish whose name has a vaguer meaning than "sole." The finest sole—and *la véritable*—is that whose natural habitat is the English Channel. Legend has it that officials once planted a few of these fish, properly tagged, in American waters. Within a matter of days the fish swam directly back where they came from. On the East Coast of America various fish from Atlantic waters, such as yellow-tail flounder, gray sole, lemon sole, plus winter and summer flounder (fluke), are legally sold as fillet of sole. On the West Coast the Pacific yields lemon sole, rex sole, and rock sole. Sole in American recipes usually means any flatfish from Atlantic or Pacific waters. In New York most of the fish sold as "fillet of sole" is a flatfish more accurately known as yellowtail flounder.

Stuffed Sole with Sauce Newburg

1¼   cups finely minced celery
1¼   cups finely minced onion
1   green pepper, cored, seeded, and finely minced
10   tablespoons butter
3   teaspoons paprika

Salt and freshly ground black pepper
½   pound raw shrimp, about 12, shelled and deveined
1½   cups fresh bread crumbs
16   small sole or flounder fillets, about 2 pounds
Sauce Newburg (see recipe)

1. Preheat oven to 450 degrees.

2. Combine the celery, onion, and green pepper.

3. Melt 6 tablespoons of the butter in a saucepan and add the vegetable mixture. Sprinkle with 1 teaspoon of paprika and salt and pepper to taste and cook, stirring, about 5 minutes. Do not overcook. The vegetables must remain crunchy.

4. Finely chop the shrimp. There should be about ¾ of a cup. Add them to the vegetables. Cook about 30 seconds, stirring, and remove from the heat. Add the bread crumbs and stir to blend. Cool.

5. Place 8 flounder fillets, skinned side up, on a flat surface and sprinkle lightly with salt and pepper. Spoon equal amounts of filling on each and pat the filling to shape it to the fillets. Cover each with another fillet, skinned side down.

6. Butter a baking dish large enough to hold the stuffed fish in one layer. Arrange the fish on it and brush with 4 tablespoons of melted butter. Sprinkle the remaining paprika through a small sieve over the fish. Bake 15 minutes or until the fish flakes easily. Serve with sauce Newburg.

Yield: 6 to 8 servings.

Sauce Newburg

    4 tablespoons butter
    1 tablespoon flour
    ¼ teaspoon paprika
    2¼ cups heavy cream
       Salt and freshly ground
       black pepper
    3 egg yolks
    ¼ cup dry sherry

1. Melt the butter in a saucepan and add the flour, stirring with a wire whisk. Add the paprika and stir. Add 2 cups of the cream, stirring rapidly with the whisk. Cook, stirring until well blended. Add salt and pepper to taste.

2. Beat the yolks lightly and add the remaining cream. Stir to blend. Add the yolk mixture to the sauce, stirring rapidly. Remove the saucepan from the heat immediately and continue stirring. The sauce should now be thick enough to coat a spoon. Do not boil, or the sauce may curdle.

3. Add the sherry and stir. Heat thoroughly but do not boil.

Yield: About 2½ cups.

Sole in White Wine Sauce with Shrimp

    5 tablespoons butter
    2 tablespoons finely chopped
       shallots
    8 fillets of sole, striped bass
       or other white-fleshed fish,
       about 2 pounds
       Salt and freshly ground
       black pepper
    2 tablespoons finely chopped
       dill or parsley
    ½ cup dry white wine
    ½ pound raw shrimp, shelled
       and deveined
       A few drops Tabasco
    1½ cups heavy cream
    1 teaspoon lemon juice
       Boiled potatoes

1. Preheat oven to 400 degrees.

2. Select a baking dish large enough to accomodate the fish in one layer. We used an oval baking dish that measured 16 by 10 inches.

3. Grease the dish with 1 tablespoon of butter and sprinkle with the shallots. Place the fish, skinned side down, in one layer. Dot with the remaining 4 tablespoons butter and add salt and pepper to taste. Sprinkle with 1 tablespoon of dill and pour the wine over all. Cover closely with a piece of wax paper. Place the baking dish on top of the stove and bring the liquid just to the boil. Place the dish immediately in the oven and bake 5 minutes. Do not bake much longer, or the fish will become dry.

4. Meanwhile, place the shrimp on a flat surface and cut them into ½-inch pieces.

5. Carefully drain the liquid that has accumulated in the baking dish into a medium-size skillet. Add the shrimp, salt and pepper and a dash of Tabasco. Simmer about 30 seconds. Using a slotted spoon, remove the shrimp and scatter them over the fish.

6. Reduce the cooking liquid over high heat about 2 minutes. Add the heavy cream and reduce it over high heat about 10 minutes or until the sauce is thickened. Add the lemon juice and a bit more Tabasco. If desired, add a little more salt and pepper. Spoon the sauce over the fish and shrimp and sprinkle with the remaining tablespoon of chopped dill. Serve with plain buttered boiled potatoes.

Yield: 8 servings.

Over the years, numerous anecdotes about food surface, some of which may be given more credence than others. One which has remained with us for years has to do with the naming of the seafood dish called Newburg. There are at least a dozen variations on this story but they are all basically the same.

It seems there was a man named Gus Wenburg, a fruit importer whose pleasure it was to dine at the old, now defunct Delmonico's restaurant in New York. The owner of Delmonico's much admired Mr. Wenburg and created a dish which he named in his honor. Years later, the story goes, the two had a bitter argument and Mr. Wenburg withdrew his patronage from the restaurant. The owner, in retaliation, revised the name of the dish on his menu by reversing the first three letters. Whether one can believe this story or not is up for grabs. We reserve a certain skepticism.

Chef Luigi Nanni

When Luigi Nanni, whom we consider to be one of the best Italian chefs in Manhattan, came into our home to cook one day recently, we recalled an anecdote related by an Italian journalist of the last century.

It has to do with the region of Italy known as the Abruzzi, celebrated in literature for the gargantuan nature of its feasts. In an estimable book *Italian Regional Cooking* by Ada Boni (E. P. Dutton and Company, 1969), the author makes note of the dining celebration known as a panarda. "The meal," she stated, "begins at midday and often continues far into the night. With merciless regularity, as it must seem to those of modest appetite, dish follows dish. From time to time there is a short pause for conversation, then the interminable procession of dishes, which include every kind of local specialty, starts again.

"A famous Neapolitan journalist of the nineteenth century, Edoardo Scarfoglio, describes how he was once a guest at one of these feasts. After the thirtieth dish he felt that he could eat no more. Consequently, he refused the next dish, but in doing so he ran a serious risk. His host, quite indifferent to the limitations of Scarfoglio's digestive system, snatched up a rifle and threatened to kill him if he refused to finish the meal . . ."

We thought of the incident, but with amusement, as we made our way blissfully through a fraction of Signor Nanni's repertory. We had invited Signor Nanni—chef-padrone of Nanni's Restaurant at 146 East 46th Street—and the relatively new Il Valletto, 133 East 61st Street in Manhattan—into our kitchen to offer a small display of his talents, and arrive he did but laden with boxes and crates bearing a host of delicacies that would eventually begin with a procession of Italian good things including a delectable crostini alla provatura—hot mozzarella toast dripping with anchovy sauce; polpi moscardini—baby octopus in wine and anchovy sauce; crisp, fine flavored ocean-fresh frutti di mare or deep-fried seafood including squid and whiting, red mullet and shrimp; a splendid, irresistible kettle of fresh Italian beans in a prosciutto and wine sauce; an exceptional pasta (matagliati, meaning poorly cut) bathed in an Abruzzese tomato sauce; pollo alla campagnola—chicken sauté with prosciutto and mushrooms and a rich, crusty nut cake, marzapane made with ground almonds. Plus Italian wines, predominantly a gratifying and hearty Baròlo.

As he cooked, Signor Nanni, a soft-spoken, pixielike gentleman (5 feet, 5 inches) of sober mien, sipped his medicato, a clean-tasting aperitivo made with a dry white wine, a touch of Campari, ice, and a twist of lemon.

The chefs of Italy are equally as chauvinistic about distinguishing the places of their birth as gastronomic spawning places as are the French. Just as French chefs claim that the gastronomic center of France (if not the universe) is Lyons, so do many Italian chefs claim that the mountainous Abruzzi region of Italy has produced the preponderance of great Italian chefs.

Poor regions, Mr. Nanni claims, tend to produce fine cooks, who must exercise the greatest skill with such bounty as they have. "Where I come from," he stated, "is a very poor country. We cultivate only sheep, the best baby lamb, cheeses like pecorino and caciotta, and wine."

The chef informed us that the cooking of Abruzzi is much more refined than that of the south and, oddly, one of the few regions in the country that cultivates and makes much use of tarragon, a staple of fine French cookery.

Crostini alla Provatura

(Mozzarella toast with anchovy sauce)

Luigi Nanni used foil and napkins to create a gondola server.

The toast

½   cup peanut, vegetable, or corn oil, approximately
8   tablespoons butter, approximately
12   ½-inch-thick slices French bread

The anchovy sauce

2   tablespoons capers
8   flat anchovy fillets
4   tablespoons butter
½   cup dry white wine
1   tablespoon chicken broth
½   teaspoon freshly ground black pepper

The cheese

12   slices mozzarella cheese, about ¼-inch thick

1. Heat the oil and butter for the toast in one or two skillets and brown the bread nicely on all sides. Drain on absorbent toweling.

2. Chop together the capers and anchovy fillets.

3. Heat the butter for the sauce in a saucepan and add the caper mixture. Cook, stirring, about 3 minutes. Add the remaining ingredients except mozzarella cheese and cook about 5 minutes over high heat.

4. Arrange one slice of mozzarella on each slice of toast and run under the broiler until nicely browned and bubbling on top. Spoon the hot sauce over and serve immediately.

Yield: 6 to 12 servings.

Fagioli Freschi in Umido

(Italian beans with prosciutto in tomato sauce)

1½ *pounds shelled fresh cranberry or other fresh or dried beans*
1 *1-pound ham bone, preferably a bone of prosciutto*
2 *quarts water*
¼ *pound prosciutto*
⅓ *cup olive oil*
2 *small sprigs fresh rosemary or 1 tablespoon dried, tied in a cheesecloth bag*
1 *tablespoon finely chopped garlic*
¼ *cup chopped shallots*
⅓ *cup chopped onion*
½ *cup coarsely chopped celery*
1 *hot dried red pepper*
¼ *cup chopped parsley, preferably flat leaf*
¾ *cup dry white wine*

2 *cups drained canned tomatoes, preferably imported Italian peeled tomatoes*

1. Fresh beans are preferable in this recipe, but if dried beans are used, presoak them or not, according to package indication.

2. Place the beans in a kettle and add the ham bone and water. Do not add salt. Cook 30 minutes or until tender and turn off heat. Set aside.

3. Cut the prosciutto into ½-inch strips.

4. Heat the oil in a deep sauté pan and add the prosciutto and rosemary. Cook, stirring, about 2 minutes and add the garlic, shallots, onion, celery, red pepper, and parsley. Cook, stirring, about 3 minutes and add the wine. Cook 5 minutes and add the tomatoes and 1 cup of the cooking liquid from the beans. Cover and cook about 15 minutes.

5. Drain the beans, but reserve at least 1 cup of the cooking liquid. Discard cheesecloth bag.

6. Add the beans to the sauce and, if desired, the reserved cup of liquid. Bring to the boil and serve piping hot.

Yield: 8 or more servings.

Note: Leftover beans may be reheated and combined with cooked pasta such as macaroni to make pasta e fagioli. Fresh cranberry beans are frequently available in Italian markets in metropolitan areas.

Ragu Abruzzese

(A meat and tomato sauce
for pasta)

1   cup vegetable oil
2½ pounds veal and beef
    bones, preferably a few
    marrow bones included
    Salt and freshly ground
    black pepper
2¼ pounds flank steak, cut into
    ½-inch-thick rectangles,
    measuring about 2 by 4
    inches
½   pound butter
¾   cup finely chopped heart of
    celery
1½ cups chopped onion
½   cup chopped shallots
3   cloves garlic, chopped
3   bay leaves
2   cups dry red wine
4   quarts tomatoes, put
    through a sieve or food
    mill to eliminate seeds
1   cup tomato paste
1½ cups water
1   sprig fresh rosemary or 1
    tablespoon dried, tied in a
    cheesecloth bag
¾   cup dried Italian
    mushrooms

1. Heat the oil in a heavy kettle and add the bones. Sprinkle with salt and pepper and cook, stirring occasionally, until nicely browned, about 10 or 15 minutes.

2. Add the meat and cook, stirring occasionally, about 30 minutes or until browned. Pour off fat from kettle.

3. Add the butter, celery, onion, shallots, garlic, and bay leaves. Cook about 20 minutes, stirring occasionally. Add the wine and simmer 10 minutes. Add the tomatoes, tomato paste, and water. Cook about 30 minutes and add the rosemary.

4. Cook about 1 hour longer. Remove the bones. The meat clinging to the bones is excellent for nibbling on.

5. Remove and discard the bay leaves and cheesecloth bag.

6. Cover the mushrooms with water and bring to the boil. Simmer about 1 minute. Drain and add to the tomato sauce. Cook briefly. This sauce is now ready to be served with almost any form of pasta. The meat may be served with the sauce or separately after the pasta course. This sauce will keep for several days in the refrigerator and much longer if reheated occasionally. It freezes well.

Yield: About 4 quarts of sauce.

Marzapane

(An Italian almond cake)

7   egg whites
3   cups instant superfine
    sugar
8   cups ground almonds
2   tablespoons Arum (an
    Italian orange liqueur
    available in liquor shops)
    or Grand Marnier
5   cups flour
6   sheets rice paper

1. Preheat the oven to 350 degrees.

2. Beat the egg whites until

they stand in very stiff peaks.

3. Beat in the sugar and fold in the almonds until thoroughly blended. Add the liqueur.

4. Pour the flour into a standard jelly roll pan measuring about 10 by 15 inches. Smooth it over with a spatula and cover the flour neatly with 4 overlapping sheets of rice paper. (The flour acts as insulation to keep the rice paper from burning.) Spoon the almond mixture on top and smooth it over with a spatula almost but not quite to the edge of the pan. Cover with 2 sheets of rice paper. Bake 15 to 20 minutes. Remove the cake. Discard the flour and serve.

Yield: 12 or more servings.

Pollo alla Campagnola

(Chicken sauté with prosciutto and mushrooms)

2 3½-pound chickens, cut into serving pieces
   Salt and freshly ground black pepper
   Flour for dredging
   Oil for shallow frying
¾ cup dried Italian mushrooms
12 tablespoons butter
2 cloves garlic, finely minced
⅓ cup finely chopped onion
¼ cup chopped shallots
¼ pound prosciutto, cut into fine julienne strips
2 teaspoons dried tarragon or 1 tablespoon chopped fresh

3 tablespoons lemon juice
¾ cup dry white wine

1. The chicken should be cut into smaller morsels than usual. For example, cut each breast half into 3 or 4 pieces. Cut the wings in half and discard the wing tips. Cut the main wing bone in 2 and cut the second wing joint in 2. Cut the thighs into 2 or 3 pieces. Cut the legs into 2 pieces and discard the meatless leg ends.

2. Sprinkle the pieces with salt and pepper and dredge lightly in flour.

3. Heat the oil to a depth of about ⅓ inch in one or two large, heavy skillets. Cook the chicken pieces, turning often, until golden brown all over. Drain.

4. Place the mushrooms in a saucepan and add water barely to cover. Bring to the boil. Simmer 1 minute and set aside.

5. Heat 8 tablespoons of butter in a skillet and add the garlic, onion, and shallots. Cook, stirring, until wilted and add the prosciutto. Cook briefly and sprinkle with tarragon. Cook about 3 minutes and add the browned chicken pieces.

6. Drain the mushrooms but reserve the cooking liquid.

7. Add the mushrooms, lemon juice, and white wine to the chicken. Add a little of the reserved mushroom cooking liquid and stir. Boil gently about 5 minutes and add the remaining butter. When it melts, stir to blend and serve.

Yield: 8 servings.

May 1975

Y OU CAN'T, TO COIN a phrase, judge a book by its cover nor a cook by any given physical attribute.

Once upon a time, we rented an office in East Hampton from a young camera enthusiast. His wife, who was pretty as Billy-be-damned, was frequently in the building and we exchanged on many mornings a few civilities and that was it. Her name was Maria Robbins. Months passed. One morning the phone rang. It was Jean Stafford, our neighbor and the Pulitzer Prize-winning author. She told us she had met a marvelous young and enthusiastic Russian cook; would we be interested in an interview? We accepted with alacrity, without even asking the young woman's name. It was agreed that I would stop by to fetch Jean and take her to this Russian meal. When we arrived, of course, there was Maria in the kitchen, uncorking a bottle of her husband's excellent vodka with lemon peel. We dined on food fit for the czars. Maria's recipes begin on page 183.

Great Bird

WITH PIERRE FRANEY

Although duck—gastronomically—is seldom thought of as America's national bird, it is without question one of the 10 or 12 most popular dishes on French menus in this country, and deservedly so. Duck is a winged creature of many virtues, not the least of which is the richness of its flesh. While duck à l'orange is by far the best-known duck preparation in the French repertoire, there are scores more—including the two dishes outlined here.

Duck in Red Wine Sauce

2 oven-ready ducks, 5–6 pounds each
    Salt and freshly ground black pepper
1 tablespoon butter
⅓ cup coarsely chopped shallots
¾ cup coarsely chopped onion
½ bay leaf
½ clove garlic
2 sprigs parsley
¼ cup flour
1 bottle (⅘ quart) dry red wine, preferably Burgundy
1 cup chicken broth
    Buttered wild rice (see recipe)

1. Preheat oven to 450 degrees.

2. Remove and discard the inner fat from the ducks. Sprinkle the ducks inside and out with salt and pepper.

3. Arrange the ducks back-side down in a roasting pan (a rack is not necessary) and bake 30 minutes. Remove the ducks and pour off the fat from the pan. Return the ducks to the oven and roast 30 minutes longer. The ducks should now be fairly crisp and free of skin fat. If they are not, return to the oven for 10 minutes or so.

4. Remove the ducks from the oven and when they are cool enough to handle, carve them as follows: Carve away and separate the legs and thighs. Carve on either side of the breast bone, carving the breast halves in whole pieces and leaving the main wing bone attached. Cut off and reserve the second joint and wing tip from the wing bone. Trim off and discard any excess fat but leave the skin intact.

5. As the ducks are carved arrange the pieces, skin side up, in one layer in a heavy casserole. Cover with a round of wax paper, then with the casserole lid, and set aside.

6. Chop up the neck and carcass and other reserved bones of the ducks. Set aside. Discard any excess fat.

7. Heat the butter in a deep, heavy saucepan and add the shallots, onion, bay leaf, garlic, and parsley. Cook, stirring frequently, until the vegetables start to take on color.

8. Add the chopped duck bones and cook, stirring often, about 10 minutes.

9. Sprinkle the vegetables and bones with flour and stir until the bones are well coated. Add the wine and broth and stir well. Bring to the boil and add salt and pepper to taste. Cook, uncovered, about 1 hour. Strain the sauce over the duck pieces, preferably through the French conical sieve known as a *chinois*, available in kitchen specialty shops. Press to extract juices from the solids. Discard the solids.

10. Cover the casserole and simmer gently about 30 minutes. Serve with buttered wild rice.

Yield: About 8 servings.

Buttered wild rice

1   *cup wild rice*
2   *cups boiling water*
    Salt and freshly ground
    black pepper
3   *tablespoons butter*

1. Place the rice, water, salt and pepper to taste, and 1 tablespoon of butter in the top of a double boiler (see note).

2. Insert the top over boiling water, cover, and steam the rice 1 hour. Fluff the rice with a fork, stirring in the remaining butter.

Yield: 8 small servings.

Note: an improvised bain-marie may be substituted for the double boiler. Place the ingredients in a small kettle or a large saucepan which will fit inside another utensil containing boiling water. Cover the ingredients closely and let simmer in the water for 1 hour.

Roast Duck au Cassis

2   *5-pound oven-ready ducks,*
    with giblets
⅓   *cup chopped celery*
⅓   *cup chopped carrot*
½   *cup chopped onion*
2   *tablespoons granulated*
    sugar
2   *tablespoons red wine*
    vinegar
2   *cups chicken broth*
    Salt and freshly ground
    black pepper
1   *tablespoon cornstarch*
3   *tablespoons water*
¼   *cup crème de Cassis, a*
    black currant cordial,
    available in fine liquor
    stores
1   *tablespoon butter*
    Buttered wild rice (see
    recipe above)

1. Remove the cavity fat from the ducks and set aside. Cut off and reserve the wing tips and second wing joints of both ducks. Leave the main wing bone attached. Quarter the gizzards and set aside. Reserve the livers.

2. To a saucepan add the duck fat and wing tips. Cut the second wing joints in half and add the pieces. Add livers and gizzards. Cook 20 minutes.

3. Add the celery, carrot, and onion. Cook, stirring about 5 minutes and drain well, discarding all fat. Return the solids to the saucepan and sprinkle with sugar. Cook, stirring frequently, until the sugar is caramelized, 5 to 10 minutes. Add the wine vinegar, cook briefly, and add the chicken broth. Add salt and pepper to taste. Simmer 1 hour and 15 minutes.

4. Meanwhile, preheat oven to 450 degrees.

5. Sprinkle the ducks inside and out with salt and pepper. Truss the ducks with string. Place the ducks on a rack breast side up and bake 30 minutes. Carefully pour off the fat from the roasting pan.

6. Return the ducks to the oven and bake 15 minutes longer. Turn the ducks breast side down and bake 25 minutes longer. Pour off the fat from the pan.

7. Return the ducks to the oven breast side up and bake 20 minutes longer. Total baking time is 1½ hours.

8. Meanwhile, when the sauce has simmered the indicated 1¼ hours, blend the cornstarch with water and stir it into the sauce. Strain the sauce through a sieve, preferably a *chinois*. Return the sauce to a saucepan and stir in the Cassis. Swirl in the butter without boiling.

9. Carve the duck. Serve with the sauce and buttered wild rice.

Yield: 8 servings.

It has long been evident that Americans are becoming increasingly sophisticated and aware when it comes to highly prized European products with long-standing reputations in their country of origin. An example is this country's new fondness for cassis. Cassis, which is made in the south of France, is a syrup of black currant. It is one of the two principal ingredients for what seems to have become the preferred aperitif with a certain class of people, principally those who dine in French restaurants and like a drink to whet the appetite but don't want hard liquor. The name of the drink is kir, and it is named for a onetime mayor of Dijon. The drink is made with a very dry white wine and a dash of crème de cassis. The generic name for the drink, which has been consumed for years in Burgundy, is cassis au vin blanc. It was a great favorite of the mayor's, a much admired and heroic figure, a crew-cut resistance fighter during World War II. Cassis is frequently used to flavor fruit desserts and it is excellent in the roast duck recipe that precedes.

Russian Cookery

"You can't have a Russian meal without herring," Maria Robbins told us as she lifted a fine, fat schmaltz herring from its milk bath, boned it, and garnished it with chopped scallions and a touch of vinegar and oil. "It goes particularly well with fau, which a lot of my Russian friends say they've never heard of," she went on. "Fau is a puree of white beans, and it is a specialty of the small Bulgarian village where my father was born. The beans are topped with soft onions fried brown and a little or a lot of cayenne pepper is sprinkled on top, depending on your taste and conscience."

Mrs. Robbins, a 34-year-old author and translator, was in the midst of preparing a Russian dinner that would include such zakuski, or appetizers, as herring and fau, eggplant caviar, cucumbers with dill, and tarragon-flavored cold mushrooms. These would be accompanied by vodka, delicately and naturally yellow in color from the lemon peel with which it had been macerated for several days.

The main course would include shchi (pronounced shkee), a rich, hearty soup made with sauerkraut and beef broth, plus piroshki, the meat-filled dumplings, a traditional accompaniment for the dish.

Mrs. Robbins, who was born in the town of Poltava in the Ukraine ("the breadbasket of Russia") averred that to her mind shchi is a more common "everyday" Russian dish than borscht, which is, of course, to most Western minds the national soup of the Soviet Union.

"Shchi is seasonal and doesn't have to be made with sauerkraut," she said. "Sometimes it is made with sorrel, sometimes with cabbage or sauerkraut, and it is served with or without potatoes and sour cream."

The young woman, whose husband, Ken, is an owner of the Old Post Office Cinema here and a professional photographer, told us that she has been cooking—and seriously—since she was nine years old.

Her father is Andre Polushkin, who reads and abstracts Soviet literature for the Library of Congress. Her mother is with the language division of McGraw-Hill, Inc., in Washington.

"When we came to this country in 1949," she explained, "mother had to work so I did all the shopping, cooking, and ironing of my father's shirts. When mother would come home from work, she would sit us down and give us lessons in Russian language and literature."

Mrs. Robbins, who is working on the manuscript of a Russian cookbook, reads and writes the language fluently. Using the name Maria Polushkin, she has written children's books and has translated several from the Russian, including the recently published *An Old Tale Carved Out of Stone,* by A. Linevski, which this year won the Mildred Batchelder award for the best translation of 1974.

Mrs. Robbins explains that her cookbook will be based on family recipes, plus recipes from Russian sources including books, family, and friends. She has an extensive collection of Russian cookbooks, including the one she considers the definitive volume for home kitchens, *Gift for Young Housewives,* by E. Molokhovetz, published several decades ago.

Mrs. Robbins told us that during the war and shortly after she had developed a curious taste in foods. "We were in a labor camp outside Munich and food was almost nonexistent," she said. "At times we could scrape together a scallion and a piece of bread with sala, which is white salted pork fat. For years it was my favorite breakfast."

Mrs. Robbins explained that the filling for her piroshki is not traditional. "Generally," she added, "the dough is filled with a mushroom or a meat stuffing. I've combined them both." The results are laudable.

Eggplant Caviar à la Russe

3 eggplants, about 1 pound each.
4 large green and/or red sweet peppers
⅓ cup peanut, vegetable, or corn oil
2 large Bermuda onions, chopped, about 4 cups
1¼ cups tomato paste
1 tablespoon sugar
Salt
2 teaspoons red pepper flakes, more or less to taste

1. Preheat the oven to 375 degrees.

2. Place the eggplants on a square of aluminum foil and place in the oven. Bake 1 hour or until the eggplants are collapsed and thoroughly tender. Let cool.

3. Meanwhile, place the peppers on a foil square and bake until they are tender. Or roast them over charcoal or a gas flame until the skin is slightly charred, turning often. Remove the peppers and place in a brown paper bag. When cool, peel the peppers, discarding the skin and seeds but saving all juices.

4. Peel the eggplants and put the pulp through the coarse blade of a food mill. Chop the peppers and add them along with accumulated juices.

5. Heat the oil in a casserole and add the onions. Cook, stirring, until they are golden, about 10 minutes. Add the eggplant mixture, tomato paste, sugar, salt, and pepper flakes. Let cook 15 minutes, stirring frequently. Cool, then chill thoroughly. Serve as an appetizer.

Yield: 6 to 8 servings.

Fau

(A Russian puree of beans)

2 20-ounce cans cannelini
   beans, undrained
4 yellow onions, about 1
   pound, peeled
⅓ cup peanut, vegetable, or
   corn oil
   Cayenne according to taste
   and conscience

1. Put the beans through a food mill or use a food processor to blend.

2. Pour the puree into a bowl.

3. Cut the onions in half and slice each half as thinly as possible. There should be about 4 cups loosely packed.

4. Heat the oil in a skillet and add the onions. Cook, stirring, until the onions are nicely browned. Spread the onions evenly over the pureed beans. Sprinkle lightly or heavily with cayenne and serve at room temperature as an appetizer.

Yield: 4 to 6 servings.

Schmaltz Herring à la Russe

1 whole schmaltz herring
   with skin on
   Milk
3 or 4 scallions
2 tablespoons peanut,
   vegetable, or corn oil
1 tablespoon wine vinegar

1. Rinse and pat the herring

dry. Place it in a bowl and add milk to cover. Let stand 3 hours.

2. Drain the herring. Using the fingers and a paring knife, skin the herring on both sides. Carefully fillet the herring by cutting along both sides of the backbone with the knife. Remove as many bones as possible. Rinse well and drain.

3. Place the fillets on a flat surface and cut on the diagonal into slices about 1½ inches thick. Arrange the herring on a platter.

4. Chop the scallions, white part only, and scatter over the herring. Sprinkle with oil and vinegar. Do not add salt. Serve as an appetizer.

Yield: 4 servings.

Note: Schmaltz herring are available in delicatessens and appetizer stores.

Shchi

(Sauerkraut and beef soup)

2   pounds sauerkraut
10 cups beef broth (see
    recipe)
1   tablespoon plus 1 teaspoon
    sugar
2   tablespoons tomato paste
4   tablespoons butter
2   cups chopped onion
⅓   cup chopped celery
1   cup chopped carrots
1   cup chopped parsnip,
    optional
½   bay leaf
    Salt
1   tablespoon lemon juice

1. Drain the sauerkraut. Rinse

it in cold water and squeeze to extract most of the moisture.

2. Put the sauerkraut in a Dutch oven or heavy casserole and add ½ cup of broth, the tablespoon of sugar, and tomato paste. Stir and cover. Cook about 45 minutes. Add a little more broth if the sauerkraut starts to become dry.

3. Heat the butter in a skillet and add the onion. Cook, stirring, until wilted. Add the celery, carrots, and parsnip. Add this to the sauerkraut. Cover and let cook about 10 minutes.

4. Add the remaining broth, the bay leaf, remaining teaspoon of sugar, salt, and lemon juice. Cover and cook 1 hour. Serve hot with piroshki.

Yield: 4 to 6 servings.

Beef broth

2 *pounds chuck*
4 *marrow bones*
2 *carrots, scraped and quartered*
1 *onion, peeled and stuck with 4 cloves*
1 *parsnip, trimmed and quartered, if available*
3 *ribs celery, trimmed and quartered*
5 *quarts water*
Salt
12 *peppercorns*

Combine all the ingredients in a kettle and bring to the boil. Simmer 3 to 4 hours. Skim the surface frequently to remove foam and scum. Strain and reserve both the broth and the beef. Discard the vegetables. Skim the surface to remove excess fat.

Yield: About 3 quarts.

Note: Leftover beef broth can be frozen.

Piroshki
(Meat filled dumplings)

The dough

1½ *cups milk*
4 *tablespoons butter*
1 *envelope dry active yeast*
⅓ *cup warm water*
3 *tablespoons sugar*
4 *to 5 cups unbleached flour*
1 *tablespoon salt, or to taste*
3 *eggs, slightly beaten*

The filling

2 *pounds chuck, cooked until tender (see recipe for beef broth above)*
⅓ *cup oil*
2 *cups finely chopped onion Salt and freshly ground black pepper*
4 *tablespoons butter*
1 *pound fresh mushrooms, cut into very fine dice or chopped*

1. To prepare the dough, put the milk in a saucepan and bring just to the boil. Remove from the heat and add the 4 tablespoons butter. Let stand until the butter melts and the mixture is just warm.

2. Combine the yeast with the water and ¼ teaspoon of sugar. Stir to dissolve the yeast.

3. Measure out 4 cups of flour

into a large bowl and add the remaining sugar and the salt. Stir. Make a well in the center and add 2 eggs, warm milk and butter mixture, and the yeast. Start combining the flour with the center liquid ingredients, working rapidly and beating with a wooden spoon until well blended. Scoop out onto a floured board and start kneading. Add more flour, up to 1 more cup, until the dough is smooth and no longer sticky. Add the flour about ¼ cup at a time. Gather the dough into a ball. Rub a warm bowl with butter and add the ball of dough.

4. Cover the dough with plastic wrap and let rise in a warm place until double in bulk, about 1½ hours. Punch down and let rise again, about 1 hour.

5. Meanwhile, to make the filling grind the beef, using the fine blade of a good grinder. There should be about 4 cups.

6. Heat the oil in a skillet and add the onions. Cook until golden brown and add the beef. Blend well, adding salt and pepper to taste.

7. Heat the butter in another skillet and add the mushrooms, salt and pepper to taste. A good deal of liquid will come from the mushrooms. Cook this down briefly. The mixture should not be very dry. Add this to the meat mixture. Blend well.

8. Preheat the oven to 350 degrees.

9. Turn the dough out onto a lightly floured board when it is ready. Knead it briefly and divide it into 4. Work one part at a time and keep the remainder covered. Roll out one piece at a time into a long, snakelike rope. Cut this off into 1½-inch lengths. Roll each piece into a ball and flatten with the fingers, turning it around and around into a 3-inch circle. Add to each circle 1 level teaspoon of filling. Fold the dough over to enclose the meat. Press around the edges to seal, tucking the pointed edges under. Place on a baking sheet. Continue making piroshki until all the dough and filling are used. Brush with remaining beaten egg and bake 25 minutes. Serve hot. These are also good cold and can be reheated.

Yield: About 45 piroshki.

Vodka with Lemon Peel

1 *lemon*
1 *bottle vodka*

1. Peel the lemon and carefully cut away the white pulp.

2. Add the yellow peel to the vodka. Seal and let stand at room temperature for 24 hours. Place in the freezer for several hours before serving.

Yield: 1 bottle of vodka.

A Well-Seasoned Liverwurst

Perhaps it is part of the natural foods movement, "do-it-yourself" era, or whatever you may call it, but we have received more requests for homemade sausages during the past year than ever in the history of our career in food reporting.

In reply to such requests, we frequently recommend a book with excellent recipes and advice on sausage-making French-style. It is an inspired work titled *The Art of Charcuterie* (Alfred A. Knopf, 1968, $8.95, virtually out of print but hopefully to be reprinted in paperback), written by a distinguished English food authority, Jane Grigson, and it contains a complete repertory of French cold and hot meat specialties including terrines, pâtés, as well as numerous sausages.

In our own kitchen we have recently created a fine batch of well-seasoned liverwurst, which has long been one of our favorite kinds of sausage. There are several things that liverwurst is not. It is definitely not low calorie and should you decide to make it at home, you will have to avail yourself of liverwurst casings, which are known in the trade as hog bung ends. We make note at the end of the liverwurst recipe that the manager of the G. Esposito pork store in New York will supply the casings on special request to those who order them in advance.

Although the stuffing for liverwurst can be pureed in a blender, a little at a time, the ideal machine for doing this in the home is the Cuisinart Food Processor, about which so much has been written lately.

Liverwurst

5 pounds pork liver
5 pounds fresh lean, unsmoked bacon (boneless)
2 teaspoons white pepper
1 teaspoon cardamom
¾ teaspoon powdered ginger
1¼ teaspoons mace
1 teaspoon crushed marjoram
½ teaspoon crushed thyme leaves
¼ cup salt, or to taste
¼ pound onion, chopped (about 1 cup) and blended to a puree
3 tablespoons white corn syrup
1 tablespoon saltpeter
Enough liverwurst casings (hog bung ends) for 6 liverwurst (see note)

1. Cut the pork liver and bacon into 1- or 2-inch cubes and blend to a fine puree. This is best done by using a food processor.

2. Pour the mixture into a large bowl and add the remaining ingredients except the liverwurst casings. Blend well.

3. Use a large pastry bag outfitted with a large tube (No. 6 or larger). Slip the end of a casing over the end of the tube, fill the bag with the meat mixture, and squeeze it into the casing, packing it in. When the casing is filled to a length of about 10 or 12 inches, tie that end. Continue filling the casing, tying after filling, to make about 6 sausages weighing about 1½ pounds each.

4. Bring enough water to the boil in a large kettle to cover the sausages when added. The temperature of the water should be approximately 180 degrees, never considerably hotter. Add the sausages and then add a lid or other contrivance to keep the sausages submerged as they cook. Cook about 1 hour. The internal temperature of the sausages when cooked through is 160 degrees. If a thermometer is inserted in the sausages, however, the sausage casings may split, so it is best to estimate the cooking time. Drain and let cool.

Yield: 6 sausages.

Note: Hog bung ends or liverwurst casings are not easily obtainable from retail outlets. We spoke to the manager of G. Esposito's notable pork store, 500 Ninth Avenue (at 38th Street), and he stated that he could supply the casings on special request. He does, of course, sell the unsmoked, boneless bacon and pork liver called for in this recipe.

We think that one of the best quick meals conceivable is a liverwurst sandwich made with thin slices of the sausage, superthin slices of sweet-flavored onion, fresh mayonnaise, and freshly baked rye bread.

If you are not equipped or not in the mood to make your own liverwurst, we can recommend the liverwurst made by the Jones Sausage Company. It is called Braunschweiger liver sausage and an 8-ounce package of liverwurst sells for about 79 cents. It is widely available and is perhaps the best commercially produced liverwurst we know.

As we have noted before, during the past year or so, we have become absolutely enamored of French breadmaking and would only buy a commercially produced French loaf in cases of emergency. Not so with rye bread. We think the best rye bread we've ever eaten anywhere, out of our oven or elsewhere, is a frozen—repeat frozen—loaf made by Kasanof's Baking Co., Inc., 219 Blue Hill Avenue, Roxbury, Massachusetts.

It is called Kasanof's Jewish Caraway Rye and is sold frozen in many supermarkets as well as in some specialty markets on the East Coast.

Sherry Wine Vinegar

About 10 years ago in a restaurant in Spain, we tasted an excellent gazpacho unlike any sampled elsewhere in the world. We decided that the difference stemmed from the vinegar used and determined that it must have been made from sherry wine. We brought back a bottle of vinegar made in Jerez, where sherry is made, and used it on random occasions. As time passed, the bottle was empty and over the years it slipped from memory.

We had forgotten about that until a short time ago when a friend told us he had an absolute passion for sherry wine vinegar. It had been stocked at all the fine food shops in Manhattan, he said, but was no longer readily available. We found the name of an importer who stated that indeed he had brought in the product from Spain but no longer did because of soaring prices. A Spanish consulate official told us, however, that there still exists in Manhattan an importer of sherry wine vinegar. As far as he knows, there is only one and her name is Susan Wagner.

We contacted Miss Wagner, who unfolded one of the most amusing stories of entrepreneurism we've heard in many a decade. "A few years ago," she began, "I was in London visiting in the home of the Baron and Baroness John Bachofen von Echt, and they served the best salad I'd ever tasted. I asked my hostess if she could tell me her secret, and she said it was because of the vinegar made with sherry wine. She told me that they had discovered the vinegar through Carter Burden in New York and that they had uncovered their own source in Paris at Hédiard Frères on the Place Madeleine across from Fauchon. I made up my mind to find a bottle, one way or another, before going back to New York.

"I came back by way of Spain and stopped at Jerez de la Frontera where, of course, sherry is made. It was smack in the middle of the grape harvest and everybody was celebrating what they call the *feria de la vendimia*.

"I learned in a hurry that most of the winemakers don't want to admit they make vinegar, even if they do. If you ask them, it's like asking sotto voce, 'Is there anybody mad in your family?' I'm told that a lot of bodegas, if they find their wine is too acid or thin after harvest, throw it away. Some bury it, they say, so nobody will know. In any event, I found one or two bodegas that did blend vinegar and admit it, so I ordered a ton.

"I had it shipped back in the passenger baggage section of an airline charter flight. The plane landed at seven in the evening and, when the cases arrived at customs, the agent looked at me and said, 'Lady, you gotta be kidding.'

"I told him I wasn't and I discovered one incredible thing that night. In an emergency, if you don't panic, if you don't scream, it's amazing what people will do for you."

Miss Wagner said that the passengers on the flight had been a group of metal roofers. "A great, burly group, and they were marvelous in giving me a hand," she recalled. "It took seven taxis to accommodate all the wine and four hours of customs and loading, but I had it stored in my apartment basement by eleven that night. Early the next morning the super knocked on my door to say I had to move the wine because it was a violation of the fire laws. I moved it up to my apartment. The next shipment weighed two tons, and I had it picked up by truck. That year I stored it in the apartment here, wall to wall and floor to ceiling. See that crack along the wall there?"

Sherry wine vinegar with its specialized taste smacks definitely of its wine origin. It is an interesting, expensive kitchen curiosity along the lines of pickled walnuts, quail eggs, and anchovy-stuffed olives. For anyone who cares about such exotics and can afford it, this vinegar is worth exploring and, as Miss Wagner has observed, one bottle goes a long way.

Miss Wagner, a reed-slender woman, states that she delivers the vinegar personally in taxis and by foot. Her principal customers include the Four Seasons and Forum restaurants, which use five cases a month. Her product is also carried by Maison Glass, Cheese 'n Things, William Poll, Balducci's, and The Cheese Shop in Manhattan. Mr. Poll was her first customer and he makes and sells a special salad dressing using her vinegar, which carries the label Juan Santamaria Vinaigre de Yena.

The cost of the vinegar varies in that the price and stock are in a current state of flux. A 1½-pint bottle costs between five and six dollars and can be ordered by mail through Maison Glass at 52 East 58th Street.

Miss Wagner adds that her vinegar is very strong and less is necessary than of an ordinary vinegar. She also states that the vinegar improves with age.

We recently devised a gazpacho using the vinegar, which we labeled Mexican-style in that we use chopped hot green chilies and chopped coriander. The recipe for the potato salad dressing is an excellent novelty and was given to Miss Wagner by Seppi Renggli, chef of the Forum and Four Seasons restaurants. There are also recipes for liver sautéed with the vinegar and sherry pickled peppers.

Susan Wagner

Gazpacho Mexican-Style

2 pounds red, ripe tomatoes, cored and finely chopped
2 tablespoons sherry wine or red wine vinegar
2 tablespoons chopped red onion
2 tablespoons chopped scallions
2 tablespoons chopped long green hot or mild chilies
2 cloves garlic, finely minced
1 cup cucumber chopped into ¼-inch dice
2 tablespoons chopped coriander leaves
2 tablespoons chopped fresh basil leaves
¼ cup olive oil
Salt and freshly ground black pepper
Garlic croutons (see recipe)

Combine all the ingredients in a mixing bowl except the garlic croutons. Quantities of various ingredients may be increased ac-cording to taste. Serve sprinkled with garlic croutons.

Yield: 4 to 6 servings.

Garlic croutons

2 cloves garlic
4 tablespoons butter
1½ cups bread cut into ½-inch cubes

1. Peel the garlic and crush each clove slightly.

2. Heat the butter in a heavy saucepan and, when it is hot, add the garlic and bread cubes. Cook, stirring and shaking the skillet, until the cubes are golden brown all over. Drain the cubes and discard the garlic.

Yield: 1½ cups.

Sherry Pickled Peppers

1½ pounds red, firm, unblemished sweet peppers
2 hot red dried peppers
2 tablespoons salt
1½ cups sherry wine vinegar or cider vinegar
1 teaspoon sugar

1. Core the peppers and split them in half lengthwise. Remove the inner fibers and seeds.

2. Cut the peppers widthwise into ½-inch strips.

3. Bring enough water to the boil to cover the peppers when they are added. Add the peppers and let stand about 5 seconds.

Drain immediately and run under cold running water to stop any cooking action. Drain well.

4. Pack the peppers into 2 pint jars and add 1 hot red pepper and 1 tablespoon salt to each jar. Bring the vinegar to the boil and add the sugar. Pour the boiling vinegar over the peppers. The jars should be filled to the brim with vinegar. Seal and store. Serve chilled and drained with anchovy fillets.

Yield: 2 pints.

Sautéed Calf's Liver with Vinegar Glaze

1   *pound calf's liver, sliced (see note)*
½   *cup flour*
    Salt and freshly ground black pepper
8   *tablespoons butter*
¼   *cup finely chopped parsley*
¼   *cup sherry wine or red wine vinegar*

1. The liver may be cut into 4 to 8 slices according to taste. We prefer it sliced thin.

2. Blend the flour with the salt and pepper and dredge the liver slices on all sides with the mixture.

3. Heat half the butter in a heavy skillet and add the liver. Cook on one side, 2 minutes or according to taste. Turn the liver and cook that side 2 minutes more. Transfer the liver to a heated platter and sprinkle with the parsley.

4. Add the remaining butter to the skillet. Let it brown briefly. Pour this over the liver. Add the vinegar to the skillet and bring to the boil, swirling it around in the skillet. Pour this over the liver. Serve with boiled potatoes or rice.

Yield: 4 servings.

Note: If you can persuade your butcher to remove the nerves or veins in each slice of liver, so much the better. Or this may be done at home with a small, sharp knife or scissors.

Salad Dressing

1   *firm potato, about ¼ pound*
    Salt
⅓   *cup coarsely chopped onion*
½   *cup fresh or canned beef broth*
    Freshly ground black pepper
½   *cup olive oil*
2   *tablespoons sherry wine or red wine vinegar*

1. Place the potato in a saucepan and add cold water to cover. Add salt to taste and bring to the boil. Simmer until the potato is tender but not mushy. Drain and let cool.

2. Peel the potato and mash it. There should be about ½ cup. Add this to a blender or food processor and add the onion, beef broth, pepper, oil and vinegar. Blend well. Chill thoroughly. This dressing keeps well in the refrigerator and will not separate.

Yield: About 2 cups.

Southern Gumbo

With a certain reservation we will print an inquiry about gumbo from a reader and former New Yorker now living in Louisiana who asks that his name not be mentioned. We acknowledge the touch of reluctance because we know gumbo is almost as sensitive a dish as Indian pudding and clam chowder, about which amateurs have expressed very strong opinions. The inquiry, in any event, is whether filé powder is an essential ingredient to all gumbos and the answer is a resounding "No."

Filé powder is, as any food dictionary will attest, the pulverized dried sassafras root. It has thickening qualities when added to soups, gumbos, or whatever. It is equally important for its flavor, which is distinctive.

The word gumbo derives from an African word meaning okra. In the strictest sense, okra, which also has thickening properties, is an essential ingredient in gumbo. Okra is frequently omitted in Louisiana gumbos and as a substitute filé powder is added. The powder, when used, should be stirred after the gumbo is cooked and ready to be served. There are recipes extant that call for both okra and filé powder, but the use of both is unreasonable and unnecessary.

Here, in any event, is an excellent gumbo using fresh okra. Frozen okra may be substituted. We know that clams are not a characteristic ingredient of the Southern gumbo, but they do add a delicious flavor.

Seafood Gumbo with Okra

⅓ cup plus 3 tablespoons vegetable oil, bacon fat, or lard
⅓ cup flour
1 pound raw shrimp in the shell
4 cups fish stock (see note)
2 cups finely chopped onions
1 cup chopped green pepper
¼ cup chopped long hot or mild green chilies, optional
1 cup chopped celery
½ cup chopped scallion
1 tablespoon finely chopped garlic
1 cup oysters in their liquor
1 cup chopped tomatoes, preferably Italian peeled tomatoes, if canned
1 bay leaf
1 or 2 dried red peppers or ½ teaspoon red pepper flakes
16 whole allspice berries
6 whole cloves
4 sprigs fresh thyme or ½ teaspoon dried
⅛ teaspoon grated nutmeg

Salt and freshly ground
black pepper

¾ pound fresh okra, trimmed
and cut into ½-inch pieces,
or 1 10-ounce package
frozen cut okra

8 cherrystone clams,
optional

⅓ cup dry white wine or dry
vermouth, optional

Juice of ½ lemon

½ to 1 teaspoon
worcestershire sauce

½ pound cooked crab meat or
1 6-ounce package frozen
and defrosted crab meat,
optional

1. The essential thing about a Southern gumbo is the use of a properly made roux. This is a combination of flour and fat cooked and stirred constantly over low heat until the flour is the color of light chocolate or dark caramel. The roux should be cooked from about 20 to 40 minutes and care must be taken that it does not burn, or it will be bitter. If the roux burns, start over. To prepare the roux for this recipe, add ⅓ cup of oil and the flour to a heavy 4- or 5-quart casserole or Dutch oven. Cook, stirring with a wooden spoon and over low heat, 20 to 40 minutes or longer until the flour is nicely browned.

2. Peel and devein the shrimp and reserve the shells. Refrigerate the shrimp until ready for use. Combine the shells and fish broth and simmer about 5 minutes. Strain and set aside.

3. When the roux is ready, add the onions, stirring with the spoon. Cook, stirring, until the onions wilt. Add the green pep-

per, chilies, celery, scallion, and garlic and continue stirring—it will be a thick mass—about 5 minutes to brown lightly. Add the oysters, tomatoes, and strained fish broth, stirring constantly with a wire whisk. When the mixture is thickened and boiling, add the bay leaf and red peppers. Tie the allspice, cloves, and thyme in a small cheesecloth bag and add it. Add the nutmeg, salt and pepper to taste. Let simmer. The shrimp may be added now or reserved until later if you wish them to remain firm.

4. Heat the remaining 3 tablespoons of oil in a skillet and add the okra. Add salt and pepper to taste. Toss and stir until the okra starts to brown. Add it to the gumbo.

5. If the clams are to be used, rinse them under cold water. Place them in a saucepan and add the wine. Bring to a boil and simmer until clams open. Add the clam liquid to the gumbo. You can add or discard the clams. It is really the clam broth's flavor you are after. Add the lemon juice and worcestershire. Add the crab meat if it is to be used.

6. Add more salt and pepper if desired, according to taste. Cook the mixture about 45 minutes to an hour. If the shrimp have not been added, add them at least 5 minutes before serving. While the gumbo cooks it must be stirred frequently from the bottom to make sure it does not stick and burn, and it is best to cook it on a flame-guarding device such as a Flame-Tamer. When the gumbo is ready, remove the bay leaf and

spice bag. Add more worcestershire sauce and lemon juice to taste. Serve with fluffy rice.

Yield: 6 to 8 servings.

Note: Fish stock is made by simmering fish bones in water with such seasonings as chopped celery, carrots, salt and pepper to taste, and parsley. This is strained. If fish stock is not available, bottled clam broth diluted with water could be substituted. A recipe for a typical fish stock appears on page 156.

A Few Fine Cooks Revisited

It has long been apparent that people who dote on cooking are among the most generous people on earth. We have found them in Alaska sharing with us a favorite recipe for muktuk, the edible "black and white" of whale; enjoyed a long conversation in Hong Kong, our host discussing the fine points of making snake soup; relished the details of watching a turtle being readied for the kettle in the flatlands of New Jersey. It is scarcely surprising then that we have, over the years, accumulated a few notebooks full of keen and delectable ideas that have never seen the light of print in this newspaper. The reasons have varied and have included slovenliness and sloth, to name but two of our seven deadly sins that will not wash. Sometimes we feel a surging need for accountability, and this column is a result of some remembered pleasures of recent months.

Two splendid and dissimilar recipes were shared with us by Christina Drechsler, one fine rainy day, in her home in New Canaan, Connecticut. One is for what was perhaps the best lentil soup we've ever tasted. Another was for Mrs. Drechsler's formidably good Koenigsberger klopse or German meat balls in a caper sauce. Other of Mrs. Drechsler's recipes appear on pages 133–136.

Some of the ingredients for Christina Drechsler's lentil soup.

Lentil Soup

1 *pound dried lentils*
3 *quarts water*
   Salt
1 *roast duck, goose, or turkey carcass, broken up, optional*
1 *2–2½-pound smoked pork butt*
1 *cup chopped onion*
1 *cup sliced carrots*
2 *cups thinly sliced leeks, optional*
2 *cups cubed knob celery (stalk celery may be substituted)*
4 *sprigs parsley Red wine vinegar*

1. Place the lentils in a bowl and add cold water just to cover. Let stand 2 hours or longer. Most of the liquid should be absorbed.

2. Add the lentils and their soaking liquid to a kettle and add the 3 quarts of water.

3. Add salt, the duck carcass if available, and smoked pork butt. Bring to the boil and simmer, uncovered, 20 minutes, skimming the surface frequently until little or no scum rises to the surface. Cook, uncovered, about 15 minutes longer.

4. Add the onion, carrots, leeks, knob celery, and parsley. Cover and cook 1 hour, turning the pork butt occasionally. Cook until the pork butt is thoroughly tender, 1½ to 2 hours in all.

5. Remove and discard the parsley sprigs and duck carcass if used. Remove the pork butt and cut half of it into ¾-inch cubes. Use the remaining meat for sandwiches and so on.

6. Return the cubed meat to the soup and serve piping hot. Serve with red wine vinegar on the side to be added at will.

Yield: 12 or more servings.

Koenigsberger Klopse
(German meat balls in caper sauce)

1 *pound ground veal*
1 *pound ground pork Salt and freshly ground black pepper*
2 *eggs*
1 *hard roll, at least a day old*
1 *cup water*
10 *tablespoons butter*
¾ *cup finely chopped red onion*
½ *cup finely chopped parsley*
1¼ *teaspoons anchovy paste or more to taste*
½ *cup flour*
4 *cups fresh or canned beef broth*
1 *cup Rhine or Moselle wine*
½ *cup drained capers*
2 *egg yolks*
½ *cup sour cream Juice of ½ lemon Mashed potatoes, optional*

1. In a mixing bowl, combine the veal, pork, salt, pepper, and 2 whole eggs.

2. Soak the hard roll in the water. Drain and squeeze dry.

Tear the roll into small pieces and add it to the meat.

3. Melt 2 tablespoons butter in a saucepan and add the onion and parsley. Cook, stirring, until wilted and add it to the meat. Add the anchovy paste and blend well.

4. Shape the mixture into 16 balls.

5. Melt the remaining 8 tablespoons butter in a saucepan and add the flour, stirring with a wire whisk. When blended, add the broth, stirring rapidly with the whisk. When blended and

smooth, add the wine. Simmer 10 minutes.

6. Add the meat balls one by one to the sauce. Let cook 25 minutes, stirring gently from the bottom to prevent sticking. Simmer 25 minutes, covered.

7. Remove the balls and add the capers to the sauce. Blend the yolks with the sour cream and stir in. Cook briefly over gentle heat without boiling. Add the lemon juice, salt and pepper to taste. Add the meat balls and heat gently. Serve hot with mashed potatoes.

Yield: 8 to 12 servings

In one of our most recent interviews with Luigi Nanni of Nanni's restaurant in New York, we were regaled with an excellent stew made of baby octopus in a wine and anchovy sauce, a touch of tomatoes and hot red peppers. Nanni's recipe for deep-fried seafood—frutta di mare—is also included. Other recipes by Chef Nanni appear on pages 172–175.

Polpi Moscardini
(Baby octopus in wine and anchovy sauce)

3   *pounds baby octopus (see note)*
1   *cup olive oil*
3   *tablespoons chopped garlic*
¾   *cup chopped onion*
⅓   *cup chopped shallots*
10 *parsley sprigs, tied in a bundle*
1   *tablespoon chopped fresh basil or 2 teaspoons dried basil*
10 *flat anchovy fillets, chopped*
2   *cups dry white wine*

1½ *cups fresh or bottled clam juice*
¾   *cup coarsely chopped parsley, preferably flat leaf*
1   *teaspoon dried oregano*
2   *dried hot red peppers*
1   *cup imported canned tomatoes*
1   *cup water*

1. Rinse the octopus well and drain thoroughly.

2. Heat the oil in a kettle and add the garlic, onion, and shallots. Cook, stirring often, about 5 minutes. Add the parsley sprigs, basil, and octopus. Cook, stirring, about 1 minute and add the anchovies and wine. Cover and cook, stirring occasionally, about 30 minutes.

3. Add the clam juice and continue cooking, uncovered, about 20 minutes. Add the chopped parsley. Cook 15 minutes.

4. Add the oregano, red peppers, tomatoes, and water and continue cooking about 20 or 30 minutes. Remove the parsley sprigs and serve.

Yield: 8 to 12 servings.

Note: Baby octopus is available in some Italian fish markets and at fish markets on Ninth Avenue in New York City. Leftover octopus is good cold as an appetizer. Leftover sauce is good reheated and served on pasta.

Frutta di Mare
(Deep-fried seafood)

Almost any seafood is delectable when simply cooked as follows: Select such fish and seafood as peeled raw shrimp; cleaned red mullet (available in fish markets on Bleecker Street and Ninth Avenue); fresh cleaned squid cut into rounds; whole whitebait; small cleaned whiting and so on. Sprinkle the fish or seafood generously with lemon juice and let stand briefly. Sprinkle with salt and pepper to taste and coat with flour, shaking off the excess. Deep fry in very hot fat from 1 to 10 minutes, depending on the size. Drain and serve with salt and lemon wedges.

Although fresh trout may not be as common as sole or cod in markets, they are at times available, and they could scarcely be turned into a more toothsome or tempting morsel than in a recipe obtained from Jean Banchet, the owner of a fine French restaurant, Le Français in Wheeling, Illinois. This is a recipe he had, in turn, from the late and lamented Fernand Point, by any odds one of the greatest chefs in French history. The details are a bit elaborate, but the dish is worth the effort and time. Other recipes by M. Banchet can be found on pages 154–156.

Truites Farcis Fernand Point
(Stuffed trout in the style of Fernand Point)

4   *fresh trout*
1   *or 2 carrots, scraped*
2   *or 3 ribs celery*
¼   *pound fresh mushrooms*
1   *large truffle, optional*

*Salt and freshly ground
black pepper*
3   *tablespoons butter*
2½ *cups heavy cream*
2   *egg yolks*
5   *tablespoons flour*
3   *tablespoons finely chopped
shallots*
3   *cups fish stock (see recipe,
page 156)*
1   *cup port wine*
1   *cup dry white wine*

1. To prepare this dish properly, the trout when purchased should be opened up and boned but without splitting them down the back. The heads and tails should be left on.

2. Cut the carrots into 2-inch lengths. Cut the slices into very thin matchlike strips. There should be about 1 cup. Set aside.

3. Cut the celery into 2-inch lengths. Cut the slices into very thin matchlike strips. There should be about 1 cup. Set aside.

4. Cut the mushrooms into thin slices and cut the slices into very thin strips. There should be about 1½ cups. Set aside.

5. Sprinkle each batch of vegetables with salt and pepper.

6. If the truffle is used, slice it and cut it into thin strips. Set aside.

7. Preheat the oven to 500 degrees.

8. Heat the butter in a skillet and add the celery and carrots. Cover and cook, stirring as necessary, about 10 minutes. The vegetables must not be overcooked. The strips should be crisp-tender, or al dente, when ready.

9. Heat ¼ cup of cream and add the raw mushrooms. Add salt to taste and bring to the boil. Cook about 12 minutes or until cream is almost totally reduced. Add this, scraping the skillet, to the carrot mixture. Add the truffle, if used. Cook briefly.

10. Beat the egg yolks with ¼ cup heavy cream. Add salt and pepper to taste. Off heat, stir into vegetable mixture. Stir in the flour. Stir until thoroughly blended. Return to heat and cook about 3 minutes and remove from heat. Let cool.

11. Place the trout opened up and skin side down on a flat surface. Sprinkle with salt and pepper. Add equal portions of the stuffing and fold over to enclose the filling.

12. Butter 4 rectangles of wax paper (Chef Banchet uses Marcal dry, unshiny wax paper although any brand will do). Do not skewer the trout, but cover the belly opening of each fish with a buttered rectangle of wax paper. Fold the paper over so as to partially enclose the fish.

13. Butter a baking dish and sprinkle with shallots, salt, and pepper. Arrange the fish over it. Add the fish stock, port, and white wine. Cover with a buttered oval or round of wax paper. Cover loosely with a lid and bake on the bottom rack of the oven about 30 minutes or until the fish flakes easily when tested with a fork.

14. Pour the cooking liquid from the fish into a saucepan or skillet and cook over high heat about 5 minutes. The liquid should be almost completely reduced. Add the remaining 2 cups of cream and cook over high heat about 5 minutes or until it has a nice saucelike consistency. Season with salt and pepper. (At this point Chef Banchet stirs in a tablespoon or so of hollandaise into the sauce, off heat.)

15. When ready to serve, remove the fish from the baking dish. Remove the skin from the main body of the fish. It comes off easily when pulled with the

fingers. Strain the sauce over the fish and garnish if desired with

pastry crescents and truffle slices.

Yield: 4 servings.

A young lawyer, David Liederman, whom we interviewed in February (page 77), gave us a highly special and delectable recipe for a green bean salad distinctly seasoned and of his own creation. The fresh beans are steamed and flavored with a cumin and shallot sauce. David also shared with us a fine lobster dish, which he attributed to Paul Bocuse.

Green Beans with Cumin and Shallots Vinaigrette

1   *pound fresh green beans*
    Salt
1   *teaspoon dry mustard*
1   *teaspoon ground cumin*
1   *tablespoon finely chopped shallots*
    Freshly ground black pepper
2   *tablespoons wine vinegar*
6   *tablespoons olive oil*

1. Unless the green beans are very small, cut them into 2-inch lengths. Steam briefly over boiling salted water until crisp-tender. Drain. Let stand until lukewarm or at room temperature.

2. Combine the mustard, cumin, shallots, salt, pepper, and wine vinegar in a small mixing bowl. Stir rapidly with a wire whisk, gradually beating in the oil. Serve the sauce over the beans.

Yield: 2 to 4 servings.

Baked Lobster with Herb Butter

1   *1–1½-pound lobster*
1   *teaspoon olive oil*
    Salt and white pepper
½   *cup butter*
1   *tablespoon finely chopped shallots*
1   *tablespoon finely chopped parsley*
1   *teaspoon finely chopped fresh tarragon*

1. Preheat the oven to 450 degrees.

2. Turn the lobster on its back and split it lengthwise. Remove and discard the small sac inside the lobster near the eyes.

3. Arrange the lobster halves, split-side up, in a baking dish and brush with oil. Sprinkle with salt and pepper.

4. Bake 15 minutes and remove.

5. Combine the butter with the remaining ingredients. Using a fork, lift up the tail sections from the shell. Spoon the butter into the shell and replace the tails in the shell. Serve immediately.

Yield: 1 to 2 servings.

All Goulash

WITH PIERRE FRANEY

There are probably more recipes for Hungarian goulash throughout the world than there are for sauerkraut, coq au vin, and bouillabaisse—not to mention baked beans—put together. Actually, both a soup and a meat stew go by the name goulash. George Lang explains in his immensely edifying book, *The Cuisine of Hungary* (Outlet Book Company, Bonanza Books, 1971, 1975, $4.98), that originally a gulyas was a shepherd's dish made with meat cooked with onions until all the liquid disappeared. The dish was then put in a bag made of sheep's stomach and placed in the sun to dry. When the shepherds got hungry, they simply added a little water to make a meat stew (gulyashus), a lot of water to make a soup (gulyasleves). Our versions on these dishes appear below.

Hungarian Veal Goulash

    2 tablespoons lard, salad oil,
       or butter
    4 cups halved and sliced
       onion, about 1 pound
    4 pounds boneless veal or
       pork, cut into 2-inch cubes
    1 to 3 tablespoons paprika
       (see note)
    2 tablespoons finely chopped
       garlic
       Salt and freshly ground
       black pepper
    2 tablespoons flour
 2½ cups chicken broth
 1½ cups cored, seeded green
       peppers, cut into 1-inch
       strips
    1 cup sour cream at room
       temperature, optional

1. Preheat oven to 350 degrees.

2. Heat the lard in a Dutch oven or deep, heavy saucepan and add the onion. Cook, stirring, until wilted. Add the veal and stir. Cook, stirring often, until the veal loses its red color.

3. Sprinkle with the paprika and stir. Cook 5 minutes and sprinkle with garlic and salt and pepper to taste. Stir briefly and sprinkle with flour. Stir to coat the pieces of meat and add the chicken broth. Bring to the boil. Cover with a round of wax paper and put the lid on. Place in the oven and bake from 1½ to 2 hours. Cooking time will depend on the quality of the veal. Best-quality veal cooks more rapidly than that of a lesser quality. Pork cooks quickly.

4. Meanwhile, drop the green pepper strips into boiling water and blanch about 15 seconds. Drain immediately and set aside.

5. Thirty minutes before the

stew is fully cooked sprinkle with the pepper strips. Continue cooking until veal is tender.

6. If desired, add the sour cream. Preferably, it should be beaten with a whisk before adding and stirred in gradually. Serve the stew, if desired, with spaetzli (see recipe).

Yield: 8 or more servings.

Note: The best Hungarian paprika is available in bulk. It comes in three strengths: sweet, medium, and hot. It should be added to taste. Imported paprika can be purchased or mail-ordered from Lekvar by the Barrel, 1577 First Avenue (at 82d Street); The Spice Box, 968 Second Avenue (between 51st and 52d Streets); and Aphrodisia, 28 Carmine Street, all in New York City.

Spaetzli

    2 cups sifted flour
    3 eggs
    ⅔ cup milk
       Salt
    ⅛ teaspoon grated nutmeg
    2 tablespoons butter

1. Place the flour in a mixing bowl. Beat the eggs and add them to the flour, stirring with a wire whisk or an electric beater. Gradually add the milk, beating or stirring constantly. Add salt and nutmeg.

2. Bring a large quantity of water to a boil in a kettle and add salt. Pour the spaetzli mixture into a colander and hold the colander over the boiling water. Press the mixture through the holes of the colander with a rubber spatula or large spoon. Or use a spaetzli machine (see note) and put the noodle mixture through, following the manufacturer's directions. The spaetzli are done when they float on the top. Drain the noodles and spoon them onto a clean towel or paper towels to dry briefly.

3. Heat the butter in a skillet and when it is hot, add the spaetzli, tossing and stirring 3 to 5 minutes. Serve hot.

Yield: 4 to 6 servings.

Note: Spaetzli machines are available at Lekvar by the Barrel and The Spice Box.

Goulash Soup

    2   tablespoons butter
    1   cup finely chopped onion,
         about ¼ pound
    1   teaspoon finely chopped
         garlic
    2   tablespoons sweet paprika
    3   cups cubed green or red
         sweet peppers, about ¾
         pound
    1   teaspoon crushed caraway
         seeds
    2   tablespoons flour
    1½   cups potatoes, about ½
         pound, peeled and cut into
         ½-inch cubes
    1   cup chopped tomatoes,
         preferably Italian peeled
    4   cups veal or beef broth (see
         recipe)
    2   cups cubed cooked veal or
         beef reserved from the veal
         or beef broth (see recipe)
         Sour cream as a garnish,
         optional

1. Melt the butter in a large saucepan or kettle and add the onion. Cook, stirring, until wilted. Add the garlic and sprinkle with paprika, stirring. Add the peppers and caraway seeds. Sprinkle with flour and cook, stirring, to distribute the flour evenly. Cook over low heat, stirring occasionally, about 5 minutes.

2. Add the potatoes and tomatoes, stirring rapidly. Add the broth, stirring, and the meat. Simmer 20 minutes, skimming the surface as necessary. Serve with sour cream if desired.

Yield: 8 or more servings.

Veal or beef broth

3½   *pounds meaty veal or beef bones (there should be enough meat to make 2 cups when the bones are cooked)*

6   *cups chicken broth, diluted with water if concentrated*

3   *carrots, about ½ pound, scraped and quartered*

2   *onions, about ¾ pound, each stuck with 2 cloves*

4   *celery ribs, trimmed and quartered*

1   *bay leaf*

10   *peppercorns*

2   *sprigs fresh thyme or ½ teaspoon dried*

4   *sprigs parsley Salt*

½   *cup chopped fresh or canned Italian peeled tomatoes*

1. Put the bones in a kettle and add cold water to cover. Bring to the boil and simmer about 5 minutes. Drain quickly and chill under cold running water. Rinse out the kettle.

2. Return the bones to the kettle and add the chicken broth, carrots, onions, celery, bay leaf, peppercorns, thyme, and parsley. Add salt to taste. Bring to the boil and cook 2 to 2½ hours or until the meat almost falls from the bones.

3. Strain the broth, reserving the bones. Pull or cut the meat from the bones and reserve. Discard vegetables. The broth will keep several days in the refrigerator and for several months in the freezer.

Yield: About 2 quarts of broth plus the equivalent of 2 cups of cubed meat.

June 1975

D URING THE DECADES in which we have written about food, we have had a long and we hope honorable association with the truffle. Never, in our life, however, have we approached such a surfeit of "black diamonds" as in the year 1975. Truffles are, we must confess, one of our favorite subjects. We are endlessly intrigued by the mystery that surrounds them. The primary sources for truffles, in this country at least, are France and Italy. Although we have heard frequent rumors about the discovery of truffles in America, in such places as Vermont and California, we remain skeptical. We have also been told the story of a wealthy Greek shipowner who imported several tons of Italian soil from truffle country in an old landing craft such as was used in World War II. The earth was shoveled into some field and, though waited upon patiently, not one truffle made itself known.

June was the month when Paul Bocuse, almost without question the most famous chef in the world today, came into our kitchen and made a truffle soup which was uncommon, to say the least. He brought his own truffles with him—one enormous can packaged in his own kitchen in Lyon and valued at something in excess of $200. Months later, when we dined at Chez Denis in Paris, truffles seemed to appear in every third if not to say every second course, but more of that later.

We will herewith tell the truth about black truffles. When black truffles are taken and used fresh from the earth they have an indescribably delicious and subtle perfume and taste. Unfortunately, much of this aroma and flavor dissipates once the truffles are processed either in cans or other containers. Thus they become an expensive conceit. There is, however, no substitute for black truffles either fresh or canned.

We have been speaking specifically of black truffles which are a staple of the classic French kitchen. There is also such a thing as a white truffle which is enormously tantalizing in flavor and almost wholly dissimilar where taste in concerned. Their great similarity lies on their scarcity and manner of propagation. White truffles, to our mind, have an almost decadent taste. They are much prized in Italian cooking. Both black and white truffles may be purchased fresh and at great cost during the late autumn and early winter months. They are flown into this country and sold at luxury markets. Both are highly perishable and their flavor loss is rapid.

Recipes for Lamb

"I sometimes feel that this kitchen must be one of the oldest in America," Jeanette Seaver was saying. "The drawers stick and you can't regulate the oven heat. You have to keep shifting things from one shelf to another to keep it from burning. But it's my contention that you can cook with poetry and invention under the most absurd conditions.

"When Dick and I were first married," the Paris-born Mrs. Seaver went on, "we lived in a small apartment in Chaumont, a dreadful little town outside Paris, and we dined very well with only an alcohol burner for a stove."

Mrs. Seaver is the author of an engaging and soundly written cookbook, *Jeanette's Secrets of Everyday Good Cooking* (Alfred A. Knopf, Inc., $10). The book is a fascinating volume that, besides recipes ranging from brioche doughs to excellent roasts to fruit tarts, offers a chapter on wines written by her husband. The book is also full of recipes for using leftovers and on that day we were dining on three of her lamb dishes— an original roast lamb flamed with Pernod and served with a tomato and Pernod sauce; a fine dish of leftover lamb with lemon; and another of leftover lamb with vegetables baked in pastry.

Mrs. Seaver recalled that she grew up in Paris after World War II, a time, she said, when it was taken for granted that young women would know their way about the kitchen. "We certainly weren't pampered with appliances," she said. "I remember the day my family bought its first refrigerator. It was a tremendous event in our lives." She laughed. "I saw it recently. It's a tiny little Fridge, the kind you might hesitate to put in a guest house."

The couple maintain two residences, a century-old house here that was originally a stable, and an apartment in Manhattan where, since last December, Mrs. Seaver has taught French cooking.

"I try to teach my students and I try to stress in my book that you can produce an inspired dish simply by improvising with materials and equipment on hand," she said. "If you don't have a blender, you can use a fork or a whisk. If you don't have a rolling pin, use a bottle. And if you don't have a fish poacher, use the largest kettle or roasting pan. You don't need a machine to make yogurt; you need good milk."

Mrs. Seaver limits her classes to five students so that the instruction can be on a one-to-one basis. "As I cook, the students cook," she said, "We start off first with bread-making and everyone makes a loaf of bread in each subsequent class. The first lesson includes such basics as coq au

Jeannette Seaver

vin, chocolate mousse, vegetable soups—traditional, everyday-dish food. The second lesson includes poached fish with mousseline sauce, apple tart, cream puffs, and so on. Each class lasts three hours—two in cooking, one in the pleasure of eating. With appropriate wines, of course.

Mrs. Seaver, a raven-haired woman, was a professional concert violinist for several years. "When we met," she said, "I was studying violin at the Paris Conservatory and Dick was running an English language magazine—a literary journal—and acquiring French culture. He acquired a French wife instead."

Mrs. Seaver said she has never had a cooking lesson in her life, that her interest in cooking—which is considerable and solid—began in her home. Her mother is a fine cook and her father, a journalist and Paris correspondent for a German newspaper, the *Frankfurter Allgemeiner Zeitung,* was a genuine gourmand (in the best sense of that word) who fussed a good deal over what he ate.

Mrs. Seaver and her husband, who is the owner of Richard Seaver Books, distributed by Viking Press, are the parents of three children, age 5 to 18. Mrs. Seaver recalled that her husband's introduction to the techniques of her cookery came about in an amusing way. He was busy at work in the office in their apartment and by that time, the students in the class had gone to the dining-and-wining phase of the class.

"Dick apparently was distracted by the giggling in the kitchen," Mrs. Seaver said. "I decided to join them," he replied. "The trouble is," Mrs. Seaver added, "I de-mythed Dick's mind not only about French cooking but my talents as a cook as well."

Mr. Seaver broke off another morsel of the French bread he had made that morning, dipped into the Pernod sauce and grinned.

Gigot au Pastis
(Leg of lamb with Pernod or Ricard)

1 7-pound leg of lamb, boned and rolled
2 cloves garlic, peeled and cut into slivers
2 tablespoons vegetable oil
Salt and freshly ground black pepper
½ teaspoon or more dried rosemary
⅛ teaspoon dried thyme
½ cup Pernod or Ricard
2 cups sauce tomate au pastis (see recipe)

1. Preheat the oven to 350 degrees.

2. Using a sharp, pointed knife, make slight incisions in the lamb. Press slivers of garlic into the incisions. Rub the lamb all over with oil and sprinkle with salt and pepper to taste, rosemary and thyme.

3. Roast the lamb 15 minutes per pound if you wish the lamb rare. Roast longer for well-done

lamb. Let the lamb rest 15 minutes after it is removed from the oven. When ready to serve, warm the Pernod or Ricard in a saucepan and pour it over the lamb, igniting it immediately with a match. Slice the lamb and serve with tomato sauce with Pernod.

Yield: 6 to 8 servings.

Sauce tomate au pastis
(Tomato sauce with Pernod or Ricard)

1 tablespoon olive or vegetable oil
1 shallot, finely chopped
¾ cup finely chopped onion
2 cups fresh or canned tomato sauce
½ teaspoon dried thyme
½ teaspoon crushed bay leaves
1 teaspoon sugar
Salt and freshly ground black pepper
½ cup Pernod or Ricard

1. Heat the oil in a saucepan and add the shallot and onion.

Cook, stirring, until onion is golden brown.

2. Add the remaining ingredients and bring to the boil. Simmer briefly and serve hot in a sauceboat.

Yield: About 2 cups.

Lamb in Lemon Sauce with Scallions and Walnuts

⅓   cup olive oil
2   cups cooked cubed lamb
1   cup thinly sliced onion
½   lemon, seeded and sliced
6   scallions, trimmed, rinsed and cut into 1-inch lengths
½   cup whole or broken walnut halves
    Salt and freshly ground black pepper
1   cup water
2   egg yolks, lightly beaten
    Juice of 1 lemon
½   cup heavy cream

1. In a Dutch oven or heavy casserole, heat the oil and cook the lamb, stirring, about 5 minutes. Add the onion, lemon slices, scallions, walnuts, salt and pepper to taste. Add the water and cover. Cook over gentle heat about 35 minutes. Uncover.

2. Combine the yolks, lemon juice and cream. Blend well. Add this to the lamb mixture, stirring. Bring just to the boil, but do not boil. Serve piping hot with dumplings or rice.

Yield: 4 servings.

Leftover Lamb and Vegetables in Brioche

1   brioche dough (see recipe)
⅓   cup olive oil
2   cups finely chopped onion
2   Italian sausages, preferably hot
1   small eggplant, peeled and cubed
1   zucchini, trimmed and cubed
1   to 1½ cups ground cooked lamb
4   to 5 red ripe tomatoes, cored and halved, or 1 16-ounce can, drained
½   cup bread crumbs
1   green pepper, diced
1   clove garlic, finely minced
1   cup finely chopped parsley
2   tablespoons chopped fresh basil or half the amount dried
1   teaspoon dried thyme
1   teaspoon dried oregano
    Salt and freshly ground black pepper
1   egg yolk
2   tablespoons water

1. Prepare the dough.

2. When ready to cook, preheat the oven to 350 degrees.

3. Heat the oil in a skillet and add the onions. Cook, stirring, until golden brown. Remove the sausage meat from the casings and add it to the onions. Cook, breaking up lumps, about 10 minutes. Add the eggplant and zucchini and cook, stirring, about 8 minutes. Add the lamb, tomatoes, bread crumbs, green pepper, garlic, parsley, basil, thyme, oregano, salt and pepper to taste. Blend well.

4. Roll out the brioche dough on a lightly floured board to a thickness of approximately ½ inch. Cut it into 2 roughly equal rectangles. Lift one rectangle and place it on a buttered cooky sheet. Use a slotted spoon to drain excess liquid from the meat mixture and add the mixture to the dough, leaving at least a ½-inch margin. Cover with the second rectangle of dough and press all around to seal the edges of the pastry with the fingers.

5. Blend the egg yolk with water and brush over the top of the dough. Bake 50 minutes.

Yield: 6 to 8 servings.

Brioche dough
(For foods to be baked in pastry)

1   *envelope dry active yeast*
¼   *cup warm water*
3½ *cups flour*
2   *eggs*
¾   *teaspoon salt*
2   *tablespoons sugar*
8   *tablespoons melted butter*

1. In a small bowl, combine the yeast and water. Stir to dissolve yeast.

2. In another bowl, combine the flour, eggs, salt, sugar, and butter. Scrape in the yeast mixture. Knead the dough until it is smooth and elastic. Place it in a warm bowl and cover with plastic wrap or a damp towel. Place it in a draft-free place (temperature about 70 degrees) and let rise 3 hours.

3. When ready to use, punch the dough down and roll it out onto a floured board to the necessary shape for wrapping food in pastry. This dough can be securely wrapped and frozen.

Yield: About 1 pound of dough; enough for the preceding recipe or 2 average-size fish or 2 5-pound hams.

The Sausage Patty

After we wrote of a fairly recent and uncommon revival of interest in home sausage-making, we received a communication from Fred Devine, the deputy executive director of CARE in New York.

"Having read your article on sausage-making, liverwurst, etc., reminds me that even though I have over 100 cookbooks, I have yet to find a good sausage patty recipe. If you have one readily available, I'd certainly appreciate receiving it."

We are pleased to print two recipes for sausage patties or sausage cakes, one made from pork chops of the standard sort purchased in supermarkets. The other calls for the traditional quantities of lean pork and pork fat. The standard proportion is one part fat to two parts lean. The second recipe was contrived while preparing recipes for an article on using a food processor.

Rosemary and Sage Sausage

2   pounds pork chops, with fat.
    Salt
1   tablespoon dried sage leaf
1   teaspoon chopped fresh rosemary or ½ teaspoon dried
½   teaspoon coarsely ground black pepper or to taste
½   teaspoon hot red pepper flakes or to taste, optional

1. Remove the meat and fat from the bones. Reserve the bones for another use, such as tomato sauces, if desired.

2. Put the lean and fat through a meat grinder and put it through again. Add the remaining ingredients to the ground meat and mix well. Shape the mixture into 4 or 6 patties.

3. To cook, put the patties in a cold skillet. Cook on both sides until well browned and the meat is thoroughly cooked.

Yield: 4 to 6 servings.

Pork Sausage
(For sausage cakes)

⅔   pound lean pork
⅓   pound pork fat (see note)
    Salt and freshly ground black pepper
1   tablespoon chopped dried sage leaf or half the amount ground (see note)
1   teaspoon dried red pepper flakes, optional

1. Cut the lean pork and pork fat into 1-inch cubes. Equip the container of a food processor with the steel knife blade and add the pork cubes and blend. Or grind the lean and fat, using a meat grinder.

2. Add the remaining ingredients and blend 15 to 30 seconds or until the meat is coarse-fine. Do not overblend or the consistency will be too fine. Store the sausage in a container in the refrigerator for future use or shape it into 4 or 6 patties and fry in a skillet, turning as necessary, until the sausage cakes are thoroughly browned and cooked through.

Yield: 4 to 6 sausage cakes.

Note: You may omit the sage and add about a teaspoon or more crushed fennel seeds. If you wish leaner sausage cakes, simply decrease the amount of pork fat and increase the lean pork.

The Japanese Grill

Semantics has a curious way of coloring thought and history. The United States, of course, is the land of what is known as the barbecue world, and many learned treatises have been written as to the origin of the word. Some sources say it is from an American-Spanish word, barbacoa, which describes a grill consisting of rotary sticks set on posts. Less believably, it is said to be creole and derives from a French phrase, barbe à queue, meaning head to tail, referring to an entire animal cooked on a spit.

Whatever the case, barbecue seems synonymous in many American minds with grilled foods of any sort; thus the false assumption that

For yakitori, chicken, some grilled and some waiting to be grilled.

grilled dishes are of Yankee origin. Nothing, obviously, is further from the truth. It takes little enough reason to know that grilled foods must have come about shortly after man began to use fire and many thousand years before Charles Lamb wrote his famed dissertation on roast pig.

A short while back during a visit to Japan, we made frequent excursions to yakitori restaurants and reflected then that yakitori, which must go back a few hundred years, must be a relatively advanced and sophisticated example of cooking grilled foods. Actually, yakitori is a combination of two Japanese words, yaki, meaning grilled, and tori, meaning birds. The most usual bird used for yakitori is chicken, which is, more often than not, cut into boneless cubes and arranged on skewers before grilling. The pieces include not only the flesh but the hearts, livers, gizzards and so on as well. The skewered portions are brushed when grilling with a fairly sweet sauce composed generally of sake, mirin, soy sauce, and honey among other things. The sauce is known as yakitori-no-tare.

Yakitori
(Grilled fowl)

Bone the light and dark meat of a chicken, setting aside the heart, liver, gizzard and so on. Cut the light and dark meat into bite-size cubes. Arrange the cubes on skewers. If desired, arrange one- or two-inch lengths of scallions alternately on some skewers with the chicken pieces.

Trim and cut away the tough, muscular parts of the gizzards if used. Arrange the tender gizzard pieces on skewers. Arrange the liver and heart on skewers. Grill the unseasoned chicken pieces, brushing as necessary with yakitori-no-tare (see recipe). Cook, turning often, until the chicken pieces are done. Remove from the heat, sprinkle with lemon and serve hot.

Yield: A varying number of servings, depending on the quantity of chicken used.

Note: Although strictly speaking only chicken or other fowl is used for yakitori, many restaurants also include other skewered foods, mushroom caps, asparagus wrapped in bacon, steak bits and so on.

Yakitori-no-tare
(Sauce for yakitori)

Chicken bones, optional
½ *cup sake*
½ *cup mirin (sweet Japanese cooking wine), available in wine and spirit shops in Japanese communities*
⅓ *cup or slightly more coarsely cracked rock sugar (see note)*
1 *cup dark soy sauce (see note)*
2 *to 3 tablespoons honey*

1. If chicken bones are used, cook them over a charcoal fire turning often and without burning. Crack them and add them to a saucepan. Add the sake, mirin, rock sugar, and soy sauce. Bring to the boil and cook 3 minutes.

2. Stir in the honey and boil 2 minutes longer. Strain before using. Use to brush chicken on skewers as it is grilled.

Yield: About 2½ cups.

Note: Rock sugar and dark soy sauce are available among other sources in many Oriental food shops.

One of the finest and most delicate of Japanese grilled foods is shioyaki, which is perhaps even more primitive than yakitori. Shioyaki is a notably low-calorie dish, and the name is a blend of *shio,* meaning salt, and *yaki,* which, as indicated, means grilled or broiled.

Shioyaki is, in effect, a piece of fish, generally salmon, that has been salted without aging before it is grilled over charcoal until just cooked through. It can be made with almost any edible fish and it is both grilled and served without oil or butter. Only a small wedge of lemon.

Shioyaki
(Salt grilled salmon)

1½ *pounds salmon*
1   *tablespoon salt*
¼   *cup sake, optional*
6   *lemon wedges*

1. Place the salmon on a board, preferably wooden, and sprinkle it with salt on all sides. Tilt the board at a small angle so that any liquid given up by the fish because of the salt will drain. Let the fish stand in a very cool place 3 or 4 hours.

2. Cut the salmon into individual serving pieces of about ¼ pound each. Rinse each individual piece quickly in cold water and pat dry.

3. Skewer the fish, preferably using 2 skewers for each serving so that they do not break while cooking. Grill it over hot coals skin side down, about 2 minutes. Continue grilling, turning the pieces as necessary so that they cook evenly throughout.

4. When cooked, douse the fish with sake and flame it. Serve with lemon wedges.

Yield: 6 servings.

Historically, to the Western mind at least, one of the principal differences between a "barbecue" and grilled dishes in the United States and Japan is that barbecues and similar occasions specializing in grilled foods are almost invariably open-air functions.

More often than not these foods are cooked over hot coals indoors throughout Japan. The foods are generally part of a menu that almost always includes rice and perhaps a clear or bean soup. For those who wish to dine on these dishes in or out of doors, here are recipes for both clear and bean soups.

Fish and Mushroom Soup

3   cups dashi or soup stock
    (see recipe)
    Salt
⅛   teaspoon monosodium
    glutamate, optional
½   teaspoon light soy sauce
12 thin slices fresh mushroom
3   shrimp (see recipe for
    shrimp to garnish Japanese
    soups)
    Grated lemon peel

1. Put the dashi in a saucepan and add the salt, monosodium glutamate, and soy sauce. Add the mushrooms and bring to the boil.

2. Arrange 1 shrimp in each of 3 soup bowls and add a few shreds of lemon peel. Pour equal quantities of boiling hot soup into the bowls and cover. Serve immediately.

Yield: 3 servings.

Dashi or soup stock

5   cups cold water
1   large square or rectangle
    kombu (kelp), measuring in
    the vicinity of 7 by 7 inches
    (see note)

3   cups loosely packed
    packaged katsuobushi or
    dried bonito shavings (see
    note)

1. Place the water in a saucepan and add the kombu. Bring to boil and immediately remove the kombu. Do not let the kombu cook.

2. Add the katsuobushi and stir. Remove from the heat immediately. Strain immediately through flannel.

Yield: About 5 cups.

Note: Both kombu and katsuobushi are available in Japanese markets.

Shrimp to garnish Japanese soups

If the shrimp are whole, tear off the head. In any event, peel the shrimp tail, leaving the last tail section intact. Butterfly the shrimp without cutting through. Score each shrimp on the underside at ½-inch intervals. Sprinkle with salt and dip lightly in cornstarch. Drop the shrimp into rapidly boiling water and cook 30 to 40 seconds just until heated through. Drain and drop immediately into ice water. Drain and pat dry. Use one shrimp in each serving of piping hot soup.

Misoshiru

(Bean soup)

3   cups dashi or soup stock
    (see recipe above)
⅓   cup miso (bean paste),
    available in Japanese food
    outlets
⅛   teaspoon monosodium
    glutamate, optional
½   cup thinly sliced fresh
    mushrooms (see note)
2   or 3 tablespoons chopped
    scallions for garnish

1. Pour the dashi into a saucepan and add the bean paste, stirring constantly. Taste the soup. If it is not strong enough, stir in a little more bean paste. If it is too strong, thin it with more dashi.

2. When ready to serve, strain the soup into another saucepan. Add the monosodium glutamate and mushrooms. Bring to the boil and pour equal quantities into 3 soup bowls. Garnish each serving with chopped scallions.

Yield: 3 servings.

Note: Many ingredients can be added to this soup including bean curd cut into cubes (available in Oriental groceries) and shrimp or eel. Very small cherrystone clams, cooked just until they open, are also excellent served in the shell.

Eel to garnish Japanese soups

Place one small cleaned and boned eel skin side down on a flat surface. Using a knife, make widthwise parallel gashes close together through the flesh of the eel cutting down to but not through the skin. At one-inch intervals cut through the skin and set the cut portions aside. Drop the pieces into boiling water and cook quite briefly just to cook through. Drain and drop immediately into a basin of ice water to chill rapidly. Drain and pat dry. Use one piece in each serving of piping hot soup.

Chef Paul Bocuse

When Paul Bocuse, who is almost indisputably the most famous chef in the world, made his presence known in our kitchen he had in his satchel a kilogram of Stygian-black truffles, valued at slightly in excess of $200. He would combine these with cubes of truffled fois gras, a hastily made but rich and full-bodied chicken consomme, and a topping of butter-layered puff pastry. This soup would be placed in the oven at 2:15 P.M. and 20 minutes later 16 guests would sit down to dine on the soup in individual dishes marked "Palais de l'Elysée, 25 Février 1975, soupe aux truffes V.G.E. Paul Bocuse."

Mr. Bocuse, a tall broad-shouldered, handsome man who is 49 years old and stands 5 feet 11 inches without his toque blanche, is a great cele-brator of occasions. The soup dishes commemorated the occasion a few months ago when he was awarded the Legion of Honor by France's President, Valéry Giscard d'Estaing. Mr. Bocuse himself had created the soup for the occasion.

The gentleman, who has doubtless done more to "propagandize" French cooking throughout the world than anyone else of his generation, had come to New York to celebrate the opening of Manhattan's newest French restaurant, Le Colisée at 36 East 60th Street. In France he is the proprietor of the Paul Bocuse restaurant in Lyons.

There were two of America's best-known chefs assisting Paul Bocuse in the kitchen, Pierre Franey and Jacques Pépin. Interestingly, the present chef of the Elysée Palace in Paris replaced Mr. Pépin when the latter came to America.

One question frequently put to those who toil in the kitchen vine-yards so to speak, is why throughout history have there been so few women chefs? We have always taken the soft—and we feel reason-able—position that in the old days at least the average restaurant kitchen was a fiery furnace that only a dumb male would endure; that many pro-fessional pots and pans are of an intolerable weight requiring muscle with which most women are not endowed. But that is certainly not the view of Mr. Bocuse, who is regarded among his colleagues as being heavily macho and with a high profile sex image. (His face bears a strong resemblance to Jacques David's famed portrait of Napoleon. However, he is more often referred to as le roi Paul than as l'empéreur Bocuse.)

"Women," he states, "lack the instincts for great cooking. It follows in the same sense that there are so few great women architects and orchestra leaders. Women who become chefs are limited in their ac-

Gourmet cooking, insists Paul Bocuse, doesn't call for a battery of helpers and a dozen foundation sauces.

complishments. They have one or two dishes they accomplish very well, but they are not great innovators." A fellow chef from Lyons stated later that he found the view surprising in that Lyons, where Mr. Bocuse was born and served part of his apprenticeship, is celebrated as the city of *les mères*—La Mère Fillioux, La Mère Brazier, and so on.

Before Mr. Bocuse arrived on the day in question we had spent the morning shopping for *les primeurs*, the finest and freshest vegetables available at our local market, the Green Thumb, in Watermill. The overflowing baskets included radishes, carrots, string beans, two kinds of lettuce, and strawberries that had been picked that morning. We purchased lobsters from Stewart's Fish Market in Amagansett. These would be turned into an excellent navarin of lobster—a sort of stew based on the traditional and more common navarin of lamb. The freshly killed chickens came from Iacono's farm in East Hampton.

The chef was obviously impressed with the fare, which was in all respects of first quality. "Impeccable," he stated, a word that he uses with enthusiasm and cunning abandon as he works. He sips the lobster sauce from a wooden spoon. "Impeccable," he exclaims. The sauce for the chicken pleases him. "Impeccable." But when he broke into the puff pastry that glorified the truffle soup, the host to his right beat him to the draw.

"Impeccable," he said.

Navarin de Homards

(Baked lobsters with vegetables)

1½ cups small potatoes, peeled
and quartered or cut into
chunks
Salt
¾ pound green beans,
trimmed at the ends and
cut into 1-inch lengths
1 cup shelled peas, the
fresher the better
1½ cups carrots cut into
bâtonnets (see note)
1 cup fresh turnips cut into
bâtonnets (see note)
3 or 4 live lobsters, about
1–1½ pounds each
6 tablespoons butter
¼ cup olive oil
⅓ cup finely chopped shallots
8 to 10 very small white
onions, peeled and cut into
quarters or eighths
Freshly ground black
pepper
¾ cup dry white wine
1¼ cups chicken broth,
preferably freshly made
3 tablespoons flour

1. In a saucepan, bring to the boil enough water to amply cover the potatoes. Add salt to taste and a bit more than seems logical. Add the potatoes and simmer until cooked but still a bit firm to the bite, about 10 to 15 minutes. Drain well.

2. In a saucepan, bring to the boil enough water to cover the green beans amply. Add salt as indicated above. Add the beans and cook until tender but still a bit firm to the bite, about 10 minutes, depending on size and age. Drain and rinse under cold water until well chilled. Drain well.

3. Bring enough water to the boil to cover the peas thoroughly. Add salt as indicated above. Add the peas and simmer about 4 minutes or longer until tender but still firm. Drain and rinse under cold running water. Drain well.

4. Combine the carrots and turnips and add cold water to cover. Add salt to taste and bring to the boil. Cook as above, about 10 minutes. Drain and rinse until cold. Drain well.

5. Plunge a knife into the center of each lobster where the tail and body meet. This will kill the lobster instantly. Cut the lobsters in half at midsection between the carcass and tail. Cut the tail section into 3 pieces each. Cut the carcasses in half lengthwise. Remove and reserve the soft coral and liver portion of the lobster. Discard the sac. Crack the claws. Place the lobster pieces in a mixing bowl.

6. Heat 4 tablespoons of butter and the oil in a large, heavy casserole or Dutch oven and add all the lobster pieces. Cook about 3 to 4 minutes. Add the shallots and onions and stir. Add the blanched vegetables—potatoes, green beans, peas, carrots, and turnips. Add salt and pepper to taste. Cook, stirring, about 5 minutes to blend the flavors.

7. Add the wine and broth and cover. Cook about 10 minutes. Remove from the heat. Using a lid to hold the solids in place, drain off the liquid into a large, heavy saucepan. Bring liquid to the boil and let simmer about 15 minutes.

8. Meanwhile, add remaining 2 tablespoons butter to the coral and liver and blend well with the fingers. Add the flour and blend well. Add to the sauce, stirring vigorously. Bring to the boil and cook, stirring constantly, about 5 minutes.

9. Pour this mixture over the lobster mixture and bring to the boil. Cook, stirring, about 5 minutes. Serve.

Yield: 10 servings.

Note: In French cooking, bâtonnets are vegetables that are cut into the size of tiny *bâtons*. Vegetables cut bâtonnet-style include carrots, turnips, celery, and others that are first cut into any given small length, such as an inch or two, and then cut into small rectangles about ¼ to ½ inch on all sides.

Poulet Sauté au Vinaigre

(Sautéed chicken with tomato sauce)

2 *chickens, about 3½ pounds each, cut into serving pieces*
   Salt and freshly ground black pepper
4 *tablespoons butter*
6 *whole, peeled cloves garlic*
6 *whole, unpeeled cloves garlic*
½ *cup red wine vinegar*
¾ *cup dry white wine*
1 *cup fresh or canned chicken broth*
3 *tablespoons tomato paste*

1 *pound fresh, red, ripe tomatoes, peeled, seeded, and cut into 1-inch cubes, about 2 cups*
2 *tablespoons tarragon wine vinegar*
3 *tablespoons chopped fresh tarragon or 1 tablespoon dried*

1. Preheat the oven to 400 degrees.

2. Sprinkle the chicken pieces with salt and pepper.

3. Heat equal amounts of the butter in two heavy skillets and add the chicken pieces skin side down. Brown on one side, 6 to 8 minutes, and turn. Add equal amounts of peeled and unpeeled garlic to both skillets. Cook the chicken, turning the pieces often, about 10 minutes. Using a slotted spoon, transfer the chicken from one skillet to the other. Pour off and discard the fat from the first skillet. Place the skillet containing all the chicken in the oven, uncovered. Let bake 10 minutes. Remove from the oven and cover.

4. Meanwhile, add the red wine vinegar to the first skillet, stirring to dissolve the brown particles that cling to the bottom and sides of the pan. Cook over high heat until reduced by half and add the wine and chicken broth. Add the tomato paste and stir to dissolve.

5. Cook about 15 minutes and add the tomatoes and tarragon wine vinegar. Bring to the boil over high heat and cook 10 minutes. Add the tarragon and cook about 3 minutes.

6. Pour off the fat from the skillet containing all the chicken. Pour the tomato and tarragon sauce over the chicken and stir to blend. Bring to the boil stirring, and make sure the chicken pieces are well coated. Serve.

Yield: 6 servings.

Soupe aux Truffes Elysée

(Truffle soup in the style of the Elysée Palace)

4   *tablespoons butter*
1   *cup finely diced white onion*
½   *cup finely diced celery*
1½   *cups finely diced carrots*
2½   *cups finely diced fresh mushrooms*
¼   *cup Smithfield ham, cut into ¼-inch cubes, optional*
1   *pound canned truffles (see note)*
¼   *pound fresh or tinned foie gras, more or less, optional*
6   *tablespoons dry white vermouth*
6   *tablespoons truffle liquid*
⅓   *cup chicken broth for each serving*
     Salt and freshly ground black pepper
1   *pound or less puff pastry, made according to any standard recipe*
1   *beaten egg*

1. Melt butter in a heavy skillet and add the onion, celery, and carrots. Cook about 15 minutes and add the mushrooms. The mushrooms will give up quite a bit of liquid. Cook about 10 minutes longer and add the ham. Cook 10 to 15 minutes longer.

2. Meanwhile, drain the truffles, reserving the liquid. Cut the truffles into very thin slices, into ¼-inch cubes or into fine ¼-inch julienne strips.

3. If used, cut the foie gras into 16 equal cubes.

4. When ready to assemble the dish, add about ⅓ cup of the mushroom mixture to the bottom of each of 8 small, individual soup dishes such as French onion soup crocks. Add equal portions of truffles to each dish and 2 cubes of foie gras, if used.

5. Blend the vermouth and reserved truffle liquid and pour equal portions of the mixture into each dish. Add the broth, salt and pepper to taste.

6. Roll out the puff pastry to a thickness of ⅛ inch and cut it into 8 rounds, about 6 or 7 inches in diameter, enough to cover the top of each dish with about half an inch hanging over the sides. Brush the rounds with beaten egg. Invert the rounds over the dishes so that the egg-brushed portion covers the dish. Press all around to seal the dough onto the soup dishes. Place on a baking sheet or sheets and refrigerate until ready to use.

7. When ready to cook, preheat the oven to its highest heat, 500 to 550 degrees. Brush the top of each serving with more egg and place in the oven on the bottom shelf. Bake 20 to 25 minutes or until the pastry is puffed and quite nicely browned.

Yield: 8 servings.

Note: It almost goes without saying that a soup as costly as this is only for a once-in-a-lifetime occasion.

As we have mentioned several times, there are many dishes, mostly imported, that enjoy a tremendous vogue in America. When we first came onto the food scene, curried dishes were the great fad coast to coast. In the intervening years, Americans have adopted such foods as boeuf bourguignonne, steak tartare, quiche lorraine, beef Wellington, and so on. One of the most recent of these dining diversions is a chicken sauté served in a sauce lightly laced with vinegar. It is a dish that is found in most of the first-rate restaurants in Europe and as you can see in the foregoing article, in the month of June we came into an original source for that dish—Paul Bocuse.

July 1975

I F WE HAD TO name the one dish in this volume that is the easiest, tasti-est, the most interesting for a large and imaginative group, it would be a pork and hominy stew called pozole that appears in this month of July. For years we have sought out, on our various visits to Mexico, an assortment of sources for the dish. The authentic version, which we describe on page 254, calls for a whole pig's head and a highly laborious technique of soaking dried corn. Shortly after that recipe appeared, a reader sent us the streamlined version (page 260) which is absolutely delicious and infinitely simpler in preparation. It is made with almost any meaty cut of pork with bone. The dried corn can be purchased in cans already prepared as whole kernel hominy. It is a meal in itself although there might be a few traditional side dishes such as guacamole and tortillas. Ideally, we would preface such a meal with perfectly iced and potent margaritas, and serve the dish with ice cold beer, preferably of Mexican import such as Carta Blanca or Bohemia.

A Summer Bounty

If the meal seems somewhat incongruous in midsummer, it could not be faulted from the standpoint of taste. It began with mackerel caught in front of the house last May; cold sliced smoked pheasant from last November's hunt; and a casserole of wild rice with oysters, the oysters also fresh from the waters in front of the house.

The table was that of Jane and Clifton Phalen and the meal had been assembled, by special request, of dishes we had enjoyed in times past plus a few we knew only by reputation.

Both the mackerel and the pheasant were the bounty of the host and had been kept for several months in a well-stocked freezer in the basement. The dessert for the occasion included a very much in season strawberry tart plus a timely and delectable English trifle, a recipe that had been in Mrs. Phalen's family for a couple of generations.

"My father came from Wisconsin, but became a British citizen and I was born in Canada," Mrs. Phalen explained. "My mother was from Missouri but she always served trifle on special occasions. I honestly don't know where the recipe originated, but Cliff and I have traveled all over England and Scotland and I've never found a trifle to equal it."

We would concur with that. The Phalen trifle consists of split ladyfingers smeared with raspberry jam, reshaped sandwich-fashion, and liberally doused with a sweet or semisweet imported sherry. A rich English custard is poured in and over and the whole is topped with sweetened whipped cream. "The important thing," Mrs. Phalen contends, "is that the custard be refrigerated for a considerable length of time. It must be ice cold."

Mr. Phalen retired as president of the New York Telephone Company in 1960. He still serves on the board of several prestigious firms including Eastern Airlines and W. R. Grace. The couple, who have been married 18 years, entertain frequently and often with members of their family at table. Mrs. Phalen is the mother of three children and Mr. Phalen is the father of two. Together they have nine grandchildren.

Mr. Phalen, an avid hunter and fisherman, manages to keep the family larder in generous supply. In fall and winter it is filled with wild duck, pheasant and quail and partridge plus four-footed game. In spring there is mackerel and, as the summer progresses, weakfish, bluefish, and striped bass.

The couple are only a short ferry ride from Greenport, the largest oyster packing facility on Long Island. They have clams for the raking, which, along with local lobster and corn, go into occasional wash-boiler clambakes.

In a large sense they are self-sufficient with a well-tended vegetable garden and a herb garden that is a study in itself. It is small but elaborate and yields such diverse flavors as sage, French thyme, tarragon, mint, oregano, parsley, rosemary, chives, fennel, lovage, and dill. Among the decorative herbs there is tansy; among the medicinal, wormwood and hyssop. There is lavender for potpourri and woodruff for, if anyone wishes, May wine. "I don't like it," Mrs. Phalen states flatly, and we can scarcely agree more.

We will confess that until we sampled Jane Phalen's smoked pheasant some months ago we had also not been all that keen on smoked game. It was she who directed us to our present smoker, which we purchased at the time, a Little Chief manufactured by Luhr Jensen and Sons, Inc. in Oregon. Home smokers are available from a number of sources. Addresses and prices are listed on page 66.

Jane Phalen removes smoked pheasant from the smoker.

Smoked Pheasant

2   pheasants weighing about
    2¾ pounds each (see note)
3   quarts water
1½ cups salt
¾   cup sugar
½   tablespoon freshly ground
    black pepper
4   bay leaves

1. If the pheasants are frozen, defrost them. Tie the legs together so that they are neatly shaped.

2. Combine the water, salt, sugar, pepper, and bay leaves, and stir to dissolve the salt and sugar. Add the pheasants and let them stand in the brine for 3 hours. Use a weight to make sure no portion of the birds is not immersed in the brine.

3. Remove the pheasant and rinse in cold water. Do not pat dry, but place them on a rack and let them dry in the air.

4. Prepare the smoker as indicated on the manufacturer's instructions. Place the pheasant in the smoker and smoke 3 hours.

5. Meanwhile, preheat the oven to 300 degrees.

6. Remove the pheasant from the smoker and bake on a rack in the oven for 45 minutes.

Yield: 8 to 12 servings.

Note: If you don't have a pheasant in the freezer, a nice, plump chicken will do.

Mackerel au Vin Blanc

2   tablespoons oil
⅔   cup thinly sliced carrots
1½   cups thinly sliced onions
2   cups dry white wine
3   tablespoons lemon juice
3   sprigs fresh parsley
2   sprigs fresh tarragon
3   sprigs fresh thyme
3   whole cloves
10   peppercorns
4   mackerel, about 1¼ pounds
     each, filleted but with the
     skin left on
     Salt and freshly ground
     black pepper
12   tablespoons capers
     Lemon wedges

1. Heat the oil in a saucepan and add the carrots and onions. Cook about 5 minutes or until wilted.

2. Add the wine and lemon juice. Add the parsley, tarragon, thyme, cloves, and peppercorns. Cook about 10 minutes.

3. Oil a metal pan large enough to hold the fish in one layer. Arrange the fish skin side down and sprinkle with salt and pepper. Pour the hot liquid with the solid ingredients over the mackerel and cover closely with foil. Bring to the boil and simmer 5 to 7 minutes. Let cool. Chill thoroughly. Serve sprinkled with capers and use the lemon wedges as a garnish.

Yield: 8 or more servings.

Wild Rice and Seafood Casserole

2 *pints raw oysters, or 1 pound cooked shrimp or crab meat*
1½ *cups raw wild rice, cooked (cooked in twice the amount of beef broth or half broth and half water)*
¼ *pound butter, at room temperature*
3 *cups, more or less, mushroom and oyster sauce (see recipe)*

1. Preheat the oven to 325 degrees.

2. Drain the oysters well and reserve the liquid to make the mushroom and oyster sauce. If crab meat or cooked shrimp are used, eliminate the oyster liquor and use milk and cream to make the cream sauce.

3. Place the oysters in a casserole or skillet and cook them over moderate heat just until the edges curl. Drain.

4. Combine the rice and butter and toss. Spoon half the wild rice over the bottom of an oval or rectangular baking dish and add the oysters. Add the remaining rice and smooth it over. Spoon the sauce over all and bake 30 minutes or until the casserole is piping hot.

Yield: 6 to 8 servings.

Mushroom and oyster sauce

2½ *tablespoons butter*
1½ *tablespoons flour*

1 *cup oyster liquor or a combination of oyster liquor and enough milk to make 1 cup (see note)*
Salt and freshly ground black pepper
4 *large fresh mushrooms*
2 *tablespoons finely chopped onion*
1½ *tablespoons finely chopped shallots*
1½ *teaspoons curry powder*
¾ *teaspoon dried thyme*
¾ *cup heavy cream*

1. Heat 1½ tablespoons butter in a saucepan and add the flour, stirring with a wire whisk. When blended, add the oyster liquor, stirring vigorously with the whisk. When thickened and smooth, add salt and pepper to taste.

2. Slice the mushrooms, then chop them. There should be about 1½ cups.

3. Heat the remaining tablespoon of butter and add the onion and shallots. Add the mushrooms, salt and pepper and cook until the mushrooms give up their liquid. Continue cooking until most of the liquid evaporates. Sprinkle with curry powder and thyme. Add the oyster sauce and heavy cream. Cook, stirring, about 5 minutes. Add salt and pepper to taste.

Yield: About 3 cups.

Note: If you are using shrimp or crabmeat in the casserole, substitute a combination of milk and cream for 1 cup of oyster liquor.

Trifle

12 *ladyfingers*
¾ *cup raspberry preserves*
4 *cups, more or less, English
     custard (see recipe), chilled*
1½ *cups Amontillado or other
     sweet or semisweet sherry*
12 *tablespoons or more
     sweetened whipped cream*

1. Split the ladyfingers in half. Smear the split side of each half with raspberry preserves and re-shape the ladyfingers sandwich-fashion.

2. Douse each sandwich liberally with sherry. Arrange 2 of the sandwiches in each of 6 individual dessert bowls. Spoon equal amounts of the custard and chill thoroughly.

3. When ready to serve, top each serving with 2 tablespoons or more of whipped cream.

Yield: 6 servings.

English custard

4 *whole eggs*
2 *egg yolks*
⅓ *cup sugar*
3 *cups milk*
¼ *teaspoon salt*
1 *teaspoon vanilla extract*

1. Combine the eggs, egg yolks, and sugar in a saucepan. Beat with a wire whisk until thick and lemon colored.

2. Meanwhile, bring the milk almost but not quite to the boil.

3. Gradually add the milk to the yolk mixture, beating constantly, this way and that, making certain that the spoon touches all over the bottom of the saucepan. Cook, stirring, and add the salt. Cook until the mixture has a custardlike consistency and coats the sides of the spoon. Do not let the sauce boil, or it will curdle.

4. Immediately remove the sauce from the stove, but continue stirring. Add the vanilla. Set the saucepan in a basin of cold water to reduce the temperature. Let the sauce cool to room temperature. Chill.

Yield: About 4 cups.

The Fresh Coriander Leaf

One of the most fascinating aspects of the palatal revolution that has occurred in the United States during the last couple of decades has been an extraordinary increase in the use of herbs, spices, and other natural seasonings. We can well recall the days when a shallot was considered an exotic and—it was before the days when pesto genovese became a commonplace—fresh basil was all but an unknown quantity. A few years ago we ran a statistic stating that imports of oregano had increased 2000 percent after pizza became almost as American as the hamburger. And that was a phenomenon that dates back two or three decades.

We are currently impressed with the status of fresh coriander leaves, long a staple flavor in international cookery, but until quite recently—except in the most adventurous homes—a rare ingredient in American kitchens. In the kitchens of India, China, and Mexico—to choose a few random nations—the fresh leaf of the coriander plant is as common as parsley (which we presume to be this country's commonest herb) is here.

In his excellent book, *Herbs, Spices and Flavorings* (an International Wine and Food Society guide, first published in this country in 1973 by McGraw-Hill, $9.95), Tom Stobart observes as follows: "Green coriander," which is to say the fresh leaf, "is not much used in Europe, and in England it is usual to dismiss it as 'unpleasant' or 'not a kitchen herb.' This is nonsense."

What really impresses us is the author's statement that fresh coriander "is probably the most commonly used flavoring herb of any in the world." It is, he continues, found in almost every market from Beirut to China and "loved, not only in the whole of southern Asia, but also in the Americas in Mexico and South America."

Although the coriander leaf and the dried coriander seed—which is widely used in American kitchens—come from the same plant, their flavors are wholly different and, thus, so are their uses. Fresh coriander is one of those flavors you do or don't become addicted to. It is not one of those ordinary, predictable flavors like parsley and chives.

There are, in fact, those for whom the perfume of the coriander leaf is anathema. The scent is undeniably droll, and we have mused at times that it smells musty, and relate it to an old trunk in a damp and little-used attic. The origin of the name is also droll. It stems from the Greek word koris, which means a bug, and it is said that those who coined the name a few thousand years ago related the scent of the coriander leaf to that of bed bugs.

Since we are enthusiastic in depth for the cooking of China, Mexico, India, and so on, we find fresh coriander absolutely essential to our peace of mind. In midsummer we have two sources for it: the groceries and the supermarkets in Chinatown and the *bodegas* in Hispanic communities, and our own small herb garden in East Hampton. Fresh coriander (also known as Chinese parsley, cilantro, and culantro), is purchasable by the bunch, and it will keep fresh and in excellent condition in the refrigerator if treated as follows: Place the coriander bunch in a jar and add enough water to immerse the stems at least halfway up. Cover the leaves with clear plastic and refrigerate, snipping off leaves as necessary.

Coriander is as easy as any other herb to grow, and the coriander seeds are widely available.

There are some recipes for which fresh coriander is a sine qua non, and these include the irresistible hot and sour fish soup at Uncle Tai's Hunan Yuan Restaurant and chicken chat, a kind of salad/appetizer at the Gaylord restaurant.

We offer recipes for these, plus Mexican meat balls to be sprinkled with chopped coriander leaves, and an Armenian yogurt soup adapted from Eva Zane's estimable cookbook, *Middle Eastern Cookery* (101 Productions, 1974, $7.95).

Chicken Chat

(An Indian appetizer made with chicken)

1 *large chicken breast, about ¾ pound*
3 *cups fresh or canned chicken broth, approximately*
½ *cup chopped mint leaves*
½ *cup chopped fresh coriander leaves*
2 *mild or hot long green chilies*
½ *cup plus ⅓ cup chopped onion*
½ *cup chopped tomato*
1 *teaspoon grated fresh ginger*
¼ *teaspoon ground coriander seeds*
1 *teaspoon finely chopped garlic*
  Salt and freshly ground black pepper
⅛ *teaspoon cayenne, or more to taste*
3 *tablespoons lemon juice, or more to taste*
2 *tablespoons yogurt*
2 *tablespoons grenadine syrup*
½ *cup seeded diced tomato*
⅓ *cup finely diced seeded cucumber*
1 *very sweet seedless naval orange, optional*
½ *banana, optional*
  Lettuce leaves
  Coriander leaves

1. Place the chicken breast in a saucepan and add chicken broth to cover. Bring to the boil. Par-

tially cover and simmer 15 minutes. Turn off the heat and let
stand until cool.

2. Combine the chopped mint
and coriander leaves in the container of an electric blender. Split
the chilies in half and chop
coarsely. Add them to the blender.
Add ½ cup chopped onion, ½ cup
chopped tomato, ginger, ground
coriander seeds, garlic, salt, pepper, cayenne, lemon juice, yogurt,
grenadine syrup. Blend thoroughly.

3. Skin and bone the chicken
breast. Pull the meat into sizable
bite-size pieces. Refrigerate
chicken broth for other use. Place
the chicken pieces in a mixing
bowl. Add the diced tomato, remaining ⅓ cup chopped onion,
and cucumber. If the orange and
banana are used, peel them and
cut into small cubes. Add them to
the chicken. Add the blender
sauce and toss well. Refrigerate
until ready to use. Serve on a bed
of lettuce leaves and garnish with
coriander leaves.

Yield: 4 to 6 servings.

Hot and Sour
Fish Soup

(A Chinese dish from Hunam
Province)

3 to 4 pounds very fresh fish
   bones, preferably with
   head but with gills
   removed
   Water
1 1½-inch length fresh ginger
4 scallions

*Hot and sour soup ingredients include
fresh coriander leaves.*

20 sprigs fresh coriander
    leaves
 3 to 4 tablespoons white
    vinegar
 ⅛ to ¼ teaspoon ground
    white pepper
 ½ teaspoon sesame oil
    Salt
 ½ pound skinless, boneless
    nonoily fish such as
    flounder, fluke, sole,
    striped bass, etc.

1. Place the fish bones in a
kettle and let cold running water
flow over them to remove all
traces of blood. When the water
runs clear, drain and add enough

cold water to barely cover the bones. Do not add salt.

2. Bring to the boil and let simmer over very gentle heat about 20 minutes. Strain. Reserve broth and discard bones.

3. Add 6 or 7 cups of the broth to a saucepan and bring to the boil.

4. Meanwhile, scrape the ginger. Cut the ginger into the thinnest possible slices. Stack the slices and cut them into the finest possible shreds. Set aside. Add scrapings to the soup.

5. Trim the scallions and cut into 2-inch lengths. Cut the lengths into very fine shreds. Set aside.

6. Pluck or cut off the coriander leaves from the stems. Set leaves aside. Crush the stems and add to the soup. Strain the soup into another saucepan and add the shredded ginger, scallions, coriander leaves, vinegar, white pepper, sesame oil, and salt. Stir to blend the flavors, but do not cook.

7. Cut the fish into ½-inch cubes and add it. Bring just to the boil and cook just until the fish loses its raw look. Spoon into individual soup bowls and serve piping hot.

Yield: 6 servings.

Albondigas

(Mexican meatballs in tomato and chili sauce)

1 *pound twice-ground pork*
1 *egg*

1 *teaspoon dried oregano*
½ *teaspoon ground cumin*
Salt and freshly ground black pepper
1 *small zucchini*
3 *tablespoons finely chopped onion*
2 *cloves garlic, finely minced*
3 *cups drained imported canned tomatoes*
2 *or 3 chipotle chilies, available in tins (see note)*
2 *tablespoons peanut, vegetable, or corn oil*
½ *cup fresh or canned chicken broth*
¼ *cup finely chopped fresh coriander*

1. Place the pork in a mixing bowl. Beat the egg, and add the oregano and cumin. Stir and add this mixture to the pork. Add salt and pepper to taste.

2. Trim off the ends of the zucchini. Cut the zucchini into thin slices. Stack the slices and cut them into strips. Cut the strips into fine cubes. There should be about ¾ cup. Add the zucchini, onion, and garlic to the meat. Blend well with the hands. Using lightly oiled fingers and palms, shape the mixture into 18 meat balls.

3. Combine the tomatoes and chilies in the container of an electric blender. Blend thoroughly.

4. Heat the oil in a Dutch oven or casserole. Add the tomato mixture. Add salt and pepper to taste and cook, stirring, about 5 minutes. Add the chicken broth and bring to the boil. Add the meat balls one at a time and bring to the boil. Cover closely and simmer about 45 minutes. Serve

sprinkled with chopped coriander. Serve with hot rice.

Yield: 4 servings.

Note: Chipotle chilies en escabèche have a smoked taste. They are smoked before canning. They are available in stores that cater to Mexican or Mexico-oriented clientele.

Eva Zane's Tanabour

(Armenian yogurt soup with coriander leaves)

1 *cup barley*
3 *cups water*
  Salt
¼ *teaspoon freshly ground black pepper*
7 *tablespoons butter*
1 *cup finely chopped onions*
4 *cups plain yogurt*
1 *egg*
1 *tablespoon flour*
4 *cups chicken broth*
1 *cup chopped fresh coriander*

1. Place the barley in a bowl and add water to cover. Soak overnight.

2. Drain the barley and place it in a saucepan with the 3 cups of water, salt, and pepper. Bring to the boil, lower heat, and simmer until tender. Add more water if necessary to keep the barley from sticking.

3. Heat 3 tablespoons of butter in a skillet and add the onions. Cook until lightly browned. Set aside.

4. Add the yogurt to a large saucepan and cook over low heat.

5. As it heats, beat the egg with the flour and add it to the yogurt. Add the chicken broth and bring to the boil. Add the barley and onions.

6. Heat the remaining butter in a small skillet and add the coriander leaves. Add this to the soup and season to taste with salt and pepper.

Yield: 6 to 8 servings.

We are, as we have stated, totally addicted to the flavor of that marvelous herb, fresh coriander. We grieved as the summer waned and the end of our crop came near. But then we made a remarkable discovery—with enough sunlight and good soil, the herb can be grown in the home year-round. We found that the larger the pot, the better.

The Après-Honeymoon Cookbook

WITH PIERRE FRANEY

We were impressed and by all means surprised recently to learn that June has not been relegated to the land of bustles, bloomers, and tandem bicycles where marriage is concerned. "June is still the big month for marriage," one correspondent advised us a short while ago, "and July is the month when housekeeping begins."

Call it our personal dowry to last month's brides (and bridegrooms for that matter, in that cooking by the distaff side only has long gone the way of bustles, bloomers, etc.) if we offer a hope chest of what every beginning cook should know. It includes five great and simple foundation sauces, plus a series of variations. The first recipe in the chest is the basic white sauce, to be converted into cream sauces, curry sauces, mushroom sauces, and so on. Then come an essential tomato sauce, which can be turned into anything from spaghetti with meat balls to something known (a bit racily, no?) as spaghetti whore's-style; that wondrously versatile, if not to say sublime, creation, homemade mayonnaise—with its logical palatal extensions, tartare sauce and gribiche sauce; a hollandaise, easily converted into a mousseline or maltaise sauce; and finally the traditional French salad sauce, which can become vinaigrette or ravigote sauce.

Basic White Sauce

2 tablespoons butter
2 tablespoons flour
1 to 1½ cups milk
  Salt and freshly ground pepper, preferably white pepper

1. Select a saucepan with a 3- or 4-cup capacity. Add the butter and let it heat until melted. Do not let it burn. Add the flour and immediately start stirring with a wire whisk.

2. Add the milk all at once, stirring rapidly with the whisk. Add the salt and pepper to taste. Cook, stirring frequently, about 5 minutes.

Yield: 1 to 1½ cups.

Variations

Cream sauce: When the white sauce is ready, add ½ to ¾ cup of heavy cream. Cook, stirring, about 1 minute, adding salt to taste.

For creamed foods such as chicken, meat, fish, seafood, or eggs: Cut chicken, meat, or eggs into bite-size pieces. Flake fish or seafood into bite-size morsels. For each cup of solid food such as chicken, meat, or eggs, use ½ cup or a little more of cream sauce. Fold the solid food into the sauce and heat until nice and bubbling. Serve, if desired, on toast.

Mornay sauce: Prepare the recipe for basic white sauce. Stir in ¼ cup of heavy cream. Bring to the boil and add ¾ cup grated Swiss or Gruyère cheese (Cheddar could be used). Stir until the cheese melts. Add 1 egg yolk, stirring rapidly with the wire whisk. Add about ⅛ teaspoon of grated nutmeg. Pour the sauce over hot, freshly cooked vegetables such as asparagus or cauliflower. Preferably, run the dish under the broiler until it is nicely golden on top. Do not overcook.

Curry sauce: Prepare the basic white sauce. In another small saucepan, heat 1 tablespoon butter and add 2 or 3 tablespoons finely chopped onion. Add 1 teaspoon of curry powder (use a little more if you particularly like curry), and stir until well distributed. Add the basic white sauce and ½ cup of heavy cream. For curried dishes proceed as indicated above for creamed foods.

Curried mushroom sauce: Make the curry sauce but add, along with the curry powder, 1½ cups of finely chopped mushrooms. The mushrooms will give up a lot of their natural juices, so cook, stirring, until that liquid evaporates. Do not brown. Add the basic white sauce and heavy cream as indicated in the curry sauce.

Basic Tomato Sauce

4   cups canned tomatoes,
    preferably the peeled
    imported Italian kind
    Salt and freshly ground
    black pepper
¼   teaspoon sugar, optional

1. Empty the tomatoes with their liquid into a 6-to-8-quart saucepan or a small, fairly deep skillet. Bring to the boil and let the tomatoes cook until they are reduced to 3 cups. If you want a thicker sauce, which is generally preferable, let the tomatoes cook until they are reduced to 2 cups. When ready, the sauce should not be watery. Remember that this sauce must be stirred from the bottom and often or the tomatoes might stick and burn.

2. Add salt and pepper to taste and, if desired, sugar. Proceed to one of the variations below before using. This sauce, incidentally, may be spooned into refrigerator containers. Tightly sealed it will keep for a week or longer. It also freezes well and can be kept for months.

Yield: 2 or 3 cups.

Variations

Neapolitan-style tomato sauce:
When the sauce is ready, heat 2 tablespoons of olive oil in a saucepan. Add 1 clove of garlic, finely chopped, and cook for only a few seconds. Do not boil. Add the tomato sauce and stir with a wire whisk until the oil is thoroughly blended with the sauce. Add 1 tablespoon of chopped fresh basil or 1 teaspoon dried and/or ½ teaspoon crushed dried oregano. Serve with cooked spaghetti and grated Parmesan cheese.

Spaghetti alla puttanesca (a Neapolitan dish which translates as "spaghetti whore's-style"): Prepare the Neapolitan-style tomato sauce, using the basic tomato sauce when it has been reduced to 3 cups. Add 1 or 2 cloves of garlic, finely chopped, and do not add salt. Add 1 tablespoon of drained capers, ½ cup pitted black olives (imported black olives found in many supermarkets and specialty food shops are far superior to the flavorless domestic kind), and a light sprinkling of crushed red pepper flakes. Continue to cook, uncovered, about 5 or 10 minutes. Add one 2-ounce can of flat anchovy fillets, well drained. Cook about 3 minutes longer, stirring, until the anchovies dissolve. At this point add salt to taste (not much—the anchovies are salty). Serve piping hot with freshly cooked drained spaghetti.

Spaghetti with meatballs: Prepare the Neapolitan-style tomato sauce, using the basic tomato sauce when it has been reduced to 3 cups. Combine in a mixing bowl ½ pound of ground pork or beef, 1 egg (lightly beaten), ½ cup of bread crumbs, 1 tablespoon grated Parmesan cheese, and ⅛ teaspoon grated nutmeg. If desired, add about ½ teaspoon grated lemon peel and a little finely chopped parsley. Shape into a dozen small meatballs. Dust the meatballs with flour, shaking off the excess. Brown the meatballs all over in 2 tablespoons of oil, using a heavy skillet and turning the meatballs gently in the oil as they cook. Add them to the tomato sauce, bring to the boil, and cook about 30 minutes.

Basic Mayonnaise

1 *egg yolk*
  Salt and freshly ground
  black pepper
1 *teaspoon imported*
  mustard, such as Dijon or
  Düsseldorf
1 *teaspoon vinegar or lemon*
  juice
¾ *to 1 cup peanut, vegetable,*
  corn, or olive oil

1. Place the yolk in a mixing bowl and add salt and pepper to taste, mustard, and vinegar. It is imperative that the yolk be combined with the acid provided by the mustard and vinegar before the oil is added. The acid will help prevent curdling.

2. Use a wire whisk or electric beater. Put the oil in a measuring cup with a pouring spout. Gradually add the oil while beating vigorously with the whisk or electric beater. When approximately half the oil has been added, the remaining oil can be added more rapidly. It is best to use the full cup of oil. Add more salt to taste and, if desired, more lemon juice. If the mayonnaise seems too thick, it may be thinned by beating in a little cold water. But use very little. The mayonnaise for most purposes should not be runny. The touch of water will also help to prevent curdling once the mayonnaise is refrigerated. Use the mayonnaise for sandwiches, salads and so on.

Yield: 1 cup.

Variations

Chicken, meat, fish, or seafood salads: Cut the chicken or meat into bite-size pieces. Shred or cut the fish or seafood into bite-size morsels. Place the food in a mixing bowl. Use half as much mayonnaise as there are solids. For example, use 1 cup of mayonnaise with 2 cups of chicken, meat, fish, and so on. You can also add ½ cup of finely chopped celery and a tablespoon each of chopped onion and capers to each 2 cups of solids.

Mustard mayonnaise: When the mayonnaise is finished, add ½ tablespoon or more imported mustard to taste. Use like regular mayonnaise (it is particularly good as a spread for meat sandwiches).

Tartare sauce: To 1 cup of mayonnaise add 1 tablespoon of well-drained capers, 1 tablespoon of chopped sour pickles (preferably the French pickles called cornichons), and 1 tablespoon finely chopped parsley. Other flavors may be added, including 2 teaspoons finely chopped shallots or onion or chives and 1 teaspoon chopped tarragon. Serve with fried, grilled, and cold poached fish or seafood.

Rémoulade sauce: To the preceding recipe for tartare sauce add 1 tablespoon of chopped anchovy fillets.

Gribiche sauce: To the recipe for tartare sauce add a hard-cooked egg that has been put through a sieve or finely chopped. Serve with cold poached fish or cold meats.

Niçoise sauce: To the recipe for tartare sauce add 1 tablespoon of the preceding Neapolitan-style tomato sauce after it is cooled or chilled. This is particularly good with cold sliced lamb.

Louis dressing: To 1 cup of mayonnaise add ¼ cup heavy cream, ¼ cup chili sauce, 3 tablespoons finely chopped heart of celery, 3 tablespoons finely chopped scallions or 2 teaspoons chopped onion, 2 tablespoons finely chopped stuffed green olives, ½ teaspoon of worcestershire sauce, and lemon juice to taste. Serve with cold crab, lobster, or shrimp.

Cognac and mayonnaise dressing: To 1 cup of mayonnaise add 1 tablespoon tomato ketchup and 2 tablespoons cognac. Serve with cold seafood cocktails.

constantly and vigorously, until all the butter is added. Add the remaining lemon juice and cayenne. The sauce is now ready to serve. Serve with cooked asparagus, artichokes and poached fish.

Yield: About 1 cup.

Basic Hollandaise Sauce

12 *tablespoons butter*
3 *egg yolks*
2 *tablespoons cold water*
  Salt
2 *teaspoons lemon juice*
⅛ *teaspoon cayenne*

1. Place a skillet on the stove and add about ½ inch of water. Bring the water to the simmer. Have ready a 1½-quart saucepan.

2. Place the butter in another saucepan and place it over very low heat (perhaps using an asbestos pad or a Flame-Tamer).

3. Set the 1½-quart saucepan in the simmering water in the skillet. Place the egg yolks in the saucepan. Add the cold water, salt to taste, and half the lemon juice. Start beating the egg yolks with a wire whisk, stirring in a back-and-forth and circular fashion, making certain that the whisk covers the bottom of the saucepan so that the yolks do not stick. It is imperative that the heat beneath the saucepan be moderate. When the egg yolks become custardlike and thickened, start adding the melted butter.

4. Continue beating, stirring

Variations

Mousseline sauce: To the recipe for hollandaise fold in 1 cup of whipped cream (measured after the cream is whipped).

Maltaise sauce: To the recipe for hollandaise add the juice of ½ an orange, ½ teaspoon grated orange rind, and 2 teaspoons Grand Marnier or Curaçao liqueur. Serve with asparagus.

Béarnaise sauce: Before preparing the hollandaise sauce, combine in the 1½-quart saucepan 3 tablespoons red wine vinegar with 1 tablespoon each finely chopped shallots and fresh tarragon. Or use 1 teaspoon dried tarragon. Add 1 teaspoon cracked black pepper. Bring to the boil over direct heat. Let simmer until all the vinegar evaporates. Remove the saucepan from the heat and let it cool slightly. Add the egg yolks, water, and so on and proceed with the recipe for hollandaise. Ideally, a béarnaise sauce is strained or squeezed through cheesecloth before serving, but this is a nuisance and is not necessarily recommended for beginning cooks.

Basic Salad Sauce

2 *tablespoons red wine
   vinegar or lemon juice*
6 *to 8 tablespoons peanut,
   vegetable, corn, or olive oil
   Salt and freshly ground
   black pepper*

Combine all the ingredients in a small jar. Close and shake until thoroughly blended. Serve over salad greens.

Yield: About ⅓ cup.

Variations

Piquant salad sauce: Add 1 teaspoon of prepared imported mustard to the basic sauce, plus 1 clove garlic, finely chopped, and a few drops of Tabasco.

Vinaigrette sauce: To the basic sauce add 1 teaspoon capers, 1 teaspoon chopped sour pickles (preferably the imported French pickles known as cornichons), 1 teaspoon of finely chopped onion, 1 tablespoon of finely chopped parsley. Other flavors might include a teaspoon of chopped chives and a teaspoon of chopped chervil.

Ravigote sauce: To the vinaigrette sauce add half a hard-cooked egg, coarsely chopped, and, if desired, 1 tablespoon of red, ripe tomato cut into small cubes.

The Golden Glories
of Corn

New corn, fresh from the kettle, is one of those foods which, like the first radish in spring or a woodland raspberry, are utterly irresistible. Although born in a corn belt in Mississippi, we were first instructed in the proper method of cooking corn on the cob by Ann Seranne, the cookbook author, a Canadian by birth, and one of our nicest friends. Years ago she instructed that freshly shucked corn should be dropped into a kettle of boiling water, the kettle covered with a lid. When the water returns to the boil, the kettle should be removed from the heat, the kettle left to stand five minutes. The corn, then drained, is ready to be served with melted butter, salt, and pepper.

Sometime thereafter we wrote a basic cookbook called *A Kitchen Primer* (Knopf, 1969, $6.95) and in it we repeated those instructions: "When the water in the kettle has reached a full rolling boil, carefully drop the prepared corn into the kettle. Let the water return to a boil and when it does, place the cover on the kettle. Immediately turn off the heat and let the corn stand in the water from 5 to 10 minutes. Serve immediately without further cooking. Drain the corn . . ." and so on.

A few years later the book was printed in England, and we thought little about it until a Rhodes scholar, an American, wrote to ask if we had revised our opinion of how to cook corn. Or was some British editor simply indulging in the traditional English method of vegetable cookery?

To our amusement—and chagrin—we found it had indeed been altered as follows: "Let the water return to the boil and when it does, place the lid on the pan. Boil quickly for 20-25 minutes, then drain. . . ."

Corn is, without fault, one of the glories of summer, and this year's crop promises to be excellent both in quality and quantity. A few ears from New Jersey and Riverhead, Long Island, have been sampled, and the kernels are joyously sweet, bursting with goodness, and there's the happy thought that for a few brief weeks the appetite can be recklessly gratified not only with corn on the cob but with numerous other delights in such dishes as corn omelets, corn soufflés, corn puddings, curried corn with peppers, creole corn, and so on. It is an enormously versatile vegetable.

Although corn on the cob with sweet butter, salt, and pepper is per-

haps the most delectable manner of serving corn, we have, since child-hood, had a special fondness for grated corn dishes, corn puddings, corn custards and the like.

We have recently come into possession of a simply designed, hand-some and marvelously functional device for grating corn. It was sent by Ivan R. Cousins of Sausalito, California, who informed us in a letter that accompanied the gadget that he is a cousin of Julia Child, who had rec-ommended he send it to us in the first place.

The corn scraper consists of a small, polished, unpainted slab of wood resting on wooden legs, benchstyle. A round hole in the center is bisected with a small metal bar and before that a row of nails.

"To use it," Mr. Cousins advises, "place the grate over a dish with the row of nails on the far side of you. Draw a fresh, uncooked ear of corn toward you across the nails and the bar. This deposits the corn es-sence through the hole and into the dish. You are now ready to prepare corn pudding, fritters or chowder."

We can heartily endorse the grater, which is made by a small com-pany in northern California of which Mr. Cousins is the sole represen-tative. A grater may be obtained by sending a check or money order for $12 plus postage, F.O.B.; the address is Ivan R. Cousins, 139 Currey Av-enue, Sausalito, California 94965.

Fresh Corn and Fish Chowder

6   to 8 ears of corn on the cob
2   potatoes, about ¾ pound
3   tablespoons cubed salt
    pork
1½ cups finely chopped onions
1½ cups water, fish broth, or
    chicken broth
¼   pound nonoily, white-
    fleshed fish such as striped
    bass, flounder, etc.
    Salt and freshly ground
    black pepper
    Tabasco
3   cups milk
2   tablespoons butter

1. Drop the corn into boiling water and cover. When the water returns to the boil, remove from the heat. Let stand 5 minutes and drain.

2. When the corn is cool enough to handle, cut and scrape the kernels from the cob. There should be about 2 cups.

3. Peel the potatoes and cut them into ½-inch cubes. Drop into cold water and let stand until ready to use.

4. Place the salt pork in a saucepan or small kettle over low heat and when it is rendered of its fat, add the onions and cook until wilted. Drain the potatoes and add them and the 1½ cups of water or broth and bring to the boil. Simmer until tender, 5 minutes or longer.

5. Cut the fish into ½-inch cubes and add it. Add salt and pepper to taste and Tabasco to taste. Cook about 5 minutes and add the milk. Bring to the boil and add the corn. Add the butter and swirl it in. Serve piping hot.

Yield: 4 to 6 servings.

Curried Corn and Cheese Soufflé

6   to 8 cooked ears of corn
¼   pound sharp Cheddar
    cheese
3   tablespoons butter
3   tablespoons flour
2   tablespoons curry powder
1½ cups milk
    Salt and freshly ground
    black pepper
2   teaspoons cornstarch
1   tablespoon water
6   eggs, separated
¼   cup grated Parmesan
    cheese

1. Preheat the oven to 400 degrees.

2. Using a knife, cut the kernels from the corn. Set aside.

3. Grate the cheese. There should be about 1½ cups loosely packed.

4. Melt 2 tablespoons of butter in a saucepan and add the flour and curry powder, stirring with a wire whisk. When blended and smooth, add the milk, stirring rapidly with the whisk. Blend until thickened and smooth and add salt and pepper. Blend the cornstarch and water and stir it in.

5. Add the egg yolks, stirring constantly. Cook only until the

mixture boils and remove it from the heat. Let cool. Add the Cheddar cheese and fold in the corn.

6. Rub the inside of a 1½-quart soufflé dish with the remaining 1 tablespoon butter. Add the Parmesan cheese and shake the cheese around until bottom and sides are lightly coated. Shake out excess cheese. Place the dish in the freezer until ready to use.

7. Beat the egg whites until stiff. Add half the whites to the soufflé mixture, stirring rapidly. Fold in the remaining whites. Spoon the mixture into the prepared soufflé dish. Place the soufflé in the oven and immediately lower the oven heat to 375 degrees. Bake 25 to 35 minutes, depending on whether you wish a soufflé with a moist or firm center.

Yield: 4 to 6 servings.

Corn Pudding

8 to 10 *ears shucked, uncooked corn*
½ *cup heavy cream*
2 *egg yolks*
2 *whole eggs*
½ *cup grated Cheddar cheese, optional*
⅛ *teaspoon grated nutmeg Salt and freshly ground black pepper*
1 *to 2 tablespoons diced green chilies (available in 4-ounce cans in many groceries and supermarkets), optional*
1 *tablespoon butter*

1. Preheat the oven to 375 degrees.

2. Grate and scrape the corn. There should be about 2½ cups. Add the corn pulp to a mixing bowl.

3. Add the cream, yolks, eggs, cheese, nutmeg, salt, pepper, and green chilies. Beat well.

4. Butter a baking dish with the tablespoon butter (we used a 9-inch ceramic pie plate) and pour in the corn batter. Bake 25 minutes. Serve hot.

Yield: 6 servings.

Curried Corn with Green Peppers

6 *ears corn on the cob*
3 *tablespoons butter*
¼ *cup finely chopped green pepper*
1 *teaspoon curry powder Salt and freshly ground black pepper*
¼ *cup heavy cream*

1. Drop the corn into boiling water. When the water returns to the boil, cover and turn off the heat. Let the corn remain in the water 5 minutes. Drain and let the corn cool.

2. Cut and scrape the corn off the cob. There should be about 1½ cups.

3. Heat 2 tablespoons of butter in a skillet and add the green peppers. Cook, stirring, about 1 minute. Sprinkle with the curry powder and cook, stirring, about 30 seconds. Add the corn and salt and pepper to taste. Add the re-

maining 1 tablespoon of butter and the heavy cream. Serve hot.

Yield: 2 to 4 servings.

Cold Corn, Zucchini, and Tomato Salad

2   to 4 ears of corn
1   small zucchini, about ¼ pound (or use a portion of a large zucchini)
1   or 2 red, ripe tomatoes, about ½ pound
¼   cup chopped, seeded, hot or mild chilies or green peppers
¼   cup chopped red onion
2   cloves garlic, finely minced
¼   cup chopped parsley
1   tablespoon chopped fresh basil
1   to 2 tablespoons red wine vinegar
2   tablespoons olive oil
    Tabasco, optional
    Salt and freshly ground black pepper

1.   Shuck the corn and drop the ears into boiling water without salt. Cover and when the water returns to boil, turn off the heat. Let stand 5 minutes. Drain and let cool.

2.   Using a sharp knife, cut the corn kernels from the cob. There should be about 1 cup. Add to a mixing bowl.

3.   Trim off the ends of the zucchini. Cut the zucchini into ¼-inch slices. Cut the slices into ¼-inch strips. Cut the strips into ¼-inch cubes. Add this to the corn.

4.   Core the tomato and slice it in half. Squeeze gently to remove the seeds. Cut the pulp into small cubes. Add this to the corn mixture.

5.   Add the remaining ingredients and toss with a salad fork and spoon to blend. Chill until ready to serve.

Yield: 4 servings.

Corn and Zucchini au Gratin

1½   pounds zucchini
7   or 8 ears of corn
3   tablespoons butter
3   tablespoons flour
1¾   cups milk
⅓   cup heavy cream
⅛   teaspoon grated nutmeg
1/16   teaspoon cayenne
3   tablespoons grated Cheddar or Gruyère cheese
    Salt and freshly ground black pepper
¼   cup grated Parmesan cheese

1.   Preheat the oven to 350 degrees.

2.   Trim off the ends of the zucchini. Split them lengthwise into halves, then into quarters. Cut each quarter into ½-inch or bite-size pieces.

3.   Place the zucchini in the top of a steamer over boiling water. Cover closely and steam 5 minutes. Do not overcook. The pieces must remain firm and not mushy.

4. Shuck the corn and drop the ears into boiling water without salt. Cover and when the water returns to the boil, turn off the heat. Let stand 5 minutes. Drain and let cool.

5. Using a sharp knife, cut the corn kernels from the cob. There should be about 2¼ cups.

6. Melt 2 tablespoons butter in a saucepan and add the flour, stirring with a wire whisk. When blended, add the milk all at once, stirring rapidly with the whisk. When thickened and smooth, add the cream, nutmeg, and cayenne. Cook about 5 minutes, stirring occasionally. Add the Cheddar cheese, stirring, and turn off the heat. Add salt and pepper to taste.

7. Fold the zucchini and corn into the cream sauce. Pour the mixture into a baking dish and sprinkle with Parmesan. Dot with the remaining 1 tablespoon butter and bake 25 to 30 minutes or until golden brown and bubbling throughout. If desired, run the casserole under the broiler to get a better glaze on top.

Yield: 6 servings.

How to Cook Corn on the Cob

Add enough water to a kettle to cover the shucked corn. Do not add salt but bring the water to the boil. Add the corn and cover. When the water returns to the boil, remove the kettle from the heat. Let the corn stand in the water 5 to 10 minutes and serve immediately without further cooking.

The corn may stand in the water for as long as 20 minutes without damage to its flavor and quality.

While browsing through these recipes for corn, it occurred to us that we ignored one of the techniques we use to facilitate (or expedite) the eating of corn on the cob. Before we sit down, we prepare a kind of seasoned butter to be smeared on the corn. This eliminates the need of serving salt and pepper separately. To prepare the butter, you simply soften it and beat in any given quantity of freshly ground black pepper plus salt. The butter keeps indefinitely in the refrigerator and may be served melted or as a spread.

Cold Soups

WITH PIERRE FRANEY

Numerous changes in the eating and drinking habits of Americans occurred shortly after World War II, notably cocktails on the rocks and cold savory soups. Prior to the war, a martini or manhattan on the rocks would have seemed downright peculiar. When the late chef Louis Diat created vichyssoise (it was purely and simply the traditional potage parisienne of his childhood, chilled and with cream added), it was in a sense revolutionary. Since that period, cold soups have become very much a popular staple for summer. Here are a few of them to serve cold or hot. And cold garlic soup isn't as far out as it may seem. They've been serving garlic soup in France for generations.

Chilled Tomato and Yogurt Soup

2 tablespoons butter
2 cups chopped onion
2 cups peeled, seeded, cubed cucumbers
3 cups peeled, cored, cubed tomatoes
3 basil leaves or 1 teaspoon dried
2 cups chicken broth
2 cups yogurt
Salt
1 teaspoon chopped fresh mint, optional

1. Melt the butter in a saucepan and add the onion. Cook, stirring frequently, about 10 minutes. Do not brown.

2. Add the cucumber, tomatoes, basil, and chicken broth. Cook, stirring frequently, about 30 minutes.

3. Put the mixture, including the vegetable solids, through a sieve, or blend in an electric blender.

4. Empty the mixture into a bowl and add the yogurt and salt to taste. Chill thoroughly. Add the mint and serve.

Yield: About 6 servings.

Jacques Pépin's Cold Zucchini Soup

5 or 6 small-to-medium-size zucchini
1 large onion, peeled and thinly sliced, about 1 cup
1½ teaspoons curry powder
3 cups chicken broth
1 cup heavy cream
½ cup milk
Salt and freshly ground black pepper
Finely chopped chives

1. Rinse the zucchini and pat dry. Trim off the ends. Cut one zucchini in two and thinly slice one half. Stack the slices and cut them into very thin matchlike strips. There should be about 1 cup. Place in a saucepan and add cold water to cover. Boil 3 to 4 minutes and drain. Set aside.

2. Cut the remaining zucchini half and the other zucchini into 1-inch lengths. Cut each length into quarters.

3. Place the pieces of quartered zucchini in a kettle or saucepan and add the onion slices. Sprinkle with curry powder and stir to coat the pieces. Add the chicken broth and bring to the boil. Cover and simmer about 45 minutes.

4. Spoon and scrape the mixture into a blender or food processor and blend to a fine puree. There should be about 4 cups. Add the cream, milk, and salt and pepper to taste. Add the reserved zucchini strips. Chill thoroughly. Serve sprinkled with chopped chives.

Yield: 6 to 8 servings.

Cold Garlic Soup

1   *quart rich chicken broth*
2   *large cloves garlic*
2   *cups heavy cream*
4   *egg yolks*

Salt and freshly ground black pepper
¼   *teaspoon grated nutmeg or to taste*
1½   *cups garlic croutons (see recipe)*

1. Pour the broth into a 2-quart heavy casserole.

2. Peel the garlic and crush each clove slightly. Add it to the broth. Simmer 10 minutes.

3. Blend the cream and yolks and add the mixture to the broth, stirring rapidly. Bring just to the boil, stirring constantly, and remove from the heat. Add salt and pepper to taste and the nutmeg. Serve very cold with a garnish of croutons on each serving. (Can also be served piping hot.)

Yield: 6 to 8 servings.

Garlic croutons

2   *cloves garlic*
4   *tablespoons butter*
1½   *cups bread cut into ½-inch cubes*

1. Peel the garlic and crush each clove slightly.

2. Heat the butter in a heavy saucepan, and when it is hot, add the garlic and bread cubes. Cook, stirring and shaking the skillet, until the cubes are golden brown all over. Drain the cubes and discard the garlic.

Yield: 1½ cups.

A Weekend
with Diana Kennedy

Question: What do 50 pounds of slaked powdered lime, a pound of dried whole hominy, four pigs' heads, crumpets, and English muffins add up to?

Answer: A weekend with Diana Kennedy.

This saga began about three months ago when, during the course of a visit to Mexico, we dined with the British-born Diana at a market in Guadalajara. The dish of the day was pozole, a profoundly Mexican dish of which we have long been especially fond. Its two principal components happen to be dried hominy and the cooked flesh of a pig's head.

As we dipped our spoons in the deep bowls garnished with fresh lime wedges, chilies, and chopped onion, Diana told us of her childhood in Sussex and of the marvelous, insidiously good English muffins and crumpets, drenched in butter and taken with tea. She had, she related, recently been able to duplicate both in her Manhattan kitchen and she would be happy to share the recipes with us on our return.

Weeks passed and one morning while shopping for dried chilies and other condiments at Casa Moneo on 14th Street, our eyes fell on a package of dried hominy. We salivated with memories of Guadalajara, bought the hominy and telephoned Diana to come out for the weekend. She accepted with alacrity, cautioning us to buy a bit of slaked lime and order a pig's head in advance.

Diana's position in the food field need scarcely be outlined, of course. She is an authority on Mexican cooking and the author of the excellent *The Cuisines of Mexico* (Harper & Row, 1972, $12.50) and *The Tortilla Book* (Harper & Row, 1975, $4.95 paperback, $10 hard cover).

Well, a short while ago we stopped by our local meat market and asked our butcher to order a pig's head for the weekend. Half a head would do, for that is what the recipe calls for, but we added, with a shrug, we supposed we would have to take the whole head. After all, half a pig's head in the Hamptons is not the easiest thing in the world to give away, much less sell for profit. Our butcher told us he would see what he could do.

Then we started out for the "large teaspoon" of slaked lime the recipe called for. We traveled to Bridgehampton where, we were told, the local Agway store sells such essentials.

"We would like," we told the man, "to buy some slaked lime."

"How much would you like?"

"One large teaspoonful," we replied.

"Mister," he said, "that stuff only comes in 50-pound bags. What do you want it for anyway?'

"We cook," we said humbly, "and we need it for a hominy dish."

He shook his head in stunned disbelief and marched away to bring us the 50-pound bag of lime, which was tossed into the trunk of the car.

The Friday following, a telephone call from the meat man informed us that he had not only one pig's head, he had four, the smallest number his distributor would supply him with. We agreed to buy one and he agreed to freeze the others for some future need.

As the weekend progressed, the kitchen adventures became, if not more eventful, a study in dining well. Diana made her crumpets and muffins which were soaringly good, a special delight. She termed them "the most British of food, gut-sticking stuff." The pozole was masterful, although she decided against using the lime anyway.

Diana Kennedy duplicates the English crumpets of her childhood.

"The purpose of the lime," she explained, "is to soften the corn, which facilitates removing the 'eye' at the base of each kernel. When the 'eye' is removed and the hominy cooked, each kernel 'opens like a flower' as the Mexican expression goes." After an overnight soaking, the hominy was soft enough, she decided, so that the "eyes" could be removed with her fingernails, although it took some three hours of doing.

It must be added that the Mexican dinner was prefaced by an exceedingly piquant and tasty clam cocktail made with fresh jalapeño peppers and littleneck clams fresh from the local market. We were especially intrigued by the clam cocktail, for we have always sported the theory that cold shucked clams, for one esthetic reason or another, never tasted as good as clams on the half shell. Diana's clams in a palate-tingling green chili and fresh tomato sauce were an unalloyed pleasure.

P.S. We used the lime on the lawn. The disposition of the other half of the pig's head must wait for another installment.

Diana Kennedy's English Muffins

(Adapted from a recipe in Mrs. Beeton's *Book of Household Management*)

---

1 *small potato in the skin*
1 *pound all-purpose, unbleached flour plus 1 cup extra for kneading*
1 *teaspoon finely ground rock salt or kosher salt*
1¼ *cups warm water (100 degrees Fahrenheit)*
½ *ounce moist bulk yeast (see note) or 1 package granular yeast*
   Cornmeal

1. Place the potato in a small saucepan and add cold water to cover. Bring to the boil and cook 15 to 20 minutes or until tender. Drain and let cool. Peel the potato and mash it by putting it through a food mill or potato ricer. Set aside.

2. Meanwhile, preheat the oven to 300 degrees. Place the flour in a heatproof bowl and let it bake about 15 minutes to dry out. Let stand until thoroughly cool.

3. Dissolve the salt in the water.

4. Combine 5 level teaspoons of the mashed potato with approximately 2 tablespoons of the salted warm water and the yeast. Stir to blend thoroughly, taking care there are no lumps. Add the yeast mixture and the remaining water to the pound of flour and beat for about 3 minutes, using an electric mixer, or knead by hand about 6 minutes. The dough should come away cleanly from the sides of the bowl but it will be somewhat stiff and sticky. Do not overbeat or the result will be too spongy and the muffin will be too "cakey" when cooked.

5. Scrape the dough onto a floured surface and let it rest

briefly. The bowl should be clean. Sprinkle the dough with a little flour. Knead the dough quickly and pat it into a round cushion shape. Return it to the bowl, lightly floured.

6. Cover the bowl tightly with plastic wrap and set it aside in a warm place (about 80 degrees) and free from drafts, until it is almost double in bulk. The rising time is about 1 hour. When ready the dough should be soft and springy to the touch.

7. Scrape the dough onto a lightly floured surface. Sprinkle it lightly with flour to make certain it is not sticky to the touch. Flatten and pat it into a circular shape with both hands. Knead it firmly for about 3 minutes until it is quite resilient. Cut it into 11 pieces of equal weight, about 2½ ounces each. A small scale, such as a postal scale, is good for this.

8. Sprinkle a large baking sheet liberally with cornmeal, available in all supermarkets.

9. Roll each of the 11 pieces of dough, one at a time, into an even ball using lightly floured hands. Press the balls flat like biscuits or small cushions. Place them onto the prepared baking sheet allowing space between the muffins for expansion.

10. Let the muffins rise in a warm place for about 45 minutes to 1 hour. When ready the muffins will be well puffed and springy to the touch.

11. Meanwhile, preheat a heavy black iron skillet or a griddle over a medium but not too hot flame. Turn the heat to low.

Lightly oil the surface of the griddle. Carefully transfer the muffins, using a broad, metal spatula and with the cornmeal side down. Cook slowly about 10 minutes, cornmeal side down. Care should be taken that the muffins do not cook too fast and burn.

12. Turn the muffins and let cook about 10 minutes on the other side, taking care they do not burn. Transfer to a wire rack and let cool completely before splitting and toasting.

13. When ready to toast, insert the tines of a fork all around the perimeter of each muffin, going to the center. Break or pull the muffins apart with the fingers. Toast under the broiler neatly on both sides, butter the split side generously and serve hot. They are delicious with bitter marmalade or other preserves.

Yield: About 11 muffins.

Note: Bulk yeast or "yeast cakes" are more and more becoming available in supermarkets and are generally found in a refrigerated area. Mrs. Kennedy strongly advises using scales to measure all ingredients such as flour and yeast. The muffins will keep for several days if properly stored in the refrigerator and they may be frozen for future use.

Pozole de Jalisco

(A pork and
hominy soup or stew)

---

1 *pound whole dried hominy (see note)*

2 teaspoons calcium
   hydroxide U.S.P., also
   called slaked lime, optional
   (see note)
½ pig's head, 3 pounds or less
1½ pounds pork tenderloin or
   boneless fresh pork butt
1 pound pork neck bones
2 cups dried, small, hot red
   pepper pods, about 3
   ounces
   Salt
2 cups finely chopped onion
16 radishes, trimmed and
   thinly sliced
3 cups chopped or shredded
   crisp lettuce
16 lime wedges

1. Approximately 2 days before this dish is to be made, place the hominy in a deep bowl and add cold water to cover. If the lime is to be used, drain the hominy, add more water to cover and bring to the boil. Dilute the lime in a little cold water and add it through a strainer to the hominy. Boil 10 minutes. Cover and let soak ½ hour. Rinse the hominy in numerous changes of cold water to remove all traces of lime. Rub the corn between the hands so that the thin transparent sheath surrounding each kernel is removed. If the lime is not used, carefully remove the peaked "beak" of each kernel and the thin transparent sheath.

2. The night before the dish is to be prepared, place the pig's head in a kettle and add cold water to cover. Cut the pork tenderloin into large serving pieces and add to the pig's head. Add the neck bones and let soak overnight.

3. Cover the red pepper pods

with cold water and soak overnight.

4. Drain the hominy and add cold, unsalted water to cover. Bring to the boil and cook, uncovered, until the kernels open up like a flower, about 1 hour. Skim the surface as necessary.

5. Meanwhile, cover the head and other meat with fresh unsalted water and bring to the boil. Simmer uncovered until the meat can be removed from the bone, about 1 hour. Do not overcook for the meat will cook longer with the hominy. Set aside to cool. Reserve the cooking liquid.

6. When the head is cool enough to handle, remove all the meat and skin from the bones. Discard the bones. Cut the meat and skin into serving pieces. Cut the ear into pieces. There should be at least one piece of ear for each guest.

7. Add all the meat including that from the neck bones and the cooking broth to the hominy. Add salt to taste. Cook, uncovered, about 4 hours, over very low heat. Skim the fat from the surface as necessary and, if the dish becomes too dry, add boiling water as necessary.

8. Pour the red peppers and their liquid into a blender and blend thoroughly.

9. Serve the meat and hominy with the hot pepper sauce and remaining ingredients as garnish.

Yield: 12 to 14 servings.

Note: Hominy is available at Spanish and Mexican markets. Calcium hydroxide is available in some drugstores.

Diana Kennedy's
Crumpets

(Adapted from a recipe in Mrs.
Beeton's *Book of Household
Management*)

---

1   *small potato in the skin*
12 *ounces all-purpose,
    unbleached flour, about 2¾
    cups.*
½   *ounce moist bulk yeast (see
    note) or 1 package granular
    yeast*
1¾ *cups warm water (100
    degrees Fahrenheit)*
¾   *teaspoon ground rock salt
    or kosher salt*

1. Place the potato in a small saucepan and add cold water to cover. Bring to the boil and cook 15 to 20 minutes or until tender. Drain and let cool. Peel the potato and mash it by putting it through a food mill or potato ricer. Set aside.

2. Meanwhile, preheat the oven to 300 degrees. Place the flour in a heatproof bowl and let it bake about 15 minutes to dry out. Let stand until thoroughly cool.

3. Spoon 5 level teaspoons of the mashed potato and the yeast into a mixing bowl. Cream the two together. Measure out 1¼ cups of the warm water. Add 2 tablespoons of this water to the yeast mixture and stir to smooth out any lumps. Add this mixture to the flour along with the remaining measured water. Beat 2 minutes using an electric mixer, or beat by hand about 4 minutes, until dough is fairly smooth, soft, and sticky.

4. Cover the bowl tightly with plastic wrap and set it aside in a warm place—about 80 degrees— and free from drafts for about 30 minutes. It will take on a slightly fermented appearance.

5. Beat the dough as before and set aside covered with plastic wrap. Let stand about 30 minutes.

6. Blend the remaining ½ cup of warm water with the salt and stir to dissolve. Add this to the dough and beat well as before about 2 minutes. The batter will be loose and somewhat lumpy. Cover closely again and let rest a third time, about 20 minutes.

7. Heat a heavy black iron skillet or a griddle over a medium flame. If crumpet rings, which resemble napkin rings and measure about 3½ inches in diameter, are available, use them. Otherwise use the metal rings of wide-mouth canning jars. Just before cooking, lightly oil the skillet or griddle. Lightly oil the inside of the crumpet rings or canning jar rings.

8. Place the rings on the griddle and ladle into them slightly less than ½ cup of the batter. The batter should almost but not quite come to the brim of the rings. Cook over a medium flame about 10 minutes. As the crumpets start to cook, if the flame is sufficiently high, bubbles will appear on the surface of the batter. The flame must not be high enough to burn the bottom of the crumpets. The tops of the crumpets will take on a honeycomb effect.

9. Let the crumpets cook until the top of the batter has completely dried and is not moist to the touch. Remove the ring and turn the crumpets to cook for 2

more minutes on the second side. Properly cooked, the bottom should be solid and lightly browned while the top should have a pattern of holes and be just lightly colored.

10. Transfer the crumpets to a wire tray to cool completely. When ready to serve, toast them under the broiler without splitting, on both sides. While piping hot spread them lavishly with butter. Properly the crumpets should be slightly chewy if not to say a bit rubbery.

11. Untoasted, cooled crumpets will keep for days if properly stored in the refrigerator. Or they may be frozen.

Yield: Approximately 10 crumpets.

Note: Bulk yeast or "yeast cakes" are more and more becoming available in supermarkets and are generally found in the refrigerated section.

Tortilla and Chorizo "Dry Soup"

12 *tortillas, preferably left over from a day or two earlier*
1 *tablespoon melted lard or peanut oil*
2 *chorizo sausages, skinned and crumbled*
1¼ *cups skinned and chopped fresh red, ripe tomatoes or imported canned tomatoes*
¼ *cup finely chopped onion Peanut oil for shallow frying*
1 *cup fresh or canned pork or chicken broth*
2 *sprigs fresh mint, chopped, or about 1 teaspoon crumbled dried mint leaves Salt*
⅓ *cup crumbled farmer cheese*
½ *cup thinly sliced onion*

1. Cut the tortillas into thin strips.

2. Heat the lard and add the chorizos. Cook, stirring, about 4 minutes. Drain the meat and set aside. Reserve the cooking fat.

3. Combine the tomatoes and onion in a blender and blend. Heat about 7 tablespoons of the chorizo fat in a skillet and add the tomato mixture. Cook, stirring about 3 minutes. Set aside.

4. Heat the peanut oil to a depth of about ½ inch. Add the tortilla strips, about one-third at a time, and cook until wilted and starting to stiffen but without browning. Drain on absorbent toweling.

5. Combine the tortilla pieces with the tomato sauce in a saucepan. Add the chorizos, broth, mint, and salt. Cook gently, stirring occasionally and gently, about 5 to 8 minutes. Garnish with the cheese and sliced onions and serve immediately.

Yield: 4 servings.

Mexican Clam "Coctel"

2½ *dozen littleneck or small cherrystone clams*

1 *cup fresh, cored, unpeeled, red, ripe tomato cut into ½-inch cubes*
3 *tablespoons finely chopped onion*
1 *teaspoon finely chopped garlic*
1 *or 2 hot fresh long red or green chili peppers, preferably jalapeño peppers, chopped with their seeds*
¼ *cup fresh lime juice*
3 *tablespoons olive oil
Salt
Freshly ground black pepper*
⅓ *cup chopped fresh coriander*

1. Open the clams or have them opened and save both the clams and their juice.

2. Combine the clams and their liquid with the remaining ingredients. Serve in cocktail glasses with spoons.

Yield: 2 to 4 servings.

Food columns can take curious and unexpected turns. This article on Diana Kennedy grew out of a casual conversation in Mexico about English crumpets. We were interested in the subject matter and decided to make it the topic of what was projected to be a full-length discourse. When we happened to mention to Diana that we were overcome by a hunger for pozole, she offered to prepare it for us in the authentic manner during her visit to our home. While she was out in East Hampton, we happened to stop by the local fish market at the moment a fresh shipment of small clams arrived. We purchased a couple of dozen of the bivalves taken fresh from local waters and carried them home. Diana spoke with great enthusiasm of the marvelous clam "coctel" remembered from the years when she kept house in Mexico City. As it just happened to be lunchtime and we happened to have half a case of Mexican beer chilling in the refrigerator, what transpired, as is always the case when dining with Diana, was an occasion to remember.

Another bit of serendipity: The main point of Diana's visit being the English crumpet, she had arrived with crumpet rings, round bands of metal especially made for shaping crumpets, that she had purchased in England. We realized that locating these rings would prove an obstacle to Americans and while pondering this dilemma, we suddenly recalled the manuscript cookbook Mother had written many years ago. We searched in the pages of that book, and there, alongside a recipe for crumpets sent to her from a friend in England, was a handwritten notation, "Mason jar rings work very well for making these crumpets."

Subsequent to this article, which includes a recipe for Diana's pozole calling for half a pig's head and dried hominy, we received a letter from George Biderman of Manhattan who said, "I have been reading with some amusement your recent discussions and recipes for pozole, which we discovered in a different version at Gay Head, Martha's Vineyard, in 1950, and have been enjoying ever since. We were introduced to pozole through our friendship with a Gay Head family, the Adrian Vanderhoops, who had four beautiful daughters. One of these, Bertha, on a Mexican vacation, married a silversmith called José Giles. One evening, José prepared and cooked what he said was a favorite fiesta dish in his native village, which was somewhere south of Taxco.

"As José explained it, at fiesta time pozole stalls were set up in the street. The basic ingredient was a hog's head soup with whole hominy. This was served in a bowl. On the counter were the following ingredients, which each individual added to the shredded pork and hominy to his own taste: red chili pepper, oregano, diced onion, sliced lime, diced avocado, tacos, fried bacon rind, salt.

"Tequila was an obligatory aperitif and beer the equally obligatory accompaniment. José used canned whole hominy, Fritos, and the packaged fried bacon rind sold as a snack. Instead of a hog's head, he used a loin of pork. (The canned hominy is sold at Casa Moneo in Manhattan, although they sometimes have only the diced hominy, which is not an adequate substitute.)

"Ever since, pozole has been one of our favorite festive meals. My wife Beth has found that fresh ham serves as well as a loin for the shredded pork, and she added garlic to José's recipe for the broth.

"We serve broth, pork, and hominy in a large bowl to each guest; after that, they're on their own. We caution that the oregano be used sparingly at first, since we've found that it dampens the appetite when used in large quantities in this dish. It makes for a busy table as the ingredients are passed around and each person adjusts the ingredients to his taste, adding more lime juice or avocado or onion, for example, to contrast with the pork and hominy."

José Giles's Pozole
(Modified for 6 to 8 persons)

Pozole

1 4–5-pound fresh ham or
   pork loin
1 or 2 cloves garlic, crushed
2 tablespoons coarse salt
4 quarts water
4 14-ounce cans whole
   hominy

1. In a kettle, add the pork, garlic, salt, and water. Bring to the boil and simmer until meat is tender.

2. Remove pork and shred. Cool the broth and skim accumulated fat.

3. Put the pork in a large, flat baking dish and add approximately a soup ladle of broth to keep the pork moist. Cover with aluminum foil.

4. Bring remaining broth to boil again and add the hominy, discarding half the liquid in the cans. (This step may be reserved until just before serving.) Simmer 20 minutes.

5. Warm pork in oven before serving.

Extra ingredients

4 large limes, cut into
   eighths
4 medium-size avocados,
   diced into 1-inch chunks
1 large Spanish onion, diced
2 packages Fritos
2 packages fried bacon rind
¼ cup crushed red chili
   pepper
¼ cup oregano

1. To keep diced avocado, save the pit and place in serving dish with the diced avocado. This will prevent it from turning brown.

2. Place all other ingredients in appropriate serving dishes. If onion and lime are prepared in advance, cover with foil or plastic wrap.

Serving

1. In a large soup bowl, serve a small portion of shredded pork and hominy with enough broth to fill approximately half the bowl.

2. Instruct guests that they are to add ingredients gingerly until each finds the taste combination that suits his/her palate. Fried bacon rinds and Fritos may be crushed or added whole. Lime is squeezed for juice.

3. Free-for-all. Everyone is invited to help himself to experiment with combinations.

Note: All the quantities are approximations based on experience. If guests are delicate eaters, you'll have leftover pozole, which is delicious. If they are heavy eaters, add more meat and ingredients.

August 1975

I T MAY SEEM curious to a lot of casual readers if we say that one of the highs, one of the most engaging assignments in almost twenty years of writing about food for *The New York Times*, was a visit to Saigon shortly before the end of the Vietnam War. We are still haunted with remembrances of that visit, about which we wrote extensively in the first volume of this series. At that time, because of space limitations, it was possible to print only a fraction of the marvelous recipes we found during our brief stay in Vietnam.

One of the dishes we were to admire most entered our consciousness early one morning at a small crowded restaurant where we were taken by a native of the country who was intensely anxious that we sample the genuine and traditional food of his homeland. The dish is called pho ga and it is a staple in even the poorest homes. It consists basically of chicken broth, bits of chicken, rice noodles, and a glorious assortment of fresh herbs such as mint, basil, scallions, and fresh coriander leaves. The soup is served with a sauce called nuoc mam which is as essential to the Vietnamese palate as salt to Western cuisine. Unfortunately, the genuine sauce is available in only the most limited quantities in America since it is no longer imported. We have contrived an excellent substitute for that sauce using bottled fish sauce which may be purchased in most Chinese grocery stores in metropolitan areas. The soup on which we dined that morning was the basis for one of the most memorable meals of our lives. We would like to encourage you to try it for the briefest sample of what Vietnamese cookery is all about. The recipe for pho ga appears on page 269.

Spiked Pie

Years ago, a reader sent us a recipe for what was called a brandy Alexander pie. It consisted of a mousse or charlottelike filling flavored with brandy and crème de cacao poured into a graham-cracker-crumb crust before chilling. It proved to be one of the most popular desserts printed in *The New York Times* over a 10-year period. A short while ago we received a detailed compilation of similar pies with various cordial flavors. It was the contribution of an enormously resourceful reader from College Park, Maryland, Richard C. Taeuber. Mr. Taeuber submitted his list with the added information that "the pie freezes, or more important, thaws, quite well, which means that it can be made further in advance of use than the night before, as has been the custom in my home." The results of his prolonged kitchen experiments are reprinted here.

Dick Taeuber's Cordial Pie

1½ *cups crumbs (graham crackers, chocolate wafers, or gingersnaps)*
¼ *cup melted butter (⅓ cup with graham-cracker crumbs)*
½ *cup cold water*
1 *envelope unflavored gelatin*
⅔ *cup sugar*
⅛ *teaspoon salt*
3 *eggs, separated*
½ *cup of liqueurs or liquor, as directed on chart*
1 *cup heavy cream*
   Food coloring

1. Preheat oven to 350 degrees.

2. Combine crumbs with butter. Form in a 9-inch pan and bake for 10 minutes. Cool.

3. Pour the water in a saucepan and sprinkle gelatin over it. Add ⅓ cup sugar, salt, and egg yolks. Stir to blend.

4. Place over low heat and stir until gelatin dissolves and mixture thickens. DO NOT BOIL! Remove from heat.

5. Stir the liqueurs or liquor into the mixture. Then chill until mixture starts to mound slightly.

6. Beat egg whites until stiff, then add remaining sugar and beat until peaks are firm. Fold meringue into thickened mixture.

7. Whip the cream, then fold into mixture. Add food coloring if desired.

8. Turn mixture into crust. Add garnish, if desired. Chill several hours or overnight.

Yield: 6 servings.

Options

	Liquors (Equal parts, ½ cup total)	Crust (Graham can be used for any)	Garnish
1. Brandy Alexander	Cognac, brown crème de cacao	Graham cracker	Chocolate curls
2. Chocolate mint	White crème de menthe, brown crème de cacao	Chocolate cooky	Chocolate curls
3. Grasshopper	White crème de menthe, green crème de menthe	Chocolate cooky	
4. Eggnog	Rum	Gingersnap	Nutmeg
5. Banana mint	Crème de banana, white crème de menthe	Graham cracker	
6. Pink squirrel	Crème d'almond, white crème de cacao	Graham cracker	
7. Brown velvet	Triple sec, brown crème de cacao	Chocolate cooky	
8. Irish coffee	Irish whisky (use double strength coffee in place of water)	Graham cracker	
9. Golden dream	Galliano, Cointreau (use ¾ cup of orange juice in place of water, add 2 tablespoons grated orange peel)	Graham cracker	Toasted coconut
10. Midnight cowboy	Chocolate mint, brandy	Chocolate cooky	
11. Italian mousse	Chocolate mint, vodka	Chocolate cooky	
12. Fifth Avenue	Apricot brandy, brown crème de cacao	Chocolate cooky	
13. Raspberry Alexander	3 ounces raspberry brandy, 1 ounce white crème de cacao	Graham cracker	
14. Blackberry Alexander	3 ounces blackberry brandy, 1 ounce white crème de cacao	Graham cracker	
15. Banana chocolate cream	Crème de banana, white crème de cacao	Chocolate cooky	
16. George Washington	Chocolate mint, cherry brandy	Chocolate cooky	
17. Shady lady	Coffee-flavored brandy, triple sec (use coffee in place of water)	Chocolate cooky	
18. Cheri Suisse	Cherry Suisse (cherry chocolate)	Chocolate cooky	
19. Vandermint	Vandermint (chocolate mint)	Chocolate cooky	
20. Sabra	Sabra (orange chocolate)	Chocolate cooky	

Scrambled Stuffing

WITH PIERRE FRANEY

Several years ago we dined on an uncommonly interesting dish in an Italian restaurant in Boston. It was roast chicken with a custardlike stuffing that proved to be extremely palatable, not only because of its delicate flavor but also because of its tender, gossamerlike texture. We honestly don't recall the name of the restaurant and would not name it if we did, for it was otherwise undistinguished. After numerous tries in our kitchen, we discovered that the filling was nothing more than well-seasoned scrambled eggs, which, when cooked in the bird, achieved that sought-after and notably compelling stuffing. We further learned that a similar scrambled-egg filling, lightly seasoned with tarragon, is delectable in a veal roll.

Chicken Stuffed with Scrambled Eggs

5   *eggs*
¼   *cup heavy cream*
½   *teaspoon chopped tarragon*
    Salt and freshly ground
    black pepper
3½ *tablespoons butter*
1   *2½-pound chicken*
1   *small onion, peeled*

1. Preheat oven to 450 degrees.

2. Beat the eggs in a mixing bowl until well blended. Add the cream, tarragon, and salt and pepper to taste.

3. Heat 1 tablespoon butter in a skillet and add the egg mixture. Cook over low heat, stirring with a rubber spatula, until the eggs are almost set. Do not overcook. Remove from the heat. Stir in ½ tablespoon of butter. Cool.

4. Sprinkle the inside of the chicken with salt and pepper and stuff the chicken with the egg mixture. Truss the chicken. Sprinkle the outside with salt and pepper to taste.

5. Melt 2 tablespoons of butter in a shallow roasting pan and turn the chicken around in it until coated. Add the onion to the pan. Rest the chicken on one side and place it in the oven. Bake 15 minutes, basting occasionally.

6. Turn the chicken to the other side and continue baking about 15 minutes, basting occasionally. Turn the chicken once again and bake 15 minutes, basting often.

7. Untruss the chicken and carve it. Serve the stuffing on the side.

Yield: 4 servings.

Roast Veal Stuffed with Tarragon-Flavored Scrambled Eggs

1   *4-pound shoulder of veal, boned and with pocket*
6   *eggs*
1   *teaspoon dried tarragon Salt and freshly ground black pepper*
⅓   *cup heavy cream*
4   *tablespoons plus 1 teaspoon butter*
¼   *pound thinly sliced boiled or baked ham or prosciutto*
16   *small pickles, preferably cornichons (sour French gherkins), or a few larger sour or dill pickles*

2   *onions, about ½-pound, peeled and cut into thin rounds*
2   *carrots, about ½-pound, scraped and cut into thin rounds*
1   *clove garlic, cut in half*
1   *rib celery, cut into 1-inch lengths*

1. Preheat oven to 450 degrees.

2. Open up the roast for stuffing.

3. In a mixing bowl, combine the eggs with the tarragon, salt and pepper to taste, and heavy cream. Beat well until blended.

4. In a saucepan heat 1 tablespoon of butter and add the eggs. Cook, stirring, to the soft stage. Remove from the heat and stir in 1 teaspoon of butter.

5. Sprinkle the veal with salt and pepper. Line it well with the thin slices of ham, covering the open surface. Spoon the eggs up and down the center. Arrange the pickles down the center of the eggs. Overlap the edges of the meat so that they enclose the egg mixture. Tie securely up and down with string so that the stuffing does not come out.

6. Sprinkle the veal outside with salt and pepper.

7. Rub a flameproof baking dish with remaining 3 tablespoons of butter. Scatter the onions, carrots, garlic, and celery over the bottom of the dish. Add the veal. Heat the dish on top of the stove and put it in the oven. No liquid is necessary. Bake uncovered 1½ hours.

8. Cover with foil and bake 30 minutes longer, basting occasionally. Then reduce oven heat to 400 degrees.

9. Bake 30 minutes longer. Cut away the trussing string. Slice and serve with the natural juices and pan vegetables. Serve with buttered noodles or mashed potatoes.

Yield: 6 to 8 servings.

The recipe for stuffed chicken—the bird's cavity filled with scrambled eggs—struck a responsive note in the minds of numerous readers, particularly those of European background.

"The recipe for the chicken," Mrs. A. M. Aksoy of Sewickley, Pennsylvania, wrote, "brings to mind a Volhynian stuffing I learned to make before World War II while a student at the University of Krakow in Poland, and which I have encountered nowhere else. Very little seems to have been written about the cuisine of Poland, where, before the war at least, one could eat splendidly, ignoring completely kielbasa and pierogi. (Someone ought to write an article about the leached-out ethnicity of American ethnic groups!)

"An authentic Polish cook who taught me how to stuff chicken Volhynian-style was the late Mrs. Wilhelmina Stachowicz. She was the daughter of a Polish forester and grew up in southeastern Poland, now gobbled up by the Soviets. In her memory and on behalf of authentic Polish cuisine in general, I should like to pass on to you for your consideration chicken stuffed Volhynian-style."

We had the pleasure of testing Mrs. Aksoy's recipe in our own kitchen recently and, though it differs considerably from our version, we can label hers a Polish treasure.

Roast Chicken Volhynian-Style

1   3-pound chicken
    Salt and freshly ground
    black pepper
1   cup French or Italian
    bread, preferably a day or
    so old, cut into 1-inch
    cubes
¼   cup milk
2   cups loosely packed
    parsley leaves

1   chicken liver
6   tablespoons butter
2   eggs, separated
    Juice of ½ lemon

1. Preheat the oven to 425 degrees.

2. Sprinkle the chicken inside and out with salt and pepper.

3. Place the cubed bread in a bowl and add milk. Work with the fingers to remove lumps.

4. Put the parsley leaves and

chicken liver in the container of an electric blender or food processor and chop until fine.

5. Cream together 4 tablespoons of butter with the yolks. Add to this mixture the bread and parsley mixtures. Blend thoroughly. Add salt and pepper to taste.

6. Whip the whites until stiff and fold them into the stuffing. Stuff the cavity of the bird and if there is more, stuff it in the neck opening. Truss the bird.

7. Heat the remaining 2 tablespoons of butter in a heavy skillet and add the chicken, turning it in the butter. Place the chicken on one side and add the gizzard and neck if used. Add the lemon juice to the basting liquid. Roast 15 minutes and turn the chicken to the other side. Baste occasionally. Roast 15 minutes and turn the chicken on its back. Roast 15 minutes longer or until golden brown. Serve hot or cold.

Yield: 4 servings.

Barbara A. Pagano of Yorktown Heights, New York, wrote to say that "A stuffing similar to the one you had in Boston (perhaps it is the same) has been passed down in my family for several generations. I believe it originated with my great-grandmother, who came from Stigliano, near Salerno in Italy." The following measurements are approximate. The ingredients are combined and stuffed into the cavity of the bird.

Stuffing Stigliano

1   *pound ricotta cheese*
1   *large or 2 small eggs (the mixture should be firm, not wet, so 2 eggs might be too much)*

1   *cup fresh bread crumbs*
½   *cup grated Parmesan cheese*
    Salt and freshly ground black pepper
¼   *cup chopped parsley*
2   *tablespoons raisins, optional*

Jo Mottola of New York wrote, "This is an old Italian recipe which I have used for many years, and it was taught to me by my mother. My mother's father and mother came from Avellino (a small town near Naples). My mother also stuffed turkeys this way; a sort of Italian Thanksgiving specialty.

"I make it exactly as you described it only the seasonings are different. My mother has always made it with eggs, parsley, and Italian grated cheese. In recent years, I have made variations, and have added chopped sautéed mushrooms, which is just fabulous, and on other occasions chopped liver or crumbled bacon. Each time, however, the scrambled eggs always include parsley and Italian grated cheese."

Hot Summer, Hot Soup

WITH PIERRE FRANEY

One of the great dishes of summer is, curiously enough, a hot soup of Vietnamese origin—elegant, humble, and eminently edible. It is essentially a summer dish in that its goodness is based, as with so many Vietnamese dishes, on fresh raw herbs, which are now at their peak of flavor. The basic herbs for our version are the ones generally available in America—fresh basil and fresh mint along with fresh coriander, usually obtainable throughout the year in Chinese and Spanish markets. Made with rice noodles, the soup is called pho. When served with chicken, it is called pho ga; with beef it is pho bo.

Pho Ga

(Rice-noodle soup with chicken)

1   3–3½-pound chicken
     Water or, preferably,
     chicken broth to cover (see
     note)
16 to 20 fresh mint leaves
16 to 20 fresh basil leaves
16 to 20 fresh coriander leaves
1   cup chopped scallions
2   cups fresh bean sprouts
1   4-inch length of trimmed,
     peeled cucumber, optional
1   small red onion
1   tablespoon red wine
     vinegar
1   or 2 limes
1   or 2 long, hot, green or red
     chilies
1   cup nuoc mam sauce (see
     recipe) or pure nuoc mam
     or Chinese fish sauce
     straight from the bottle
     (see note)
½ teaspoon monosodium
     glutamate, optional

1   pound rice noodles,
     preferably Vietnamese or
     Thai (see note)
⅓ pound very lean and tender
     beef such as rib or shell
     steak, sliced as thinly as
     possible, optional (if beef is
     used, the name of this dish
     would be pho bo)
4   to 6 raw eggs, optional
     Freshly ground black
     pepper

1. Place the chicken in a kettle and add the water or, preferably, chicken broth to cover. Do not add salt. Bring to the boil and simmer about 20 minutes. Turn off the heat and let the chicken stand 30 minutes or so.

2. Meanwhile, rinse the mint, basil, and coriander leaves separately. Pat dry and arrange in separate bowls. Put the scallions in a bowl.

3. Pour boiling water over the bean sprouts. Drain immediately.

Rinse under cold water and drain. Arrange in a bowl.

4. Cut the cucumber into thin slices. Stack the slices and cut them into thin strips. Place in another bowl.

5. Peel the onion and slice it thin, top to bottom rather than crosswise into rings. Arrange the onion slices in a bowl and toss in the vinegar.

6. Cut the limes top to bottom and off center to avoid the seedy portion. Each lime should produce 4 seedless wedges. Arrange in a bowl or add them to the mint bowl.

7. Cut the chilies into ⅛-inch slices crosswise. Arrange in another bowl.

8. Add the nuoc mam or fish sauce to another bowl or to a pitcher.

9. Skin the chicken and remove the meat from the bones. Tear the meat into bite-size pieces.

10. Strain the broth and add it to a saucepan. Bring it to the boil and add the monosodium glutamate. Do not add salt. The fish sauce or nuoc mam will add the salty flavor. Add a little of the broth to the chicken meat to keep it moist.

11. When ready to serve, place the noodles in a large bowl and add boiling water to cover. If the water from the tap is steaming, that is hot enough. Let the noodles stand briefly and drain. Add more very hot water; let stand briefly and drain. Continue adding hot water and draining about 7 times or until noodles are thoroughly tender without being mushy. They overcook easily.

12. When ready to serve, arrange all the bowls of seasonings in the center of the dining table. Heat the chicken meat.

13. Drain the noodles and add equal portions to each of 4 to 6 hot soup bowls, the deeper the better to help retain the heat. Top with equal amounts of chicken. Ladle the boiling broth over all. If the beef is used, add equal amounts to each serving. If the eggs are used, put the meat on one side of the noodles and break an egg on the opposite side. Ladle the boiling broth over the meat and eggs. The eggs will remain almost raw; otherwise the eggs may be prepoached before adding to the bowls. Serve immediately. This dish must be eaten piping hot.

14. Let each participant at the table add seasonings, including lime juice, cucumber, freshly ground pepper, nuoc mam and so on, according to individual taste.

Yield: 4 to 6 servings.

Note: College Inn brand chicken broth, if available, is a preferred brand.

Bottled fish sauce and rice noodles are available in groceries and supermarkets in Chinese communities. Bottled nuoc mam is available by mail at Viet Nam Center, Inc., 3133 Wilson Boulevard, Arlington, Virginia 22201, and Saigon Market, Inc., 3147 Wilson Boulevard, Arlington, Virginia 22201.

Nuoc mam sauce

2   *tablespoons sugar*
¼   *cup water*

1   *cup fish sauce (see note)*
6   *¼-inch-thick slices peeled
    fresh ginger, finely
    chopped*
2   *cloves garlic, finely
    chopped*
1   *teaspoon hot red pepper
    flakes (or use a little
    cayenne to taste)*
3   *tablespoons lemon juice*

Combine all the ingredients and stir to blend. Place equal portions into individual bowls and serve with Vietnamese dishes. Leftover sauce may be kept refrigerated for a week or longer.

Yield: About 1½ cups.

Note: Fish sauce is widely available in Chinese groceries and supermarkets.

Seafood Trio

WITH PIERRE FRANEY

It has always seemed to us that fish and shellfish are more toothsome in the summer than in any other season of the year. We offer here a trio of fish and shellfish dishes contrived during the recent warm months. They include a fish soup delicately flavored with saffron; a creole dish with a base of tomatoes, onion, and sweet peppers plus capers; and a special fish and shellfish "stew," or ragout andalouse.

Fish Soup

3   tablespoons olive oil
1   cup chopped onion
1   teaspoon finely minced garlic
½   tablespoon loosely packed saffron stems
¼   cup flour
2   cups fish stock or water
2   cups peeled, chopped, red, ripe tomatoes, fresh or canned
1   cup dry white wine
1¼ pounds fillet of white-fleshed, non-oily fish such as weakfish or sea bass
1   pint scrubbed, well-cleaned mussels or very small littleneck clams
½   teaspoon dried thyme
1   cup heavy cream
    Salt and freshly ground black pepper
    Tabasco

1. Heat the oil in a kettle and add the onion, garlic, and saffron.

Stir in the flour, using a wire whisk.

2. Add the fish stock, tomatoes, and wine, stirring rapidly with the whisk. When blended, cook, stirring frequently, about half an hour.

3. Cut the fish into 1½-inch cubes (there should be about 3 cups). Add the fish and cook about 5 minutes or until fish flakes easily. Add the remaining ingredients and simmer about 5 minutes longer.

Yield: 8 servings.

Fish Creole

1¾ pounds skinless, boneless
     fish fillets such as
     weakfish, sea bass, cod, red
     snapper, or hake
6   tablespoons butter
1   cup quartered, thinly
     sliced onion
1   teaspoon chopped garlic
3   cups chopped green and
     red sweet peppers
     Salt and freshly ground
     black pepper
2   cups chopped fresh or one
     17-ounce can imported
     peeled tomatoes,
     preferably with tomato
     paste and basil
2   tablespoons capers
     Tabasco
¼   cup finely chopped parsley

1. Preheat oven to 450 degrees.

2. Cut the fish into 6 individual serving pieces and set aside.

3. Melt half the butter in a saucepan and add the onion. Cook, stirring, until wilted and add the garlic and sweet peppers. Sprinkle with salt and pepper to taste. Toss well and add the tomatoes, capers, Tabasco to taste, and parsley. Cover and cook 15 minutes. Uncover and cook 5 minutes longer.

4. Rub a baking dish with half the remaining butter and sprinkle with salt and pepper. Add the fish pieces and dot with the remaining butter. Spoon the sauce over and bake 15 minutes.

Yield: 6 servings.

Fish and Seafood Andalouse

4   pounds red and/or green
     sweet peppers
5   tablespoons butter
     Salt and freshly ground
     black pepper
1   tablespoon flour
1   cup fish stock (see note) or
     bottled clam juice
1   pound raw shrimp
1   pound fresh skinless and
     boneless weakfish or sea
     bass fillets or other white-
     fleshed, nonoily fish fillets
½   pound (1 cup) scallops
1   tablespoon chopped
     shallots
1   teaspoon loosely packed
     stem saffron or ½ teaspoon
     powdered saffron, optional
½   cup chopped, drained
     canned tomatoes,
     preferably imported plum
     tomatoes

1. Core and seed the peppers. Cut the peppers into ½-inch strips. There should be about 4 cups loosely packed.

2. Heat 2 tablespoons butter in a large skillet and add the peppers and salt and pepper to taste. Cook quickly, tossing and stirring, about 8 minutes. When ready, the peppers should be crisp but tender. Set aside.

3. Heat 1 tablespoon of butter and add the flour. Stir with a whisk until blended. Add the fish stock, stirring rapidly with the whisk. When the sauce is thickened and smooth, season to taste with salt and pepper. Set aside.

4. Peel and devein the shrimp. If they are large, cut them in half lengthwise. Set aside.

5. Cut the fish fillets into 1½-inch cubes. Set aside.

6. If bay scallops are used, leave them whole. If ocean scallops are used, cut them in half or quarter them. Set aside.

7. Heat remaining 2 tablespoons butter in a large skillet and add the shallots. Cook, stirring, and add the shrimp, fish, scallops, and peppers. Sprinkle with salt and pepper and cook, stirring as necessary, about 2 minutes. Add the saffron and tomatoes. Stir in the fish sauce.

8. Add salt and pepper to taste. Cover and cook about 3 minutes, no longer. Serve immediately with rice.

Yield: 8 to 10 servings.

Note: Fish stock is easily made with fish bones or perhaps the head with gills removed. Simply add water to cover the bones, chopped carrot, onion, celery, salt, pepper, and parsley sprigs. Simmer 20 minutes and strain. (If you prefer a more detailed recipe, see page 156). This dish is excellent made with mussels if available. The mussel liquid may be substituted for the fish stock. Put 2 pounds of cleaned mussels in a saucepan and add about ½ cup dry white wine. Cover and simmer until mussels open, 5 to 10 minutes. Drain and reserve the mussels and cooking liquid. Remove the mussels from the shell and set aside. Use 1 cup of the liquid for the fish sauce. Add the mussels to the dish for the last 3 minutes of cooking.

A Summer Picnic

Dear Diary: Well, it's the end of summer, and we guess the thing we remember most about it was Claudia's wedding. That's Claudia Franey, Pierre's daughter. She married a nice young man named Rick Jensen, and there was a big striped tent and 170 guests and a four-foot wedding cake that was made by Albert Kumin, one of the world's greatest pastry chefs. There were also six great chefs in the kitchen—Jacques Pépin, Jean Vergnes, Raymond Bruballa, Jean-Jacques Paimblanc, Jean-Louis Todeschini, plus the father of the bride. Roger Fessaguet, chef of La Caravalle, was tied up in traffic, but he got there in time for the wedding march. The chefs spent a couple of days—and a couple of nights, for that matter—preparing the food, a cold buffet with lots of aspic dishes and a hot buffet that included 10 fillets of beef with truffle sauce, 15 roasted racks of lamb and a chicken and veal Burgundy tart. The cold buffet, indecently delicious, included cold striped bass with salade russe, mussels vinaigrette, terrines of sweetbreads, pâtés of venison, galantines of duck, a salad of pork rind pâté (would you believe it is one of the greatest pâtés ever devised?), and garlic sausages with lentils. A most amusing thing happened the next day. We looked in the refrigerator and found enough leftover venison pâté and sweetbread terrine to feed a small crowd, so we called up some of our favorite picnic people (we've observed that there are some people who simply aren't picnic types) to come over for a feast and lots of them came with picnic food and wine. The weather looked threatening and the tent was still intact, so we decided to stage the picnic there. The guests included Josephine Premice and Jane White, the actresses, and Alfredo Viazzi, the restaurateur. There was Sam Aaron, the wine and spirits man (he owns Sherry-Lehmann), plus his wife, Florence, and Sarah Lewis, a grand cook and neighbor. Josephine made a seductive smoked herring vinaigrette, a Haitian dish; Florence brought a delectable cold salad of hard-cooked eggs with salmon, and Sarah showed up with her famous cold steamer clams with mustard mayonnaise appetizer plus her notable black beans vinaigrette and a fine chicken dish Mexican-style, which she had learned from the late Paula Peck. We rounded out the menu with tomatoes and anchovies vinaigrette. There seemed to be an awful lot of vinaigrette dishes, but then it was catch as catch can. Sam brought the picnic wines, a California white, Del Mar Ranch, Monterrey Vineyard, 1974; and a French Château de la Chaize, 1973. It wasn't the weather that threatened the day's bliss so much as the tent moving-men who loomed exceedingly large in the driveway. There is more than one way, we learned, to stall a tentmover's mission. With a dispatch that would have heartened Amphytrion, some glasses of wine were thrust into the moving-men's hands, and they were invited to dine and a couple of hours later we were still being urged not to rush.

Josephine Premice's Haitian Smoked Herring Salad

16   *dried, smoked herring fillets, about ⅓ pound (see note)*
1   *small red onion, peeled and cut into rings*
½   *carrot, scraped and cut into very thin julienne strips*
1   *hot green chili pepper, unseeded and thinly sliced into rings*
1   *cup white vinegar*
2   *cloves garlic, finely chopped*
¾   *cup peanut, vegetable, or corn oil*

1. Cut the herring in half widthwise. Place the herring in a saucepan and add cold water to cover. Bring to the boil and remove from the heat. Let stand 30 minutes or so. Drain.

2. Make layers of onion, carrot, and herring in a mixing bowl.

3. Combine the chili pepper, vinegar, and garlic in a saucepan and bring to the boil. Pour the mixture over the herring salad and add the oil. Refrigerate.

Yield: 6 to 8 servings.

Note: Dried smoked herring is available in many specialty shops that sell pickled fish products.

Sarah Lewis's Black Bean Salad

The beans

2 pounds dried black beans,
   preferably turtle beans
½ pound salt pork, cut into
   small cubes
2 cups finely chopped onion
1 cup chopped green pepper
1 tablespoon finely chopped
   garlic
½ teaspoon dried oregano
1 cup dry red wine

The vinaigrette sauce

2 tablespoons red wine
   vinegar
6 tablespoons olive oil
1 clove garlic, finely minced
1 teaspoon Dijon mustard
   Salt and freshly ground
   black pepper

1. Bring 3 quarts of water to the boil. Add the beans and return to the boil. Remove from the heat and let stand 1 hour.

2. Return the beans to the boil and simmer 1½ to 2 hours until beans are soft but not mushy.

3. Meanwhile, cook the salt pork in a heavy skillet until the fat is rendered and the pork is crisp. Remove the pork with a slotted spoon and set aside. To the fat in the skillet add the onion and cook 5 minutes, stirring. Add the green pepper, garlic, and oregano and continue cooking, stirring, until onions are golden. Add this to the beans. Add the red wine and bring to the boil. Simmer half an hour. Let cool.

4. Combine the ingredients for the vinaigrette sauce and stir it into the beans. Add more salt and pepper to taste, if desired, and chill.

Yield: 8 to 12 servings.

Paula Peck's Chicken Breasts Mexican-Style

6 whole chicken breasts,
   boned, skinned and cut
   into 1-inch squares
4 cloves garlic, finely minced
1 onion, finely chopped
2 cans peeled green chilies,
   chopped
3 tablespoons curry powder
½ cup brown beef gravy
1 teaspoon soy sauce
   Salt and freshly ground
   black pepper
2 teaspoons chopped fresh
   coriander, optional

1. Place the chicken pieces in a bowl. Combine the remaining ingredients and add to the chicken. Cover and refrigerate for at least 1 hour.

2. Preheat the broiler for 20 minutes. Arrange chicken in metal pan large enough to hold the pieces placed close together in one layer. Broil 6 minutes or until top is brown. Do not turn the pieces.

Yield: 6 servings.

Note: This recipe is from Paula Peck's *Art of Good Cooking* (Simon & Schuster, 1966, $7.50).

Florence Aaron's Salmon and Egg Salad

10   hard-cooked eggs
¼   to ½ pound thinly sliced
     smoked salmon
1   cup thinly sliced red onion
     rings
⅔   cup olive oil
½   cup chopped fresh dill
4   tablespoons wine vinegar
     Salt and freshly ground
     black pepper

1. Peel and slice the eggs. Cut the salmon into 1-inch pieces.

2. Arrange the egg slices in a dish and cover with pieces of smoked salmon. Sprinkle with onion rings, and ¼ cup chopped dill.

3. Blend the olive oil, vinegar, salt and pepper to taste and pour this over the salad. Let stand 2 hours before serving. When ready to serve, sprinkle with remaining chopped dill.

Yield: 6 to 8 servings.

Note: This dish is best if made a day in advance.

Tomato and Anchovies Vinaigrette

3   to 4 red ripe tomatoes,
    sliced
    Salt and freshly ground
    black pepper
8   anchovies, chopped
⅓ cup finely chopped parsley

2   tablespoons red wine
    vinegar
7   tablespoons olive oil

1. Arrange the tomatoes on a platter and sprinkle with salt and pepper. Scatter the chopped anchovies over the tomatoes and sprinkle with parsley.

2. Sprinkle the vinegar and oil over all.

Yield: 6 to 8 servings.

Steamer Clams with Mustard Mayonnaise

2   quarts soft-shell or steamer
    clams
2   tablespoons salt
3   tablespoons vegetable oil
½ to ¾ cup fresh mayonnaise
    (see recipe)
2   tablespoons imported
    mustard, such as Dijon or
    Düsseldorf

1. Place the clams in a large mixing bowl and add cold water to cover. Add the salt and oil and cover with a clean cloth. Let stand 6 or 7 hours. In time the clams will start to spew out a liquid.

2. Drain the clams and place them in a kettle. Add about 1 cup of cold water and cover. Bring to the boil and steam 5 to 10 minutes, or until the clams are partially opened. Drain and save the broth for drinking, if desired. Chill the clams.

3. Remove the clams from the shell and pull off the tough "shield" attached to each clam neck. Discard it. There should be about 2 cups of cleaned clams. If desired, the clams may be rinsed individually as they are cleaned to insure ridding them of any trace of sand. Drain the clams well.

4. Place the clams in a mixing bowl. Blend the mayonnaise and mustard. Add it to the clams and stir to blend.

Yield: 8 picnic servings.

Mayonnaise

1   *egg yolk*
    Salt and freshly ground
    black pepper
1   *teaspoon prepared*
    mustard, preferably an
    imported mustard such as
    Dijon or Düsseldorf
1   *teaspoon vinegar or lemon*
    juice
¾   *to 1 cup peanut, vegetable,*
    corn, or olive oil

1. Place the yolk in a mixing bowl and add salt and pepper, mustard, and vinegar.

2. Use a wire whisk or elec-tric beater. Put the oil in a measuring cup with a pouring spout. Gradually add the oil while beating vigorously with the whisk or electric beater. When approximately half the oil has been added, the remaining oil can be added more rapidly. It is best to use the full cup of oil. Add more salt to taste and, if desired, more vinegar or lemon juice. Chill.

Yield: 1 cup.

Bing Cherries with Liqueurs

2½   *quarts Bing cherries with*
     stem
⅔   *cup Cassis syrup, available*
     in wine and spirits shops
⅓   *cup framboise, available in*
     wine and spirits shops

Rinse the cherries and drain well. Place in a bowl and pour the liqueurs over them.

Yield: 8 or more servings.

In memory of Sarah Lewis's steamed clams, we will make an awful confession: We had never dined on a clam until we arrived in the big town of Chicago at the ripe old age of twenty-six. Now that we live in clam country with a house on Gardiner's Bay on the eastern tip of Long Island, we are fairly passionate clam eaters and sometime clam diggers. Needless to say, it was rather late in life that we learned the differences between hard-shell and soft-shell or steamer clams.

We have one great peeve about soft-shell clams and that is that they are, under the best of circumstances, devilishly sandy, even after numerous rinses in changes of water. We know all the old-fashioned techniques for getting rid of the sand—adding cornmeal to the water on the theory that the clams will eat the cornmeal while simultaneously disgorging the sand within; adding flour to the water, and so on. To our mind, the clams still come out sandy. The best technique we learned was from our Chinese cooking teacher Virginia Lee with whom we authored a Chinese cookbook. Virginia rinses the clams many times in very cold water and then puts them in a bowl with more cold water to cover. She then adds a few spoonfuls of salad oil to the bowl and lets it sit for a while at room temperature. After a few hours, the clams start spuming and spurting (to prevent suffocation, we suppose) and, in this manner, rid themselves of a maximum amount of sand.

We have indicated that instruction in Sarah Lewis's receipe for steamer clams and recommend it for any steamer clam recipe you may encounter. Because we loathe the feeling of even a single grain of sand between our teeth, we propose an even further refinement: if the clams, as in our recipe, are to be served cold, we rinse them once more after they are taken out of their shells.

The shell of a soft-shell clam is almost as fragile as that of an egg, whereas the hard-shell clam is, as its name implies, a lot harder. Hard-shell clams are marketed under three names: there are the table clams, which are, more often than not, served on a half shell or chopped and served with a white or red sauce on linguine or another form of pasta. The table clams can be either littlenecks, which are about one to two inches in width, or cherrystones, which are about two to three inches in width. The third type is the chowder clam which also goes by the American Indian name of Quahog. These clams are larger than three inches across at the widest part of the shell. They are tough when raw and are almost always cooked and chopped or ground before turning them into chowders and clam pies. Except for their size, all the hard-shell clams are the same, which is to say, a littleneck clam is simply a chowder clam as a baby. With rare exceptions, hard-shell clams do not contain internal sand. To prepare them, it is only necessary to rinse them briefly in cold water, no soaking necessary, and open. A brief discussion on opening clams can be found on page 23.

September 1975

IT IS AN indisputable fact that various flavors, some of which may be universal, are more closely identified with one culture than another. For example, as we have observed earlier in this book, the cooking of Vietnam is keenly based on fresh herbs such as mint, basil, and fresh coriander. The food of both the south of Italy and the south of France is staunchly based on garlic, olive oil, and tomatoes. The cooking of Mexico uses fresh chilies astutely but in depth, and it would be a far poorer cuisine without them.

In this month, we speak of the cooking of Greece and offer a brief discourse on the essential nature of lemon to the Greek kitchen. That realization first struck us when we traveled to Greece many summers ago with Leon Lianides, the proprietor of the distinguished Coach House restaurant in Manhattan, and his wife. Wherever we went, in Athens or through the islands of the Aegean, Leon, who is native born, would have a seizure of discomfort if he ever sat at a table and didn't have at least a wedge of lemon in sight. Some of the most delectable Greek food we've ever eaten has been in his home; the food prepared by his elegant wife, Aphrodite. Needless to say, in their kitchen the lemon literally flourisheth. Her avgolemono soup is sublime and as far as we recall, we were introduced to taramosalata, which is one of the world's most irresistible appetizers, in their home. Tarama is made with carp roe, olive oil, and, of course, lemon juice. *Avgo,* incidentally, is a Greek prefix for egg; *lemono* is a Greek suffix for the national staple.

Sorrel

A long time ago we developed a theory that most people who truly care about what they eat fall into two groups, those who invariably save the tastiest tidbit (the heart of watermelon, for example) for the very last bite; and those who gobble up the most flavorsome morsel of a dish at the moment of sitting down to dine.

Some time ago we read in a medical journal an amusing and enlightening explanation of such habits: "Guarding the most toothsome part of a meal for last could be an infantile expression of security; downing the best part first or eating excessively fast is a show of insecurity, the exhibition of a fear as to whether or not there will be a next meal."

We quite unequivocally belong to the group that saves the best to the end, working up slowly to that last exquisite swallow. We were reflecting on that this week while eying our small plot of herbs just outside the kitchen window of our place in East Hampton, Long Island.

With autumn in the van we continue to have a flourishing, emerald green patch of fresh sorrel growing between the tarragon and thyme and we are saving the sorrel among our herbs for the last of the best.

Oddly enough, with one notable exception, sorrel has never enjoyed the reputation in this country that it has in Europe. The exception is schav, a soup whose principal ingredient is sorrel and a dish most commonly appreciated, and associated with Russian and Polish Jews or those of Russian and Polish descent.

Schav is traditionally made with sorrel and chicken or veal broth plus eggs. The name of the soup derives from szczaw, the Polish word for the herb; the vulgar English name for sorrel is sour grass.

Next to schav, the most famous soup in the world containing sorrel is the French potage Germiny, also made with chicken broth and shredded sorrel, plus eggs as a thickener. It is one of the absolute marvels of soupdom and can be eaten hot or cold.

In decent soil sorrel grows like weeds, thus the name sour grass. The seeds are widely available in garden supply houses and in seed catalogues; the leaves, which are rounded and sometimes slightly pointed, resemble the leaves of young mustard or turnip greens and have a distinctly sour or acid taste. This acidity offers a welcome counterpoint to foods noted for their fat content, eel, for example, which is splendid in a green sauce cooked with sorrel, among other flavorings.

The name "sorrel" had its origins in a Teutonic word meaning sour and it is said to have been known to the inhabitants of ancient Egypt.

During the last decade as part of that much bruited thing called *la nouvelle cuisine,* fish (salmon in particular) cooked with sorrel has been very much in vogue and is associated in particular with the Troisgros Restaurant in Roanne, France. The French appellation for sorrel is oseille.

To tell the truth, the present small harvest of sorrel in our garden to be gathered for early autumn feasting is a third growth. The initial planting was in early spring and it has endured through two cuttings during the summer.

For what it is worth, fresh sorrel is more often than not cut into very thin shreds known as a chiffonade. The sorrel thus treated is then cooked briefly in butter and at this point it may be placed in tightly sealed containers; it will freeze well to be used with such abandon as quantity permits as the winter progresses.

Sorrel is enormously compatible with many foods. It is delectable when freshly shredded and served on tomatoes with oil and vinegar and a touch of salt. It harmonizes elegantly with the likes of chicken, fish and seafood as in the recipes offered here.

One added note: Most herbs have been catalogued with symbols. Sorrel is said to symbolize affection.

Potage Germiny

(A cream of sorrel soup with egg yolks)

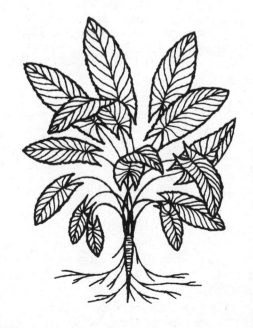

½ pound fresh sorrel
5 egg yolks, lightly beaten
1 cup heavy cream
⅛ teaspoon freshly grated nutmeg
3 cups hot chicken broth
1 tablespoon butter
Salt and freshly ground black pepper

1. Remove the leaves from the stems of the sorrel, leaving only portions of the stems that are very tender. Discard the tough stems.

2. Shred the sorrel leaves and set aside. The shredded leaves are called chiffonade. There should

be about 2 cups loosely packed.

3. In a saucepan, combine the yolks, cream, and nutmeg and stir with a whisk to blend. Add the hot broth and beat with the whisk over low heat. Cook, stirring, until thickened to the consistency of a light custard. Do not boil or the yolks will curdle.

4. In a small saucepan, heat the butter and add the chiffonade. Cook briefly, about 45 seconds, and sprinkle with salt and pepper to taste. The sorrel will discolor. Add this to the soup and bring just to the boil. Serve piping hot.

Yield: 6 to 8 servings.

Striped Bass
with Sorrel

6   *tablespoons butter*
1   *4–6 pound striped bass,*
    scaled, cleaned and gills
    removed
    Salt and freshly ground
    black pepper
3   *mushrooms, sliced*
½   *cup thinly sliced or*
    chopped shallots
½   *cup chopped onion*
1   *bay leaf*
3   *sprigs fresh thyme or 1*
    teaspoon dried
6   *sprigs parsley*
2   *cups dry white wine*
2   *cups heavy cream*
2   *cups shredded sorrel or*
    finely diced mushrooms
1   *egg yolk*

1. Preheat the oven to 425 degrees.

2. Butter a baking sheet with 2 tablespoons butter.

3. Sprinkle the fish inside and out with salt and pepper to taste. Place the fish on the baking sheet and dot it with 3 tablespoons butter. Scatter the mushrooms, shallots, and onion around the fish. Place the bay leaf, thyme, and parsley in the cavity of the fish.

4. Pour the wine over and around the fish and cover closely with heavy-duty aluminum foil. Place in the oven and bake 20 to 30 minutes. Remove the foil and continue baking 20 to 30 minutes longer.

5. Pour off the cooking liquid and the vegetables with herbs into a saucepan. Cover the fish and keep it warm while preparing the sauce.

6. Reduce the cooking liquid to ½ cup. Strain it into a skillet. Add 1½ cups heavy cream and cook, stirring, about 15 minutes. The sauce should be reduced to about 1 cup.

7. Meanwhile, heat the remaining tablespoon of butter and add the sorrel or mushrooms. Cook until sorrel is wilted. Or cook the mushrooms until almost all the liquid evaporates. Add this to the sauce.

8. Blend the remaining ½ cup cream with the egg yolk. Add it to the sauce and cook briefly without boiling.

9. To serve the fish, it is preferable to remove the small bone line down the back of the fish plus the skin of the fish. Both are easily removed simply by pulling and scraping neatly with the fingers.

Serve the fish in individual serving portions with a little of the hot sauce spooned over.

Yield: 6 to 10 servings.

Sautéed Chicken with Sorrel

2　2½–3-pound chickens, cut into serving pieces
　Salt and freshly ground black pepper
2　tablespoons butter
1　tablespoon olive oil
4　to 5 cups loosely packed sorrel leaves
3　tablespoons finely chopped shallots
1　cup dry white wine
½　cup plus ⅓ cup heavy cream
1　egg yolk

1. Sprinkle the chicken pieces with salt and pepper.

2. Heat the butter and oil in a heavy skillet with a lid. Add the chicken pieces skin side down, and cook about 5 minutes or longer until golden brown. Turn the pieces and reduce the heat. Cook about 10 minutes, uncovered.

3. Meanwhile, stack the sorrel leaves and cut them into fine shreds. This is called a chiffonade of sorrel. Set aside.

4. Scatter the shallots around the chicken pieces and cook briefly. Sprinkle the chicken with the chiffonade and add the wine. Cover and cook about 5 minutes. Uncover and add ½ cup of cream.

Turn the chicken pieces in the sauce, but leave them skin side up. Cover and remove from the heat.

5. When ready to serve, uncover. Cook the chicken in the sauce over high heat about 5 minutes. Blend the remaining ⅓ cup of cream with the egg yolk and stir it into the sauce. Cook just until the sauce bubbles up. Do not cook longer or the sauce may curdle. Serve the chicken with the sauce spooned over.

Yield: 6 servings.

Shrimp with Sorrel

1¾　pounds raw shrimp, in the shell
1　pound fresh sorrel (see note)
5　tablespoons butter
⅓　cup finely chopped onion
3　tablespoons finely chopped shallots
1　tablespoon flour
1　cup dry white wine
3　tablespoons tomato paste
2　cups heavy cream
　Salt and freshly ground black pepper
¼　cup cognac or bourbon
2　egg yolks
　Toast rounds, optional (see note)

1. Peel and devein the shrimp. Rinse well and pat dry. Reserve the shrimp shells.

2. Pick over the sorrel, remove and discard any tough stems. Rinse well and pat dry. On a flat surface, cut the sorrel into fine shreds. This is called a chiffonade. Set aside.

3. Heat 2 tablespoons butter in a small, deep skillet and add the shrimp shells, stirring. Cook briefly and add the onion and shallots. Cook about 2 minutes, stirring frequently, and sprinkle with flour, stirring. Add the wine and tomato paste, stirring until well blended. Cook about 5 minutes.

4. Add the cream and cook about 5 minutes over high heat. Strain through a sieve, pushing down to extract as much liquid as possible from the solids.

5. Heat 1 tablespoon of butter in a small saucepan and add the sorrel. Cook, stirring, just until wilted.

6. Heat the remaining butter in a saucepan and add the shrimp. Sprinkle with salt and pepper and cook briefly, stirring, just until the shrimp change color. Add the cognac and ignite it. When the flame dies down, stir in the cream sauce and sorrel. Bring to the boil and simmer about 1 minute.

7. Beat the yolks and add a little of the hot sauce, stirring constantly. Return the mixture to the sauce and stir without boiling. Remove from the heat immediately. Serve on toast rounds.

Yield: 6 to 8 servings.

Note: If sorrel is not available, substitute one tablespoon chopped fresh tarragon or dill, but do not cook the herb before adding. Or sprinkle with chopped chives before serving.

The best way to make toast rounds is to cut fresh white bread slices with a bread cutter. Brush with butter and bake in a 400-degree oven until toasted.

Delectably Greek

WITH PIERRE FRANEY

Lemon is the vanilla of Greek cooking. We have certain Greek friends who would sooner do without salt than the juice of a freshly squeezed lemon. This fondness for the sour citrus is nowhere more apparent in the Greek kitchen than in those celebrated dishes that bear the name avgolemono. Avgolemono (the name derives from avgo, meaning egg, plus lemon) comes in the form of soups and sauces, and one of the best uses to which it can be put is as a sauce for stuffed cabbage. A recipe for the cabbage and sauce is given here, accompanied by recipes for an assortment of complementary dishes and a menu.

Melitzanes me yiaourti
(Eggplant and yogurt salad)

Angourosalata me yiaourti
(Cucumber and yogurt salad)

Taramosalata
(Carp-roe spread)

Lahanodoimathes avgolemono
(Stuffed cabbage with egg and lemon sauce)

Baklava

Iced Ouzo
Retsina wine

Melitzanes me Yiaourti

(Eggplant and yogurt salad)

---

2 cups plain yogurt
1 eggplant, about 1¼ pounds
3 tablespoons chopped fresh dill
½ cup chopped scallions
1 clove garlic, finely minced
3 tablespoons olive oil
   Juice of ½ lemon
   Salt

1. Line a mixing bowl with cheesecloth and empty the yogurt into it. Bring up the edges of the cheesecloth to make a bag. Tie the bag with string and suspend the bag over the bowl to let the yogurt drip. Let stand in a cool place 2 or 3 hours. The yogurt will become thick like sour cream.

2. Meanwhile preheat the oven to 375 degrees. Place the eggplant on a square of aluminum foil and bake about 1 hour until the eggplant is totally soft throughout.

3. Remove the eggplant and let it cool. Peel it. Place the soft interior of the eggplant in the bowl of an electric beater. Beat on high speed. Add the yogurt and continue beating to blend well. Add the remaining ingredients and chill thoroughly. Garnish, if desired, with tomato wedges and imported Greek olives.

Yield: 4 to 6 servings.

Lahanodolmathes Avgolemono

(Stuffed cabbage with egg and lemon sauce

---

2 heads cabbage, about 2
   pounds each
   Salt
1½ cups milk
¼ cup raw rice
1 pound ground lamb
⅓ cup finely chopped onion
3 tablespoons chopped fresh
   dill or 1 teaspoon dried
½ teaspoon ground cinnamon
   Freshly ground black
   pepper
6 tablespoons olive oil
1 teaspoon dried oregano
2 cloves garlic, chopped
½ cup coarsely chopped
   onion
2½ cups chicken broth
3 egg yolks
⅓ cup lemon juice

1. Pull off the tough outer leaves from the head of cabbage. Use a knife to cut away the tough white center core. Drop the cabbage into boiling salted water to cover and let cook about 5 min-

utes, or until the leaves separate easily. Invert the cabbage in a colander and let stand until cool and thoroughly drained.

2. Combine 1 cup of the milk and the rice in a small saucepan and bring to the boil. Stir and cover. Cook over low heat until all the liquid is absorbed and the rice very soft. Stir as necessary. Uncover and let cool.

3. Combine the lamb with the rice, finely chopped onion, dill, cinnamon, salt and pepper to taste, 2 tablespoons olive oil, remaining ½ cup of milk, and oregano.

4. Separate the leaves of cabbage and pat dry. Use a sharp knife to make a V cut at the tough center end of each large leaf. Leave the tender smaller leaves intact. Rinse out a large square of cheesecloth in cold water, then squeeze dry and place on a flat surface. In the center place a large cabbage leaf, curly edge up. Arrange a smaller cabbage leaf in the center of the large leaf. Spoon 1 or 2 tablespoons of the filling into the center of the small leaf.

5. Bring the 4 corners of cheesecloth together and twist the ends together over a bowl. This will shape the leaves into a compact round. Remove the cabbage ball from the cheese cloth. It will not be necessary to use any string. Continue making the balls until all the cabbage leaves and filling are used.

6. Shred any remaining cabbage leaves.

7. Heat the remaining 4 tablespoons of oil in a heavy casserole

or Dutch oven large enough to hold the stuffed cabbage rolls in one layer. Add the garlic, coarsely chopped onion, salt to taste, and shredded cabbage. Arrange the stuffed cabbage seam side down and sprinkle with salt and pepper to taste. Add the chicken broth and bring to the boil. Cover and cook until the cabbage is tender, 1 to 1½ hours.

8. Pour off and save the cooking liquid. Keep the cabbage warm. Skim fat from cooking liquid. Pour reserved cooking liquid into a saucepan and reduce it to about 1½ cups.

9. Beat the yolks and lemon juice together. Add them, off heat, to the sauce, stirring rapidly. Return sauce to the burner and bring it just to the boil, stirring, but do not boil or it will curdle. Serve the sauce over the cabbage.

Yield: 16 to 18 cabbage rolls.

Taramosalata
(Carp-roe spread)

2 or 3 slices fresh bread
1½ tablespoons water
1 10-ounce jar tarama (1¼ cups), available in Greek groceries and stores that specialize in imported Oriental foods
   Juice of ½ lemon
1 cup olive oil

1. Trim the crusts from the bread and cut the bread into ½-inch cubes. There should be about ½ cup. Place the bread in a bowl and add the water. Add half a cup of tarama and the lemon juice.

2. Start beating the mixture with an electric mixer. Add the oil in a thin stream. The sauce should thicken like mayonnaise.

3. Beat in the remaining tarama. Spoon into a serving dish and chill thoroughly.

Yield: About 2½ cups.

Angourosalata me Yiaourti
(Cucumber and yogurt salad)

3 cups plain yogurt
1 cup peeled, seeded, diced cucumber
   Salt
2 cloves garlic, finely minced
1 tablespoon chopped fresh dill
¼ cup olive oil
2 teaspoons wine vinegar

1. Line a bowl with cheesecloth and empty the yogurt into it. Bring the edges of the cheesecloth together and tie to make a bag. Suspend the bag over the bowl and let drain for an hour or longer. The yogurt will take on a much thicker consistency, like heavy cream.

2. Empty the yogurt into a clean bowl and add the remaining ingredients. Blend thoroughly. Chill well.

Yield: About 2½ cups.

Side Dish, Front and Center

WITH PIERRE FRANEY

The standard procedure in menu planning is, of course, to determine an entrée and then select an assortment of foods to complement it. There are times, however, when we find a so-called lesser or side dish so tempting it is worth contriving a main dish to go with it. That is the way we felt recently after preparing a traditional grated potato dish we discovered while perusing a faded volume by Austin de Croze, *The Regional Dishes of France,* published in the early 1920s. The recipe, attributed to the region of Morvan, came from a Mme. Laurent of the Château Chinon, so we have dubbed it potatoes Château Chinon. The main dish we offer is a pot roast.

French Pot Roast with Red-Wine Sauce

- 1 *5–6-pound round beef roast*
- ½ *cup red wine vinegar*
- 2¼ *cups chopped onion*
- 2¼ *cups chopped carrots*
- 1⅓ *cups chopped celery*
- 2 *cups chopped leeks, optional*
- 2 *cloves garlic, crushed*
- 3 *sprigs parsley*
- 1 *teaspoon each of leaf sage, dried rosemary, marjoram, and coriander seeds*
- 4 *to 5 cups dry red wine Salt and freshly ground black pepper*
- ¾ *cup diced salt pork or 2 tablespoons vegetable oil*
- ¼ *cup flour*
- 2 *cups beef broth Potatoes Château Chinon (see recipe)*

1. Place the beef in a mixing bowl.

2. Combine the vinegar, 1½ cups each chopped onion and carrots, 1 cup of celery, the leeks, garlic, and parsley in a saucepan. Tie the sage, rosemary, marjoram, and coriander seeds in a cheesecloth bag and add the bag. Bring to the boil, stirring.

3. Pour the vinegar mixture over the meat and add enough wine to barely cover the meat. Sprinkle with salt and pepper to taste. Cover closely and refrigerate overnight or longer, up to 3 days.

4. Remove the meat and pat it

dry. Strain and reserve 3 cups of the liquid. Discard the remaining liquid and vegetables.

5. Heat the pork in a heavy Dutch oven or casserole and cook, stirring, until it is rendered of fat. Scoop out and discard the solids.

6. Sprinkle the beef with salt and pepper. Add it to the Dutch oven or casserole and brown well on all sides. Transfer the meat to a warm place.

7. Add remaining ¾ cup each of chopped onion and carrots and remaining ½ cup of celery. Cook, stirring, until onion is wilted. Sprinkle with the flour and stir to blend thoroughly. Add the reserved marinade and beef broth, stirring with a wire whisk. When the mixture is thickened, add the meat. Cover closely and cook over low heat about 3 hours or until the roast is thoroughly tender.

8. Remove the meat and keep it warm. Cook the sauce down to the desired consistency. Slice the meat and serve with the sauce and with potatoes Château Chinon.

Yield: 6 to 10 servings.

Potatoes Château Chinon

5 potatoes, about 1¾ pounds
   Salt
2 eggs, lightly beaten
2 tablespoons flour
⅛ teaspoon grated nutmeg
½ cup cheese, Gruyère or Swiss, cut into the finest possible dice
4 tablespoons oil

1. Peel the potatoes and grate them, using the fine blade of the grater. Spoon the potatoes into cheesecloth and squeeze to extract most of the moisture. There should be about 1¾ cups of pulp remaining.

2. Empty the potato pulp into a bowl and add salt to taste, the eggs, flour, and nutmeg. Add the cheese and blend well.

3. Heat the oil in a skillet and drop the potato mixture into the skillet, using about 3 tablespoons at a time. Cook until golden on one side; turn and cook on the other side.

Yield: 6 to 8 servings.

The foregoing article on the makings of what might be called a French potato pancake elicited an impressive response from readers. In fact, to judge from the volume of correspondence received on the subject, it would seem that potato pancakes are as dear as cheesecake to the New York appetite. Susan Kopald of La Gourmande, a cooking school and pots-and-pans shop in Forest Hill, Fort Montgomery, New York, wrote and enclosed a potato-pancake recipe based on one that was her grandmother's.

"I have added the parsley, which I think gives the pancakes a great flavor," she said. "Also, I feel that the secret to the Old World potato pancake is in the matzo meal."

Susan Kopald's Potato Pancakes

6 *Idaho or Russet potatoes (medium to large)*
2 *large yellow onions*
2 *eggs, slightly beaten*
4 *to 6 tablespoons matzo meal*
   Salt and white pepper
4 *tablespoons minced fresh parsley*
   Vegetable oil

1. Grate the potatoes and onions in a food processor, but do not puree them. They must be rough. Put in a mixing bowl.

2. Add the eggs and matzo meal. Add the seasonings and parsley.

3. Fry the pancakes in vegetable oil in a skillet or on a greased griddle until golden brown. The pancakes should be thin.

Yield: 4 to 6 servings.

Note: When you are ready to fry the second batch, it may be necessary to add more matzo meal to the potato mixture to absorb some of the accumulated liquid. If these are eaten as a meal with a salad, they are often served with homemade applesauce; that is the tradition.

We then heard from a Manhattan acquaintance who said that "The recipes that call for onions, flour, bread crumbs, matzo meal, and other fillers are rubbish. A true potato pancake, though it takes more work and time, is prepared, according to the gospel passed on to my wife from my mother, as follows:

"Hand-grate the potato into a colander. This allows excess water and starch to drain. Completing this, empty the colander into a large bowl. Add 1 egg per potato, salt, and stir until well blended.

"In frying, never use peanut oil. It smells. Cover the frying pan with about ⅛ inch oil and heat. Drop the mixture into the hot oil, cook until golden. Never brown.

"Those claiming that not adding flour or bread crumbs will leave the mixture runny are those who do not drain the potatoes. These ingredients were added by the poor to stretch the potatoes. A European version of Hamburger Helper. The eggs are enough of a binder to prevent running."

Pauline Gleichenhaus of the Bronx sent us her favorite potato pancake recipe, one which she says she has "used for more years than I care to remember. If prepared and used immediately," she continues, "the potatoes do not get soggy. They are also not peeled, which seems to make them crisper." Here is the Gleichenhaus version:

Potato Pancakes

3 *medium-size Idaho*
   potatoes, about 1 pound
1 *small onion, about ¼*
   pound, optional
1 *large egg*
2 *tablespoons flour*
¼ *cup bread crumbs*
   Salt and freshly ground
   black pepper
¼ *cup peanut, vegetable, or*
   corn oil

1. Rinse the potatoes well and dry them. Do not peel. Cut the potatoes into ½-inch cubes. There should be about 2 cups.

2. Peel and chop the onion.

Add the potatoes, onion, and egg to the container of a food processor or electric blender and blend to make a coarse puree. Do not overblend.

3. Spoon the mixture into a bowl and add the flour, bread crumbs, salt and pepper to taste. Blend well. If the mixture proves to be thin, it may be necessary to add up to a teaspoon more flour.

4. Heat a small amount of oil in a skillet and spoon about ⅛ of the potato mixture into the skillet. Cook until brown on one side and turn to brown on the other side. Continue making pancakes, adding more oil as necessary, until all the potato mixture is used.

Yield: 8 potato pancakes.

Susan Renoir of Manhattan, champion of her own version, wrote to say that "All of this controversy regarding potato pancakes is silly. The ultimate potato pancake is the zucchini potato pancake made according to the following recipe. Hope this settles the issue!"

Zucchini-Potato Pancakes

4 *boiling potatoes*
2 *medium zucchini*
2 *eggs, lightly beaten*
1½ *tablespoons flour*
¼ *teaspoon baking powder*
1 *teaspoon salt*
   Freshly ground black
   pepper
2 *tablespoons finely grated*
   onion
   Oil for frying

1. Peel the potatoes, grate

coarsely, and drop into cold water.

2. Trim zucchini, grate coarsely, and put in a mixing bowl.

3. Drain potatoes thoroughly, squeezing between towels and add to zucchini.

4. Add eggs. Blend the flour, baking powder, salt, and pepper, and stir into potato-zucchini mixture. Stir in grated onion.

5. Shape the mixture into patties. Heat the oil and fry on both sides until golden brown. Drain and serve immediately.

Yield: 6 to 8 servings.

Chef Wen Dah Tai

Keenly observant students of Chinese cookbooks printed in English may note that a dominant number of recipes calling for beef specify flank steak. Similarly, a vast majority of the recipes calling for stir-fried dishes made with beef, pork, chicken, shrimp, or whatever call for the addition of one or more egg whites. We were, therefore, vastly amused, a short while ago, when someone asked us, "What, in the name of heaven, happens to the rest of the beef and the yolks of the eggs?" It was a thought we had not previously pondered, and it took the occasion of a visit to our kitchen of one of New York's finest Chinese chefs to find out.

The chef is Wen Dah Tai, better known as Uncle Tai, chef of and a principal in Uncle Tai's Hunan Yuan, 1059 Third Avenue (between 62d and 63d Streets).

He is Peking-born, 56 years old, and is known as uncle, we discovered, because uncle is a title of respect in his native land. Hunan is, of course, the Chinese province whose food is, like that of Szechuan, characteristically fiery-hot to the palate. Proprietors of Hunanese restaurants tend to claim it is even more so.

Uncle Tai has numbered among his clientele such figures as Danny Kaye and Robert Redford, Shirley MacLaine, Rusty Staub, Jacqueline and the late Aristotle Onassis.

The chef, who is sober-minded and portly, told us over a cup of tea that flank steak in America most closely resembles in flavor and texture the hip steak that is most commonly used in China and Formosa. He hastened to add—through an interpreter, he does not speak English—that the remainder of the cow was in no sense wasted or ignored in the Chinese kitchen.

"The fillet, which is the most expensive, is always cut into neat cubes and used in high-class banquet dishes; the shin of beef, the juiciest part of the beef, goes into a cold appetizer, five-flavored beef; and the rest of the animal goes into casserole dishes." Beef, he added, is expensive in China, which is one reason for the number of pork and chicken dishes on Chinese menus.

As for those egg yolks, they are directed toward fried rice, a few tons of which are consumed in Chinese restaurants throughout America each day.

Chef Tai, who is married and has four children, said that his wife was an excellent cook to whom he had never offered instruction. But when they entertain, it is more often than not in a restaurant.

The gentleman came to visit us in the company of Norman Chi, the maître d'hôtel and partner in the restaurant, who acted as interpreter. (Mr. Chi, as it turns out, has an interesting background on Broadway. A producer once thought he looked Japanese and engaged him to act as an understudy for the lead in John Patrick's play, "Teahouse of the August Moon." He starred in the role for 80 performances.)

We learned that hot Hunanese cooking is not only a professional outlet, it is a predilection for the chef. "Each night," Mr. Chi informed us, "we dine together on dishes that contain lots of garlic, scallions and hot pepper." They attribute the association of hot, spicy food and Hunan, to the province's climate, which is very damp.

"It is empirically true that hot food pleases the body and appetite in hot, humid climates," Mr. Chi observed.

We learned the chef's unwavering yardstick for determining the quality of a Chinese restaurant. "If a meat dish is prepared with 70 percent meat and 30 percent vegetables, the restaurant is probably first class, all other things being equal; if the ratio is fifty-fifty, the place is probably mediocre. If the meat-to-vegetable ratio is reversed, stay away."

Norman Chi, right, watches with some fascination as Uncle Tai meticulously slices fresh ginger.

During the course of his stay in our kitchen, the chef prepared several of his restaurant's most prestigious dishes including duck with young ginger; lamb with scallions; Uncle Tai's beef; Uncle Tai's shrimp, and shredded chicken with bean sprouts.

Several of the chef's cooking concepts were apparent throughout the day. Most of the initial preparation for several of his dishes requires blending the meat or seafood or whatever with cornstarch and egg white. These dishes are best left to marinate in the refrigerator overnight before cooking. Bicarbonate of soda is frequently added to beef dishes although the meat must be thoroughly rinsed to remove any flavor of soda before cooking. The soda tends to tenderize the beef.

He invariably uses the "pass through once" cooking technique. This is a technique that involves dropping the cornstarch-and-egg-white blended foods into warm-to-slightly hot fat and stirring vigorously and briefly to separate the bite-size pieces prior to a final cooking. The food is only partially cooked and the purpose is to prevent the pieces from sticking together during the final cooking, which is done in seconds.

Uncle Tai's Beef

1½   pounds flank steak
⅔   cup plus 3 tablespoons water
½   teaspoon bicarbonate of soda
¼   teaspoon salt
3   tablespoons dry sherry or shao hsing wine
1   egg white
3½   tablespoons cornstarch
4   cups plus 2 tablespoons peanut, vegetable, or corn oil
2   scallions, cut into ½-inch lengths, about ⅓ cup
3   tablespoons dried orange peel (see note)
3   thin slices fresh ginger, cut into ½-inch cubes
1   long, thin, fresh, hot red pepper, chopped, optional
3   tablespoons soy sauce
¼   teaspoon monosodium glutamate, optional
2   tablespoons sugar
1   teaspoon sesame oil
¼   cup chicken broth
10   dried small hot red pepper pods

1. Place the flank steak on a flat surface and, holding a sharp knife parallel to the beef, slice it in half widthwise. Cut each half into very thin strips, about ¼ inch each. There should be about 4 cups loosely packed.

2. Place the beef in a mixing bowl and add ⅔ cup water blended with the bicarbonate of soda. Refrigerate overnight or for at least 1 hour. When ready to cook, rinse the beef thoroughly under cold running water. Drain thoroughly and pat dry.

3. To the meat add the salt, 1 tablespoon wine, and egg white.

Stir in a circular motion until the white is bubbly. Add 1½ tablespoons of cornstarch and 2 tablespoons of oil. Stir to blend.

4. Combine the scallions, dried orange peel, fresh ginger, and fresh red pepper. Set aside.

5. Combine the remaining 2 tablespoons wine, soy sauce, monosodium glutamate, sugar, remaining 2 tablespoons of cornstarch blended with remaining 3 tablespoons water, sesame oil and chicken broth. Stir to blend.

6. Heat remaining 4 cups of oil in a wok or skillet and when it is almost smoking, add the beef. Cook about 45 seconds, stirring constantly, and scoop it out. Drain the meat well, but leave the oil in the wok, continuously heating. Return the meat to the wok and cook over high heat about 15 seconds, stirring. Drain once more. Return the meat a third time to the hot oil and cook, stirring. Drain the meat. The purpose of this is to make the meat crisp on the outside but retain its juiciness within.

7. Drain the wok completely. Return 2 tablespoons of the oil to the wok and add the hot pepper pods, stirring over high heat until brown and almost blackened, about 30 seconds. Remove. Add the scallion mixture and stir. Add the beef and cook, stirring constantly, about 10 seconds. Add the wine mixture, stirring, and cook about 15 seconds until piping hot and the meat is well coated.

Yield: 4 to 8 servings.

Note: Dried orange peel is available in many oriental grocery and spice stores. It may be made at home, however, by peeling an orange, eliminating as much of the white pulpy part as possible. The peel is cut into pieces, placed on a baking sheet and baked in a 200-degree oven until dried. It may be stored for months in a tight container.

Uncle Tai's Shrimp

10	giant shrimp, about 1¼ pounds, available in Chinese fish markets
4½	tablespoons dry sherry or shao hsing wine
2	egg whites
4	cups plus 1½ tablespoons peanut, vegetable, or corn oil
½	teaspoon salt
2½	tablespoons cornstarch
2	scallions, white part only, trimmed and shredded
5	very thin slices fresh ginger, shredded
2	tablespoons water
2	tablespoons soy sauce
2½	tablespoons white vinegar
2	tablespoons sugar
½	teaspoon sesame oil
⅓	cup chicken broth
½	cup loosely packed fresh coriander

1. Peel the shrimp and split them in half. Rinse well to remove the dark vein. Pat dry.

2. Place the shrimp in a mixing bowl and add 1½ tablespoons wine, the egg whites, and 1½ tablespoons oil. Stir in a circular motion until whites become bubbly and add half the salt and 1½ tablespoons cornstarch. Stir to blend.

3. Prepare the scallions and ginger and set aside.

4. Combine the remaining 3 tablespoons wine, remaining 1 tablespoon cornstarch blended with the water, soy sauce, vinegar, sugar, remaining salt, sesame oil, and chicken broth.

5. Heat remaining 4 cups of oil in a wok or skillet and add the shrimp, one at a time. Cook about 1 minute and scoop out, leaving the oil in the wok, continuously heating. Return the shrimp to the oil and cook about 30 seconds. Drain wok completely.

6. Return about 1 tablespoon of oil to the wok and add the scallions and ginger, stirring constantly. Cook about 5 seconds and add the shrimp and the vinegar mixture. Toss and stir until piping hot and the shrimp coated evenly. Serve garnished with coriander leaves.

Yield: 4 to 8 servings.

Shredded Chicken with Bean Sprouts

2 or 3 large chicken breasts, about 2 pounds
  Salt
3½ tablespoons dry sherry or shao hsing wine
2 egg whites
3 tablespoons cornstarch
4 cups plus 1½ tablespoons peanut, vegetable, or corn oil

⅓ pound bean sprouts, about 3 cups
2 tablespoons water
⅛ teaspoon sugar
½ teaspoon sesame oil
⅓ cup chicken broth
2 tablespoons chopped scallions
1 teaspoon chopped fresh ginger
1 teaspoon white vinegar

1. Skin and bone the chicken breasts. There should be about 1½ pounds after skinning and boning. Place the chicken breasts on a flat surface and, using a sharp knife, cut them against the grain into thin slices. Cut the slices into very thin shreds. There should be about 2 cups. If desired, the chicken may be partially frozen to facilitate the slicing and shredding.

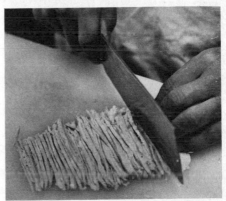

Slicing the chicken before it's shredded.

2. Place the meat in a mixing bowl and add salt, 1½ tablespoons wine, and the egg whites. Stir in a circular motion until the whites become a bit bubbly. Add 2 tablespoons of cornstarch and 1½ tablespoons of oil. Stir to blend well. Refrigerate, preferably overnight, or for at least 1 hour.

3. Ideally, the tips of the bean sprouts should be plucked, leaving only the firm white center portion. This is tedious, however, and is not necessary. Set aside.

4. Combine the remaining 2 tablespoons of wine, remaining 1 tablespoon of cornstarch mixed with the water, salt, sugar, sesame oil, and chicken broth. Stir to blend. Set aside.

5. Heat the remaining 4 cups of oil in a wok or skillet and add the chicken mixture. Cook over high heat, stirring constantly and vigorously to separate the shreds, about 1 minute. Drain almost completely, leaving about 1 tablespoon of oil in the wok.

6. Add the scallions and ginger, stir for a second and add the bean sprouts. Cook, stirring vigorously, about 15 seconds. Add the chicken, sesame oil mixture and vinegar and cook, stirring, until piping hot and lightly thickened. Serve hot.

Yield: 4 to 8 servings.

Lamb with Scallions

1¼   pounds very lean lamb, cut from the leg and in one piece
¼   teaspoon salt
2   small egg whites
2½   tablespoons cornstarch
4   cups plus 3½ tablespoons peanut, vegetable, or corn oil
30   scallions
3   large cloves garlic

2   tablespoons dry sherry or shao hsing wine
2   tablespoons water
3   tablespoons soy sauce
⅛   teaspoon monosodium glutamate, optional
½   teaspoon sugar
1   tablespoon red wine vinegar
½   teaspoon sesame oil
⅓   cup chicken broth

1. Place the lamb on a flat surface and, using a sharp knife, cut it against the grain into ¼-inch-thick slices. If desired, the lamb may be partly frozen to facilitate slicing.

2. Place the slices in a mixing bowl and add the salt and egg whites. Stir in a circular motion until the whites become a bit bubbly. Stir in 1½ tablespoons cornstarch and 1½ tablespoons of oil. Refrigerate, preferably overnight, or at least 1 hour.

3. Trim the scallions at the white tips, but otherwise leave them whole. Flatten them by pounding lightly with the flat side of a cleaver or heavy knife. Cut the scallions on the diagonal into 1-inch lengths. There should be about 4 cups. Set aside.

4. Chop the garlic coarsely. Set aside.

5. Combine the wine, remaining 1 tablespoon of cornstarch blended with the water, the soy sauce, monosodium glutamate, sugar, vinegar, sesame oil, and chicken broth. Stir to blend and set aside.

6. Heat the 4 cups of oil in a wok or skillet and when it is almost smoking, add the lamb, stir-

ring to separate the slices. Cook, stirring constantly, for a total of about 45 seconds, no longer, and drain the meat. Drain the wok completely.

7. Heat the remaining 2 tablespoons of oil in the wok and when it is very hot, add the scallions and garlic and cook, stirring and tossing, about 30 seconds. Add the lamb, stirring, and the vinegar mixture. Cook, tossing and stirring, until piping hot and slightly thickened. Serve hot.

Yield: 4 to 8 servings.

Sliced Duck with Young Ginger Root

1 4–5-pound duck, the smaller the better
1 teaspoon salt
1 tablespoon plus 4 teaspoons cornstarch
6 water chestnuts, sliced, about 1½ cups
1 sweet red pepper, cored, seeded and cut into ½-inch cubes, about ½ cup
2 scallions, trimmed and cut into ½-inch lengths, about ½ cup
5 pieces bottled young ginger root in syrup, available in 1-pound jars in Chinese markets
15 whole fresh asparagus spears for garnish, optional
4 cups peanut, vegetable, or corn oil
¾ cup chicken broth
¼ teaspoon monosodium glutamate, optional

2 tablespoons dry sherry or shao hsing wine
2 tablespoons water
2 tablespoons soy sauce
½ teaspoon white vinegar
½ teaspoon sesame oil
1 tablespoon finely chopped fresh ginger
2 teaspoons hot pepper or chili oil, available in bottles in Chinese markets

1. Using a sharp knife, carefully remove and discard the skin from the duck. Bone the duck, reserving the bones, if desired, for soup. To facilitate slicing, the duck meat may be partially frozen. In any event, cut the duck meat into very thin slices, about 3 cups. To this, add ½ teaspoon salt and 4 teaspoons of cornstarch and blend well.

2. Prepare the water chestnuts, sweet peppers, and scallions and set aside.

3. Rinse off the ginger and slice thinly. There should be about ⅔ cup. Set aside.

4. Scrape the asparagus spears, leaving the tips intact. Drop the spears into boiling water for about 50 seconds. Drain and immediately run under cold water to crisp. Drain thoroughly.

5. Heat 2 cups of oil in a wok or skillet and add the asparagus. Cook about 45 seconds and drain completely. Reserve the oil. Add ½ cup of chicken broth to the wok and the asparagus. Cook about 10 seconds and sprinkle with remaining salt and monosodium glutamate. Drain and transfer to a platter.

6. Combine the wine, remain-

ing cornstarch blended with the water, soy sauce, vinegar, sesame oil, and remaining ¼ cup chicken broth. Set aside.

7. Heat the remaining oil, including reserved oil, in a wok or skillet and add the water chestnuts. Cook about 10 seconds and add the duck, stirring and tossing constantly. Cook about 30 seconds. Add the sweet red peppers and ginger pieces and cook, stir-

ring, about 10 seconds. Drain completely.

8. To the wok add 2 teaspoons of hot pepper oil or regular oil and add the scallions and fresh ginger. Add the duck mixture and the vinegar mixture, stirring rapidly. Cook until piping hot and until the duck pieces are thoroughly coated. Serve on the platter with the asparagus spears as a garnish.

Yield: 4 to 8 servings.

Having been somewhat immersed in Chinese cooking during recent years, we are asked over and over again, "How on earth can one person turn out a proper Chinese meal for more than two?" In the first place, it is best to plan a menu that is not too elaborate. A proper menu might start with a cold appetizer which may be made, or for that matter, purchased, ahead of time—for example, thousand year eggs which are available in Chinese markets. A hot soup might follow which could be prepared in advance (there are many such soups in the Chinese repertoire). Then a long-cooked casserole dish such as Hunam lamb (see page 57) or beggar's chicken which can be baked in a clay dish; and one or two, but no more, stir-fry dishes, that is to say, those dishes which must be cooked quickly and at the last moment. There are numerous Chinese desserts that can be made in advance, but we find ice cream quite appropriate for the end of a casual Chinese meal.

Pork as Caviar

WITH PIERRE FRANEY

We have long been bemused by a commentary attributed to the late great chef Auguste Escoffier: "However deservedly pork may be praised, it could never have been included among the preparations of first-class cookery (except subsidiarily) had it not been for the culinary value of hams." While that may be the ultimate accolade for a cured leg of pig, the gentleman obviously does not share our intense enthusiasm for the remainder of the animal. We find pork in almost any of its myriad forms—from those delectable sausages made with pig's chitterlings to an irresistible roast loin—almost as appealing as caviar. Two excellent pork dishes are printed here—one for pork chops stuffed with herbs, another for pork chops Esterhazy, a Hungarian-inspired dish made with sour cream and capers.

Herb-Stuffed Pork Chops

4 loin, center-cut pork chops, each about 1 inch thick and weighing about ¾ pound
¼ cup peeled pistachios, optional
¼ pound ground pork
¼ cup finely chopped onion
1 cup thinly sliced mushrooms
1 small clove garlic, peeled
3 tablespoons parsley
½ teaspoon dried marjoram or sage
¼ cup fine bread crumbs
1 raw chicken liver
   Salt and freshly ground black pepper
1 egg, beaten
   Flour for dredging

1 tablespoon butter
1 cup chicken broth

1. Preheat oven to 350 degrees.

2. Open the chops for stuffing "butterfly" fashion. To do this, use a sharp knife and slice the chops through the center down to the bone, top to bottom. Open them up and, using a flat mallet, pound the opened-up flaps to flatten lightly. Do not break the meat, however, in pounding.

3. Drop the pistachios into boiling water. Let stand a few seconds and drain. Rub off the skins. Set the pistachio meats aside.

4. Cook the ground pork in a saucepan, stirring, until it loses its red color. Add the onion and mushrooms and cook, stirring.

5. Chop the garlic with the parsley and marjoram and add

them to the pork mixture. Stir in the bread crumbs.

6. Chop the chicken liver and add it, stirring. Add salt and pepper to taste and the pistachios. Cook briefly and remove from the heat. Let cool. Add the egg and blend well.

7. Sprinkle the opened-up chops with salt and pepper to taste. Add equal amounts of the filling to the chops and bring the flaps together to enclose the stuffing. Skewer the ends of each chop with toothpicks or sew with string.

8. Dredge the chops on all sides in flour seasoned with salt and pepper.

9. Heat the butter in a large, heavy skillet and brown the chops well on one side, 5 minutes or longer. Turn and brown on the other side. Cover loosely with aluminum foil.

10. Place the skillet in the oven and bake 1 hour. Remove the chops briefly and add half the chicken broth to the skillet, stirring it into the brown particles on the bottom of the skillet. Return the chops to the skillet. Cover with foil and bake 15 minutes longer. Turn the chops in the pan glaze; then transfer them to a hot serving dish. Add the remaining broth to the skillet and cook, stirring, to dissolve the brown particles remaining. Strain this over the chops.

Yield: 4 servings.

Pork Chops Esterhazy

8 thick loin pork chops,
about ½ pound each
Salt and freshly ground
black pepper
2 tablespoons peanut,
vegetable, or corn oil
½ cup chopped carrots
½ cup chopped celery
1 cup chopped onions
2 tablespoons finely minced
garlic
½ teaspoon dried thyme
1 bay leaf
6 sprigs parsley
½ cup dry white wine
1 cup chicken broth
1 tablespoon tomato paste
1 tablespoon imported
mustard, such as Dijon or
Düsseldorf
1 cup sour cream
¼ cup drained capers

1. Sprinkle the chops with salt and pepper to taste. Heat the oil in a large skillet and add the chops. Brown on both sides, about 10 minutes each side. Pour off the fat.

2. Scatter the carrots, celery, onion, garlic, thyme, bay leaf, and parsley around the chops. Cover and cook 10 minutes. Add the wine and the chicken broth blended with tomato paste. Cook 45 minutes and turn the chops. Continue cooking about 45 minutes or until the chops are quite tender.

3. Remove the chops and keep them warm. Add the mustard and sour cream and stir. Bring just to the boil, but do not boil or the sour cream will curdle. Put the sauce through a fine sieve, pressing down with a wooden spoon to extract the liquid flavorings from the vegetables. Add this to a small saucepan and stir in the capers. Add salt to taste and reheat gently without boiling. Spoon this over the chops and heat gently without boiling. Serve hot.

Yield: 8 servings.

October 1975

HERE ARE SOME dishes that have given us so much pleasure, some which remain so sublimely in the mind, that we would literally like to walk into kitchens all over America and say to cooks, "Try this, try this." That's the way we feel about a certain Mexican fish soup we wrote about early in the month of October.

Although we did not mention it previously, our chief reason for going to Guadalajara, Mexico, was to discover the ins and outs of tequila making. Tequila is perhaps the fastest growing spirit in America, and we're right there on the bandwagon. (A margarita, made with 1½ ounces of tequila, 1 ounce of Triple Sec, and the juice of half a lemon, shaken with ice and strained into a glass rimmed with salt, is one of the greatest elixirs in the world of cocktails.)

In any event, we were staying in Guadalajara because it is less than an hour's drive from the small, dusty hot town of Tequila where the spirit is produced. We had spent the morning with a tequila producer watching the production of tequila from the harvest of the *agave* through its pressure cooking, squeezing, and fermentation. The friend who had us in tow spent the morning extolling the virtues of what he called a sort of soup, a kind of appetizer, made with numerous fish and served with a spicy cold sauce, lime juice, and cold avocado. Along about noon, we were utterly famished and our acquaintance drove us back to Guadalajara to an odd little place at a busy intersection in town. It is inconceivable to us that we ever would have made such a momentous and worthwhile discovery under any other auspices. We were absolutely enchanted with the soup prepared by Chino, the proprietor, at his unlikely looking food stand. Perhaps because he did not understand our Spanish (who does?), he refused to part with his recipe. We tried to persuade him that if he came to New York and peddled the same soup he would make a fortune. We are not sure he understood that either. Happily, we were able to assemble all the ingredients necessary for Chino's dish and we recreated it down to the last squeeze of lime in our own kitchen. We urge you to turn the next page and try it.

Roadside Find

WITH PIERRE FRANEY

One of the best soups in Mexico and one of the best fish soups we've tasted anywhere can be found at a small, tacky roadside stand here that would not command a second glance from a finicky and unadventurous tourist. It is called Chino's and is located at the corner of Calle Libertad and 8 de Julio. It is an open-air, sidewalk affair with one rectangular oilcloth-covered table that is shared by random customers. Overhead is a torn cloth canopy to shield the patrons from sun (or rain), and the principal sound is that of a stereo—generally the voices of Frank Sinatra, Peggy Lee, or other American idols, piped from a small room somewhere in the rear.

Chino's is named after the industrious, young, affable owner and chef, who dispenses, in addition to his soup, a good, fine-textured but moist seviche made with flaked fish in lime juice, frequently spread on a tostada or fried tortilla with hot sauce; a delectable salsa cruda made

with cubed, seeded, unpeeled tomatoes, chopped onion, chilies, and chopped cilantro (fresh coriander leaves); plus slices of pickled jalapeño peppers (optional) and avocado slices for garnish and lime wedges on the side.

The real pièce de résistance, however, is the chavela, a sort of soup or appetizer or main course, depending on your appetite. The base consists of morsels of assorted fish and shellfish—generally poached robalo or huachinango or any white fish fillet, small shrimp, cooked cubed octopus, and fresh raw oysters. These are spooned into a thick glass or mug like a beer mug and to this is added a boiling hot fish broth containing cubed vegetables, which is deftly flavored with tomato and bay leaf. A spoonful or so of Chino's salsa cruda—hot sauce optional—is added, plus a garnish of cubed avocado. Lime wedges are served on the side and, preferably, warmed fresh tortillas are served separately. Here is our version of Chino's soup.

Chino's Chavela

7 cups fish stock (see recipe, page 156)
1 tablespoon olive oil
1 cup finely chopped onion
½ teaspoon chopped garlic
2 cups chopped tomatoes, preferably canned, imported, Italian peeled tomatoes
2 carrots, scraped and cut into ½-inch cubes, about 1½ cups
3 or 4 ribs celery, scraped and cut into ½-inch cubes, about 1½ cups
Salt and freshly ground black pepper
4 bay leaves
2 potatoes, peeled and cut into ½-inch cubes, about ½ cups
1 skinless and boneless fillet of fish such as fluke, sea bass or red snapper, cut into 1-inch cubes

12 to 18 raw shrimp, peeled, deveined and cut into thirds
6 to 12 raw oysters
3 cups salsa cruda (see recipe), more or less
2 avocados, peeled and cut into 1-inch cubes
Lime wedges as garnish
Tabasco or other hot sauce, optional

1. Prepare the fish stock and set it aside.

2. Heat the oil in a kettle and add the onion. Cook until wilted. Add the garlic and stir briefly. Add the tomatoes, carrots, celery, and fish stock. Add salt and pepper to taste and the bay leaves. Bring to the boil and simmer 15 minutes.

3. Add the potatoes and cook 20 minutes longer or until the potatoes are tender.

4. Add the fish and simmer about 3 minutes.

5. When ready to serve, bring the soup to the boil and add the shrimp and oysters to the soup. Do not cook further, but spoon the soup into very hot deep beer glasses or bowls. To each serving add a spoonful or two of the cold salsa cruda. Add equal amounts of the cold avocado as a garnish and serve with lime wedges on the side, to be squeezed into the soup according to taste. Tabasco or other hot sauce may also be added at will.

Yield: 6 servings.

Note: At Chino's place, cooked octopus cut into ½-inch pieces is also added to the soup, along with the shrimp. To cook octopus, place the cleaned octopus in a saucepan and add cold water to cover and salt to taste. Simmer about 1½ to 1¾ hours, until tender.

Salsa cruda

2 *fresh tomatoes, about 1 pound*
¾ *cup chopped onion*
Salt
⅓ *cup chopped fresh coriander leaves, available in Mexican and Chinese markets, or use chopped parsley*
1 *to 4 tablespoons chopped, fresh, long, hot or mild green chilies or chopped canned seranno peppers to taste*

1. Do not peel the tomatoes. Cut them in half and squeeze each half gently to remove the seeds. Cut the tomatoes into small cubes. Add them to a bowl.

2. Add the remaining ingredients and stir to blend.

Yield: About 3 cups.

Egg Power

WITH PIERRE FRANEY

All in all, in the world of food, there may be nothing more versatile than the egg. The yolk provides the emulsion of the world's most basic and elegant sauces—mayonnaise and hollandaise; the white is the essence of a multitude of meringues, including the candy meringue known as divinity; and almost all foods that are breaded or cooked *à l'anglaise,* as French chefs term it, are dipped in beaten egg before they are "crumbed." The thickening power of the egg for soups and sauces and stuffings and custards—both savory and sweet—is universal, and the uses of a hard-cooked egg are varied. Where, historically, without hard-cooked eggs, would picnics be? Following is a random selection of egg dishes: that marvelous all-in-one dish, Scotch eggs, with the egg encased in sausage meat; a first-rate canapé of eggs with seafood; and that old-fashioned standby of the corner saloon, the pickled egg.

Pickled Eggs

12 hard-cooked eggs
3 cups cider vinegar or
enough to cover the eggs
Salt
3 small, dried, hot red
peppers
10 whole allspice berries
2 blades mace, optional
6 whole cloves
12 coriander seeds
2 bay leaves
1 tablespoon sugar

1. Peel the eggs and pack them in sterilized jars.

2. Combine the remaining ingredients in a saucepan and simmer 5 minutes. Pour the vinegar over the eggs and seal tightly. Store for a week or more before serving.

Yield: One dozen pickled eggs.

Scotch Eggs

6 hard-cooked eggs
Flour for dredging
1 pound sausage meat
Hot pepper flakes to taste,
optional
½ cup bread crumbs
2 egg yolks
Peanut, vegetable, or corn
oil for deep frying
Tomato sauce (see recipe)

1. Peel the eggs and leave them whole. Gently roll each egg in flour to coat. Set aside.

2. Combine the sausage meat with the pepper flakes, crumbs, and yolks. Blend thoroughly.

3. Divide the sausage mixture into 6 equal portions. Using moistened fingers, shape each portion around an egg. The eggs should be thoroughly and evenly coated with the mixture.

4. Heat the oil and before it is piping hot (if the oil is too hot in the beginning, the sausage meat may cook too fast and split), add the eggs, one at a time, turning gently with wooden spoons. Let cook, turning as necessary, until the eggs are piping hot throughout and the sausage nicely crisped and brown outside. Serve hot with tomato sauce.

Yield: 6 servings.

Tomato sauce

2 tablespoons peanut,
vegetable, or corn oil
½ cup finely chopped onion
1 teaspoon finely minced
garlic
½ teaspoon dried basil
½ teaspoon dried thyme
¼ cup tomato paste
1 teaspoon flour
1 cup fresh or canned
chicken broth
1 cup chopped tomatoes,
preferably canned,
imported, Italian peeled
tomatoes
Salt and freshly ground
pepper
1 tablespoon butter

1. Heat the oil in a saucepan and add the onion and garlic. Cook, stirring, about 3 minutes or until onion is translucent. Add the

basil, thyme, and tomato paste. Stir about 1 minute and add flour, stirring.

2. Add the chicken broth, stirring constantly until the mixture is thickened and smooth. Add the tomatoes, salt and pepper to taste, and cook, partly covered, about 15 minutes. Put the sauce through a food mill or sieve. Swirl in the butter. Serve hot.

Yield: About 2 cups.

Egg and Seafood Canapé

1   cup plus 2 tablespoons
    mayonnaise (see recipe,
    page 239)
2   tablespoons ketchup
1   teaspoon cognac
3   tablespoons chopped onion
1   ounce fresh caviar,
    lumpfish, or salmon roe
    (see note)
¾   cup chopped and mashed
    sardines, tuna, cooked
    shrimp, crab, or lobster
    meat

6   rounds fresh buttered toast
6   slices tomato
3   hard-cooked eggs, peeled
    and split in half
6   rolled fillets of anchovy,
    optional

1. Combine the 1 cup of mayonnaise with the ketchup, cognac, chopped onion, and caviar. This is Russian dressing. Set aside.

2. Combine the mashed fish or seafood with the 2 remaining tablespoons of mayonnaise. Spread equal portions of the mixture on the toast rounds. Arrange the toast rounds on 6 small plates.

3. Top each round with a tomato slice and place 1 hard-cooked egg half, split side down, on each tomato slice. Spoon the Russian dressing over all. Garnish with a rolled anchovy fillet and serve.

Yield: 6 servings.

Note: Fresh caviar is ideal for this dressing, although it is expensive. Black lumpfish caviar has an artificial coloring that, while harmless, darkens the sauce.

As we have noted before, it is probably a sure sign of senility that we reflect and relate so often on the foods of our childhood. Nonetheless, for the record, we would like to mention that the egg and seafood canapé above was one of the "party" dishes served in our home for special occasions.

We would also like to add that we have revised the recipe for Scotch eggs. In the original printed version, the eggs were not coated with flour before they were enclosed in sausage meat and fried. We received a letter from Jean Bayrock, The English Epicure of Elizabeth, New Jersey, who explained to us that the flour helps the sausage meat adhere. It was a splendid suggestion.

The Culinary Challenges of the South

It has long been our persuasion that Southern cooking in the home, whether it be soul food or conventional bourgeois dishes such as beaten biscuits with baked country ham, is the best and most varied in America. We grew up in the land of corn pones and hominy grits, and we can hear the hoots and jeers of our colleagues when we say that we have an unabashed passion for the likes of hush puppies and spoon bread.

Since fried chicken, collards, and mustard greens were mother's milk, so to speak, in our infancy, we never dreamed that the day would arrive when we would state that some of the best Southern cooking we've ever tasted would be cooked by a Yankee born and bred.

And by someone who, until 11 years ago had never so much as put her hands to a saucepan or skillet. Her name is Laura Benson, whose husband, Robert, is an artist.

The Bensons live here in a splendid, brightly lit home made of four connected geodesic domes. It is fascinating architecturally. It is situated on the beach and is in stunning contrast to the prosaic wood frame buildings that border it on either side.

"In the beginning there was a problem with tourists who would simply wander in for a look," Mr. Benson declared. "We pretty much stopped that with the sign in front." The sign, which looks awfully official, states "U. S. Electrovisual Studies. Do not enter." Today they don't, although random tourists do seem to feel that the sand in front of the house is a great place to picnic.

There is a handsome, functional kitchen with a professional range (South Bend) complete with six burners, a large oven, and a salamander, an upper—and to our mind indispensable—broiler unit for glazing dishes. There is a large, solidly constructed center island for chopping and knife storage; open wall shelves for utensils, and ingredients within easy reach.

We had come to Nags Head on the advice of friends who said that Mrs. Benson, born in Westbury, Long Island, is a first-rate cook who delves in many cuisines. We had also been told that the waters around here are a fisherman's—or rather a fish cook's—paradise. We learned that both facts are patently true.

"I had never cooked a day in my life," Mrs. Benson declared, "until

I married Bob. I started cooking with Dione Lucas, French, of course, and subsequently I took seven courses in Chinese cooking with Virginia Lee."

The Bensons spend approximately six months a year here, the remainder of the year in New York, where she has a weekly yoga session with Yogi Vithaldas, who has in turn a considerable reputation as an Indian cook. Thanks to his influence, the young woman has a number of Indian dishes in her repertoire. They also have the services of a marvelous Southern cook, Phenas Manuel, the source of many of Mrs. Benson's Southern dishes.

Both the Bensons are ardent fishermen, and at least once a week they charter a deep-sea fishing vessel which they board around 5:30 A.M. for a 12-hour outing. Their annual haul reads like a catalogue of Atlantic fish—blue and white marlin, striped bass, bluefish, channel bass, pompano, sport, weakfish or speckled trout, flounder, tuna, wahoo, dolphin, and Spanish mackerel. They also have access to quantities of fresh catfish, an unbelievably delicious fish of excelling texture and sweet flesh; freshly shucked and delicious oysters; fresh crab meat (she generally steams the crabs herself and takes them to a local picker to have the meat taken from the shells); and genuinely fresh shrimp, which are enormously scarce in New York.

Laura Benson makes preparations for a Nags Head red drum stew.

Robert Benson keeps a watchful eye on the grill where he is cooking a fillet of king mackerel.

The Bensons' guests have included some fairly weighty names in the arts—Jasper Johns, a close friend; Merce Cunningham, the dancer; John Cage, the composer; and Calvin Tomkins, the writer.

At our request the majority of the dishes sampled in the Benson home were in-depth Southern. Someone had given the hostess a dozen quail, and scuppernong, a traditional Southern grape with a pronounced fruity flavor, was available, so we dined on braised quail with Port wine and scuppernongs.

There was a distinguished Nags Head fisherman's soup made with a local catch (some of the seasonings, which included saffron, fennel and turmeric, were a trifle exotic for the traditional Southern kitchen). There were sautéed, fresh soft shell crabs and a delectable, hearty fish stew made with channel bass, also known as drum and red drum. The most Southern of dishes included fried catfish; Phenas Manuel's custardlike cornmeal and egg bread; the most gossamer hush puppies we've ever eaten; a she-crab soup, thus called in that it is traditionally made with the roe or coral that comes only from female crabs; and steamed rutabagas.

Robert Benson, too, plays a role in the cooking activities of the U. S. Electrovisual establishment. He is an excellent grill man, particularly with fresh-caught fish such as king mackerel.

Nags Head Fisherman's Soup

½ cup olive oil
2 cups finely chopped onion
1½ cups seeded, chopped sweet green or red pepper
1 cup cubed carrot
1 small, hot green or red pepper, chopped, optional
1½ pounds potatoes, peeled and cut into ¼-inch slices
2 pounds fresh red, ripe tomatoes, cored and cut into ½-inch cubes, or use 4 cups imported canned tomatoes, chopped
 Salt and freshly ground black pepper
7 cups fish broth (see recipe)
2 teaspoons loosely packed stem saffron

1 tablespoon water
1 teaspoon fennel seeds, crushed
½ teaspoon turmeric
1 thin slice orange peel, white pulp removed
1 teaspoon sugar
1½ pounds fresh scallops, cut in half or quartered, if desired
1 whole, cleaned 2-pound salt water fish such as weakfish, preferably with head on
1¼ pounds raw shrimp, the smaller the better, shelled and deveined
24 littleneck clams, well scrubbed to remove sand

1. Heat the oil in a kettle and add the onion, sweet pepper, carrot, and the hot pepper if used.

Cook, stirring, about 5 minutes. Add the potatoes and cook about 1 minute. Add the tomatoes and salt and pepper to taste. Add the fish broth and bring to a boil.

2. Combine the saffron with the tablespoon of water and add it. Add the fennel, turmeric, orange peel, and sugar. Simmer about 10 minutes and add the scallops and the whole fish. If the fish won't fit, cut it into pieces.

3. Cover and simmer 5 minutes. Add the shrimp and clams and cook about 10 minutes or until clams open. If desired, the clams may be steamed separately and added to the soup, layered with the other ingredients. Add salt and pepper to taste and serve piping hot.

Yield: 6 servings.

Fish broth

2 *pounds fresh fish bones, preferably with head, but gills removed (see note)*
1 *cup dry white wine*
1 *cup dry white vermouth*
6 *cups water*

Combine all the ingredients and simmer, uncovered, about 30 minutes. Strain.

Yield: About 7 cups.

Note: Mrs. Benson, who has an ample supply of fish at all times, uses one whole 2-pound weakfish instead of fish bones. After cooking, fish is discarded.

Nags Head Channel Bass or Red Drum Stew

2½ *pounds skinned and boned channel bass or use another fish such as blackfish (see note)*
6   *strips bacon*
2½ *cups thinly sliced onions, about 1 pound*
6   *tablespoons flour*
2   *hot, fresh, red or green peppers, chopped, or ¼ teaspoon or more cayenne added to taste*
3   *cups peeled potatoes, cut into 1-inch cubes, about 1 pound*
5   *cups water, approximately Salt and freshly ground black pepper Finely chopped parsley for garnish*

1. Cut the fish into 1-inch cubes and set aside.

2. Cut the bacon into fine cubes and add it to a Dutch oven. Cook the bacon, stirring, until crisp.

3. Add the onion to the Dutch oven and cook, stirring, until wilted. Sprinkle with flour and stir. Add the hot peppers and potatoes.

4. Add the water, stirring constantly, until thickened and smooth. Add salt and pepper. Cover and simmer about 15 minutes or until the potatoes are nearly tender. Watch carefully and stir often from the bottom to prevent sticking. The stew should be

thick, but it may be desirable to add a little water.

5. Add the cubed fish and cover. Cook about 6 minutes. Serve in hot soup bowls sprinkled with parsley.

Yield: 6 servings.

Note: Channel bass or red drum, like blackfish, is a firm-fleshed fish whose flesh does not flake easily when it is cooked. These fish are best for this dish, although other fish such as striped bass could be substituted.

Avocado with Crab Meat

⅓ cup sour cream
⅓ cup mayonnaise
3 tablespoons lemon juice
¼ teaspoon paprika
   Salt and freshly ground
   black pepper
¾ pound fresh crab meat,
   preferably lump or
   backfin, picked over to
   remove all traces of shell
   and cartilage
2 or 3 ripe, unblemished
   avocados, halved and
   seeded.

1. In a mixing bowl, combine the sour cream and mayonnaise. Stir in the lemon juice, paprika, salt, and pepper.

2. Fold in the crab meat, stirring as little as possible so as not to break up the lumps. Fill the avocado halves with the mixture and serve.

Yield: 4 to 6 servings.

Hush Puppies

1 cup white cornmeal
1 teaspoon bicarbonate of
   soda
1 teaspoon baking powder
1 teaspoon salt
1 teaspoon sugar
⅛ teaspoon cayenne
1 egg, well beaten
3 tablespoons chopped onion
1 cup buttermilk
   Oil for deep frying

1. Combine the cornmeal with soda, baking powder, salt, sugar, cayenne, egg, onion, and buttermilk. Stir to blend well.

2. Heat the oil for deep frying and drop the batter by rounded spoonfuls into the hot fat. The hush puppies should be about 1½ inches in diameter. Cook the hush puppies, turning them in the hot fat until golden brown all over.

Yield: 8 servings.

Sautéed Soft Shell Crabs

12 cleaned soft shell crabs
   Flour for dredging
   Salt and freshly ground
   black pepper
⅛ teaspoon cayenne
6 tablespoons butter
   Chopped parsley
6 lemon wedges for garnish

1. Dredge the crabs all over with flour seasoned with salt and pepper and cayenne.

2. Heat the butter in a large, heavy skillet and add the crabs. Cook until golden brown on one side. Turn and brown on the other side. Serve garnished with parsley and lemon wedges.

Yield: 6 servings.

She-Crab Soup

2   *tablespoons butter*
3   *tablespoons flour*
3   *cups milk*
¼   *teaspoon freshly grated nutmeg or more to taste*
¼   *teaspoon paprika*
Salt and freshly ground black pepper
⅛   *teaspoon cayenne*
2   *cups picked-over crab meat, preferably with a certain amount of coral or roe*
10   *lemon slices*
¼   *cup Amontillado sherry*

1. Melt the butter in a large saucepan and add the flour, stirring with a wire whisk. Add the milk, stirring rapidly with the whisk. Cook, stirring, until thickened and smooth.

2. Add the nutmeg, paprika, salt, pepper, and cayenne and stir. Add the crab meat, stirring gently, and bring just to the boil. Add the lemon slices and sherry and pour into a soup tureen or serve in individual bowls.

Yield: 6 to 8 servings.

Note: This is called she-crab soup because the soup traditionally is made with the meat and coral or roe that comes only from female crabs.

Steamed Rutabaga

1½   *pounds rutabaga*
4   *tablespoons butter*
3   *cups water*
3   *tablespoons lemon juice*
Chopped parsley for garnish

1. Pare the rutabaga and cut into 1-inch cubes. There should be about 5 cups. Place the rutabaga in a saucepan and add the butter and water. Cover as tightly as possible.

2. Bring the liquid to the boil and cook over low heat until all the liquid has evaporated and the rutabaga is tender. Check occasionally to make certain the rutabaga does not burn towards the end. Pour the lemon juice over the rutabaga.

3. Turn the rutabaga out into a serving dish and sprinkle with parsley.

Yield: 6 to 8 servings.

Braised Quail
with Scuppernongs

12   *cleaned quail*
Flour for dredging
Salt and freshly ground black pepper
4   *tablespoons butter*

½ cup chopped scallions,
green part and all
½ cup chopped celery
½ cup chopped onion
⅓ cup port wine
¾ cup chicken broth
1 cup scuppernongs or
seedless white grapes

1. Dredge the quail in flour seasoned with salt and pepper.

2. Heat the butter in a large, heavy skillet or casserole. Add the quail and cook, turning frequently, until lightly browned all over. Add the scallions, celery, and onion and continue cooking, turning frequently, until golden brown all over.

3. Add the port wine and cook until the wine almost evaporates. Add the chicken broth, salt and pepper and cover closely. Cook about 20 minutes. Add the grapes and cover. Cook briefly, just until the grapes have heated through.

Yield: 6 servings.

Laura Benson's Trifle

2 large, ripe, unblemished
peaches
1¼ cups sugar
1 cup red, ripe strawberries
2 cups milk
2 whole eggs
2 egg yolks
1½ teaspoons vanilla extract
¼ teaspoon almond extract
2 tablespoons medium-dry
sherry
1 frozen poundcake,
defrosted

¾ cup apricot preserves,
approximately
½ cup strawberry or currant
preserves, approximately
1 cup sweetened whipped
cream

1. Drop the peaches into boiling water for about 12 minutes. Drain immediately. Skin the peaches by pulling off the peel with a paring knife. Slice and pit the peaches. Add ½ cup of sugar and refrigerate.

2. Rinse, hull, and drain the strawberries. Add ½ cup of sugar and refrigerate.

3. Bring the milk just to the boil. Add the whole eggs and egg yolks to a mixing bowl. Beat until light and lemon colored. Add remaining ¼ cup of sugar. Pour half of the near-boiling milk over the eggs, beating vigorously. Return this mixture to the remaining milk and return the saucepan to the heat. Cook, stirring constantly this way and that over the bottom, using a wooden spoon. It may be best to use a heat-proof pad under the saucepan. Cook the custard until it is slightly thickened, like thick cream, and coats the spoon. Strain the sauce into a mixing bowl. Add the vanilla, almond extract, and sherry. Chill.

4. Cut the poundcake into ½-inch-thick slices. Spread enough slices with apricot preserves to arrange the slices spread-side up over the bottom and sides of a crystal bowl. Cut additional slices into convenient sizes as necessary to fill empty spaces.

5. Add the peaches to the lined bowl and pour in the custard almost to the top. Spread any remaining poundcake slices with strawberry preserves and arrange spreadside up on top of the cake. Arrange the strawberries on top of this. Pipe sweetened whipped cream over the top.

Yield: 8 to 12 servings.

Laura Benson's Gingerbread

1   cup molasses (do not use
    blackstrap molasses)
½   pound butter
1   egg
1   cup sugar
2¼ cups flour
1½ teaspoons baking soda
1½ teaspoons ground ginger
1   teaspoon ground cinnamon
½   teaspoon ground cloves
¼   teaspoon grated nutmeg
    Grated peel of 1 orange
    Salt
½   cup boiling water
3   tablespoons sour cream

1. Preheat the oven to 350 degrees.

2. Combine the molasses and butter in a saucepan and bring just to the boil, stirring. Let cool.

3. Combine in the bowl of an electric mixer the egg and granulated sugar. Beat to blend.

4. Sift together the flour, baking soda, ginger, cinnamon, cloves, and nutmeg. Add the orange peel and salt.

5. Gradually add the dry ingredients to the egg mixture. Spoon and scrape in the molasses mixture while beating. Add the boiling water and sour cream. Blend well.

6. Pour the mixture into a buttered 9-by-13-inch pan. Bake 50 minutes. The center of the gingerbread will sink when it cools. Serve, if desired, with applesauce, a lemon sauce thickened with cornstarch, or sweetened whipped cream.

Yield: 8 to 12 servings.

Phenas Manuel's Egg Bread

7   tablespoons butter, at
    room temperature
1   cup white cornmeal
1   teaspoon salt
2   tablespoons sugar
1   cup boiling water
3   eggs
1   cup milk

1. Preheat the oven to 375 degrees.

2. Place 3 tablespoons of butter in a 10-by-2-inch round baking dish. Place it in the oven until piping hot, but do not let the butter burn.

3. Place the cornmeal, salt, and sugar in the bowl of an electric mixer. Add the remaining butter and start beating on low speed. Add the boiling water, gradually increasing the mixer speed. Add the eggs, one at a time, beating constantly. Beat in the milk.

4. Pour the mixture into the

hot baking dish and return it to the oven. Bake 30 minutes or until set.

Yield: 6 to 8 servings.

Concord Grape Aspic

  5 *cups concord grapes*
4½ *cups water*
  2 *envelopes unflavored gelatin*
  2 *cups sugar*
  2 *cups sweetened whipped cream for garnish*
     Candied violets for garnish, optional

1. Combine the grapes and 4 cups of water in a saucepan and bring to the boil. Simmer about 40 minutes.

2. Strain the mixture, pressing the grapes gently with the back of a spoon to extract more juice. Discard grapes.

3. Combine the gelatin with the remaining ½ cup of water and stir to soften. Add this to the grape liquid. Add the sugar and bring to the boil, stirring. Simmer until the sugar is dissolved. Pour into a 1½-quart mold, preferably crystal. Let cool and chill until firm. Garnish with whipped cream and, if desired, candied violets.

Yield: 8 servings.

Caterers' Choice

Sometime ago a magazine ran an article that detailed the names of various caterers in the city who would serve "breakfast in bed" to be offered as a gift. And generally as a surprise. One of those who agreed to provide such a service was Stephen Bierman and his wife, Elizabeth.

"I delivered about thirty breakfasts," the young man said recently, "and each delivery was at times as much a surprise for me as for the recipient. The breakfasts were served around noon or shortly thereafter—freshly squeezed orange juice, hot black coffee, warm croissants, decadently buttered and slathered with apricot marmalade.

"I would arrive dressed to the nines in a blue blazer. Once on a Sunday I had an order to deliver a surprise breakfast to Sheepshead Bay. When I arrived at a two-family house on Nostrand Avenue and emerged from the car, a venetian blind shot up and quickly went down again. I could tell they were peering at me as I unloaded my canvas catering bags, and when I knocked on the door, a man's voice asked, as forbiddingly as possible, 'Who's there?'

"I said: 'Breakfast in Bed.'

" 'You're what?' he asked.

" 'I'm the surprise from Joe.' Well, anyway, they opened the door and when I explained the situation, he retreated to the bedroom and not, I might add, in the best of humor.

"After the orange juice and so on I re-entered with mushrooms stuffed with steak tartare and caviar and poured the champagne. Then the eggs Florentine with hollandaise and truffles and a side order of velvety smoked salmon. I poured more champagne and served the dessert, strawberries with raspberry sauce. Then black coffee and brandy.

"After I'd packed the dishes and was about to stalk out into the afternoon sunshine, I glanced back. You've never seen two more blissful looking people in your life. Total nirvana."

These days, the Biermans are less involved with breakfasts and cater mostly dinners and buffets. The first order of business is to visit the kitchen to establish what is and what isn't necessary. The Biermans charge an average fee of $15 per guest but on a sliding scale. The amount increases or decreases in relation to the kinds of foods, the time involved in preparation and the size of the staff required. They are equipped to provide all services including table service, bar service, all food, beverages, and so on. Menus and prices are discussed in detail with a prospective client. The couple may be reached by telephone at (212) 249-4594.

3 tablespoons finely chopped
parsley
½ cup coarsely chopped
celery
½ cup finely chopped leeks,
optional
1 cup dry vermouth
½ cup heavy cream
1 cup chicken broth
1 tablespoon imported
mustard, preferably Dijon
1 tablespoon chopped chives

1. Skin and bone or have the chicken breasts skinned, boned, and halved.

2. Sprinkle the pieces with salt and pepper.

3. Melt the butter in a skillet large enough to hold the pieces in one layer. Add the onions, carrots, and garlic and cook, stirring, about 10 minutes without browning.

4. Sprinkle with flour and stir to blend. Arrange the chicken pieces, boned side down, in the skillet and sprinkle with thyme, bay leaf, parsley, celery, and leeks. Cover closely and let cook 5 minutes.

5. Add the vermouth, cream, and broth and cover once more. Simmer 20 minutes.

6. Remove the chicken pieces to a platter and keep warm. Spoon and scrape the sauce into the container of a food processor or blender and blend to a fine puree. Return this sauce to a saucepan and add salt to taste. Add the mustard, stirring, and remove from the heat. Sprinkle with chives and pour the sauce over the chicken. Serve hot.

Yield: 8 servings.

Stephen Bierman

Chicken au Poivre

4 large whole chicken
breasts, the larger the
better
Salt
1 tablespoon coarsely ground
black pepper
6 tablespoons butter
1 cup thinly sliced onions
1 cup thinly sliced carrots
1 clove garlic, crushed
2 tablespoons flour
½ teaspoon dried thyme
1 bay leaf

Stuffed Chicken Breasts with Tomato Sauce

4   *large whole chicken
     breasts, the larger the
     better
     Salt and freshly ground
     black pepper*
9   *tablespoons butter*
¼   *cup finely chopped onion*
1   *pound spinach or 1 10-
     ounce package frozen*
1   *cup ground cooked ham*
1   *cup ricotta cheese*
1   *egg yolk*
½   *cup freshly grated
     Parmesan cheese*
¼   *teaspoon grated nutmeg*
¼   *pound ground sausage*
1   *clove garlic, finely minced*
1   *teaspoon dried basil*
¼   *cup dry sherry
     Tomato sauce (see recipe)*

1. Preheat oven 375 degrees.

2. Skin and bone or have the chicken breasts skinned, boned, and halved.

3. Using the fingers, make a pocket on the under or boned side of the chicken breasts for stuffing. Salt and pepper the breasts.

4. Heat 3 tablespoons of butter in a skillet and add the onion. Cook until wilted.

5. If fresh spinach is used, rinse well and cook, covered, in the water that clings to the leaves, stirring so that it cooks evenly, about 1 minute. If frozen spinach is used, cook according to package directions. In any event, drain the cooked spinach and when cool enough to handle, squeeze to extract excess moisture. Chop finely.

6. Add the spinach to the onions in the skillet. Add the ham, ricotta, egg yolk, Parmesan, nutmeg, sausage, garlic, and basil. Blend thoroughly.

7. Stuff the 8 pieces of chicken breast with 2 or 3 tablespoons of the mixture. Fold the ends of the chicken to enclose the filling. It is not necessary to tie the pieces. Arrange the pieces close together in a baking dish, stuffed side down.

8. Melt the remaining 6 tablespoons of butter and dribble it over the chicken. Sprinkle with wine. Do not cover, but bake 45 minutes to 1 hour, basting often. Serve hot with hot tomato sauce.

Yield: 8 servings.

Tomato sauce

¼   *cup olive oil*
¾   *cup finely chopped onion*
1   *or 2 cloves garlic, finely
     minced*
6   *cups crushed imported
     canned peeled tomatoes
     with tomato paste*
¼   *cup dry white wine*
½   *teaspoon dried basil*
¼   *teaspoon dried thyme*
½   *teaspoon dried oregano*
1   *piece orange peel, white
     pulp removed
     Salt and freshly ground
     black pepper*
1   *teaspoon sugar*
2   *tablespoons sour cream*

1. Heat the oil in a large saucepan and add the onion.

Cook, stirring, until onion wilts. Add the garlic and cook briefly. Add the tomatoes, wine, basil, thyme, oregano, orange peel, salt, pepper, and sugar. Simmer over low heat for about 40 minutes, stirring occasionally to prevent sticking and burning.

2. Pour the sauce into the container of a food processor or electric blender and blend. Return to a saucepan and bring to the boil. Stir in the sour cream and serve.

Yield: About 4 cups.

Pâté de Campagne

1 pound sausage links or bulk sausage
1 pound fresh spinach or 1 10-ounce package frozen spinach, optional
1 pound beef or pork liver
½ pound chicken livers
½ pound pork shoulder or very lean and boneless loin of pork, cubed
1 whole chicken breast, about ½ pound, skinned, boned, and cubed
1 onion, about ¼ pound, chopped
2 eggs
3½ tablespoons cognac
¼ teaspoon cayenne
¼ teaspoon ground allspice
¼ teaspoon grated nutmeg
¼ teaspoon dried thyme
¼ teaspoon basil
¼ teaspoon dried marjoram
Salt and freshly ground black pepper
1 to 2 tablespoons chopped garlic
½ pound twice-ground lean veal
½ pound piece cooked ham Enough thin slices of fatback to line a loaf pan and cover the pâté
3 bay leaves
Croutons (see recipe, page 332)

1. Preheat oven to 350 degrees.

2. If link sausages are used, split the casings. Remove and discard the casings. Set the sausage meat aside.

3. If fresh spinach is used, rinse well and cook, covered, in the water that clings to the leaves, stirring so that it cooks evenly, about 1 minute. If frozen spinach is used, cook according to package directions. In any event, drain the cooked spinach and when cool enough to handle, squeeze to extract excess moisture. Set aside.

4. Use a small paring knife and remove all the veins and tough fibrous parts from the beef and chicken livers. Cut the livers into pieces.

5. Use an electric blender or, preferably, a food processor. Add the pieces of liver. Add the pork, chicken, onion, eggs, cognac, cayenne, spices, salt, pepper, and garlic. Blend or process (it may be necessary to do this in two stages) until coarse fine. Do not overblend. There should be some texture.

6. Spoon half the mixture into a mixing bowl. Add the sausage and veal to remaining half of the

mixture in the blender or food processor and blend or process (if a food processor is used, use the white, plastic blade) just until blended. Do not overblend. Return to the mixing bowl. Chop the spinach to a pulp and add it. Cut the ham into ½-inch cubes and add it. Beat the mixture with a wooden spoon until it is thoroughly blended.

7. Line the bottom and sides of an 11-by-4½-by-2¾-inch loaf pan with thin slices of fatback. Let the slices overhang the sides of the mold. Pour the mixture in the lined pan. Arrange the 3 bay leaves over the top of the pâté. Cover with the overhanging slices of fatback plus enough additional fatback to cover.

8. Place the loaf pan in a baking dish and add boiling water to a depth halfway up the loaf pan. Place in the oven and bake for 1½ hours. Remove. Cover with foil and weigh the pâté with one or two heavy objects such as cans of tomatoes or other vegetables. Let stand until cool. Refrigerate for 1 or 2 days to mellow. Serve with croûtons, preferably homemade.

Yield: 12 to 20 servings.

Fillet of Sole en Timbales

The fillets

4   *fillets of sole, about ⅓ pound each*
    Salt and freshly ground black pepper
8   *large or 16 small shrimp*

½   *pound fresh mushrooms*
2½ *cups fresh bread crumbs*
    Tabasco
½   *teaspoon worcestershire sauce*
    Juice of ½ lemon
¼   *teaspoon grated nutmeg*
¾   *cup fish stock (see recipe, page 156)*
1   *tablespoon cognac*
3   *tablespoons finely chopped chives*
1   *tablespoon finely chopped fresh dill*
1½ *tablespoons finely chopped parsley*
2   *tablespoons sour cream*

The sauce

4   *tablespoons butter*
2   *tablespoons flour*
2   *cups fish stock (see recipe)*
    Salt and freshly ground black pepper
½   *teaspoon dried thyme*
1   *teaspoon chopped chives*
3   *egg yolks*
½   *cup heavy cream*
    Juice of ½ lemon

1. Preheat oven to 375 degrees.

2. Split the sole fillets in half, carefully cutting on both sides of the thin bone line down the center. Discard the bone line. Sprinkle the 8 fillet halves with salt and pepper.

3. Drop the shrimp into boiling water to cover. When the water returns to the boil, drain. Shell and devein the shrimp. If the shrimp are large, split them in half.

4. Butter the inside of 8 muffin tins. Arrange the 8 fillet halves circular-fashion to line the but-

tered muffin tins, letting the ends overlap. Place 1 shrimp or shrimp half in the center of each muffin tin.

5. Coarsely chop the mushrooms on a flat surface or use a food processor. Do not overblend. They must remain a slightly coarse texture.

6. Combine the mushrooms with the remaining ingredients for the fillets. Toss lightly with a fork. Stuff the sole fillets with equal portions of the mixture. Cover closely with aluminum foil and bake 20 minutes.

7. Meanwhile, prepare the sauce. Melt 3 tablespoons butter in a saucepan and add the flour, stirring with a wire whisk. When blended add the 2 cups of fish stock, stirring rapidly with the whisk. When thickened and smooth, add the salt, pepper, thyme, and chives.

8. Beat the yolks with the cream and remaining 1 tablespoon butter, softened. Add a small amount of hot sauce and return this to the saucepan, stirring. Bring just to the boil, but do not boil. Remove from heat. Add the lemon juice.

9. Carefully place a platter over the fish when it is cooked. Quickly invert the fish onto the platter. Liquid will accumulate around the timbales of fish. Pour and sponge this off. Pour the hot sauce over the fish and serve. Garnish with chopped dill or parsley if desired.

Yield: 8 servings.

Stuffed Mushrooms

24 medium-size mushrooms
 3 tablespoons olive oil or
    butter
¼ cup finely chopped onion
 1 clove garlic, finely minced
¼ cup finely chopped or
    ground cooked ham
½ cup fresh bread crumbs
 2 tablespoons grated
    Parmesan cheese
 1 egg
 1 tablespoon chopped
    parsley
½ teaspoon dried basil
½ teaspoon dried marjoram
    Salt and freshly ground
    black pepper
 2 tablespoons boiling water

1. Preheat oven to 375 degrees.

2. Remove the stems from the mushrooms and chop them. There should be about ½ cup.

3. Heat the oil in a skillet and add the onion. Cook until wilted and add the garlic and chopped mushroom stems. Cook until mushrooms give up their liquid. Cook until the liquid evaporates, stirring. Add the ham, bread crumbs, Parmesan cheese, egg, parsley, basil, marjoram, salt and pepper. Stir to blend.

4. Stuff the mushrooms caps with the mixture. Add the water to a baking dish large enough to hold the mushrooms. Arrange the mushrooms stuffed side up and bake 20 minutes or until piping hot and cooked through.

Yield: 2 dozen.

Vinegared

WITH PIERRE FRANEY

That there are vogues in food is a commonplace. Within the past couple of decades, America has adopted such dishes as quiche Lorraine, beef Wellington, salmon with sorrel sauce and, most recently perhaps, chicken with a tomato and vinegar sauce. The thought of vinegar in a main course may seem strange, but it actually can be a tempting addition. Here are a recently conceived version of chicken with a vinegar and cream sauce, a chicken sauté with vinegar and tomatoes, and a traditional Brittany fish soup lightly laced with oil and vinegar and served with croutons.

Chicken in Vinegar and Cream Sauce

2 3½-pound chickens, cut
into serving pieces
Salt and freshly ground
black pepper
4 tablespoons butter
⅓ cup finely chopped onions
⅜ cup red wine vinegar
2½ cups heavy cream

1. Sprinkle the chicken pieces on all sides with salt and pepper to taste.

2. Heat the butter in one or two large, heavy skillets and add the chicken skin side down. Cook until golden brown and turn the pieces. Cook until golden brown and cooked through, 15 or 20 minutes. Remove the chicken pieces to a dish and cover with foil to keep warm.

3. Pour off the fat from the skillet. Add the onions and cook, stirring briefly, about 3 minutes.

4. Add the vinegar and stir to dissolve the brown particles that cling to the bottom and sides of the skillet. Cook until most of the vinegar evaporates. Pour into the skillet any juices that may have accumulated around the chicken pieces.

5. Add the cream and bring to a vigorous boil. Boil rapidly about 7 minutes and add the chicken pieces. Cook, turning once, until the chicken is nicely coated with sauce and heated through.

Yield: 8 servings.

Cotriade
(A sort of bouillabaisse from Brittany)

4 potatoes, about 1½ pounds
1 large onion, about 1 pound
4 tablespoons butter
1 clove garlic, finely minced
2 quarts water
6 sprigs fresh thyme or ½
teaspoon dried
2 bay leaves
4 sprigs parsley
2 sprigs fresh marjoram or ½
teaspoon dried
Salt and freshly ground
black pepper
1¼ pounds blackfish fillets (see
note), cut into 2-inch cubes
1¼ pounds bonito fillets (see
note), cut into 2-inch cubes
1 ¾-pound striped bass (see
note), scaled, cleaned and
cut into 1-inch pieces
½ pound fresh scallops
16 croutons made with French
bread (see recipe)
2 tablespoons red wine
vinegar
3 tablespoons olive oil
3 tablespoons finely chopped
parsley

1. Peel the potatoes and split them in half. Cut each half into thirds. Drop the potatoes as they are cut into a basin of cold water. Set aside.

2. Peel the onion and cut it into 1-inch cubes.

3. Heat the butter in a large casserole and add the onion. Cook, stirring, until wilted. Add the garlic and cook over low heat about 10 minutes.

4. Add the potatoes and water. Add the thyme, bay leaves, parsley sprigs, marjoram, salt and pepper to taste. Bring to boil and simmer about 25 minutes or until potatoes are tender without being mushy.

5. Add the pieces of fish and continue cooking, ladling the soup over the fish as it cooks. Cook 5 to 10 minutes. Do not overcook or the fish will become dry. Add the scallops and cook about 5 minutes longer.

6. Arrange 2 croutons in the bottom of each of 8 hot soup bowls. Blend the vinegar and oil and spoon this over the croutons. Add the fish soup to the hot bowls and serve sprinkled with chopped parsley.

Yield: 8 servings.

Note: Any very fresh fish, including flounder or fluke, may be substituted for the fish recommended here. Use what is available.

French croutons

Preheat the oven to 400 degrees. Cut a small loaf of French bread into 16 slices. Arrange the slices in one layer on a baking dish and bake, turning and watching carefully, until the slices are nicely browned all over. If desired, the slices could be toasted under a broiler.

Chicken Sauté with Vinegar

2 *3½-pound chickens, cut into serving pieces
Salt and freshly ground black pepper*
4 *tablespoons butter*
⅓ *cup finely chopped shallots*
3 *tablespoons red wine vinegar*
2 *cups seeded, chopped fresh tomatoes*
1 *tablespoon chopped fresh tarragon, optional*

1. Sprinkle the chicken pieces with salt and pepper to taste.

2. Heat the butter in a heavy skillet and add the chicken pieces. Brown about 12 minutes on one side, turn and brown about 10 minutes on the other.

3. Sprinkle the shallots between the pieces of chicken and add the vinegar and cook until most of the vinegar evaporates. Add the tomatoes, cover and cook about 20 minutes.

4. Remove the chicken pieces to a serving platter. Reduce the tomato sauce briefly. Sprinkle with chopped tarragon. Pour it over the chicken and serve hot with rice.

Yield: 6 or more servings.

Chef Michel Guérard

Within a very short span of time, food enthusiasts from all over the world (mostly from the United States) have flocked to the spa resort in Eugénie-les-Bains to see what the young French chef, Michel Guérard, hath wrought with what is called *la cuisine minceur,* or slimming cookery. That style of cooking has been sanctified recently as a new cuisine that allegedly eschews all forms of butter, eggs, cream, and sugar and has been hailed—mostly in American periodicals and in prose as rich and thick as crème fraîche—as the salvation of the gourmet belly. We hastened here on a visit that involved flights to London, Paris and Pau and thence, via car, to the Les Prés et Les Sources d'Eugénie spa in the Pyrénées mountains.

As we waited to check into our room there was ample time to peruse the posted menu of the day's cuisine minceur, at the spa's restaurant, Le Pot au Feu. A note on the menu stated in capital letters RÉSERVÉ EXCLUSIVEMENT AUX CURES THERMALES DE MINCEUR. In other words, the menu in question was reserved exclusively for clients at the hotel taking the cure. We were aware, however, that Mr. Guérard, an acquaintance for several years, had been apprised of our arrival and would make an exception to allow us to sample his new cooking.

A short while after noon we resorted to the bar and ordered a glass of brut champagne. The chef, who is 42 years old, arrived smiling. He has small, handsome Gallic features and stands 5 feet, 4 inches tall. He was wearing his professional, neatly starched, buttoned-down jacket and white apron. We greeted each other, spoke a few pleasantries and, after ordering a Scotch over ice for himself, he extended the hotel's regular menu. A waiter appeared with a platter of hot toast au fromage crowned with ham. We perused the menu and reflected that it was just as innovative as we had recalled it at his noted and highly praised Pot au Feu restaurant in the suburb of Asnières outside Paris.

There were numerous dishes that we remembered fondly from that long-lamented establishment, torn down a few years ago to make room for a highway or some such idiocy in the name of progress. The menu contained, among many other things, first courses that included fresh foie gras stuffed puff pastry dishes and an unforgettable salad gourmande with foie gras. There was preserved goose and the Pot au Feu's famous pot au feu; desserts, such as crêpes with apricot liqueur and a granité of bitter chocolate; plus a few other sinfully caloric delectables.

Remembering our mission, we asked for the minceur or "slimming"

menu and he proffered it with some diffidence. Or so it seemed. It was
an interesting grouping of dishes that showed promise. It listed such
dishes as field salad with chives; grilled veal chop and a soufflé of pear
for midday; crawfish in court-bouillon; a pigeon soup; and a raspberry
sherbet for dessert.

In that this was our first meal in France in a long time, and in that we
have hungered for months for fresh foie gras, we gave in to our baser instincts and appetite and chose the more fattening spread. As meal followed meal during our stay, we cheated a good deal, dining dutifully
from the slimming menu but always leaving room for bouts of hedonism
if not to say gluttony.

There is, we learned, a sharp difference between Mr. Guérard's
wholly valid and inspired concepts of both cuisine gourmande, where
calorie-counting is thrown to the wind, and cuisine minceur, designed
for those who choose for reasons of health or vanity to shape up and slim
down. In the beginning there was la cuisine gourmande. . . .

One of the most glorious dishes this side of paradise is a new creation of Mr. Guérard. It is his oeufs de poule au caviar or chicken eggs
with caviar. It is a simple masterpiece—and—glory of glories—if the
purse can afford the freight, can be easily made in any home kitchen.

It consists of eggs, soft-scrambled in sweet butter with heavy cream
or crème fraîche and a touch of chopped chives added, to hoist the basic
into the sublime. While the scrambled eggs are still hot and moist they
are spooned or, using a pastry bag, piped into, to partly fill the empty egg
shell, the top round of which has been sawed away using a sharp, ser-
rated knife. Fresh caviar is then spooned into the hot eggs in the shell almost to the brim, and another small spoonful of egg is added on top. The
cap is replaced and the eggs are served in egg cups with a small spoon
on the side. After downing the last morsel you sink back in absolute bliss
chanting "God's in his heaven, all's right with the world."

On an equal plane are Mr. Guérard's puff pastry fantasies, a palate-
ravishing puff pastry dish with a filling of hot, white asparagus tips,
anointed with a satiny, butter-rich hollandaise-type sauce flavored with
chopped chervil and/or tarragon.

Another similar creation, a gossamer confection filled with stuffed
coxcombs—the red, delicate combs of roosters—cooked to tender succulence and served with a Périgourdine—which is to say truffle—sauce
containing julienne strips of tongue, carrots, and mushrooms.

At another sitting we were regaled with one of the finer foods of the
region and one of the glories of France, confit de canard or preserved
duck (a confit of goose is also available), rich, seductively seasoned and
sautéed to a turn, served with poached apple and apricot.

We found the salade gourmande a sentimental journey into the past:
It is a joyously appealing and, perhaps at first thought, quixotic blend of

such seemingly disparate ingredients as fresh foie gras, string beans, truffles, asparagus, and a sauce salade made with lemon and walnut oil.

Give a genius such as Mr. Guérard an ingredient as pedestrian as a chicken leg and he will transform it into a celestial, irresistible creation. We were blissfully regaled with gigot de poulette cuit à la vapeur de marjolaine, or stuffed chicken leg cooked over steam with marjoram. The chicken legs, without thighs, are boned almost completely and stuffed with a farce consisting of a wondrously conceived mixture of finely cubed sweetbread, chicken meat, truffles, and tiny gelatinous cubes such as are found in a steamed calf's head. The legs are steamed over a liquid containing marjoram and served with a thin, egg-enriched sauce containing a julienne of truffles, celery, string beans, and fine-textured dried morsels. It was a dish so delicate and refined, we turned with relish to the dessert list and sampled the chef's excellent praline crêpes flamed with apricot liqueur.

Michel Guérard's establishment is situated in the heart of Les Landes, a French department, noted for two of the nation's grandest contributions to the good life, fresh foie gras and armagnac. Late autumn and winter are the times when foie gras is at its finest, and we pampered ourselves with the chef's made-on-the-premises foie gras with an outer coating of cracked peppercorns. This is the only one of the chef's departures from classic cooking with which we might take exception. We found the pepper flavor interesting on first taste, but it seemed overpowering as the meal progressed and seemed not only unnecessary but distracting. With the foie gras we sipped a sauterne, that unctuous, sweet white wine that goes so happily with foie gras that it seems a spiritual liaison. The other wine we drank most often with main courses was one of the restaurant's least expensive, the Bourgogne Pot au Feu, a Volnay, 1973. It was priced at $7 a bottle. The cost of the wines ranges, generally, from about that price to $90 a bottle. The Guérards' main cellar, incidentally, is housed in an old chapel—the altar still intact—a few hundred yards from the château. There he has stored in excess of 20,000 bottles. There is also a cave du jour next to the dining rooms, with accommodation for a hundred or so bottles for immediate needs.

Another specialty of Les Landes is lamb, and we were elated by the petit agneau de lait au thym or roasted lamb with a panade made of breadcrumbs seasoned with thyme.

That, more or less, was our sampling of the young chef's haute cuisine. If we can laud this cuisine gourmande and garland the chef's head with all the laurel leaves our garden will allow, we equally do not dismiss his new, low-calorie cuisine lightly. The trouble is, from the accounts we have read in American periodicals, the impression is gained that Mr. Guérard is attempting to replace one with the other, and, the chef admits, this is patently untrue.

The genesis of his experiments in diet cookery (and he has been quoted as disliking the implications of the word diet or *régime,* which is the French equivalent) came with his raven-haired wife, Christine Barthelémy. She is the daughter of Adrien Barthelémy, who owns a chain of thermal spas, the one at Les Prés et Les Sources presided over and owned by her.

Legend has it that when the two young people met, he was overweight and afflicted with arthritis and kidney trouble. He spent a couple of months at the spa, took the cure, and the idea for cuisine minceur evolved. He is said to have gotten rid of his ailments, including 32 pounds.

As noted, we do not pooh-pooh his efforts. It is a sincere pursuit. But to call these new creations valid substitutes for classic French cooking is farcical. For anyone distressed or invalided by obesity, liver trouble, or stomach disorders, the food is quite obviously superior to any diet food that has come within our purview. Cuisine minceur can be classified as tasty and quite palatable.

One of the most talked about of the cuisine minceur dishes is the gâteau de carrottes fondantes, or carrot cake, a molded baked vegetable dish served hot as a first course. It is made with grated carrots, blended

Michel Guérard stands at the gates of his restaurant-spa in the Pyrénées.

with chopped fresh mushrooms and a touch of cheese, presumably one of low calorie content. Like several other dishes in the repertory the dish came on with considerable appeal at first bite, but the appeal diminished as the course continued. Too much of a muchness, tasty but palling.

We admire Michel Guérard and regard him with unwavering affection. He is as capable as any chef in the whole of France of producing foods to dazzle the taste buds and set the gastric juices gushing with rapture.

Les Prés et Les Sources, thus Le Pot au Feu, closes in the winter and reopens in mid-March. Already there are bookings for much of the year. The cost of accommodations at the hotel ranges from about $24 for a room to $64 for a suite. The cost of the cure is $300 for 11 days. The cost of meals is additional.

Within a few months there will be published in France and thenceforth, no doubt, throughout the world, Mr. Guérard's book on la cuisine minceur. This will be followed, he proposes, by a work which, we suspect, lies closer to his heart and stomach, *La Cuisine Gourmande.*

Here are some recipes from the kitchen of Michel Guérard. The salade gourmande is not for the calorie-conscious, but the others are for disciples of Mr. Guérard's cuisine minceur.

Salade Gourmande

(Foie gras salad)

The basic salad

½ pound green beans, the
    fresher and smaller the
    better
    Salt
24 asparagus (if fresh is not
    available, canned or frozen
    may be used)
    Lettuce leaves, preferably
    from red leaf or Boston
    lettuce, although other
    salad greens such as endive
    or watercress could be
    used
1 large or 2 small black
    truffles, sliced and cut into
    fine (julienne) strips

1 ½-pound can of pure foie
    gras

The dressing

1 teaspoon imported
    prepared mustard,
    preferably Dijon or
    Düsseldorf (do not use the
    baseball lot variety)
    Salt and freshly ground
    black pepper
2 tablespoons lemon juice
½ cup walnut oil or peanut
    oil
⅛ teaspoon sugar

1. Snip off and discard the tips of the green beans. Cut the beans into uniform 2-inch lengths. Drop the pieces into boiling salted water to cover and cook 5 to 8 minutes, depending on size. Do not overcook. When done, the pieces should be crisp-tender.

Drain and let cool to room temperature.

2. Cut the tips, about 2 inches in length, from the asparagus. Set the remaining sections of the asparagus aside for another use such as in soups, salads, and so on. Rinse the asparagus tips well under cold running water. Drain and drop them into boiling salted water to cover. Cook 3 to 7 minutes, depending on thickness. When done, the pieces should be crisp-tender. Drain and let cool to room temperature.

3. When ready to serve, arrange a few lettuce leaves on 6 chilled individual salad plates. If red leaf lettuce is available, arrange it so that the red perimeter of the lettuce will show as a border for the salads.

4. Arrange equal portions of the green beans in the center of each salad, then a layer of asparagus tips. Sprinkle each serving with the julienne truffles. If the foie gras comes in a terrine or crock, spoon equal amounts of it in the center of the salads. If it is a bloc or tunnel-shape of foie gras, cut it into 12 portions. Arrange equal amounts of the foie gras on each salad.

5. Place the mustard in a mixing bowl and add salt and pepper. Add the lemon juice, stirring with a wire whisk. Gradually add the oil, stirring rapidly with the whisk. Add the sugar and blend. Spoon the sauce over the salads and serve, preferably with buttered toast or French bread.

Yield: 6 servings.

Sea Bass with Tomato Sauce

1   *2-pound, cleaned but unscaled sea bass, preferably with head left on and gills removed*
Salt and freshly ground black pepper
2   *pounds fresh seaweed or 1 package dried laver (seaweed) containing 10 sheets, available in Chinese and other Oriental markets*
⅓   *cup water*
Sauce vierge (see recipe)

1. Sprinkle the fish with salt and pepper. If fresh seaweed is available, place a bed of seaweed in a heavy casserole large enough to hold the fish. If dried laver is used, soak it briefly in hot water and arrange half the laver over the casserole. Place the fish on top and add the remaining seaweed or laver. Add the water and cover closely. Steam 10 minutes.

2. Remove the fish. Remove the fish bones and skin. Place the fish on a serving dish and spoon lukewarm sauce vierge over. Serve lukewarm.

Yield: 2 servings.

Sauce vierge

1   *cup crushed, peeled, seeded, red ripe tomatoes*
3   *tablespoons olive oil*
1   *crushed, unpeeled garlic clove*

1 tablespoon chopped fresh
  chervil or 1 teaspoon dried
1 teaspoon each chopped
  fresh parsley and tarragon
½ teaspoon ground coriander
  seeds
  Salt
  Freshly ground black
  pepper

1. Mash the tomatoes to a pulp or blend in a food processor or electric blender. Pour and scrape the mixture into a mixing bowl.

2. Beat in the oil and add the remaining ingredients. Let sit in a warm but not hot place until lukewarm. Serve with the fish.

Yield: About 1¼ cups.

Carrot "Cake"

2 or 3 carrots, about 1½
  pounds
1 cup finely minced
  mushrooms
1 cup chicken broth, without
  fat, or water
¼ teaspoon sugar substitute,
  or more, to taste
  Salt

Freshly ground black
  pepper
1 egg
1 tablespoon chopped fresh
  chervil or 1 teaspoon dried
1 tablespoon grated fat-free
  cheese

1. Preheat the oven to 350 degrees.

2. Trim off the ends and scrape the carrots. Grate the carrots finely.

3. Place the carrots and mushrooms in a heavy saucepan and add the broth or water. Cook, stirring often, so that they cook evenly, until tender but not soft. When ready, most of the liquid should be absorbed. Add the sugar, salt and pepper to taste, and blend well.

4. Drain well and press with a heavy spoon to remove excess moisture.

5. Beat the egg with the chervil and cheese and fold it into the carrot mixture. Pour the mixture into a mold such as a baba mold. Place the mold in a basin of boiling water. Place in the oven and bake about 30 minutes. Unmold and cut into wedges. Serve as a first course.

Yield: 4 to 6 servings.

We went to Eugénie-les-Bains with the serious intent of losing a few pounds while dining gloriously on that most talked about adjunct to what is called la nouvelle cuisine—cuisine minceur. As it turned out, we were not all that taken with these new dishes, although this in no way disputes the towering and genuine talent of Michel Guérard who is not only one of the world's greatest chefs but a good friend as well.

In any event, at the end of our second day at Eugénie-les-Bains, when Michel told us he had to return to Paris the next evening, we decided we'd fly back with him. Though his new cuisine is certainly not unpalatable, we looked forward to some old cuisine in Paris.

When the airplane touched down, Michel offered us a lift into the city which we accepted. Driving along the Champs-Elysées, he turned to us and smiled. "Are you hungry?" he asked.

"Not necessarily," we stated, diplomatically we thought.

"Wouldn't you like a little caviar?" he asked.

That is the one offer we have never been able to refuse. Michel quickly turned the car onto a sidestreet that lead to La Maison du Caviar. We sat at a counter and dined on caviar and buttered toast accompanied by the one drink that is infinitely compatible with those black pearls—well-chilled imported vodka. We must have gained three pounds in that one sitting.

November 1975

T HERE IS AN account in this month of November on what was undoubtedly and understandably one of the ineradicable memories of a lifetime. It was a meal that we had at the restaurant Chez Denis in Paris, the total tab for which came to $4000 for two. It was a meal which had, for better or for worse, repercussions throughout the world. An account of that dinner appeared on the front pages of the most important newspapers in America and was duly recorded in considerable depth in newspapers and major magazines throughout the world.

Oddly enough, although we were accused of, among other things, publicity seeking, that meal, from beginning to end, was conceived as a small and amusing footnote to dining. It was conceived in innocence. Well, almost.

Many months ago, Pierre Franey and I had been asked by the New York public television station (WNET, Channel 13) to contribute a dinner for two to a fund-raising auction. The auction was funded by thousands and thousands of well-wishing New Yorkers with gifts ranging from cruises, coffee pots, precious jewels, digital watches, to automobiles, including a Mercedes Benz. The auction was of a marathon sort and lasted one week.

On the night before the auction ended, we tuned in to the station out of curiosity to find what anyone would pay for a dinner prepared in our kitchen. Seconds after the set was turned on, an offer was flashed on the screen, one of a dozen. American Express was donating dinner for two, at no matter what cost in any restaurant in the world with the provision that the restaurant accept the American Express credit card. The initial bid flashed on the screen was for $50. We did a quick summing up, the wheels were turning rather rapidly, and decided to call in a bid for $300. We felt confident that we could contrive a dinner somewhere in this world to the tune of at least one or two thousand dollars but were hugely skeptical at the possibility of acquiring such a chance at an expenditure many people would think trifling. To our great surprise, after one hour it was announced that ours was the top bid. Thus began the reverie—the dream of a gastronomic bout which endured for about six months.

As we mention in the article on that meal, it became necessary to eliminate from our thinking and dreaming several restaurants we have long admired, such as Taillevent in Paris, and the Auberge de l'Ill, a magnificent Alsatian restaurant in the small country village of Illhaeusern near Colmar, because neither of these highly revered establishments accept any credit card. (We happen to know of one restaurateur in France, who on hearing of our project, set about applying for American Express billing.) We decided to limit our search to Paris, London, Brussels, and Stockholm.

The saga of where we were to eventually dine started in America. A friend of ours had recently returned from Paris and informed us he had dined on an exquisite dish at an enormously expensive but excellent restaurant called Chez Denis. The dish he described was a chiffonade of lobster and he could not analyze the ingredients. That in itself would have been reason enough to visit Chez Denis, curious as to any mystery about the dish. We also knew that Chez Denis is much favored by a number of restaurant critics whose taste we respect.

Though we have never favored London as a gastronomic paradise, we have been told repeatedly that it does have some restaurants of grand merit. Thus we included London in our quest.

We decided on Brussels because of the Villa Lorraine which gained eminence when it was accorded its three-star rating in the *Guide Michelin* several years ago. We decided on Stockholm because of the Operakallaren Restaurant famed for its fine wine and smorgasbord.

Our first stop was Paris. We went to Chez Denis in a party of three and we dined on the chiffonade of lobster, roast game, and fine (and costly) wine. To our mind, the kitchen was of a high order indeed. So pleased were we, in fact, that when M. Denis approached our table we fabricated the following:

"The meal was splendid. We have recently passed our 55th birthday and we have a very wealthy friend in Manhattan who, before we left town, offered us dinner anywhere in the world with cost as no object. We were thinking in terms of a meal for two costing in the vicinity of two thousand dollars. Were we to have dinner in your restaurant, could you conceive of a menu that costly?"

Indeed he could. Moments later he pulled up a chair and sat down, unbidden we might add, and with machine-gun precision, he started rattling off a list of dishes with appropriate wines. How much we asked?

Between two and three thousand dollars.

We were interested.

We were en route to London and Brussels and Stockholm. We told him the names of the hotels where we would be stopping. "If you'd like to pursue this," we said, "would you send us a detailed menu, listing the wines and the cost. We'll await your reply."

In London we tried a number of restaurants but found them in an overall sense disappointing. There was no reply from M. Denis. In Brussels, the second day, a lengthy letter arrived with the menu outlined including the wines. The cost would be, for 33 courses and 9 wines, 17,600 francs, the equivalent of $4000. "Should this interest you," he advised us, "I would be pleased if you would send me a deposit of $2000."

Before leaving New York we had been provided with an American Express chit that resembled an ordinary three-copy credit card receipt to be filled in by the guest. We had no desire to send a deposit, which would have been awkward under the circumstances, so we telephoned an acquaintance in Paris whom we knew to be a friend of M. Denis's. We asked her to telephone him and reveal our association with *The New York Times* and to explain the circumstances of the arrangement with American Express. The next day a cable from M. Denis: "Must know immediately if you accept or not; otherwise, because of the time element, the dinner cannot occur on the date you proposed." We telephoned our friend again and told her to accept.

A funny thing happened in Brussels. After we had discounted the Villa Lorraine, which was quite good but not the object of our quest, we had a sensational dinner at a marvelous place with impeccable food and service called Comme Chez Soi. At that point we had already agreed to return to Paris and eat at Chez Denis. We were so taken with Comme Chez Soi we grieved throughout the meal that this wasn't where we were to have that soon to be celebrated dinner. We dined on woodcock, and wonderful pâtés, fearful to ask the inevitable question, "Do you accept American Express credit card?" At the end of the meal we were escorted out by the owner and a bit breathlessly perhaps we asked the telltale question. We got the blessed response, "No." The rest of the story appears a few pages hence.

We might add that since that dinner, the question most often asked is, "Did you leave a tip?" Payment of the meal transpired as follows: We arrived from Brussels by train the day before the dinner. We had presumed, of course, that both tips and service would be included in that somewhat awesome figure. We went directly to the restaurant, baggage in hand. We greeted the proprietor, discussed the meal in greater detail, the deal was concluded, and before leaving we wrote on the chit $4000. We signed the chit; end of payment and negotiation. As a footnote, we might add that we did go to Stockholm. We enjoyed the visit and the restaurant but with considerable qualification. We would not have been disposed to dine there under such grandiose circumstances.

Surprise à l'Anglaise

WITH PIERRE FRANEY

The phrase *à l'anglaise* generally refers to the plainest kind of cookery—i.e., cooked in water, breaded, or simply baked. One notable exception is roast quail *à l'anglaise* which involves a series of dishes, including quail, croutons spread with liver paste, a delicate brown sauce plus an English bread sauce. They all add up to a genuine autumnal regale.

Roast Quail à l'Anglaise

6   quail
½   cup brown sauce (see recipe)
    Salt and freshly ground black pepper
4   tablespoons butter
6   thin squares fatback, measuring approximately 3 by 3 inches
1   tablespoon cognac or armagnac
6   croutons spread with liver paste (see recipe)
    Straw potatoes, optional (see recipe, page 44)
½   cup golden bread crumbs for game (see recipe)
¾   cup English bread sauce for game (see recipe)
    Currant jelly

1. When the quail are cleaned, cut off the feet and necks. Reserve. Pull out any cavity fat and reserve. If the quail are already cleaned and trimmed, substitute a couple of chicken wings for the trimmings to use in the recipe for brown sauce. Prepare the brown sauce before roasting the quail.

2. Preheat oven to 450 degrees.

3. Sprinkle the quail with salt and pepper to taste.

4. Rub the bottom of a metal roasting pan with 3 tablespoons of butter and arrange the birds on it, breast side up. Cover each breast with a square of fatback.

5. Heat the roasting pan on top of the stove until the butter starts to sizzle. Place the pan in the oven and cook, turning often and basting. As the squares of fatback fall off the birds, keep replacing them. Bake 15 minutes. Do not overcook or the quail will become dry. When cooked, the birds should be golden brown and the fatback crisp.

6. Transfer the quail to a warm place and reserve the fatback. Return the pan to the top of the stove and add the remaining tablespoon of butter. Cook, stirring, 1 minute and add the cognac.

Ignite it and pour in the ½ cup of brown sauce. Stir.

7. Arrange 1 crouton spread with liver paste on each of 6 plates and top each with a quail. Stuff a square of fatback inside each quail, letting it protrude slightly. Garnish the plates with straw potatoes. Spoon the hot pan drippings over the quail and serve with the bread crumbs, bread sauce, and currant jelly separately.

Yield: 6 servings.

Brown sauce

2 chicken wings and/or an
   equivalent amount of
   trimmings from the quail,
   including the legs and
   necks and fat from the
   inside cavity
½ teaspoon peanut,
   vegetable, or corn oil
   Salt and freshly ground
   black pepper
¼ cup finely chopped carrots
¼ cup finely chopped onions
2 tablespoons chopped celery
½ clove garlic, finely minced
1 cup water
1 cup chicken broth
¼ teaspoon dried thyme
¼ bay leaf
5 juniper berries, optional
2 peppercorns

1. If the wings are used, chop or have the butcher cut them into 1-inch pieces. Heat the oil in a small saucepan and add the wings and any available trimmings. Brown, stirring often, about 10 minutes.

2. Add the remaining ingredients and bring to the boil. Do not cover but simmer about 2 hours or until the sauce is reduced to about ½ to ¾ cup. Strain and set aside.

Yield: ½ to ¾ cup.

Croutons with liver paste

6 thin slices French bread
3 or 4 chicken livers (the
   quail livers may replace 1
   or 2 of the chicken livers)
5 tablespoons butter
   Salt and freshly ground
   black pepper
¼ teaspoon fresh or dried
   chopped thyme
¼ bay leaf
1 tablespoon coarsely
   chopped shallots
2 tablespoons cognac or
   armagnac

1. Preheat oven to 450 degrees.

2. Place the bread slices on a baking sheet and bake, turning once or twice, until nicely browned. Remove.

3. Cut the livers into quarters. There should be about ⅓ cup.

4. Heat the butter and add the livers. Cook, stirring, and add all the remaining ingredients except the cognac. Cook about 1 minute and add the cognac. Stir. Cover and remove from the heat. Let cool. Spoon the mixture into the container of an electric blender. Blend well.

5. When the quail are almost ready, spread the croutons with equal portions of the liver paste. Return to the oven briefly just to heat through.

Yield: 6 croutons with liver paste.

English bread sauce for game

½ cup milk
1 small white onion stuck
     with 2 cloves
   Salt
⅛ teaspoon or less cayenne
½ cup bread crumbs

1. Combine the milk, onion, salt to taste, and cayenne in a small saucepan. Stir and bring to the boil.

2. Remove the onion and add the bread crumbs. Stir and bring to the boil. When the mixture is thickened, the sauce is ready.

Yield: About ¾ cup.

Golden bread crumbs for game

3 tablespoons butter
½ cup bread crumbs

Heat the butter in a saucepan and add the crumbs. Cook, stirring, until the crumbs are golden brown.

Yield: About ½ cup

Many times in food news reporting space limitations prevent a thorough-going appraisal of a certain dish's true merit. That was certainly the case with the recipe for roast quail à l'anglaise. To our taste, it might be included in a list of the world's greatest dishes. It is actually not one sole dish but a combination of foods that give it an extraordinary stature amongst the world's finest dishes. It is without question an elaborate preparation and nothing to be tossed off without careful thought and dedication. In any event, it offers a remarkable contrast both in textures and in foods. There is the roast quail (quail is to some minds the greatest of edible game birds) served on crusty toasted French bread slices spread with a liver paste. There are crunchy irresistible straw potatoes, a golden pile of buttered breadcrumbs, and an English bread sauce, a bit bland and yet a marvelous foil for the dish's other textures and flavors.

It was pure coincidence, wholly unforeseen, but this recipe appeared at approximately the same time we were staying at the Connaught Hotel in London, one of the world's ultimate hostelries. One evening we dined in that hotel's elegant and elegantly staffed dining room, and we felt privileged to find on the menu roast grouse à l'anglaise; the preparation is identical to that for roast quail.

Beyond Lasagna

WITH PIERRE FRANEY

Although there is no disputing the vastly increased sophistication of this nation's palate during the past two score years, it is remarkable to what extent Americans limit their indulgence in pasta to spaghetti, lasagna and macaroni. There are dozens of interesting pastas with myriad shapes, each designed to please the palate with an esthetic difference. One of the finest pasta chefs in Manhattan is Alfredo Viazzi. A short while ago we invited Alfredo into our kitchen to turn his fine Italian hand in preparation of sauces for "different" pastas. The pastas include orecchiette, or "little ears," with a tomato, anchovy and olive sauce; fettucelle, with tomatoes, tuna and capers; and green tagliarini, with chicken livers, tomatoes, and prosciutto.

Alfredo's Spaghetti à la Fettucelle

3 tablespoons olive oil
8 tablespoons butter
1 tablespoon chopped garlic
8 fillets of anchovy, minced
1 cup drained, crushed, peeled imported Italian plum tomatoes
  Freshly ground black pepper
⅓ cup drained capers
¾ cup pitted imported red olives (about 42)
1½ cups canned, undrained tuna (see note)
1 tablespoon finely chopped parsley
  Salt, optional
1 pound fettucelle or cavatelli (see note)

1. Heat the oil and 2 tablespoons of butter in a casserole. Add the garlic and cook briefly without browning.

2. Add the anchovies and stir. Add the tomatoes and pepper to taste and cook about 10 minutes.

3. Add the capers, olives, and tuna. Stir to blend. Add the remaining butter and cook about 10 minutes. Add parsley and if desired, add salt to taste.

4. Cook the fettucelle and drain. Serve with the sauce.

Yield: 4 servings.

Note: Alfredo uses Pastene brand imported tuna. Fettucelle is a small version of fettucine. Cavatelli, a short curly noodle, or spaghetti can also be used.

Orecchiette Cinque Terre

1 large sweet (bell) pepper, preferably red
1 medium-size eggplant, about ¾ pound
½ cup olive oil
2 cloves garlic, peeled
1 hot red chili, sliced
2 cups crushed, peeled imported Italian plum tomatoes
8 anchovies
2 tablespoons chopped parsley
1 tablespoon chopped fresh basil or 2 teaspoons dried
¼ cup (about 24) pitted red olives, preferably imported
1 pound orecchiette (see note) or other pasta

1. Preheat oven to 450 degrees (see note).

2. Place the sweet pepper on a sheet of aluminum foil and bake 30 minutes or until the pepper blisters and starts to blacken. Let cool.

3. Trim the ends of the eggplant. Cut the eggplant into ½-inch cubes.

4. Heat the oil and add the garlic and sliced red chili. Cook until the chili and garlic are browned. Remove and discard the garlic and chili. Add the eggplant and continue cooking.

5. Drain the tomatoes but save both the pulp and the juice. There should be about one cup each of pulp and juice. Add the pulp to the oil and eggplant.

6. Chop the anchovies and add them. Cook, stirring occasionally, about 8 to 10 minutes.

7. Add the parsley and basil and cook about 5 minutes. Add the olives and the reserved tomato juice.

8. Peel, core, and seed the sweet pepper. Cut it into ½-inch cubes. Add the pepper to the sauce. Cover and cook about 20 minutes over low heat, stirring occasionally.

9. Cook the orecchiette until tender and drain. Serve hot with the sauce.

Yield: 4 to 6 servings.

Note: Orecchiette is a flat, small, slightly oval pasta. It is available where imported pastas are sold. The pepper in this recipe may be cooked over charcoal or over a gas flame, turning often, until it is blistered and charred all over, rather than in the oven.

Tagliarini Verdi Ghiottona

½   *pound butter*
½   *cup finely chopped onion*
¼   *cup finely diced carrots*
    Salt and freshly ground black pepper
2   *tablespoons chopped parsley*
⅛   *teaspoon grated nutmeg*
½   *pound ground meat, preferably veal, although pork or beef might be used*
¼   *pound chicken livers, cut into ½-inch cubes*
1   *tablespoon dry sherry*
⅓   *cup chicken broth*
1   *cup drained, crushed peeled imported Italian plum tomatoes*
1   *tablespoon olive oil*
¼   *pound prosciutto or other ham, shredded, about 1 cup loosely packed*
1   *pound pasta, preferably green tagliarini, although spaghettini or spaghetti could be used, cooked according to taste*

1. Heat the butter in a skillet or casserole and add the onion and carrots. When bubbling, sprinkle with salt and pepper to taste. Cook gently and without browning about 8 minutes.

2. Add the parsley and nutmeg. Add the veal and cook, stirring, to bring up any lumps. When the meat loses its red color, add the chicken livers and cook, stirring, about 1 minute. Add salt to taste and the sherry. Cook about 1 minute, stirring, and add the chicken broth. Simmer about 3 minutes.

3. Add the tomatoes and cook about 5 minutes.

4. Heat the oil in another skillet and cook the prosciutto about 3 minutes, stirring. Add to the sauce and continue to cook about 20 minutes. Serve hot with the cooked pasta.

Yield: 4 to 6 servings.

Dinner for Two in Paris

Chez Denis

dîner autour de neuf vins
réalisé à Paris
le neuf novembre
mil neuf cent soixante quinze
pour
Monsieur Craig Claiborne

If one were offered dinner for two at any price, to be eaten in any restaurant anywhere in the world, what would the choice be? And in these days of ever-higher prices, what would the cost be?

By submitting the highest bid on Channel 13's fund-raising auction last June, we found ourselves in a position earlier this week to answer these questions. The place: Chez Denis in Paris. The cost: $4,000.

Our winning bid was $300.

One factor in the selection of the restaurant should be noted quickly: The donor of the dinner that Channel 13 auctioned was American Express, which set forth as its only condition the requirement that the establishment be one that accepts its credit card.

The selection of the restaurant dominated our fantasies for weeks as in our minds, we dined on a hundred meals or more. At times we were in Paris, then in Alsace. We considered Rome, Tokyo, and Hong Kong, Copenhagen and Stockholm, Brussels and London. The consideration of restaurants competed with thoughts of the greatest of champagnes and still wines, visions of caviar and foie gras, dreams of elaborate desserts. Perhaps we would choose nothing but vodka or champagne with caviar followed by foie gras with Château d'Yquem—but no, any old millionaire could do that.

In addition to excluding those that did not recognize the credit card of the donor, we dismissed from our potential list of restaurants several celebrated places, simply, perhaps, because of their celebrity. In time we considered Chez Denis, which is a great favorite among several food writers (Henri Gault, Christian Millau, and Waverly Root among them), but is nonetheless not well known. It is a tiny place on the Rue Gustave Flaubert, not far from the Arc de Triomphe.

We visited Chez Denis in a party of three to reconnoiter. It was not hard to go incognito, for we suspect that the proprietor, Denis Lahana, does not credit any Americans with even the most elementary knowledge of French wine and food.

The investigatory dinner was sumptuous. There was a chiffonade of lobster (a salad of cold lobster, cubed foie gras, a touch of cognac and, we suspect, cayenne, and a tarragon mayonnaise flavored with tomato, tossed with lettuce). In addition, there was fresh foie gras with aspic, braised sweetbreads with a light truffle sauce, roast quail and those delectable tiny birds from the Landes region of France, ortolans. There was also a great personal favorite, andouillettes served with an outstanding sorrel sauce. The wine was a fine Pommard.

The meal having passed the test, we were able to ignore the few plastic boughs and plastic flowers tucked in beams here and there. We wondered how it was that the place did not merit one, two, or three stars in the Guide Michelin. It is not even listed. Mr. Denis would not comment on a story we had heard about inspectors from Michelin having somehow offended the proprietor and having been asked to leave.

After dinner, we asked Mr. Denis, offhandedly, how much he would charge for the most lavish dinner for two that he and his chef could prepare. He spoke in terms of $2,000 to $3,000. We told him that we were about to celebrate a birthday and that money was no obstacle in ordering the finest dinner in Europe. Mr. Denis, with little hesitation, pulled up a chair and sat down. He took us seriously.

We asked him to consider the matter at his convenience and write to us with his proposal. When he did, his letter stated:

"In accordance with your demand, I propose to organize for you a prestigious dinner. In the land of my birth, the region of Bordeaux, one speaks of a *repas de vins,* a meal during the course of which a number of wines of great prestige are served, generally nine wines.

"I am suggesting nine such wines, to be served in the course of a dinner *à la Française* in the classic tradition. To dine properly in this style, many dishes are offered and served to the guests, chosen with the sole thought that each dish be on the same high level as the wines and those most likely to give pleasure as the wines are tasted."

He suggested a dinner of 31 dishes that would start with an hors d'oeuvre and go on to three "services," the first consisting of soups, savory, an assortment of substantial main dishes, and ices or sherbets to clear the palate. This would be followed by the second service: hot roasts or baked dishes, vegetables, cold, light, meaty dishes in aspic and desserts. And then the third service: decorated confections, petits fours, and fruits.

The youngest wine would be a six-year-old white burgundy, the oldest a 140-year-old madeira.

Mr. Denis set a price of $4,000. This, we must hasten to add, included service and taxes. We accepted.

The proprietor suggested that the meal be served to four persons—all for the same price—because the food had to be prepared in a certain quantity and would be enough to serve as many as ten persons, while the wines were enough for four.

We declined, because the rules set by American Express called for dinner for two. The dinner party would be made up of me and my colleague, Pierre Franey. Anything left over, we knew, would not go to waste.

Mr. Denis noted that it was not required that all foods be sampled and that the quantity of the food served would depend on the guest's appetite.

And so, we sat down to our $4,000 dinner.

The hors d'oeuvre was presented: fresh Beluga caviar in crystal, enclosed in shaved ice, with toast. The wine was a superb 1966 Champagne Comtesse Marie de France.

Then came the first service, which started with three soups. There was consommé Denis, an inordinately good, rich, full-bodied, clear consommé of wild duck with shreds of fine crêpes and herbs. It was clarified with raw duck and duck bones and then lightly thickened as many classic soups are, with fine tapioca.

The second soup (still of the first service) was a crème Andalouse, an outstanding cream of tomato soup with shreds of sweet pimento and fines herbes, including fresh chives and chervil.

The first two soups were superb but the third, cold germiny (a cream of sorrel), seemed bland and anticlimactic. One spoonful of that sufficed,

The only wine served at this point was a touch of champagne. The soups having been disposed of, we moved on to a spectacularly delicate parfait of sweetbreads, an equally compelling mousse of quail in a small tarte, and a somewhat salty, almost abrasive but highly complementary tarte of Italian ham, mushrooms, and a border of truffles.

The wine was a 1918 Château Latour, and it was perhaps the best bordeaux we had ever known. It was very much alive, with the least trace of tannin.

The next segment of the first service included a fascinating dish that the proprietor said he had created, Belon oysters broiled quickly in the shell and served with a pure beurre blanc, the creamy, lightly thickened butter sauce. Also in this segment were a lobster in a creamy, cardinal-red sauce that was heavily laden with chopped truffles and, after that, another startling but excellent dish, a sort of Provençale pie made with red mullet and baked with tomato, black olives, and herbs, including fennel or anise seed, rosemary, sage, and thyme. The accompanying wine was a 1969 Montrachet Baron Thénard, which was extraordinary (to our taste, all first-rate Montrachet whites are extraordinary).

The final part of the first service consisted of what was termed filets et sots l'y laissent de poulard de Bresse, sauce suprème aux cèpes (the so-called "fillet" strips of chicken plus the "oysters" found in the after-backbone of chicken blended in a cream sauce containing sliced wild mushrooms).

There followed another curious but oddly appealing dish, a classic chartreuse of partridge, the pieces of roasted game nested in a bed of cooked cabbage and baked in a mosaic pattern, intricately styled, of carrot and turnip cut into fancy shapes. And a tender rare-roasted fillet of Limousin beef with a rich truffle sauce. The wine with the meats was a 1928 Château Mouton-Rothschild. It was ageless and beautiful.

The first service finally ended with sherbets in three flavors—raspberry, orange, and lemon. The purpose of this was to revive the palate for the second service, and it did. We were two hours into the meal and going at the food, it seemed, at a devilish pace.

The second service included the ortolans en brochette, an element of the dinner to be anticipated with a relish almost equal to that of the caviar or the foie gras. The small birds, which dine on berries through their brief lives, are cooked whole, with the head on, and without cleaning except for removing the feathers. They are as fat as butter and an absolute joy to bite into because of the succulence of the flesh. Even the bones, except for the tiny leg bones, are chewed and swallowed. There is one bird to one bite.

The second service also included fillets of wild duck en salmis in a rich brown game sauce. The final dish in this segment was a rognonade de veau, or roasted boned loin of veal wrapped in puff pastry with fresh black truffles about the size of golf balls. The vegetables served were pommes Anna—the potatoes cut into small rounds and baked in butter—and a puree rachel, a puree of artichokes.

Then came the cold meat delicacies. There was butter-rich fresh foie gras in clear aspic, breast meat of woodcocks that was cooked until rare and served with a natural chaudfroid, another aspic, and cold pheasant with fresh hazelnuts. The wines for this segment consisted of a 1947 Château Lafite-Rothschild, a 1961 Château Petrus, and the most magnificent wine of the evening, a 1929 Romanée Conti.

The dinner drew near an end with three sweets—a cold glazed charlotte with strawberries, an île flottante, and poires alma. The wine for the sweets was a beautiful unctuous 1928 Château d'Yquem, which was quite sweet and yet "dry."

The last service consisted of the pastry confections and fruits, served with an 1835 madeira. With coffee came a choice of a 100-year-old calvados or an hors d'âge cognac.

And for the $4,000, logic asks if it was a perfect meal in all respects? The answer is no.

The crystal was Baccarat and the silver was family sterling, but the presentation of the dishes, particularly the cold dishes such as the sweetbread parfait and quail mousse tarte, was mundane.

The foods were elegant to look at, but the over-all display was undistinguished, if not to say shabby. The chartreuse of pheasant, which can be displayed stunningly, was presented on a most ordinary dish.

The food itself was generally exemplary, although there were regrettable lapses there, too. The lobster in the gratin was chewy and even the sauce could not compensate for that. The oysters in the shells, which should have been piping hot, were almost lukewarm when they reached the table, and so was the chartreuse of pheasant.

We've spent many hours reckoning the cost of the meal and find that we cannot break it down. We have decided this: We feel we could not have made a better choice, given the circumstance of time and place. Mr. Denis declined to apply a cost to each of the wines, explaining that they contributed greatly to the total cost of the meal because it was necessary to open three bottles of the 1918 Latour in order to find one in proper condition.

Over all, it was an unforgettable evening and we have high praise for Claude Mornay, the 37-year-old genius behind the meal.

We reminded ourselves of one thing during the course of that evening: If you were Henry VIII, Lucullas, Gargantua, and Bacchus, all rolled into one, you cannot possibly sustain, start to finish, a state of ecstasy while dining on a series of 31 dishes.

Wines, illusion or not, became increasingly interesting, although we were laudably sober at the end of the meal.

Donor is "mildly astonished"

"We were mildly astonished at first but now we're cheerful about it," a spokesman for American Express said yesterday after having learned that Craig Claiborne had spent $4,000 of the company's money for dinner.

The spokesman, Jess Gregory, added, "It shows what a good deal the Channel 13 auction can be for people."

He added that under an American Express offer called Be My Guest, the recipient normally receives an invitation for dinner that carries a limitation as to how much can be spent. This was not the case with Mr. Claiborne's gift. Mr. Gregory added that he would have estimated that the winner of the unlimited dinner at the Channel 13 auction would have run up a bill as high as $500.

"We've never had one reach these heights," Mr. Gregory said, but he emphasized that American Express was not upset by the size of the bill.

American Express's mild astonishment had been expressed earlier, when a message was left with the company requesting a comment on the $4,000 meal.

Iris Burkat, an official of the company returned the call and said, "Four thousand—was that francs or dollars?"

What the wines would cost here

Rare as they are, most of the wines featured at the Chez Denis dinner are available in New York. Jack Chambers, store manager at Morrell & Co., a retail wine and liquor store in Manhattan, either had in stock or could obtain the wines at the prices below.

The champagne, a special bottling, was unavailable here, but the best champagnes we do get are probably comparable and the price list here is what they would cost. The same is true of the Calvados and the cognac.

These are, of course, retail store prices. Expensive restaurants traditionally take a markup of 100 percent or more over retail price.

The wines:

Champagne Comtesse Marie de France Cuvée Denis 1966
Not available .... (equivalent, about $25)
Château Latour 1918 .... $100
Montrachet Baron Thénard 1969 .... $25
Château Mouton-Rothschild 1928 .... $135
Château Lafite-Rothschild 1947 .... $100
Château Petrus 1961 .... $85
Romanée Conti 1929 .... $500
Chateau d'Yquem 1928 .... $75
Vin de Madère 1835 .... $100
Calvados de la Vallée d'Auge 1865 .... $75
Cognac hors d'âge-réserve Denis $90

Pierre Franey and Craig Claiborne, seated, with Denis Lahana, who prepared a $4,000 dinner for two.

One of the things that appealed to us most subsequent to that dinner was the response of our friend and colleague Russell Baker. Russell, who has been justly called the Jonathan Swift of the twentieth century, wrote an incredibly humorous parody of the meal entitled "Francs and Beans." If there are those among you who were not amused by that dinner in Paris, we offer you Russell's meal as solace and consolation.

Francs and Beans by Russell Baker

As chance would have it, the very evening Craig Claiborne ate his historic $4,000 dinner for two with 31 dishes and nine wines in Paris, a Lucullan repast for one was prepared and consumed in New York by this correspondent, no slouch himself when it comes to titillating the palate.

Mr. Claiborne won his meal in a television fund-raising auction and had it professionally prepared. Mine was created from spur-of-the-moment inspiration, necessitated when I discovered a note on the stove saying, "Am eating out with Dora and Imogene—make dinner for yourself." It was from the person who regularly does the cooking at my house and, though disconcerted at first, I quickly rose to the challenge.

The meal opened with a 1975 Diet Pepsi served in a disposable bottle. Although its bouquet was negligible, its distinct metallic aftertaste evoked memories of tin cans one had licked experimentally in the first flush of childhood's curiosity.

To create the balance of tastes so cherished by the epicurean palate, I followed with a *paté de fruites de nuts of Georgia*, prepared according to my own recipe. A half-inch layer of creamy-style peanut butter is troweled onto a graham cracker, then half a banana is crudely diced and pressed firmly into the peanut butter and cemented in place as it were by a second graham cracker.

The accompanying drink was cold milk served in a wide-brimmed jelly glass. This is essential to proper consumption of the paté, since the entire confection must be dipped into the milk to soften it for eating. In making the presentation to the mouth, one must beware lest the milk-soaked portion of the sandwich fall onto the necktie. Thus, seasoned gourmandisers follow the old maxim of the Breton chefs and "bring the mouth to the jelly glass."

At this point in the meal, the stomach was ready for serious eating, and I prepared beans with bacon grease, a dish I perfected in 1937 while developing my *cuisine du dépression.*

The dish is started by placing a pan over a very high flame until it becomes dangerously hot. A can of Heinz's pork and beans is then emptied into the pan and allowed to char until it reaches the consistency of hardening concrete. Three strips of bacon are fried to crisps, and when the beans have formed huge dense clots firmly welded to the pan, the bacon grease is poured in and stirred vigorously with a large screw driver.

This not only adds flavor but also loosens some of the beans from the side of the pan. Leaving the flame high, I stirred in a three-day-old spaghetti sauce found in the refrigerator, added a sprinkle of chili powder, a large dollop of Major Grey's chutney and a tablespoon of bicarbonate of soda to make the whole dish rise.

Beans with bacon grease is always eaten from the pan with a tablespoon while standing over the kitchen sink. The pan must be thrown away immediately. The correct drink with this dish is a straight shot of room-temperature gin. I had a Gilbey's 1975, which was superb.

For the meat course, I had fried bologna *à la Nutley, Nouveau Jersey.* Six slices of A&P bologna were placed in an ungreased frying pan over maximum heat and held down by a long fork until the entire house filled with smoke. The bologna was turned, fried the same length of time on the other side, then served on air-filled white bread with thick lashings of mayonnaise.

The correct drink for fried bologna *à la Nutley, Nouveau Jersey* is a 1927 Nehi Cola, but since my cellar, alas, had none, I had to make do with a second shot of Gilbey's 1975.

The cheese course was deliciously simple—a single slice of Kraft's individually wrapped yellow sandwich cheese, which was flavored by vigorous rubbing over the bottom of the frying pan to soak up the rich bologna juices. Wine being absolutely *de rigueur* with cheese, I chose a 1974 Muscatel, flavored with a maraschino cherry, and afterwards cleared my palate with three pickled martini onions.

It was time for the fruit. I chose a Del Monte tinned pear, which, regrettably, slipped from the spoon and fell on the floor, necessitating its being blotted with a paper towel to remove cat hairs. To compensate for the resulting loss of pear syrup, I dipped it lightly in hot-dog relish which created a unique flavor.

With the pear I drank two shots of Gilbey's 1975 and one shot of Wolfschmidt vodka (non-vintage), the Gilbey's having been exhausted.

At last it was time for the dish the entire meal had been building toward—dessert. With a paring knife, I ripped into a fresh package of Oreos, produced a bowl of My-T-Fine chocolate pudding which had been coagulating in the refrigerator for days and, using a potato masher, crushed a dozen Oreos into the pudding. It was immense.

Between mouthfuls, I sipped a tall, bubbling tumbler of cool Bromo-Seltzer, and finished with six ounces of Maalox. It couldn't have been better.

As we recounted earlier, one of the reasons for going to Chez Denis in the first place was to sample a lobster chiffonade. It had been described to us as one of the best first courses in all of Paris. We dined on the dish, as well as on many other things, and found it to be, indeed, a distinguished appetizer. On returning to New York, we found it quite easy to duplicate in our home kitchen and we offer our recipe here.

Chiffonade of Lobster Chez Denis

2 1½-pound live lobsters or 2 cups cubed cooked lobster meat
1 egg yolk
1 tablespoon white wine vinegar
1 tablespoon imported mustard, such as Dijon or Düsseldorf
1 tablespoon tomato paste
   Salt and freshly ground pepper
⅛ teaspoon cayenne or Tabasco sauce to taste
1 cup olive oil
   Juice of ½ lemon
1 teaspoon chopped fresh tarragon or ½ teaspoon dried, chopped
2 teaspoons cognac
½ cup cubed foie gras, optional
¾ cup cubed, seeded tomatoes
6 to 12 leaves fresh, crisp, romaine lettuce

1. If live lobsters are used, drop them into vigorously boiling salted water and cover. Cook 10 minutes and remove from the heat. Let stand about 15 minutes. Drain and let cool.

2. When the lobsters are cool enough to handle, crack them and remove the meat from the claws and tail. Reserve and set aside any red coral. There should be about 2 cups of meat and/or coral. Refrigerate until ready to use.

3. Place the yolk in a mixing bowl and add the vinegar, mustard, tomato paste, salt and pepper to taste, and cayenne. Gradually add the oil, beating vigorously with a wire whisk. Beat in the lemon juice, tarragon, and cognac.

4. Add the lobster and foie gras and tomatoes to the mayonnaise and fold them in with a rubber spatula. This may be done in advance and refrigerated for an hour or so.

5. When ready to serve, stack the romaine lettuce leaves and cut them into the finest possible shreds, using a heavy sharp knife. There should be about two cups loosely packed shreds. Add this to the salad and fold it in. Serve immediately before the shreds wilt.

Yield: 6 to 8 servings.

Tailgate Feast

WITH PIERRE FRANEY

It is probably apparent to a few score people that we take undisciplined delight in what might be called picnic food. We revel in the likes of stuffed eggs and sandwiches as well as in the more elaborate likes of a cold bottle and a roast bird. If the air is dry and the sun shines bright, we can say "fie" to the cold winds of autumn. And to tell the truth, we frequently take more pleasure in a tailgate feast than in any old ball game. There are, on this page, a few contrivances for just such a feast, including an excellent, simply made pâté (it is good for several occasions); a tasty dish of shrimp with a tarragon and anchovy mayonnaise; a classic roast chicken with rosemary; and even a portable Bavarian cream aromatized with one of the finest and most seductively flavored of all white liqueurs, mirabelle.

Shrimp with a Tarragon and Anchovy Mayonnaise

1½   pounds raw shrimp, about 36
12   whole allspice berries
1   dried hot red pepper
   Salt
1   cup freshly made mayonnaise
2   teaspoons fresh lemon juice, or more to taste
6   anchovies, finely chopped
1   tablespoon chopped fresh tarragon or 1 teaspoon dried

1. Place the shrimp in a saucepan and add cold water to cover. Add the allspice, hot red pepper, and salt to taste. Bring to the boil and simmer 1 minute. Remove the shrimp from the heat and let cool. Drain, shell, and devein the shrimp.

2. Combine the mayonnaise with the lemon juice, chopped anchovies, and tarragon. Cut the shrimp in half and add them. Chill and serve cold.

Yield: 6 or more servings.

Roast Chicken with Rosemary

1   3–3½-pound chicken, with giblets
1   sprig fresh rosemary or 2 teaspoons dried
1   clove garlic, unpeeled
   Salt and freshly ground black pepper
2   tablespoons butter

1. Preheat oven to 450 degrees.

2. Stuff the chicken with the rosemary and whole garlic clove. Sprinkle inside and out with salt and pepper to taste. Truss with string or skewers.

3. Melt the butter in a shallow, small roasting pan on top of the stove. Add the chicken and turn it in the butter to coat on all sides. Place the chicken on one side and scatter the neck, gizzard, and liver, if used, around the chicken.

4. Place chicken in the oven and roast it 15 to 20 minutes, basting occasionally. Turn the chicken on its other side. Roast 15 to 20 minutes, basting occasionally, and turn the chicken on its back. Roast 15 to 20 minutes longer, basting. When cooked, the chicken should be golden brown all over. No red juices should flow when the joint between the thigh and leg is pierced with a fork. Use a 2-pronged fork and lift the chicken up to let the cavity juices flow into the pan. Baste the chicken with the pan juices.

5. Untruss the chicken. Remove and discard the garlic clove. If used, remove the rosemary sprig. Cut the chicken into serving pieces. If the chicken is to be served hot, remove the leaves from the main stem of the rosemary sprig. Chop the leaves and add to the pan juices. Serve hot with the chicken.

Yield: 4 servings.

Chicken Liver Pâté

1 pound chicken livers
¼ cup chopped pork fatback
Salt and freshly ground black pepper
2 tablespoons butter
1 tablespoon finely chopped shallots
½ teaspoon dried thyme
¼ bay leaf, finely chopped or ground in a small, clean spice or coffee mill
1 tablespoon cognac
1 pound ground pork
½ pound ground veal
¼ teaspoon grated nutmeg
¼ teaspoon ground allspice
3 tablespoons whole pistachios
Thinly sliced fatback or bacon to line and cover a 6-cup mold
4 to 6 very thin slices prosciutto or ham

1. Preheat oven to 400 degrees.

2. Pick over the chicken livers to remove any tough connecting tissues.

3. Heat the fatback in a saucepan and add ¼ of the whole chicken livers. Sprinkle with salt and pepper to taste and cook, turning in the fat, about 2 minutes. Do not overcook. Remove and set aside the livers. Reserve the fat in the saucepan.

4. Heat the butter in a skillet and add the remaining livers. Sprinkle with salt and pepper to taste and cook, turning, about 2 minutes. They must not become dry.

5. Add the shallots, thyme, bay leaf, and flame with cognac. Puree the mixture in an electric blender or food processor, adding the reserved fat from the saucepan and that from the skillet.

6. Spoon the mixture into a mixing bowl and add the ground pork and veal, salt and pepper to taste, nutmeg, allspice, and pistachios. Blend well.

7. Line a 6-cup oval or rectangular mold (with a lid) with the fatback slices. Spoon about ⅓ of the pureed liver mixture into the mold.

8. Arrange the prosciutto or ham on a flat surface. Spoon a little of the pureed liver over each. Arrange the whole chicken livers in a row down the center of each ham slice. Spoon on a little more of the pureed mixture and roll the slices to enclose the livers. Arrange these rolls down the center of the lined mold. Spoon in the remaining pureed liver mixture. Cover with a single layer of fatback slices.

9. Cover the mold with the lid. Place the mold in a baking dish and pour boiling water around it. Bring the water to the boil on top of the stove and place the mold in the baking dish in the oven. Bake 2 hours or until the internal temperature of the pâté measures 160 degrees.

10. Remove the pâté from the water bath and let cool. Place a weight on the pâté (we used a small, heavy meat mallet). Refrigerate until the pâté is "set." Unmold. Serve sliced with cornichons.

Yield: 8 to 10 servings.

Mirabelle-Flavored Bavarian Cream

5   egg yolks
⅔   cup plus 1 tablespoon sugar
2   cups milk
⅛   teaspoon salt
1   envelope unflavored gelatin
¼   cup mirabelle liqueur (or use kirsch, cognac, or rum)
1   cup heavy cream

1. Place the yolks in a saucepan and add the ⅔ cup of sugar. Beat with a wire whisk until thick and lemon colored.

2. Meanwhile, bring the milk almost but not quite to the boil.

3. Gradually add the milk to the yolk mixture, beating constantly. Use a wooden spoon and stir constantly, this way and that, making certain the spoon touches all over the bottom of the saucepan. Cook, stirring, and add the salt. Cook until the mixture has a custardlike consistency and coats the sides of the spoon. Do not let the sauce boil, or it will curdle.

4. Soak the gelatin in the liqueur, add a little of the hot custard and stir until completely dissolved. Combine the two mixtures and let cool to room temperature.

5. When cool, beat the cream until it is almost stiff. Add the remaining 1 tablespoon sugar and continue beating until stiff. Fold the whipped cream into the custard-gelatin mixture; then spoon the mixture into 6 or 8 serving glasses. Chill until set.

Yield: 6 to 8 servings.

The Bialy

"I've been sending your recipes for many years to my daughter in Alaska," Joseph Slotnik of White Plains writes. "Now she asks me for a formula for one of the Yiddish delights, bialys, known in English as a water roll."

In approximately the same mail we received the latest publication from our Illinois friends, Sue and Sidney Gross. Fresh off the presses is their 40-page, soft-cover pamphlet titled *The Roll Basket,* and it includes a recipe for bialys that, Mrs. Gross adds, has taken her a year or longer to perfect.

Their booklet contains recipes for many kinds of breads and rolls including salt sticks, rye rolls, onion boards (pretzels), and Arab bread. It may be ordered by sending a check or money order for $2.25 to Gross' Kitchen Harvest, Box 30, Cortland, Ill. 60112. Here is Sue Gross's recipe for the bialys.

Bialys

Dough

1 *package yeast*
2¼ *cups warm water*
1 *tablespoon salt*
1 *tablespoon sugar*
1½ *cups 41 percent gluten flour, unsifted (available at health food stores)*
3½ *cups all-purpose flour, unsifted*

Onion-garlic topping

¼ *cup dried, minced onions, soaked in water and squeezed dry*
1 *tablespoon oil*
½ *teaspoon poppy seeds*
  Pinch salt
½ *teaspoon (or to taste) garlic powder (for plain onion topping, leave out)*

1. Dissolve the yeast in 1 cup of the warm water and set aside.

2. Dissolve the salt and sugar in the rest of the water. Add the gluten flour and stir. Add the yeast water and stir. Add the all-purpose flour and stir to mix.

3. Knead (preferably by machine; the dough is slack) until smooth (10 minutes by machine). Place the ball of dough in an ungreased bowl, cover, and let rise until very light. Punch, turn the dough over, cover and let rise until very light a second time. Punch.

4. Divide the dough into 16 or 20 pieces, depending on the size roll you want (try 16). Shape the rolls as if you were making hamburger buns, that is so they look like sand dollars, thicker in the middle than at the edges, which should be about ⅜ inch thick. (A baked bialy is about 1¼ inches thick.)

5. Place the shaped rolls on lightly floured wooden boards to rise. Do not let the tops dry out; cover the rolls with plastic wrap. Let the rolls rise part way.

6. Meanwhile, combine all the ingredients for the topping.

7. Indent a circle about 1 inch in diameter in the center of each roll. Either use your thumbs or the top of a spice jar for a press. Spread the onion-garlic topping in the indentations and sprinkle the tops of the rolls with topping, too. Let the rolls rise until light.

8. Preheat the oven to 450 degrees.

9. Place the bialys on dry baking sheets and bake for 12 to 15 minutes, or until brown.

Yield: 16 to 20 bialys.

Fennel: Crisp and Aromatic

Fresh fennel, Ralph Formisano was saying, can become a sort of addiction. Mr. Formisano, who is known in some quarters as the "fennel king of New Jersey," was standing in the middle of his 40-acre fennel crop that, caressed by a late autumn wind, resembled a vast and undulating sea of green feathers.

"Most of our crop is sold commercially," he said, "but we have personal customers who come from as far away as Massachusetts, Delaware, and Pennsylvania to buy it by the crate.

"One fellow stopped by from Springfield a few weeks ago before the fennel was ready. I told him that, and he was furious. He slammed his hands down and yelled, 'Whaddaya mean it's not ready. I drove 40 miles to get here, and I'm not leaving without it.'" Mr. Formisano laughed. "Sadly, he left without it."

Fennel is a crisp, aromatic vegetable or herb that, for one reason or another, is more closely identified with the Italian table than any other. It is established that it was known in England, however, long before the Norman Conquest and that excellent source book, *Herbs, Spices and Flavorings* by Tom Stobart (McGraw-Hill, 1970), states that for centuries it has been traditional throughout Europe for use with both fresh and salted fish.

Fennel is most commonly served in America as a cold appetizer like radishes, celery ribs, and scallions, and that is the way it is most frequently served in the Formisano home.

Its association with fish is, however, undeniable, and one of the most felicitous dishes of the French kitchen is loup de mer au fenouil, which is to say, a kind of sea bass, grilled and flamed with dried fennel leaves and stalks.

Legend has it that at one point in history, fennel was inalterably associated with fish in Europe and on fast days, the very wealthy dined on fish with fennel. The poor on those days, dined, it is related, on fennel alone, the fish in absentia.

Fennel is also known locally as "anise," although it is really a different plant. It is packed and labeled "anise" at the Formisano farm. It is, with its feathery, bright green leaves and white, clustered, globe-like base, one of the most beautiful of plants. Mr. Formisano boasts, and not without reason, that the "anise" or fennel from his farm is among the finest to be grown in America. His fennel bulbs are particularly white and full, characteristics that he attributes to a family secret handed down from his grandfather who grew fennel in his native Italy.

The seeds for this crop are purchased both from California and Italy. In seed catalogues the seeds are listed as Florence fennel. The seeds, which contribute considerable flavor to several thousand dishes around the world including Italian sausages, are planted in this farming community from mid-June to mid-July for a harvest that lasts from around the first of October to the middle or end of November. When the crop expires here, there still remain shipments of the vegetable from farms in California.

Mr. Formisano, whose three sons are also involved in his extensive farming enterprises, employs ten workmen who are equipped with constantly sharpened carbon steel knives called cabbage knives. The fennel is lifted from the soil and with one quick swoop of the knife to the underside of the plant, the "anise" or fennel is ready to be crated and labeled and sold at the local auction or to would-be buyers like the customer from Springfield.

Fennel is known as fenouil in French, fenchel in German, finocchio in Italian and hinojo in Spanish. Although it is delicious eaten out of hand, it is an enormously versatile vegetable when cooked. It is excellent in salads; it makes a fine hot soup; it complements baked fish dishes; it is fine braised and served with a meat sauce; and it excels when cooked au gratin with grated Parmesan cheese.

Ralph Formisano, known as "the fennel king of New Jersey," holds some giant examples of his crop.

Creamed Fennel Soup

1¾ *pounds tender, unblemished*
    fennel bulbs with stems
    Salt and freshly ground
    black pepper
3 *tablespoons heavy cream*
2 *tablespoons butter*

1. Trim and quarter the fennel, but save the tender stems. Place all the pieces in a saucepan and add cold water to cover. Add salt to taste. Bring to the boil and simmer about 20 minutes or until tender. Drain.

2. Puree the fennel in a food processor or blender and empty it into a saucepan. Bring to the boil and add the remaining ingredients. Serve piping hot.

Yield: About 2 cups.

Fennel au Gratin

3 *to 6 fennel bulbs*
4 *tablespoons butter*
    Salt and freshly ground
    black pepper
1 *cup chicken broth*
½ *cup grated Parmesan*
    cheese

1. Preheat oven to 400 degrees.

2. Cut off the tops of the fennel bulbs and trim the base. Pull off and discard any tough outer leaves. Cut the remaining fennel into quarters, if they are large, or in half, if they are small.

3. Drop the fennel into enough boiling water to cover and when the water returns to the boil, simmer 15 or 20 minutes or until almost tender.

4. Drain the fennel and arrange the pieces symmetrically, cutside down, on a baking dish. Dot with butter. Add salt, pepper, and chicken broth. Sprinkle with cheese and bake 30 minutes.

Yield: 6 to 8 servings.

Fennel with Meat Sauce

3 *to 6 fennel bulbs*
¼ *cup olive oil*
2 *cloves garlic, finely minced*
¼ *cup chicken broth*
2½ *cups Italian meat sauce*
    (see recipe)
    Grated Parmesan cheese

1. Cut off the tops of the fennel bulbs and trim the bases. Pull off and discard the tough outer leaves. Cut the fennel into quarters, if they are large, or in half, if they are small.

2. Drop the fennel into enough boiling water to cover and when the water returns to the boil, simmer 10 minutes. Drain.

3. Heat the oil in a skillet large enough to hold the fennel in one layer. Add the garlic and cook until it starts to brown. Add the fennel, cutside down, and the chicken broth. Cover closely and simmer until fennel is tender, about 40 minutes. Spoon the meat sauce over. Serve piping hot with grated Parmesan cheese.

Yield: 6 to 8 servings.

Italian meat sauce

3 cups chopped red, ripe, peeled fresh tomatoes or an equivalent amount of canned imported Italian tomatoes
3½ tablespoons butter
1½ tablespoons olive oil
¼ cup finely chopped onion
1 clove garlic, finely minced
¼ cup finely chopped prosciutto
¼ cup finely chopped celery
¼ cup finely chopped carrot
½ pound twice-ground beef
½ pound twice-ground veal
1 cup dry white wine
½ pound fresh mushrooms, thinly sliced
¼ pound raw chicken livers, picked over and cut into small cubes
Salt and freshly ground black pepper
1 cup chicken broth
⅛ teaspoon grated nutmeg
¾ cup heavy cream

1. If fresh tomatoes are used, peel them. Squeeze out the seeds and chop the tomatoes. Whether fresh or canned, there should be 3 cups. Place the tomatoes in a saucepan and bring to the boil. Simmer, stirring often from the bottom, about 30 minutes. Tomatoes should be reduced to about 2 cups.

2. Meanwhile, heat 1½ tablespoons butter and the olive oil in a deep skillet or kettle and add the onion. Cook until wilted and add the garlic, prosciutto, celery, and carrot. Cook briefly and add the meats, stirring with the side of a heavy metal spoon to break up lumps. Cook until the meat loses its raw color. Add the wine and cook until it is almost evaporated.

3. Heat the remaining 2 tablespoons of butter in a skillet and add the mushrooms. Cook, stirring, until they give up their liquid. Continue cooking until the liquid evaporates. Add the chicken liver, salt and pepper to taste. Cook, stirring, until the livers lose their raw look. Add this to the meat mixture. Add the broth and tomatoes, salt, pepper, and nutmeg.

4. Partly cover and simmer, stirring occasionally, about 1 hour. If the mixture becomes too thick, add more chicken broth. Just before serving, stir in the cream and blend well. Bring just to the boil and serve.

Yield: About 4 cups.

Belgian Endive and Fennel Vinaigrette

6 heads Belgian endive, approximately
1 fennel bulb
2 tablespoons fresh lemon juice
1 tablespoon imported mustard, such as Dijon or Düsseldorf
6 tablespoons olive oil
Salt and freshly ground black pepper

1. Trim off the bottoms of the endive. Cut the endive into 1-inch lengths or cut it lengthwise into thin shreds. Drop the pieces into

cold water. This will keep them from turning dark. Drain and spin dry or pat dry. Put in a plastic bag and chill.

2. Trim the fennel and slice it thinly. Cut the slices into fine pieces. Rinse, drain, and spin or pat dry. Chill.

3. Combine the fennel and endive in a chilled mixing bowl. Blend the remaining ingredients and pour it over all. Add more lemon juice or oil to taste. Toss and serve on chilled salad plates.

Yield: 4 to 6 servings.

Fennel and Avocado Vinaigrette

2   fennel bulbs
1   tablespoon finely chopped garlic
1   teaspoon crushed dried oregano
7   teaspoons red wine vinegar
6   tablespoons olive oil
    Salt and freshly ground black pepper
1   cup cubed, peeled, seeded fresh tomatoes, optional
12 flat fillets of anchovies
1   ripe, unblemished avocado
24 black olives

1. Cut off the tops of the fennel bulbs and trim the base. Pull off and discard any very large, tough outer leaves. Cut the remaining fennel lengthwise into about 12 ½-inch slices. Arrange the slices in one layer in a serving dish.

2. Blend the garlic, oregano,

vinegar, oil, salt and pepper to taste. Beat rapidly with a whisk or fork. Add the tomato cubes. Set aside.

3. Arrange 1 anchovy fillet on each of the fennel slices. When ready to serve, peel the avocado and slice in half. Discard the pit. Cut the avocado lengthwise into ½-inch-thick slices and arrange these around the fennel. Add the olives. Beat the sauce lightly and pour it over all. Serve as a first course with crusty Italian bread.

Yield: 4 to 6 servings.

Marcella Hazan's Breaded and Fried Fennel

3   fennel bulbs
    Salt
2   eggs, beaten
1½ cups fine, dry, unflavored bread crumbs
    Oil for medium-deep frying

1. Cut off the tops of the fennel bulbs and trim the base. Pull off and discard any tough outer leaves. Cut the remaining fennel into slices slightly less than ½-inch thick. Rinse well and drain.

2. Bring 3 quarts of water to the boil and add salt to taste. Add the fennel slices. Cook until tender yet firm, about 6 to 10 minutes. Drain and cool.

3. Dip the slices first in egg, then in bread crumbs.

4. Heat about ½ inch of oil in a heavy skillet and when the oil is quite hot, add the slices. Do not crowd them but cook as many as possible at one time. Cook until golden brown on one side, turn and cook until golden on the other. Drain on paper toweling. Sprinkle with salt and serve hot.

Yield: 4 servings.

Sea Bass with Fresh Fennel

12 *tablespoons butter*
 3 *tablespoons olive oil*
 6 *cloves garlic, finely minced*
 2 *1½–2-pound sea bass or other small whole fish, cleaned and with head intact but with gills removed*
 1 *fennel bulb with leaves*

Salt and freshly ground black pepper

1. Heat the butter in a baking dish large enough to hold the fish. Stir in the olive oil and garlic. Let cool briefly and add the fish, turning it in the mixture. Sprinkle with salt and pepper.

2. Cut off enough of the fennel leaves to stuff the fish lightly. Add this to the cavities.

3. Cut off the tops of the fennel bulb and trim the base. Pull off and discard the tough outer leaves. Cut the bulb into quarters and arrange these around the fish.

4. When ready to cook, preheat the oven to 375 degrees. Place the fish in the oven and bake 30 minutes, basting both the fish and fennel frequently. Cook until the fish flakes easily when tested with a fork.

Yield: 6 to 8 servings.

No Turkey Thanksgiving
WITH PIERRE FRANEY

There may be no bird in the history of feasting as celebrated as a fine capon. Poring through the recipes of a couple of antiquated cookery books, we find Capons Stewed from a fifteenth-century cookbook and Capon Brewet from a book titled *The Goodman of Paris,* which has recipes dating from the 1300s. Thus, for this Thanksgiving we propose a roast capon stuffed with a filling of livers, sausage, and nuts (either pecans or walnuts). We also offer a recently conceived pumpkin pie.

Roast Capon with Nut Stuffing

1   8–10-pound capon, cleaned weight
1   cup pecans or walnuts
½   pound fresh mushrooms
½   pound chicken livers
2   tablespoons butter
1   cup finely chopped onions
2   cloves garlic, finely minced
2   teaspoons chopped fresh thyme or 1 teaspoon dried
½   cup coarsely chopped parsley
   Salt and freshly ground black pepper
1   pound best-quality sausage meat
2   eggs
2   cups bread crumbs
¾   cup coarsely chopped onions
¾   cup coarsely chopped celery
½   cup coarsely chopped carrots
1   whole garlic clove
½   bay leaf
2   sprigs fresh thyme or ½ teaspoon dried
1   cup chicken broth

1. Preheat oven to 425 degrees.

2. Remove the inner fat from the cavity of the capon. Set aside with the liver, neck, gizzard, and heart.

3. Place the pecans or walnuts on a baking dish and bake until crisp. Take care not to burn them. Remove and let cool.

4. Cut or chop the mushrooms into very small dice.

5. Cut both the capon liver and chicken livers into small pieces.

6. Heat the butter and add the finely chopped onions. Cook until wilted and add the minced garlic and mushrooms. Cook, briefly stirring, until mushrooms give up their liquid. Continue cooking until liquid evaporates. Add the chopped livers, chopped thyme, parsley, and salt and pepper to taste.

7. Cook until the liver changes color. Add the sausage meat, stirring to break up the sausage with the side of a spoon. Add the eggs and bread crumbs and blend well. Crumble the nuts and add them. Cool.

8. Stuff the capon both in the cavity and in the neck and truss.

9. Rub the roasting pan with reserved capon fat and add the capon, breast side up. Scatter the coarsely chopped onions, celery, carrots, garlic clove, bay leaf, and thyme sprigs around it. Add the capon neck, gizzard and heart. Do not add liquid. Sprinkle the capon with salt and pepper to taste.

10. Place the pan, uncovered, in the oven and bake 45 minutes, basting often. Cover loosely with a large sheet of aluminum foil. Reduce the oven heat to 400 degrees and continue cooking 45 minutes, basting often.

11. Reduce the oven heat to 375 degrees. Remove the foil or let it remain, depending on the brownness of the bird. Continue roasting and basting about 1 hour longer. The total cooking time is approximately 20 minutes per pound. When the capon has cooked about 2 hours, carefully pour off all the fat from the roasting pan. Add the chicken broth. Continue cooking until done.

12. Remove the capon and strain the liquid from the pan into a saucepan. Reduce slightly and serve hot with the carved capon.

Yield: 8 to 12 servings.

Vermont Pumpkin Pie

Pastry for a 10-inch pie
(see recipe)
1½ cups fresh or canned
   pumpkin puree
 3 tablespoons melted butter
 ½ cup sugar
 ¼ cup maple syrup
   Salt
 ¾ teaspoon ground cinnamon
 ½ teaspoon grated nutmeg or
   mace
 ¼ teaspoon ground cloves
 3 eggs, separated
 ¾ cup milk

1. Preheat oven to 350 degrees.

2. Roll out the pastry and line a 10-inch pie tin.

3. Combine the pumpkin with butter, sugar, syrup, salt to taste, cinnamon, nutmeg, cloves, the yolks of the eggs, and milk. Beat well to blend.

4. Beat the whites until stiff and fold them into the mixture. Pour the mixture into the prepared pan and bake 50 minutes to 1 hour, or until a straw inserted near the center of the pie comes out clean.

Yield: 8 servings.

Sweet pastry for pies

1½ cups flour
   Salt
 2 tablespoons sugar
 8 tablespoons cold butter
 2 egg yolks
 1 teaspoon lemon juice
 3 tablespoons water

1. If a food processor is available, place the flour, salt to taste, and sugar into the processor's container. Cut the butter into small pieces and add it. Add the yolks and lemon juice. Add the water and blend briefly, just until the ingredients are melded.

2. If a food processor is not used, place the flour, salt, and sugar in a mixing bowl. Cut the butter into small bits and add it. Using the fingers or a pastry blender, cut in the butter until it has the texture of coarse cornmeal. Add the egg yolks and lemon juice and water while kneading the dough quickly until it will hold together.

3. Shape the dough into a ball and wrap in wax paper or plastic wrap. Refrigerate until ready to use. When ready to use, let the dough return to room temperature. Although it is preferable to let this dough rest for a while, it can be used immediately.

Yield: Enough dough for 1 10-inch pie.

A Visit with Jane Grigson

We came to Swindon for one compelling reason—to meet Jane Grigson who, through her writing and cookery books, we have long considered to be one of the most civilized and admirable of English ladies since the late Mrs. Beeton.

For those who have not made her acquaintance through bookshelves, we point out that Jane Grigson has written numerous books on food and other fine points of gastronomy including *The Art of Charcuterie* (Knopf, 1968, $8.95) *Good Things* (Knopf, 1971, $8.95) and *The Mushroom Feast*, (Knopf, 1975, $8.95). She is married to Geoffery Grigson, a handsome man, portly without being corpulent, and one of England's best-known poets and anthologists.

We arrived at their farmhouse—she had described it in earlier correspondence as a "pinkish-white, seventeenth-century farmhouse, from which, alas, the farm buildings, pigs and cows disappeared long ago,"— shortly before noon. We joined her in the orchard amid quince, pear, and medlar trees, the grounds littered with a bit of nostalgia, the last of this year's apple crop. She was, as a London acquaintance had described her earlier, a "plump, golden woman who would look properly at home, like Ceres, with a sheaf of golden wheat bundled in her arms."

"I came by food writing quite by accident," she told us. And, indeed, as the genesis of her career in food unfolded, we mused we never had met another whose professional work had come to be in a more curious or less expected fashion.

The Grigsons are, to put it one way, troglodytes. That is to say they spend part of each year living in a cave in or near the French town of Trôo—an odd French name meaning "valley"—about 40 miles north of Tours.

"Geoffrey," Mrs. Grigson began, "is a polymath. He's not only a poet, he dabbles in and writes about many things. Through him I became involved in hunting wild mushrooms, but that's another story. In any event, some years ago, 1957 to be exact, he wrote a book about painted caves. Shortly thereafter he received a letter from a friend who told him about an interesting available cave in Trôo. He added that it could be bought for a small sum.

"We went to the town, visited the cave and discovered it had the most incredible view of the countryside. We bought it for almost nothing, about £450 [about $1,260 at the 1957 exchange rate].

"In the months that followed," Mrs. Grigson continued, "we saw a good deal of the friend who recommended it and he had, as we do, a tremendous interest in food and wine. We would spend hours in local shops—the ready-made food in the town, including the charcuterie, is superb. Marvelous sausages, pâtés, terrines, and so on, and I proposed that our friend write a book on charcuterie. The preparation of sausages, hams, black and white puddings, and all the rest, and he thought it was a lovely idea. On one condition. That I provide the proper weights and measures.

"I agreed and we found a publisher. Contracts were signed and then, for one reason or another, our neighbor found it impossible to continue the project."

Jane Grigson found herself obliged contractually to finish the book herself.

In the beginning, she noted, she had envisioned a book of approximately 30 basic recipes, but the more she pursued the subject, the more deeply involved she became. She discovered that "the local charcuteries did not mind working at their dawn trade under the curious eye of a foreigner, and the recipes were generously offered."

She was forced to follow up her findings, however, in the most primitive manner in their cave in Trôo. The cave has an added-on front "house." The original limestone dwelling serves as their master bedroom and cellar. The kitchen consists of gas burners such as those used on camping expeditions. Much of the cooking is done in the fireplace. Until last year there was no electricity. There is no bathroom but rather a chemical "loo." Bath water is accumulated by rainfall and the drinking water must be lugged in five-gallon jerry cans from the town of Montoire a few miles away.

"It took four years to complete that first book," She recalled. Many of the recipes were retested in the English kitchen; built in 1665, in Swindon.

Many of the dishes that she tested and retested have garlic used in large or small quantities as a characteristic ingredient, and we were intrigued and envious when we learned of her source for that kitchen basic.

"Each year in the town of Tours," she told us, "there is an annual garlic fair. It is held every Saint Anne's day on July 26. On the day of the fair, small mountains of garlic, shallots, onion, and fresh basil are for sale." They purchase enough garlic to last a year or longer.

Quite logically, after completing her work on *The Art of Charcuterie*, the seeds of another book on food had germinated in her mind. She became involved in *Good Things*, a collection of her preferred dishes "from meat pies and game birds . . . from kippers and lobsters, to parsnips and parsley."

A third book, *The Mushroom Feast*, followed and that is described as "a celebration of all edible fungi, cultivated and wild and dried." All of Jane Grigson's works printed in the United States thus far have been published by Alfred A. Knopf, Inc.

The Grigsons spend about half of each year in Swindon, the rest in their cave house in Trôo. They are the parents of one daughter, Sophie, 16, who specializes in such dishes as caraway seed cakes and barbecue sauce. Her basting sauce consists of red currant jelly, mustard, vinegar, herbs, and oil.

Here is a sampler of recipes from Mrs. Grigson's books. The recipes for spiced salt beef and her Sussex Pond pudding are from a volume titled *English Food*, never published in this country.

Jane Grigson, the British cooking expert, in the kitchen of her home

Anchovy and Mushroom Eggs

¾ pound fresh mushrooms
4 tablespoons butter
1 tablespoon flour
½ cup heavy cream
1 2-ounce can flat fillets of anchovies
  Freshly ground black pepper
4 to 6 eggs
  Salt
  Chopped fresh parsley for garnish

1. Thinly slice the mushrooms.

2. Heat half the butter in a saucepan and add the mushrooms. Cook, stirring, until they give up their liquid. Continue cooking until most of the liquid evaporates. Sprinkle with flour and stir to blend. Add the cream, stirring, and simmer about 5 minutes, stirring often.

3. Drain and chop the anchovies. Add the anchovies gradually. Add part or all of them, according to taste. Season with pepper.

4. Preheat the oven to 400 degrees.

5. Spoon equal portions of the mixture into 4 or 6 individual ramekins or baking dishes and break 1 egg on top of each. Sprinkle with salt and pepper and dot with remaining butter. Bake about 10 to 12 minutes or until the egg whites are set and yolks are still runny. Sprinkle each serving with parsley and serve hot with toast.

Yield: 4 to 6 servings.

Brioche with Mushrooms in Cream Sauce

1   *large brioche to serve 4 to*
     6 (see note)
1½ *to 2 pounds fresh*
     mushrooms
6   *tablespoons butter*
⅓   *cup dry white wine*
     Juice of 1 lemon
2   *cups heavy cream*
     Salt and freshly ground
     black pepper
1   *tablespoon arrowroot*
2   *tablespoons cognac*

1. Preheat the oven to 250 degrees.

2. Slice the top off the brioche and reserve it. Neatly hollow out the brioche, leaving about a ¾-inch-thick shell. Place the hollowed-out shell and the top on a baking sheet.

3. Slice the mushrooms. Heat 4 tablespoons of butter in a saucepan and add the mushrooms, stirring. Add the wine and lemon juice. Cook until mushrooms wilt. Continue cooking until most of the liquid evaporates. Add the cream, salt and pepper to taste. Cook, stirring often, until the cream is slightly reduced.

4. Meanwhile, place the brioche in the oven and let stand just to heat through without drying out.

5. Blend the arrowroot and cognac and add it to the simmering sauce, stirring constantly. Remove the saucepan from the heat and swirl in the remaining butter. Spoon and pour sauce while piping hot into the brioche and replace the top. Serve.

Yield: 4 to 6 servings.

Note: Large brioche can be ordered from a number of French bakeries. In Manhattan, they are available from Bonté Patisserie and Dumas Patisserie.

Spiced Salt Beef

1   *5–6-pound brisket, rump,*
     or round of beef, tied with
     string if necessary
¾   *cup dark brown sugar*
4   *teaspoons saltpeter,*
     available in drug stores
½   *cup kosher, pickling, or sea*
     salt
2   *tablespoons coarsely*
     cracked black peppercorns
2   *tablespoons crushed whole*
     allspice
2   *tablespoons crushed*
     juniper berries
     Shredded suet, enough to
     cover the beef

1. Rub the beef on all sides with sugar and place it in a stainless steel or enamel flat baking dish. Cover closely and let stand for 2 days, turning often, in the refrigerator or very cool place.

2. Crush and blend the remaining ingredients and rub them into the meat. Cover and let stand up to 9 days longer, turning the meat often in its natural marinade.

3. Preheat the oven to 375 degrees.

4. When ready to cook, scrape off excess spices or rinse quickly. Place it in a pot that has a tight-fitting lid. Cover the meat with the shredded suet. Cover with a double layer of foil or wax paper and then with the tight-fitting lid.

5. Bake 45 minutes to the pound. Remove from the oven and let stand 3 hours without removing the lid.

6. Remove the meat and place it on a board. Cover with wax paper and add a 4-pound weight. Let stand 24 hours. Serve carved into thin slices. Recommended accompaniments are potato salad with avocado slices and horseradish sauce.

Yield: 8 to 10 servings.

Sussex Pond Pudding

2   *cups self-rising flour (or use all-purpose flour blended with 1 teaspoon baking powder)*
¼   *pound fresh beef suet from the kidney, finely chopped*
¼   *cup cold water, approximately*
¼   *cup cold milk, approximately*
¼   *pound lightly salted butter, cut into small chunks*
1   *cup dark brown sugar*
1   *large lemon*

1. Place the flour in a mixing bowl and add the suet. Toss. Combine the water and milk and toss with the flour mixture, blending with the fingers to make a workable dough. It should be soft but not too soft to roll out smoothly.

2. Place the dough on a lightly floured surface and roll it out into a large circle. Cut off and set aside ¼ of the pastry circle. Line a 4-cup pudding basin with the larger portion of dough and press the cut edges together to seal firmly.

3. Add half the butter and half the sugar. Insert the lemon, stem side up, in the center and add the remaining butter and sugar.

4. Roll the reserved piece of dough into a circle to fit the top of the pudding basin. Lay it over and seal the edges of dough as firmly as possible. Pleat a large heavy length of aluminum foil and place over the pudding. Tie it securely all around with string. Make a string handle to facilitate removal of the pudding when steamed.

5. Place a large basin of water on to boil and lower the pudding into it. The water must be boiling and reach halfway up the pudding basin or slightly more. Cover and let boil 3 or 4 hours. As the water diminishes, replenish it with more boiling water.

6. To serve, remove the pudding and lift off the foil. Invert a deep dish onto the pudding basin and quickly turn it upside down, letting the pudding fall into the dish. To facilitate this, run a knife around the inside of the basin before turning it out. Serve immediately.

Yield: 4 to 6 servings.

Note: Mrs. Grigson notes that the name of this dish refers to the sauce that runs out and provides the dish with a moat of buttery brown liquid. When served, make sure everyone has a piece of the lemon.

Venison Cutlets Ardennes Style

(From *Good Things*
and attributed
to Elizabeth David)

 8   *venison cutlets or 4 thick loin chops of venison*
     Juice of 1 lemon
12 *juniper berries, crushed*
½ *teaspoon dried marjoram*
½ *teaspoon dried thyme*
     Salt and freshly ground black pepper
 8 *tablespoons butter*
½ *cup finely chopped onion*
 3 *carrots, scraped and finely diced*
½ *cup dry white wine or vermouth*
½ *cup water*
¼ *cup chopped cooked ham*
⅓ *cup fresh bread crumbs*
¼ *cup chopped parsley*
 2 *or 3 tablespoons red currant jelly or dark orange marmalade*
     Juice of ½ orange, preferably a bitter orange
     Boiled potatoes, optional

1. Sprinkle the venison with lemon juice in a suitable dish.

2. Crush together the juniper berries, marjoram, thyme, salt and pepper to taste. Rub the mixture all over the chops. Set aside for an hour or longer.

3. Preheat the oven to 300 degrees.

4. Heat 4 tablespoons butter in a skillet and add the chops. Cook until lightly browned on both sides, turning once. Sprinkle the onion and carrots around the meat and cook, stirring, until onion is wilted. Add the wine and cook, stirring, over high heat until it is reduced by half. Add the water. Sprinkle each piece of meat with ham and top with bread crumbs mixed with parsley. Pour the remaining butter, melted, over all and bake, uncovered, 45 minutes or until chops are thoroughly tender.

5. Remove the chops to a heated platter and cover.

6. Pour the pan juices into a saucepan and bring to the boil. Stir in the jelly and orange juice. If bitter oranges are not available, use a little bitter orange marmalade and less currant jelly. Pour the sauce over the chops and serve hot with boiled potatoes.

Yield: 4 servings.

Deviled

Although highly spiced foods are characteristic of many regional kitchens throughout the world, they have over the centuries generally been eschewed by the French. Perhaps the most piquant dishes contrived in France are those labeled *à la diable*, which is simply to say deviled, and even they are pale to the palate compared with the Szechuan dishes of China and the indigenous dishes of Delhi. Dishes *à la diable*, more often than not, gain their piquancy through the use of mustard and perhaps a touch of a spicy bottled Escoffier sauce, either Robert or Diable. Deviled dishes can be delectable, and two of them are printed here—one for beef ribs, the other for chicken breasts.

Deviled Beef Ribs

Ribs

10   chuck beef ribs, about 5
    pounds
    Salt and freshly ground
    black pepper
½   cup dry white wine
4   tablespoons imported
    mustard, such as Dijon or
    Düsseldorf
1½   cups fine bread crumbs

Sauce

2   tablespoons finely chopped
    shallots
¼   cup dry white wine
    Freshly ground black
    pepper
¼   cup brown sauce or canned
    beef gravy (we use Howard
    Johnson's)
½   cup heavy cream
1   tablespoon Escoffier sauce,
    either sauce Robert or
    Diable

1   tablespoon imported
    mustard, such as Dijon or
    Düsseldorf
    Salt

1. Preheat oven to 450 degrees.

2. Sprinkle the ribs with salt and pepper to taste and place them in one layer in a large roasting pan.

3. Place the ribs in the oven and bake for 1 hour. Turn the ribs in the pan and reduce the oven heat to 400 degrees. Bake 30 minutes longer.

4. Blend the ½ cup of wine and the mustard and brush the ribs with approximately half the mixture. Sprinkle the ribs generously with half the bread crumbs. Dribble the remaining mustard mixture over the ribs, then sprinkle with the remaining bread crumbs. Bake 1 hour longer.

5. For the sauce combine the

shallots and ¼ cup of wine. Cook until reduced by half and sprinkle with pepper to taste. Continue cooking until almost all the wine has evaporated. Add the brown sauce and simmer 10 minutes. Add the cream, Escoffier sauce, and bring to the boil. Remove from the heat and stir in the mustard and salt to taste. Serve the sauce over the ribs.

Yield: 5 to 10 servings.

Deviled Chicken Breasts

3   *tablespoons imported mustard, such as Dijon or Düsseldorf*
3   *tablespoons dry white wine*
1   *teaspoon Worcestershire sauce*
4   *whole chicken breasts, split, boned and skinned (8 pieces)*
   Salt and freshly ground black pepper
2½ *cups fine, fresh bread crumbs*
4   *tablespoons butter*
4   *tablespoons vegetable, peanut, or corn oil*
   Mustard cream sauce (see recipe)

1. Combine the mustard, wine, and Worcestershire sauce. Stir to blend.

2. Place the chicken pieces between layers of wax paper and pound lightly with a flat mallet. Sprinkle the chicken pieces with salt and pepper to taste and brush on all sides with the mustard mixture. Dip the pieces to coat all over in bread crumbs. Pat lightly with the flat side of a heavy knife to help crumbs adhere. Place on a rack.

3. When ready to cook, heat equal portions of butter and oil in 2 skillets. Add the chicken pieces and brown on both sides, about 5 minutes to a side.

4. Serve with mustard cream sauce.

Yield: 4 to 8 servings.

Mustard cream sauce

⅓   *cup dry mustard or to taste*
2   *tablespoons water*
⅓   *cup dry white wine*
1   *tablespoon white wine vinegar*
¼   *cup finely chopped shallots*
1   *teaspoon freshly ground black pepper*
1   *bay leaf*
¼   *teaspoon dried thyme*
2   *cups heavy cream*

1. Combine the dry mustard and water and stir until smooth. Let stand at least 20 minutes before using.

2. Combine the wine, vinegar, shallots, pepper, bay leaf, and thyme in a small saucepan and cook over high heat until most of the liquid evaporates. Add the cream and stir. Cook, stirring often, about 10 minutes.

3. Add the mustard according to taste and put the sauce through a sieve. Reheat before serving.

Yield: About 2 cups.

December 1975

A FEW PAGES back, we were discussing food legends, namely the origin of newburg sauce. Food lore has always fascinated us ever since Adam and Eve and Charles Lamb's dissertation on roast pig. In this month of December, we print a recipe for *cioppino*, the delectable California fish soup/stew. We note that the word does not appear in any standard English dictionary. We also note that we have never been able to trace the origin of the name elsewhere, although some sources speculate it may have to do with an Italian dialect word meaning "chopped fine."

A short while ago we received a letter from Lee Dulberg of Great Neck, Long Island, who informed us we should investigate one history of cioppino's origins in Morrison Wood's *More Recipes with a Jug of Wine* (Farrar, Straus & Giroux, 1956, $6.95). Mr. Wood attributes his information about the soup to Mrs. Winfield G. Wagener of Palo Alto, California, and an interesting history it is.

"Cioppino," Mrs. Wagener wrote, "was a familiar dish" in San Francisco, particularly on Meigg's Wharf, as Fisherman's Wharf was called prior to World War I. It seems that the practice in those days was for friendly natives to make the rounds of small boats moored in the bay in an effort to coax the fishermen to toss in, gratis, one or two small fish or any other edible oddment for a stew. "One fisherman," she added, "would toss into the . . . bucket a nice, fat fish, another would drop in a crab," and so on.

"The cry that instigated this wonderful stuff was 'Chip in! Chip in!' " To make the soup sound more Italian—most of the fishermen were of Italian descent—an "o" was added to the cry, thus "cioppino."

Most often we tend to discredit these home-spun legends of word origins, but somehow the above sounds as logical to our ears as it is amusing.

The Art of Preserved Goose

One of the fabled—but genuine—glories of the French table is a dish or ingredient that has received little notice in America. Except for some rare and special occasions, it is almost nonexistent in the nation's French restaurants.

The French name of the dish is confit d'oie, which in English is preserved goose, and it is a delicacy of consummate goodness that is easily, if a trifle expensively, made. For those who would, this is the season to make it, for now until the end of the year is the season when geese are available.

Like most other preserved foods including ham and sausages, the desirable flavor and texture of confit d'oie or preserved goose undoubtedly came about more as a conservation measure than as an end in themselves. The idea was to cook the goose and maintain it in natural fat throughout an extended period, long after the last goose of the season was killed.

The preparation of the goose is simplicity itself. The goose is cut into large pieces and seasoned. It is marinated overnight, and the following morning it is cooked in a boiling bath of goose fat and lard for about two hours. The goose is then cooled and stored in a cold place. It is then ready to be used, whenever desired, up to a year or longer.

Preserved goose is a specialty of the southwest of France, although it is known and admired, if not to say coveted, throughout the nation. Those Americans who may be conversant with the dish know it best as a classic ingredient for some of the traditional cassoulets of France, principally those of Castelnaudary and Toulouse. While cassoulets are fairly well known in America, that one essential taste is missing in all but the tiniest fraction of them in this country.

To the purist with only a miser's share of preserved goose in his larder, the mélange of the food with the likes of beans in a cassoulet may be quixotic. That is for those who can employ the ingredient with abandon. Ultimately preserved goose, cooked simply until it is crisp and golden brown and served with crisp, thin sliced potatoes cooked in hot goose fat, is paradise enough. It is a sublime, ethereal creation.

There are numerous other ways in which the goose is served in the provinces of France. The *Dictionnaire de l'Académie des Gastronomes*

(Paris, 1942) includes Basque-style with cèpes (fleshy, wild mushrooms), garlic, and parsley; béarnaise, with the potatoes replacing the mushrooms; sarladaise, with potatoes and truffles; landaise with a small onion, ham cut into small cubes, and petits pois.

Preserved goose, a classic ingredient of traditional French cassoulets

Confit d'Oie
(Preserved goose)

1   *12–14-pound oven-ready goose*
    Salt and freshly ground black pepper
1   *bay leaf*
½   *teaspoon dried thyme*
½   *teaspoon saltpeter, available at drugstores*
3   *pounds lard (see note)*

1. Cut off and discard the wingtips of the goose. Cut off and reserve the second wing joints. Cut or pull away any solid goose fat and reserve it.

2. Carefully cut off the thighs and legs of the goose, leaving each leg and thigh attached.

3. Carefully bone away the breast of the goose in two sections, left and right, but leaving the main wing bone attached and unboned. Reserve the gizzard.

4. Use the bony carcass of the goose for making soup or discard it. Cut off and reserve any additional pieces or scraps of goose skin.

5. Sprinkle the goose pieces— the leg and thigh pieces, the breast halves, and the second wing joints—with salt and pepper, using a fairly generous amount of salt. Rub it in on all sides.

6. Place the bay leaf on a flat surface. Using a sharp heavy knife, chop it finely. Add the thyme and chop it. Add the saltpeter. Rub the mixture into the goose pieces on all sides. Pack the pieces into a mixing bowl or other utensil. Cover closely and refrigerate 24 hours.

7. Heat 1 or 2 large, heavy, deep skillets, flameproof casseroles or Dutch ovens and add the breast and thigh pieces skin side down in one layer. Add the second wing joints, gizzard, and the reserved goose fat and skin. Add the lard and bring to a boil. The goose will be cooked in fat without any additional liquid. The goose pieces must be totally immersed in fat when the fat melts. Cover and cook 2 hours.

8. Using a 2-pronged fork, carefully remove the goose pieces (thighs with legs, breast halves, and second wing joints). By all means reserve the cooking fat.

9. Arrange equal portions of the goose pieces in 2 earthenware terrines or casseroles. The pieces should be arranged as compactly as possible.

10. Strain enough of the cooking fat over both terrines so that the goose parts are completely submerged in fat. If the goose pieces are not completely covered, it will be necessary to add more lard and pour it over. Let stand until thoroughly cool. Refrigerate. Cover closely. Properly refrigerated or stored in a cold, dry place, preserved goose should keep for weeks and even months.

Yield: 1 preserved goose.

Note: It is a minor point, but it would be preferable if all goose fat rather than lard were used for cooking the goose. For example, if you were cooking 3 geese (roasting or whatever) during the winter season, the extra fat in each goose could be reserved and frozen until ready to make the confit d'oie.

The goose's carcass can also be quartered and cooked with the other parts. When cooked, the carcass can be used when cooking bean dishes.

Cassoulet

2 *pounds dried pea beans marked "no soaking necessary"*
3 *quarts water*
1 *onion stuck with 4 cloves*
1 *bay leaf*
1 *carrot, trimmed and scraped*
   Salt and freshly ground black pepper
¾ *pound slab of lean salt pork with rind*
1 *garlic sausage (cotechine)*
3 *tablespoons goose fat or peanut oil*
1 *tablespoon finely chopped garlic*
2 *cups chopped onion*
1 *2-pound-3-ounce can tomatoes*
   Lamb stew (see recipe)
½ *preserved goose in its fat (see recipe)*
   Roast pork (see recipe)
3 *tablespoons breadcrumbs made from toasted bread*
4 *tablespoons melted butter*

1. Pick over the beans and wash them well. Place the beans in a kettle with the water, onion, bay leaf, carrot, salt, pepper, and salt pork. Prick the garlic sausage in several places with a 2-pronged fork and add it. Bring to the boil and simmer 30 minutes.

2. Remove the garlic sausage and set aside. Continue cooking the beans 30 minutes and remove the salt pork.

3. Slice off and reserve the salt pork rind. Cut the rind into ¼-inch dice and set aside. Return the salt pork meat to the kettle.

4. Heat the goose fat in a saucepan and add the diced pork rind. Add the garlic and chopped onions. Cook about 10 minutes without browning. Add the tomatoes and let simmer, stirring often, about half an hour.

5. When the beans are tender, drain them but reserve the beans, salt pork, and cooking liquid. Discard the onion and bay leaf. Put the beans in a kettle and add the tomato sauce and the lamb stew, including both meat and sauce. Stir to blend and add salt and pepper to taste. Cover and simmer about 10 minutes.

6. Cut the salt pork into neat ¼-inch-thick slices and set aside.

7. Skin the garlic sausage and cut into neat ¼-inch-thick slices and set aside.

8. Heat the goose, including the gizzard and wing if they are present. Remove the pieces and cut or pull the meat from the bones. Slice the meat as neatly as possible.

9. Cut the pork from the bones and slice it neatly. Save the pan juices from the roasting pan. Pour off the fat.

10. Spoon about a third of the beans into a large casserole and arrange the pork slices over all. Add the pan juices.

11. Add a cup of the bean liquid to the remaining beans. Spoon half the remaining beans over the pork. Arrange the sliced preserved goose over all. Add all the remaining beans. Arrange the sliced salt pork and garlic sausage over the top. Scatter the bread crumbs over the top and dribble the butter over.

12. When ready to cook, preheat the oven to 400 degrees and bake 30 minutes. If the casserole seems too dry, add a little more bean liquid as the cassoulet cooks. When ready to serve, the cassoulet should be piping hot and bubbling throughout.

Yield: 12 or more servings.

Roast pork

1   *3-pound center cut pork loin*
    Salt and freshly ground black pepper

1. Preheat the oven to 425 degrees.

2. Sprinkle the pork all over with salt and pepper.

3. Place the pork, fat side down, in a baking dish and bake about 20 minutes.

4. Turn the pork and continue cooking about 20 minutes. If

it starts to brown too quickly, cover loosely with a sheet of aluminum foil. Continue baking about 20 minutes or until thoroughly cooked and tender.

Yield: 4 servings or enough for one large cassoulet.

Lamb stew

3 *pounds shoulder of lamb with bone, cut into 2-inch cubes*
2 *tablespoons oil or goose fat Salt and freshly ground black pepper*
1 *cup finely chopped onion*
2 *cloves garlic, finely minced*
1 *cup dry white wine*
2 *cups water*
3 *tablespoons tomato paste*
1 *sprig thyme or 1 teaspoon dried*
4 *sprigs parsley*
½ *bay leaf*

1. Use a heavy skillet and brown the lamb on all sides in the oil. Sprinkle with salt and pepper to taste and add the onion and garlic. Stir to blend. Carefully pour off all fat.

2. Return the skillet to the heat and add the remaining ingredients.

3. Cover closely and cook 1 hour and 15 minutes or until the lamb is fork tender.

Yield: 6 to 8 servings or enough for 1 cassoulet.

If we were to single out those dishes we've found particularly memorable in life, confit d'oie or preserved goose would figure high on the list. We first sampled this dish years ago when traveling with the late Frank Schoonmaker, perhaps the greatest American authority on wine who ever lived. We had traveled through Burgundy and arrived in the Bordeaux region late one morning just in time for lunch. We stopped at a small hotel with an outdoor dining area. A stream ran by and there were woods in the distance. We perused the menu over a chilled bottle of white wine and Frank, who was almost as knowledgeable about French cooking as about French wines, recommended the goose. The choice was inspired.

When we moved to East Hampton to live, one of our greatest discoveries was the proximity of Iacono's Poultry Farm where geese are raised and sold each November. Our pal Sal, the proprietor, has a standing order to reserve us two geese each year. These are turned into preserved versions which we store until the next winter. There is seldom a day throughout the year that preserved goose, generally two of them, cannot be found in the refrigerator. Of course, we could dine on either of the geese at any time or any season, but we believe in the principle of delayed pleasure and we invariably hold out until the year-end holidays and celebrate with cooked preserved goose and fine bottle of Burgundy or Bordeaux.

More Sausage, Homemade

WITH PIERRE FRANEY

One of the most coveted appetizers in the French restaurants of Manhattan, particularly those of the bistro type, is listed on the menu as *saucisson à l'ail,* which translates easily as garlic sausage. Actually, the vast majority of these freshly made and semidry products are purchased from Italian pork stores that specialize in sausages. It is not all that difficult to prepare these sausages in the home, however. For those who would make their own, we offer a recipe for garlic sausages. There are also instructions for cooking the sausages, whether bought or homemade, plus a recipe for a warm potato salad, the ideal accompaniment for the dish.

Garlic Sausages

4½ *pounds lean pork, cut into 1½-inch cubes*
1¼ *pounds pork fat, cut into 1½-inch cubes*
½ *teaspoon saltpeter*
1½ *teaspoons freshly ground black pepper*
2 *tablespoons salt*
2 *teaspoons chopped garlic*
1 *bay leaf*

½ *teaspoon powdered sage*
½ *teaspoon dried marjoram*
½ *teaspoon dried thyme*
½ *cup dry white wine*
1¼ *pounds fresh pork rind*
2 *yards (approximately) large beef casings (see note)*
  Court bouillon for garlic sausages (see recipe)

1. Combine the lean pork, pork fat, saltpeter, pepper, and salt. Chop together the garlic, bay leaf, sage, marjoram, and thyme and add it to the meat. Add the wine. Cover and let stand overnight in the refrigerator.

2. Drop the pork rind into boiling water to cover. Cover and boil 2 hours. Drain.

3. Put the meat mixture through the large blade of a meat grinder. Chop the pork rind and blend it with the meat.

4. Attach a sausage-stuffer to

the grinder. Use the beef casings and put the meat through the grinder while filling the casings automatically. Use the coarse blade for this. Fill the casings to make sausages about 9 inches long and 2 inches thick. Continue until all the stuffing is used. Each sausage will weigh about 1½ to 1¾ pounds.

5. To cook, prick the sausages all over with a fork. Drop them in a court bouillon and simmer partly covered 45 minutes.

Yield: 4 sausages.

Note: Beef casings are available at G. Esposito & Sons, 500 Ninth Avenue (at 38th Street), in Manhattan.

Court bouillon for garlic sausages

5   quarts water, approximately, enough to cover the sausages when added
2   cups dry white wine
3   sprigs parsley
1   bay leaf
3   ribs celery, quartered
2   carrots, scraped and quartered
    Salt
24 peppercorns

Combine all the ingredients in a kettle and simmer about 20 minutes. Let cool.

Yield: About 5 cups.

Warm Potato Salad

10 to 14 new potatoes, about 1½ pounds
    Salt and freshly ground pepper
2   teaspoons finely chopped fresh tarragon or 1 teaspoon dried
1   tablespoon finely chopped parsley
3   tablespoons finely chopped shallots
1   tablespoon finely chopped onion
1   clove garlic, finely minced
¼   cup dry white wine
1   teaspoon red wine vinegar
¼   cup peanut or vegetable oil

1. Rinse the potatoes and put them in a kettle with salted water to cover. Bring to the boil and simmer 20 to 30 minutes or until tender yet firm. Drain.

2. When cool enough to handle, peel the potatoes. Slice the potatoes into a bowl and add salt and pepper to taste and the remaining ingredients. Toss gently and serve warm.

Yield: 6 to 10 servings.

For the Nostalgic: Salt-Rising Bread

Salt-rising bread is another of those regional American dishes for which some people have a passion and which inspire in others something short of aversion. The bread is made by a natural fermentation, and for a period it is a bit malodorous. The finished product is a bit tangy with a flavor that is at times described as "cheeselike."

Jennifer Johnson of Manhattan writes, "I was reared in the mountains of southwest Virginia where a weekend breakfast often included country ham, eggs, fried apples, and either biscuits or salt-rising toast. My taste buds had long since forgotten how delicious salt-rising or salt-risen (as it is variously called) toast could be until I encountered it again on a recent business trip to Tennessee. It seems to be available there in practically every large grocery store under the brand name of a local bakery or chain store.

"My inquiries in supermarkets in New York City, however, have all met with a 'never heard of such a thing.' Do you know of any source in the city for salt-rising bread?"

Unfortunately we have never known of a commercial source for salt-rising bread north of the Mason-Dixon Line, nor, for that matter, since our childhood in the South. For the ambitious and nostalgically inclined, however, here is a recipe printed some years ago in *The New York Times*.

Salt Rising Bread

2 medium-size potatoes, peeled and thinly sliced
2 tablespoons cornmeal
½ tablespoon sugar
1 teaspoon salt
2 cups boiling water
2 cups milk, scalded and cooled to lukewarm
⅛ teaspoon baking soda
8 cups sifted all-purpose flour, approximately
¼ cup soft shortening or butter

1. Place the potatoes, cornmeal, sugar, and salt in a 3-quart bowl. Add the boiling water and stir until the sugar and salt are dissolved. Cover with transparent wrap or foil. Set the bowl in a pan of warm water over the pilot light

of a stove, or where it will stay at about 120 degrees, until small bubbles show in the surface, for 24 hours or longer.

2. Remove the potatoes to a sieve and press out excess moisture. Add this liquid to the potato water still in the bowl. Discard the potatoes.

3. Add the milk, baking soda, and 4 cups of the flour to the bowl. Stir until smooth. Set the bowl again in the pan of warm water and let it stand for about 2 hours, until the dough is almost doubled in bulk.

4. Chop the shortening or butter into 1 cup of the remaining flour. Add this to the dough. Add enough additional flour, about 3 cups, to make a moderately stiff dough. Knead on a floured surface quickly and lightly. Do not let the dough get cold.

5. Return the dough to the bowl, grease the surface of the dough, and let it rise for about 2 hours, until doubled in bulk.

6. Turn the risen dough out on a lightly floured surface and shape into 2 loaves. Place in greased loaf pans (9 by 5 by 3 inches) and grease the tops of the loaves. Let rise again for about 2 hours, until almost doubled in bulk, or slightly above the tops of the pans. Sprinkle the tops with cornmeal if desired.

7. About 15 minutes before the loaves have finished rising, preheat the oven to 400 degrees.

8. Bake the loaves for 15 minutes, then lower the oven temperature to 350 degrees, and bake for about 35 minutes longer, or until the bread shrinks from the sides of the pans and is well browned. Cool on a rack.

Yield: 2 loaves.

Cold Weather Soups

WITH PIERRE FRANEY

We have frequently elaborated on the notion that, where our appetite is concerned, most foods know no season. We like ice cream in December, a pot roast in July. There are, of course, certain foods that are intrinsically seasonal—the first shad in spring, the first sweet basil of summer. And nothing tastes better in midwinter, after a session on the ski slopes (or simply a long walk in the woods), than a hot, masterfully made soup, particularly one that can serve as a main dish. On these pages are three soups that are, to our mind, ideally suited to cold weather. There is a tasty oxtail soup with paprika, a warming onion soup gratinée, and a soup with beef and vegetables.

Onion Soup

5   pounds meaty beef neck bones or shin bones, cracked
5   quarts water
    Salt
2   cups coarsely chopped onion
2   cups chopped, firmly packed celery ribs, leaves included
2   cups carrots, scraped and cut into 1-inch lengths
1   cup cubed turnips, optional
10 peppercorns
6   sprigs parsley
1   bay leaf
4   sprigs fresh thyme or 1 teaspoon dried
2   cloves garlic, unpeeled but cut in half
2   pounds Bermuda onions
3   tablespoons butter
    Freshly ground black pepper
3   tablespoons flour
2   cups dry white wine
8   slices French bread
½   pound grated Gruyère, Swiss or Cheddar cheese

1. Combine the beef bones with water to cover in a kettle. Bring to the boil and simmer about 3 minutes. Drain and run the bones under cold running water. Return the bones to a clean kettle and add the 5 quarts of water and salt to taste. Bring to the boil.

2. Add the chopped onion, celery, carrots, turnips, peppercorns, parsley, bay leaf, thyme, and garlic. Bring to the boil and simmer 3 hours, skimming the surface as necessary.

3. Strain the stock through a very fine sieve or cheesecloth. Discard the solids. There should be about 8 cups.

4. Peel the Bermuda onions, cut each in half, and slice thinly.

5. When ready to prepare the soup, heat the butter in a heavy 2-quart kettle and add the onions, salt and pepper to taste. Cook, stirring often, until the onions are a rich, golden brown. Do not burn. This should take about 45 minutes.

6. Preheat oven to 500 degrees.

7. Sprinkle the onions with flour and add the wine, stirring constantly. Add the stock and bring to the boil. Simmer about 15 minutes, skimming the surface often to remove foam and scum.

8. Meanwhile, toast the bread slices on both sides.

9. Spoon equal portions of the soup into 8 individual ovenproof soup bowls (see note).

10. Cover each serving with a piece of toast and sprinkle each with equal portions of cheese. Place the soup bowls in a baking dish and place in the oven for 20 minutes or until the onion soup is piping hot and bubbling and the cheese melted.

Yield: 8 servings.

Note: If desired, one large 2-quart ovenproof casserole or tureen may be used in place of the individual bowls. Empty the soup into the tureen, cover with bread, and sprinkle with the cheese. Bake until bubbling and browned.

Vegetable Soup

3   pounds raw, meaty short
    ribs of beef or an equal
    weight of shin bone with
    meat
3   quarts water
    Salt
1¼ pounds raw green or Savoy
    cabbage, chopped into
    1-inch pieces
2   cups peeled white turnips,
    cut into ½-inch cubes
2   cups carrots, scraped and
    cut into ½-inch cubes
2   cups chopped leeks,
    optional
1   cup chopped onion
2   cups finely chopped celery
    with leaves
    Fresh ground black pepper
4   potatoes, about 1 pound,
    peeled and cut into ½-inch
    cubes

1. Place the ribs of beef or shin bone in a kettle and add cold water to cover. Bring to the boil and simmer about 3 minutes. Drain and run under cold water. Return the bones to a clean kettle and add the 3 quarts of water and salt to taste. Bring to the boil and simmer 30 minutes, skimming the surface as necessary to remove the foam and scum.

2. Add the cabbage, turnips, carrots, leeks, onion, and celery tops. Sprinkle with pepper to taste and return to the boil. Simmer 1 hour and 30 minutes.

3. Add the potatoes and cook 1 hour longer, skimming the surface as necessary.

4. Remove the short ribs of beef or shin. Carve off the meat and cut it into 1-inch cubes. Return meat to the kettle. Discard the bones. Serve the soup piping hot in hot bowls.

Yield: 8 to 12 servings.

Note: One cup of dried "no

soaking necessary" pea beans may be added to the soup at the same time as the cabbage and turnips. Grated Parmesan cheese may be served on the side if desired.

Oxtail Soup with Paprika

3 pounds meaty oxtail, cut into 2-inch lengths
3 quarts water
  Salt
1 pound green or red sweet (bell) peppers (see note)
4 tablespoons butter
4 cups finely sliced onions
2 tablespoons sweet or hot paprika
2 cloves garlic, finely minced
5 tablespoons flour
  Freshly ground black pepper
2 cups sour cream

1. Trim excess fat from the pieces of oxtail. Place the pieces in a kettle and add water to cover. Bring to the boil and simmer about 3 minutes. Drain and run under cold running water. Return the pieces to a clean kettle and add 3 quarts of water and salt to taste. Bring to the boil and simmer 1 hour.

2. Core and seed the peppers. Cut them in half and cut the halves into thin strips. There should be about 5 cups. Set aside.

3. Heat the butter in a kettle and add the onions and peppers and cook briefly until wilted. Sprinkle with paprika, garlic, and flour, stirring. Gradually add about half the broth, stirring rapidly to prevent lumping. Return this mixture to the remaining broth and oxtail in the kettle. Add salt and pepper to taste. Bring to the boil and simmer about 2½ hours. The total cooking time should be about 3½ hours or until oxtail meat is tender and almost falling from the bone.

4. Beat the sour cream with a little salt to make it smooth and seasoned. Serve the hot soup in individual bowls with the sour cream on the side to be added according to taste.

Yield: 8 to 12 servings.

Note: If your taste runs to the piquant side, a few hot Hungarian or other peppers may be used to replace part of the sweet peppers in this recipe.

From the Repertoire of Dinah Shore

There is a fish soup indigenous to California that is as much a part of American culture as Boston clam chowder in the East or oyster gumbo in the South. At its best—and the best we've ever sampled was in Dinah Shore's kitchen—cioppino is delectable. The origins of the soup, its name and various components are something of an enigma, for no one can guess the date of its entrance into the native culture.

When Dinah invited us to dine in her home, we accepted with unusual alacrity. In addition to being a well-known singer, she is justly celebrated as one of the finest cooks in Beverly Hills and, to be corny as Kansas, we have long wanted to be "someone in the kitchen with Dinah," no matter how briefly. To tell the truth, we're a bit jealous of Burt Reynolds.

When she informed us that we would be dining on cioppino, we began a bit of research thumbing through a few of this country's most prestigious dictionaries. To our great surprise, we discovered the word is not listed in those standard volumes. One book of food speculates that the word derives from Italian slang or dialect and means "lightly chopped," but we strongly suspect this is speculation.

Dinah told us that she had first discovered cioppino not in California but at a small restaurant in Hawaii some years ago. She added that the finest she had ever sampled was at a food festival at San Pedro, about 18 miles from Los Angeles. While San Francisco claims to be the birthplace of the soup, the fishermen of San Pedro are equally adamant in their assertion that their ancestors are the true source. In any event, Dinah's recipe came from a San Pedro source.

Dinah Shore, whether she's stewing up a fish soup or baking corn bread for a Christmas turkey, is an intuitive—which is to say a born—cook. Her repertoire is international and runs the gamut from those admirable Russian dumplings known as piroshki and Italy's "pasta fazool" to the foods of her childhood in Winchester, Tennessee, hominy grits with cheese and red beans with rice.

To our great surprise we have discovered that Los Angeles, even more than New York, is a cook's paradise. We spent a considerable amount of time shopping at Dinah's market, which happens to be across the street from the CBS television studio where her program "Dinah!"

originates. It is the sprawling, lavishly endowed Farmer's Market, a seemingly inexhaustible source of fresh produce, including such hard-to-find things as fresh chilies, cilantro or fresh coriander plus all manner of fish and fowl and meats. It is also a place where international food stands abound, and you can spend a few minutes or an hour or so feasting on snacks that range from chili con carne to Chinese delicacies.

Dinah occasionally ducks out of the studio to dine at Bryan's, which specializes in pit barbecue pork, or Patsy d'Amore's, which dispenses an excellent pizza.

Dinah told us that when she negotiated for her new home 10 years ago, her priorities were two—first, a tennis court, and second, a spacious, well-equipped kitchen. Her kitchen and cooking facilities are, predictably, special. The stove, with restaurant-style burners, is modeled after

Dinah Shore in the kitchen of her home in Beverly Hills, California.

one she spotted and admired in a local "fry-cook" place. There is also a large, sturdy, flat grill sometimes used for cooking an international variety of sausages—chorizos, sweet and hot Italian sausages, German knockwurst, and so on—for large gatherings.

Most of her entertaining is informal and, because of a heavy schedule, anything approaching entertaining on a grand scale is rare. She prefers small gatherings with a few close friends such as the Jack Lemmons and Billy Wilders.

We don't know how it had escaped our notice during the past four years since it was published, but Dinah is the author of a fascinating relatively small, but first-rate cookbook, *Someone's in the Kitchen With Dinah*, published by Doubleday (1971, $4.95). It is a personal, well-varied book scattered with anecdotes and easy-to-follow recipes.

Eggplant Spaghetti Sauce

½   eggplant, peeled and sliced
    Salt
½   cup olive oil,
    approximately
½   pound sweet and/or hot
    Italian sausage, cut in
    chunks
½   pound ground chuck
½   onion, finely chopped
1   clove garlic, finely chopped
1   rib celery, finely chopped
1   carrot, scraped and finely
    chopped
1   35-ounce can whole
    tomatoes, mashed or
    placed in a blender quickly
6   sprigs parsley, finely
    chopped
    Freshly ground black
    pepper
1   tablespoon dried oregano
1   tablespoon fresh basil or
    half the amount dried
½   cup or more chicken broth,
    optional
½   cup heavy cream

1. Soak sliced eggplant in salted water to cover at least 30 minutes, or an hour, if you have the time.

2. Heat 1 tablespoon oil in a skillet and add the sausage and ground chuck. Cook, stirring, until lightly browned. Set aside.

3. Heat 2 tablespoons oil in a saucepan and add the onion, garlic, celery, and carrot. Cook, stirring, until onion is transparent. Add tomatoes, parsley, and meat. Let sauce come to a boil over high heat. Add salt and pepper to taste, oregano, and basil. Let sauce simmer over low heat for 1 hour or more. If sauce becomes too thick, add a little chicken broth.

4. Meanwhile, remove eggplant slices from water, pat dry and season with salt and pepper to taste. In a skillet, sauté the eggplant slices in as much oil as necessary until browned. Drain on paper toweling.

5. Just before serving, add the cream. Serve over spaghetti. Place a slice of eggplant on top of each serving.

Yield: 6 servings.

Note: This is for a main course. If you want it vegetarian or lighter and perhaps for a side dish, omit the Italian sausage and the ground chuck.

Cream of Fresh Tomato Soup

5 medium-size fresh tomatoes
3 medium-size potatoes, peeled and thinly sliced
1 small onion, finely chopped
Salt and freshly ground black pepper
1 bay leaf
1 teaspoon dried basil
2 tablespoons butter
2 tablespoons flour
1 cup milk, approximately
1 tablespoon sugar, or to taste

1. Bring water to boil in a medium-size saucepan. Plunge the tomatoes into the boiling water. Remove pan from heat and let the tomatoes stand about 30 seconds or more in the water. Remove tomatoes and run cold water over them. Skins will slip off easily. Slice the peeled tomatoes.

2. Place the tomatoes, potatoes, onions, salt and pepper to taste, bay leaf, and basil in a saucepan. Cook over medium heat until potatoes are soft. Remove bay leaf. Press the tomato-potato mixture through a sieve or pour into a blender and puree until smooth

3. Meanwhile, melt the butter in a saucepan and add the flour, stirring. Slowly add half the milk, stirring. When smooth, add the pureed tomato-potato mixture. Cook, stirring over low heat until well blended. Add remaining milk. If soup is too thick, add more milk or a little chicken broth. Add sugar to taste. Correct seasoning. Serve very hot.

Yield: 4 servings.

Cream of Broccoli Soup

1 medium-size bunch of broccoli, trimmed
1 medium-size potato, thinly sliced
Salt
2 tablespoons butter or margarine
½ medium-size onion, coarsely chopped
2 tablespoons flour
1 cup warm chicken broth
1 cup warm milk
¼ cup warm heavy cream
Freshly ground black pepper
1 teaspoon dried basil

1. Cook the broccoli and potatoes in salted water until tender. Set aside 4 flowerets of broccoli for garnish.

2. Heat the butter in a medium-size saucepan and add the onion. Cook, stirring, until onion is transparent but not brown.

3. Add the flour and cook, stirring, until blended. Add the chicken broth and milk and cook, stirring, until smooth.

4. Place the broccoli and potatoes in a blender or food processor and puree the vegetables. Gradually add the broth-milk mixture. Add the warm cream, a little at a time, until the soup is the right consistency. Return the soup to the saucepan. Add salt and pepper to taste and reheat. Serve with 2 broccoli flowerets in each bowl of soup.

Yield: 2 servings.

Baked Red Snapper

Fish

1   *4–5-pound whole red snapper with head and tail left on*
    Salt and freshly ground black pepper
    Unsalted butter, softened
    Lime or lemon juice

Stuffing

2 *tablespoons butter*
2 *tablespoons finely chopped or grated onion*
1 *tablespoon finely chopped green pepper*
1 *tablespoon finely chopped celery*
½ *cup fresh bread crumbs*
    Salt and freshly ground black pepper
½ *teaspoon dried tarragon*
1 *teaspoon dried basil*
1 *tablespoon chopped parsley*
6 *medium-size raw shrimp, shelled and deveined, cut into small chunks*
7 *tablespoons tiny bay shrimp, cooked (see note)*

¼ *cup chopped or slivered toasted almonds*
2 *tablespoons fish stock (see recipe, page 156)*

Sauce

1 *tablespoon cornstarch*
½ *cup fish stock (see recipe) or chicken broth*
    Salt and freshly ground black pepper to taste
½ *teaspoon dried basil*
½ *teaspoon chopped fresh dill, optional*
½ *cup dry white wine or vermouth*
2 *medium-size raw shrimp, shelled and deveined, cut into small chunks*
1 *tablespoon tiny bay shrimp, cooked (see note)*
¼ *cup heavy cream*

1. Scale and clean the fish thoroughly. If possible debone it without disturbing the shape. Place fish in a shallow oblong baking dish. Sprinkle inside cavity with salt, pepper, and a little lime or lemon juice. Spread with unsalted butter.

2. Preheat the oven to 400 degrees.

3. For the stuffing, heat the butter in a skillet and sauté the onion until just transparent. Add the green pepper and celery. Then add bread crumbs, salt, pepper, tarragon, and basil. Add parsley and uncooked shrimp. Continue cooking and when shrimp barely start to turn pink, add bay shrimp and almonds. Add the fish stock. Stuffing is done when the medium-size shrimp are all pink.

4. Place stuffing in fish. Secure cavity with toothpicks or skewers. Sprinkle outside of fish with salt, pepper, and a little lime or lemon juice. Dot generously with unsalted butter. Cover with foil pressed around edges.

5. Place fish in oven and bake 20 minutes. Uncover and bake 15 minutes longer or until fish flakes easily. Remove fish to hot platter.

6. For the sauce, add cornstarch to drippings in pan, stirring. Stir in the ½ cup fish stock. Add salt, pepper, basil, and dill. Add the dry white wine or vermouth.

7. Add the 2 raw shrimp and 1 tablespoon tiny bay shrimp and then the cream. Check for seasoning. Cook until shrimp turn pink. Pour a little sauce over fish, reserving the remainder to be served separately.

Yield: 8 servings.

Note: Large shrimp, cut into small pieces, may be substituted for bay shrimp. Tiny shrimp are available in jars in specialty food shops.

Dinah Shore's Cioppino

2 tablespoons olive oil
2 tablespoons butter
3 cups chopped onion
1 leek, trimmed, washed well and finely chopped
2 to 4 cloves garlic, finely chopped
2 green peppers, cored, seeded, and cut into thin strips
4 cups chopped imported peeled tomatoes

1 cup fresh or canned tomato sauce
   Salt and freshly ground black pepper
1 bay leaf
1 teaspoon dried oregano
1 teaspoon dried thyme
1 tablespoon dried basil
   Red pepper flakes
2 cups fish stock (see recipe, page 156)
1 cup fresh or bottled clam juice
1 cup dry white wine
1 pound firm-fleshed fish such as striped bass, red snapper, rock cod, or seabass, cut into bite-size pieces
½ pound fresh scallops, preferably bay scallops
1 pound raw shrimp, shelled and deveined
1 dozen well-washed small clams in the shell
¼ cup shucked oysters with their liquor
½ pound lobster tail, cooked in the shell, optional
1 hard-shell crab, cooked in the shell and cracked, optional

1. Heat the oil and butter in a kettle and add the onion, leek, and garlic. Cook, stirring often, until the vegetables are lightly browned. Add the green peppers and continue cooking, stirring, until peppers wilt.

2. Add the tomatoes and tomato sauce. Add salt and pepper to taste, bay leaf, oregano, thyme, basil, and about ¼ teaspoon red pepper flakes. Add the fish stock and cook slowly about 2 hours, stirring often to prevent burning.

More fish stock may be added if desired.

3. Add the clam juice and wine and continue cooking about 10 minutes. The soup may be made in advance to this point.

4. Twenty minutes or so before serving, return the soup to the boil and add the striped bass or other fish. Cook about 5 minutes and add the scallops and shrimp. Simmer about 8 minutes and add the clams, oysters, lobster tail, and crab. Cook, stirring gently, about 5 minutes or until the clams open. Serve in very hot soup bowls with red pepper flakes on the side.

Yield: 10 servings.

Sunday Omelet Crêpe

6 crêpes (see recipe)
  Raspberry jam or some
  kind of tart jelly
4 tablespoons butter
7 eggs
2 tablespoons heavy cream
  Salt and freshly ground
  black pepper

1. In the center of each crêpe, put a scant teaspoon of either jam or jelly. Roll up the crêpe.

2. Heat an omelet pan. Add ⅓ of the butter. While butter is melting, beat eggs and cream together lightly with a fork. Add salt and pepper. Pour ⅓ cup of egg mixture into the hot omelet pan. Stir quickly with a fork until edges begin to cook. When omelet is almost set, place the rolled crêpe in center and with a spatula quickly roll the omelet around the crepe and slide it onto a warm platter.

3. Follow same steps with the remaining egg mixture and crêpes. Allow 3 crêpes per person.

Yield: 2 servings.

Crêpes

2 eggs
1 cup milk
⅛ teaspoon salt
½ cup flour

1. Beat the eggs well in a mixing bowl. Add the milk, salt, and flour, beating all together with a rotary beater until smooth.

2. Heat a 5-inch skillet and brush with butter. Pour in 1 tablespoon of the batter and tip quickly to coat bottom of skillet. Cook over medium heat until small bubbles appear. Shake the crêpe out of skillet onto a clean dish towel until ready to use or store. When you've made a few and they have cooled, they can be stacked without sticking together. Wrap 6 in aluminum foil and freeze. They thaw out quickly.

Yield: About 15 crêpes.

Party Pâté

WITH PIERRE FRANEY

There are some foods in this world which are, for no easily accountable reason, "festive." Among them we would count high on a list any of scores of well-seasoned pâtés. A particular favorite is a pâté of pork rind, which has a marvelous gelatinous consistency and is made with the inexpensive rind of pork available at butcher shops that specialize in pork products. We also like a somewhat coarse and not-so-subtly-seasoned country pâté. Both of them are outlined here.

Pâté of Pork Rind

2 pounds fresh pork hocks
1 pound fresh pork rind
1 teaspoon saltpeter
3 whole cloves garlic,
   unpeeled
10 black peppercorns
1 bay leaf
3 cloves
   Salt
2 carrots, trimmed, scraped,
   and halved
2 ribs celery, finely chopped
6 sprigs parsley
3 sprigs fresh thyme or ½
   teaspoon dried
   Freshly ground black
   pepper
¼ cup finely chopped parsley
⅛ teaspoon freshly grated
   nutmeg
1 clove garlic, finely minced

1. Combine the pork hocks and pork rind in a kettle and add cold water to cover, about 3 quarts. Add the saltpeter, whole garlic cloves, peppercorns, bay leaf, cloves, salt to taste, carrots, celery, parsley, and thyme; bring to the boil. Partially cover and cook 2 hours or longer until the meat is tender. Let stand until cool.

2. Remove the hocks, pork rind, and carrots from the kettle. Set aside. Strain and reserve the broth. You should have 8 cups. Discard solids.

3. Remove the meat from the pork bones and cut it into ½-inch cubes. Slice the pork rind into 1½-by-¼-inch strips. Cut the carrots into rounds.

4. Combine the meat and carrots with the reserved broth and bring to the boil. Simmer about 30 minutes to reduce to 7 to 8 cups. Add salt and pepper to taste. Add the chopped parsley, nutmeg, and minced garlic. Pour the mixture into a 2-quart pâté mold. Let cool to room temperature. Cover with wax paper, then with a lid. Chill until ready to serve. Unmold, if desired.

Yield: 12 to 24 servings.

Country Pâté

3 pounds pork liver
2 pounds boneless pork butt,
   both lean and fat
2 cups coarsely chopped
   onion (about ½ pound)
1 clove garlic, chopped
1 teaspoon chopped fresh
   thyme or ½ teaspoon dried
1 cup flour
½ teaspoon saltpeter
2 teaspoons salt
½ teaspoon freshly ground
   black pepper
½ cup dry white wine
4 eggs, lightly beaten
¼ teaspoon grated nutmeg
12 or more slices very thinly
   sliced unsalted fatback (see
   note)
   Quick aspic, optional (see
   recipe)

1. Preheat oven to 375 degrees.

2. Put the pork liver, pork butt, onion, and garlic through a meat grinder, using the fine blade of the grinder. Grind the mixture into a mixing bowl.

3. Add the thyme, flour, salt-peter, salt, pepper, wine, eggs, and nutmeg. Mix well with the hands until thoroughly blended and no lumps remain.

4. Select a 10- or 12-cup rectangular pâté mold. (This recipe was tested in a mold that measures 14 by 3¾ by 3½ inches.) Line the bottom and sides of the mold with the fatback slices, letting them hang generously over the sides of the mold. Spoon the mixture into the mold and smooth it over. Fold the fatback overhanging over the filling to completely enclose it.

5. Set the mold in a large basin and pour boiling water around it. Bake 2 hours. The pâté is done when the internal temperature registers 160 degrees on a meat thermometer. Remove from water bath. Cover with foil and weigh the pâté with one or two heavy objects. Let stand until cool and then refrigerate.

6. Pour the aspic in a jelly-roll pan and refrigerate. Let it set.

7. When ready to serve, unmold the pâté and scrape away the fat. Chop the aspic finely and put it around the pâté.

Yield: 18 or more servings.

Note: If unsalted fatback is not available, bacon may be used, although it will give a smoky flavor to the pâté.

Quick aspic

3   *cups chicken broth*
1   *cup tomato juice*
4   *envelopes unflavored gelatin*
    Salt and freshly ground black pepper
1   *teaspoon sugar*
2   *egg shells, crushed*
2   *egg whites, lightly beaten*
2   *tablespoons cognac*

1. In a saucepan, combine the chicken broth with the tomato juice, gelatin, salt and pepper to taste, sugar, egg shells, and egg whites. Heat slowly, stirring constantly, until the mixture boils up in the pan.

2. Remove the pan from the heat and stir in the cognac.

3. Strain the mixture through a sieve lined with a flannel cloth that has been rinsed in cold water and wrung out. If the aspic starts to set or become too firm, it may be reheated, then brought to any desired temperature.

Yield: About 1 quart.

Chili con Carne

To our mind, no matter how Texans and assorted citizens of the West and Southwest may boast otherwise, there is no such thing as "the one real, authentic recipe" for chili con carne. And part of the fun is in composing your own version.

We must admit to a keen fancy for almost all honestly conceived chilies, and that would not include the curries, slurries, kedgerees, and so on.

We have enjoyed dozens of chilies made with ground meat, many of them containing tomatoes in one form or another. Our personal favorite version came to us from a friend, Mrs. Margaret Field, who lives in San Antonio, Texas.

"Meat for chili," Mrs. Field told us many years ago, "must always be cut in cubes. When you add cumin and oregano, you should always rub them between the palms of the hands, because that brings out the flavor. The chili should also be made at least twenty-four hours in advance."

Mrs. Field's chili contained neither tomatoes nor beans, although beans were frequently served on the side.

When we read Carter Rochelle's recipe for chili con carne, we noted that it bears a keen resemblance to the Field version, although he adds masa harina, a flour made of dried, finely ground corn.

A colleague and well-known food enthusiast, the writer Calvin Trillin, mentioned his favorite chili in *The New Yorker* in August 1973. It was the chili served him by Sandra Wolf of New York, our neighbor and friend. Mrs. Wolf uses ground meat for her chili, but there are no tomatoes.

We've thought for years that if there's such a thing as a national American dish, it isn't apple pie, it's chili con carne. In one form or another, chili in America knows no regional boundaries. North, South, East, and West, almost every man, woman, and child has a favorite recipe. Or at least a favorite source for the dish. Some of the best-publicized food events in this country are the chili-making contests that occur, generally in midsummer, in Texas and California.

One of the most memorable essays on chili we've ever read was printed some years ago in *The Houston Chronicle*. The author was Mr. Rochelle and the object of his outrage and vituperation was the publication of a book called *The Chili Cook Book* (Price Stern, 1972, $3.95), by a couple of supposed chili fanciers named Johnrae Earl and James McCormick.

After perusing the recipes included in the book, Mr. Rochelle wrote, "Maybe half a dozen palatable and veritable chili formulas are scattered among these grotesqueries. The others are curries, slurries, soups, gravies, sauces, chowders, ragouts, paprikashes, salamagundies, kedgerees, slumgullions, and the like."

The columnist was appalled at the author's description of "Houston's best chili" which, he asserted, included flour, paprika, tomatoes, and tomato juice. In other recipes he discovered such diverse elements as mutton, scallops, currant jelly, cocoa, white bread, cornstarch, and tomato soup. Plus macaroni, chicken gumbo soup, onion soup, pickling spices, chicken fat, barley, raisins, sour cream and—perish the thought—potatoes.

Ingredients for chili

Over the years we have been (and doubtlessly will continue to be) put down by certain purists who insist that no side dishes other than beans and rice should be served with good chili. We happen to have a passion for a choice of things to be added to chili when it is served— among them a raw tomato sauce served cold, chopped lettuce, sour cream, grated Cheddar cheese, chopped fresh coriander leaves when available, and hot pepper flakes.

We print herewith recipes for our version of Mrs. Field's chili, for Mrs. Wolf's chili, and for our version of an all-American chili made with ground beef and tomatoes and a recipe for a Mexican raw tomato sauce.

Margaret Field's Chili con Carne

5   pounds lean chuck roast
½   cup olive oil
½   cup flour
½   cup chili powder, more or less to taste
2   teaspoons cumin seeds
2   teaspoons dried oregano
6   to 10 cloves garlic, finely minced
4   cups fresh or canned beef broth
    Salt and freshly ground black pepper
    Pinto beans, optional (see recipe)

1. Trim the meat and cut it into 1-inch cubes.

2. Heat the oil in a deep kettle and add the cubed meat. Cook, stirring, just until the meat loses its red color.

3. Sift together the flour and chili powder and sprinkle the meat with it, stirring constantly so that the pieces are evenly coated.

4. Place the cumin and oregano in the palm of one hand.

Rub the spices between the palms, sprinkling over the meat. Add the garlic and stir. Add the broth, stirring the meat constantly. Add salt and pepper and bring to the boil. Partly cover and simmer 3 to 4 hours or until the meat almost falls apart. If necessary, add more broth as the meat cooks. This chili should not be soupy, however. Serve with pinto beans (see recipe) if desired.

Yield: 8 to 12 servings.

Pinto beans

1   pound dried pink or pinto beans
1   large onion, chopped
½   pound chunk salt pork
    Salt

1. Soak the beans in water to cover for about 1 hour, then drain them.

2. Cover again with water, about 2 inches above the beans, add the onion and salt pork and simmer until the beans are tender, about 2 hours. Add salt to taste.

Yield: 8 servings.

All-American Chili

Yield: 8 to 16 servings.

2 tablespoons peanut, vegetable, or corn oil
6 to 8 onions, about 3 pounds
5 pounds ground beef chuck
20 cloves garlic, finely minced
½ cup chili powder, more or less to taste
1 tablespoon ground cumin
1 tablespoon oregano, crushed
2 cloves
1 teaspoon celery salt
Salt and freshly ground black pepper
6½ cups canned, whole, peeled, undrained tomatoes
6 tablespoons tomato paste (unless the tomatoes include tomato paste in can)

1. Heat the oil in a very large, heavy skillet or kettle and add the onions. Cook, stirring, until wilted, about 3 minutes.

2. Add the meat and stir with a large metal spoon, cutting into the meat with the side of the spoon to break up any lumps.

3. Add the garlic, chili powder, cumin, oregano, cloves, celery salt, salt, and pepper. Stir until well blended and add the tomatoes and tomato paste. Stir to blend. Cook, stirring often, about 1 hour or longer. If the chili becomes too thick, thin it with a little fresh or canned beef broth. Like all chili, this is best if reheated.

Side garnishes for chili

(To be served separately)
Sour cream
Grated Cheddar cheese
Cooked pinto, black, or kidney beans (see recipe, page 409)
Cooked rice
Chopped onions
Hot pepper flakes
Chopped lettuce
Chopped fresh coriander leaves

Raw tomato sauce

2 cups drained, canned tomatoes (see note)
2 tablespoons red wine vinegar
½ cup finely chopped onion
Salt and freshly ground black pepper
1 or 2 fresh or canned serrano chilies, finely chopped
1 ice cube
1 tablespoon or more chopped fresh coriander, optional

Chop the tomatoes and combine with the remaining ingredients. Stir until the ice melts.

Yield: About 2 cups.

Note: If red, ripe, tasty tomatoes are available, core them and cut into cubes. Use in lieu of the canned tomatoes.

Sandra Wolf's Texas Chili

2 tablespoons peanut oil
3 pounds ground chuck
1 tablespoon celery salt
2 tablespoons chili powder
2 tablespoons flour
2 teaspoons ground cumin
4 cloves garlic, finely minced
   Minced jalapeño peppers
   or crushed small red dried
   peppers to taste, or about
   ½ teaspoon cayenne
   Pinto beans (see recipe
   above)

1. Heat the oil in a deep kettle. Add the meat and stir to break up lumps. Cook until the meat loses its red color. Sprinkle generously with celery salt as it browns.

2. Add the chili powder and flour mixed together and stir the meat so that it is well covered with the chili powder and flour. Add all remaining ingredients except pinto beans. Add enough water to cover. Simmer very slowly 30 minutes or longer. Add more liquid if necessary. Serve the chili and pinto beans separately with a bowl of hot rice on the side. Serve with bowls of sour cream, finely grated Monterrey Jack or Cheddar cheese, shredded lettuce, and finely chopped scallions or onions.

Yield: 8 servings.

Note: To increase the quantity, add to each additional pound of meat the following: 2 teaspoons chili powder, 2 teaspoons flour, ½ teaspoon cumin, and more garlic to taste.

Sources for Foreign Ingredients

The stores listed below accept mail orders; some of them make catalogues available for that purpose. When making inquiries, find out if there is a minimum mail order charge. Order by mail only if the ingredients you need are unavailable in your community. In urban areas ethnic foods are usually not hard to find.

Caribbean, South American, and Mexican

District of Columbia
Pena's Spanish Store
1636 17th Street, N.W.
Washington 20009

Illinois
La Preferida, Inc.
177–181 West South Water Market
Chicago 60608

Louisiana
Central Grocery Company
923 Decatur Street
New Orleans 70116

Massachusetts
Cardullo's Gourmet Shop
6 Brattle Street
Cambridge 02138

Michigan
La Paloma-Tenorio and
Company
2620 Bagley Street
Detroit 48216

New York
Casa Moneo Spanish Imports
210 West 14th Street
New York 10011

Ohio
Spanish and American Food Market
7001 Wade Park Avenue
Cleveland 44103

Ontario
Cooks Gourmet
226 Rideau Street
Ottawa

Quebec
Librería Española
3779 St. Dominique Street
Montreal

Chinese

Alberta
Kim Sang Company Limited
218 Centre Street South
Calgary

British Columbia
Wing Hing Co., Ltd.
3640 East Hastings Street
Vancouver

California
Wing Chong Lung Co.
922 South San Pedro Street
Los Angeles 90015

District of Columbia
Tuck Cheong Company
617 H Street, N.W.
Washington 20001

Illinois
Star Market
3349 North Clark Street
Chicago 60657

Manitoba
Wah Hing Co., Ltd.
231 King Street
Winnipeg

Massachusetts
Wing Wing Imported Groceries
79 Harrison Avenue
Boston 02111

New York
  Yuet Hing Market, Inc.
  23 Pell Street
  New York 10013

Quebec
  Leong Jung Co., Ltd.
  999 Clark Street
  Montreal

Texas
  Oriental Import-Export Company
  2009 Polk Street
  Houston 77003

Indian

British Columbia
  Ageet Market
  3190 Quadra Street
  Victoria

California
  Haig's
  441 Clement Street
  San Francisco 94119

Manitoba
  House of India
  41 Shrebrook Street
  Winnipeg

Michigan
  Delmar and Company
  501 Monroe Avenue
  Detroit 48226

New York
  Kalustyan Orient Export Trading
    Corporation
  123 Lexington Avenue
  New York 10016

Texas
  Antone's
  Box 3352
  Houston 77001

Washington
  House of Rice
  4112 University Way Northeast
  Seattle 98105

Indonesian

California
  Holland American Market
  10343 East Artesia Boulevard
  Bellflower 90706

District of Columbia
  Tuck Cheong
  617 H Street, N.W.
  Washington 20001

Illinois
  Mee Jun Emporium
  2223 Wentworth Avenue
  Chicago 60616

New York
  Toko Garuda
  997 First Avenue
  New York 10022

Ohio
  Sun Lee Yuen
  1726 Payne Avenue
  Cleveland 44114

Pennsylvania
  Yick Fung Imports
  210 North 9th Street
  Philadelphia 19107

Italian

California
  R. Fazzi and Co.
  225 South Spring Street
  Los Angeles 90027

Florida
  Joseph Assi's Imported Foods
  3316 Beach Boulevard
  Jacksonville 32207

Indiana
  Guy Montani Fine Foods
  12 West 27th Street
  Indianapolis 46208

Manitoba
  DeLuca Bros. Canadian and
    Imported Foods
  950 Portage Avenue
  Winnipeg

New York
  Manganaro Brothers
  488 Ninth Avenue
  New York 10018

Ontario
  Guzzo and Adamo
  362 Preston Avenue
  Ottawa

Tennessee
  Barzizza Bros. Inc.
  351 South Front Street
  Memphis 38103

Texas
Cappello's
5328 Lemmon Avenue
Dallas 75209

Japanese

Alberta
Japanese Food Mart
1111 McLeod Trail South
Calgary

British Columbia
Matsuyama Asako
577 East Hastings Street
Vancouver

California
Enbun Company
248 East First Street
Los Angeles 90012

Colorado
Pacific Mercantile Company
1946 Larimer Street
Denver 80202

Illinois
Diamond Trading Company
1108 North Clark Street
Chicago 60610

Louisiana
Oriental Trading Company
2636 Edenborn Avenue
Metairie 70002

Massachusetts
Yoshinoya
36 Prospect Street
Cambridge 02139

Missouri
Maruyama's
100 North 18th Street
St. Louis 63103

New York
Katagiri Company
224 East 59th Street
New York 10022

Ohio
Soya Food Products
2356 Wyoming Avenue
Cincinnati 45214

Ontario
Japan Food Store
465 Somerset Street West
Ottawa

Quebec
Miyamoto Provisions
5997 St. Hubert Street
Montreal

Middle Eastern

California
Mediterranean and Middle East
Import Company
233 Valencia Street
San Francisco 94103

Louisiana
Progress Grocery Company
915 Decatur Street
New Orleans 70116

Massachusetts
Cardullo's Gourmet Shop
6 Brattle Street
Cambridge 02138

Michigan
American Oriental Grocery
20736 Lahser Road
Southfield 48075

Missouri
Demmas Shish-Ke-Bab
5806 Hampton Avenue
St. Louis 63109

New York
Malko Brothers
197 Atlantic Avenue
Brooklyn 11201

Ontario
Azzi's Pastry and Lunch Box
342 Elgin Street
Ottawa

Jerusalem Delicatessen
967 Eglinton Avenue West
Toronto

Tennessee
Barzizza Brothers, Inc.
351 South Front Street
Memphis 38103

Washington
Angelo Merlino and Sons
816 Sixth Avenue South
Seattle 98134

Specialty Shops

New York
H. Roth and Son
1577 First Avenue
New York 10028

Paprikas Weiss
1546 Second Avenue
New York 10028

Quebec
World Wide Imported Foods, Inc.
6700 Cote des Neiges Road
Montreal

Kitchenware

British Columbia
Woodward Stores, Ltd.
3125 Douglas Street
Victoria

New York
The Bridge Kitchenware Corp.
212 East 52nd Street
New York 10022

California
Williams–Sonoma
576 Sutter Street
San Francisco 94102

Index

A

Aaron, Florence, 275, 278
Abgushteh limon, *128*
Acaraje sauce, *60*
Aksoy, Mrs. A. M., 267
Albert Street restaurants, *333*
Albondigas, 235
Albuféra chicken, *87, 88, 90*
Alexandre sauce, *276*
Alfredo's spaghetti à la fettucelle, *349*
All-American chili, 410
All-Maine Cooking, 28
ALMOND(S)
  cake, 171, 174
  eggplant with, *150*
  manicotti with chicken and, *117, 120*
  shrimp quiche with, 140
  toasting, *164*
Alsatian meat pie, *344*
Amsterdam, *187–192*
ANCHOVY(IES)
  appetizer with shrimp and oranges, 165,
    167
  butter, *79*
  eggs with mushrooms and, 377
  mozzarella cheese with tomatoes and, 33
  mushrooms stuffed with spinach and, *123*
  octopus with, *198*
  peppers and, *236*
  sauce
    with garlic, for cold vegetables, *146, 147*
    mozzarella toast with, 171, 172
  and tarragon mayonnaise, shrimp with,
    361
  and tomatoes vinaigrette, 278
Andalouse-style fish and seafood, 273
Angourosalata me yiaourti, 290
Anise, *see* Fennel
APPETIZERS
  bean purée, 182, 184
  carpaccio, *170*
    alla Veneto, 32
  carp-roe spread, 290
  caviar, eggplant, 182, 183
  chicken
    with coriander, 233

cubed, in lettuce leaves, 59
pon pon, 56
skewered, *267, 268*
wings, with honey, 158
crêpes Belvedere, *146, 149*
crostini dello chef, *168*
eggplant and yogurt, 85
eggs
  pickled, 313
  and seafood canapé, 314
lamb on skewers, *267, 269*
meat rolls, *339, 341*
mozzarella toast with anchovy sauce, 171,
  172
pâté, 404–406
  de campagne, 327
  chicken liver, 362
  country, 405
  pork rind, 405
peppers and anchovies, *236*
quiche
  Alsace, *344*
  Lorraine, quick, *221, 224*
raw fish with green peppercorns, *240, 241*
schmaltz herring, 182, 184
shrimp
  with mustard and dill sauce, *168, 169*
  oranges and anchovies with, 165, 167
  tangy spicy, 57
taramosalata, *133, 136*
turnovers, yucca, *102*
vegetables with anchovy and garlic sauce,
  146, 147
APPLE(S)
  ice cream with Calvados and, 156
  tart, *142, 144*
Ardennes-style venison cutlets, 380
Armenian-style yogurt soup with coriander,
  233, 236
Art of Charcuterie, The (Grigson), 187, 375,
  376
Art of Cookery, Made Plain and Easy, The:
  Which far exceeds any Thing of the
  Kind ever published (Glasse), 350
Art of Good Cooking (Peck), 277
ARTICHOKE(S)
  bottoms, with oyster stuffing, *35, 36, 38*
  alla Giudea, *46, 48*
  stuffed, *117, 118*

(All page numbers in italics refer to Volume I)

Asparagus Milanaise, *108*
ASPIC
concord grape, 323
quick, 406
Au Pactole, *172–173*
Au Quai d'Orsay, *171–172*
Auberge de l'Ill, 78
Aux Deux Magots, *171*
AVOCADO
with crab meat, 319
and fennel vinaigrette, 370
soup, with cucumber and tomato, *180*

B

Bagels, *166*
"Bagels, Bagels, Bagels" (booklet), 38
Bagna caôda, *146, 147*
BAHIA-STYLE, *55–61*
acaraje sauce, *60*
caipirinha, *55, 57, 61*
coconut blanc mange, *57, 60*
haussa rice, *57, 59*
prune compote, *61*
vatapá jodo, *57*
xin xin, *57, 59*
Baker, Russell, 357–359
Bakhara pasanda, *271*
BALI, *316–320*
soto ajam, *316–318, 319*
Bali Restaurant, *190*
Banchet, Jean, 152–154, 199
Bangan bartha, *271*
BARBECUE
Genghis Khan grill, *250, 251*
Japanese-style, 214–218
grilled fowl, 215
grilled fowl, sauce for, 215
salmon, salt grilled, 216
spareribs with ginger, 237
Vietnamese-style, 247–250
lemon duck, *249*
nuoc mam sauce, *249*
pork patties grilled in lettuce leaves, 247
shrimp patties grilled in lettuce leaves, 248
Bareh meveh, *125, 129*
Basil and nut sauce for pasta, *260*
BASS
channel, stew, 318
sea
with fennel, 371
with tomato sauce, 338
BASS, STRIPED
ceviche with scallops and, *221, 223*

with champagne, *13*
court bouillon for, *89, 243*
fermière, *142*
poached, *87, 88, 89*
cold, *243*
raw, with green peppercorns, *240, 241*
salad, with tarragon, *246*
with sorrel, 285
with tomato vinaigrette sauce, 81
Bâtonnet-style vegetables, 222
Bavarian cream, mirabelle-flavored, 363
Bayrock, Jean, 314
BEAN(S)
green beans vinaigrette, 201
soup, Japanese-style, 218
sprouts
shredded chicken with, 299
and shrimp soup, 94
BEANS, DRIED
black bean salad, 277
lamb stew with, *114*
pinto, 409
with prosciutto in tomato sauce, 171, 173
purée of, *182, 184*
red beans and rice, 95
soup
lamb-shank, 108
and pork, *147*
with sage, 109
Béarnaise sauce, 241
BEEF
appetizer, raw, 32, *170*
barbecued, 235
birds, in brown sauce, *117, 118*
broth
Hungarian-style, 204
Russian-style, 185
carpaccio, *170*
alla Veneto, 32
casings, 391
casserole
with macaroni, *43*
with noodles, *42*
cured
corned, *211, 219*
pastrami, *211, 218, 220*
spiced salt, 378
dumplings, 182, 185
ginger, 96
grilled, *250, 251*
hamburgers
with cognac and cream sauce, 289
Russian-style, *289*
Stroganoff, 288
leftover, with ginger, 96
meatballs and duck in walnut sauce, 125, 127

(All page numbers in italics refer to Volume I)

raw, 32, *170*
ribs, deviled, 381
roast
　eye round, 96
　recipes from readers, 97–99
　with red wine, 291
rolls
　braccioli, *117, 118*
　rouladen, 133
sauce, for pasta, 171, 174
soup, with sauerkraut, 182, 184
steak, pan broiled, *73*
Uncle Tai's, 297
zucchini stuffed with, *139*
Bee's Knees cocktail, 40, 41
Bee-sting liqueur, 39
Beeton, Mrs., 253, 256, *346*
Beignets de crabe, *282*
BELGIAN ENDIVE
braised, *16*
and fennel vinaigrette, 369
veal chops with, *40*
Bengal Sweet House, 267
Bengalese-style cabbage with mustard
　seeds and coconut, *156*
Benson, Laura and Robert, 315–323
Bernstein, Jonine, 103–105
Berquist, Jane, 228–229
Berry and fruit compote, 136
Betty Quaker Cookbook, The (ed. Man-
　ocherian), 84
Beurre blanc, 89
BEVERAGES
Bee's Knees cocktail, 40, 41
bee-sting liqueur, 39
caipirinha, *55, 57, 61*
cider, hot spiced, *352*
eggnog, *349*
pisco, *159*
rum punch, *230, 231*
Bialys, 364
Biderman, George, 259
Bierman, Stephen and Elizabeth, 324
Biftocks à la russe, *289*
Birrenbach, Cleopatra (Bourmand), *125–
130*
Black bean salad, 277
Black Forest cake, 75
Black mushrooms, rice with, *230, 233*
Black Sheep Restaurant, *187–188*
Blackstrap molasses, whole wheat bread
　with, *78*
Blue Book of Canning, The, 258
Bocuse, Paul, 30, 78, 111, 153, 201, 205,
　219–224
Boni, Ada, 171
Book of Great Desserts (Heatter), *284–287*

Book of Household Management (Beeton),
　253, 256
Borscht, 50
Boston clam chowder, *162*
Bouillabaisse with vinegar, 331
Bouillon, *see* Broth; Court bouillon
Boulettes of beef Stroganoff, *288*
Braccioli in brown sauce, *117, 118*
Brandade de morue, 119
Brazil, *55–61*
　See also Bahia-style
BREAD
corn bread
　Southern, *322*
　stuffing, *307, 321*
egg, 322
French, *80–84*
　baking, *84*
　Clyde Brooks's, *82*
　sourdough, *82, 83*
salt-rising, *392*
sauce, *347*
whole wheat
　with blackstrap molasses, *78*
　orange, *73*
Bread crumbs, 75–76, *347*
Brezolles à la maurette, *142, 143*
Brillat Savarin, Anthelme, *34*
BRIOCHE(S), 71
dough, 211
leftover lamb and vegetables in, 207, 210
with mushrooms, 378
Broccoli soup, cream of, 400
Broodje van Kootje, *191*
Brooks, Clyde, *80–84, 337*
BROTH
beef
　Hungarian-style, 204
　Russian-style, 185
chicken, 151
chicken and tomato, 129
fish, 318
Brown Derby Restaurant, 124
BROWN SAUCE
for beef, *118*
for fowl, *15*
for game, 346
veal, *143*
Brownies, honey, 39
Brussels sprouts in cream, *324*
Bryan's Restaurant, 398
Burgoon, Richard, *18*
BURGUNDY-STYLE
lamb and bean stew, *114*
soup, main course, 23
BUTTER
anchovy, 79

(All page numbers in italics refer to Volume I)

BUTTER (*Continued*)
  caper, 79
  clarified, 156
  for corn on the cob, 248
  herb, 201
  sauce, white, 89

C

CABBAGE
  with mustard seeds and coconut, 156
  red, braised with chestnuts, 325
  stuffed, 126
    with egg and lemon sauce, 289
Café Chauveron, 39
Café de Flore, 171
Caffe da Alfredo, 30
Caipirinha, 55, 57, 61
CAKE
  almond, 171, 174
  Black Forest, 75
  carrot, 336, 339
  cheesecake, 255
  chocolate, 96
    Black Forest, 75
    -honey, 38
    spongecake, 76
  fruitcake, 346
  pepper poundcake, 285
  prune-pecan, 287
  spongecake, 97
    chocolate, 76
    Italian-style, 50
  zuccotto alla Michelangelo, 29, 46, 49
Calf's liver with vinegar glaze, 192
Canapés, *see* Appetizers
CAPER
  butter, 79
  sauce, meat balls in, 197
Capon with nut stuffing, 372
Car Park, 332–333
Caramel, pears in, 54
CARAWAY SEEDS
  potatoes with, 42
  sauerkraut with, 135
Carême, 87
Carimañolas, 102
CARPACCIO, 170
  alla Veneto, 32
Carp-roe spread, 290
CARROT(S)
  cake, 336, 339
  ring, 96
  soup
    with coriander, 143

  cream of, 181
  and tomato, cream of, 106
  Vichy, 121
CASSEROLE
  beef
    with macaroni, 43
    with noodles, 42
  chicken and sausage, 92
  mushroom and noodle, 124
  rutabaga and sweet potato, 43
  wild rice and seafood, 230
CASSIS, 181
  roast duck with, 180
Cassoulet, 385, 387
CAVIAR, 166, 340
  scrambled eggs with, 334
Ceviche, 221, 223
Cha Gio, 339, 341
CHAMPAGNE
  chicken with tarragon and, 64
  mango slices with, 237
  sauce, 65
  striped bass with, 13
Chandoha, Walter, 110–113
Channel bass stew, 318
Chao tom, 341, 343
Charosis, 96
Château Chinon potatoes, 291, 292
Chauveron, Roger, 39
Chavela, Chino's, 310
CHEESE
  corn and zucchini with, 247
  eggplant with, 152
  fennel with, 368
  green tagliarini with, 33
  and sausage pie, 164
  soufflé with corn, curried, 245
  sweet dessert, 272
  timbales, Roquefort, 228
  zucchini with, 140
  zucchini stuffed with mushrooms and,
    105
  See also names of cheese
Cheesecake, hazelnut, 255
Chello, 125, 126–127, 129
Cherries with liqueurs, 279
CHESTNUTS
  buttered whole, 324
  red cabbage braised with, 325
Chez Denis, 205, 341–343, 351–355, 359
Chez Paul Bocuse, 175
Chi, Norman, 296
CHICKEN
  general data on, 262–263
  appetizer
    with coriander, 233

(All page numbers in italics refer to Volume I)

cubed, in lettuce leaves, 59
pon pon, 56
skewered, *267, 268*
wings, with honey, 158
breasts
with bean sprouts, 299
deviled, 382
loaf with watercress sauce, *276*
Mexican-style, 277
with mushrooms, *266*
au poivre, 325
stuffed, with tomato sauce, 326
broth, 151
with tomatoes, sour cream, and herbs,
129
casserole with sausage, *92*
Chinese-style
with bean sprouts, 299
crazy, 114
pon pon, 56
Soong, 59
wings, in oyster sauce, 159
creamed, with manicotti, *117, 120*
curry, *270*
fat, rendered, 122
grilled
Genghis Khan, *250*
Japanese-style, 215
gumbo, 52
Haitian-style, *231, 232*
Indian-style
chat, 233
curried, *270*
skewered, *268*
legs, baked with herbs, *263*
with lemon, *92*
liver
mousseline of, 122
pâté, 362
roast
Albuféra, *87, 88, 90*
Italian-style, 268
with rosemary, *301*
stuffed with scrambled eggs, 265
stuffed Stigliano-style, 268
stuffed Volhynian-style, 267
with watercress, *21*
rolls stuffed with spinach, *263*
salad, 240
sautéed
with prosciutto and mushrooms, 175
with sorrel, 286
with tomatoes, 222, 224
with vinegar, 332
skewered, *267, 268*
smoked, 66

soup
-noodle, with tortellini balls, *110, 112*
rice-noodle, 261, 269
soto ajam, *316–318, 319*
with spaghetti, 149
stew, xin xin, *57, 59*
with tarragon
and champagne, 64
and cream, *93*
thighs
ketjap, 73
stuffed, *265*
and tomato samp, 91
in vinegar and cream, 331
wings, 157–159
chasseur, 157, 158
curried, 157
oven-baked, with honey, 158
in oyster sauce, 159
CHILI CON CARNE, 407–411
all-American, 410
Margaret Field's, 409
Sandra Wolf's, 411
Chili Cook Book, The (Earl and McCormick), 407–408
Chinese Cooking for American Kitchens
(Lee), 159
Chinese parsley, *see* Coriander
CHINESE-STYLE, 54–60, 295–302
beef, Uncle Tai's, 297
chicken
with bean sprouts, 299
crazy, 114
pon pon, 56
Soong, 59
chicken wings in oyster sauce, 159
duck with ginger root, 301
fish soup
hot and sour, 232, 234
tart-flavored, *327, 329*
lamb
Hunam-style, 57
with scallions, 300
meatballs (lion's head), 114
planning a meal, 302
pork and shrimp balls in soup, 327
scallions, batter-fried, 113
shrimp
and crab meat, 58
and oysters, stir-fry, 112
paste, *76*
tangy spicy, 57
Uncle Tai's, 298
Chino's Restaurant, 307, 309–311
Chocolate cake, *see* Cake
Chorizo and tortilla soup, 257

(All page numbers in italics refer to Volume I)

Cho-shoku, *301*
CHOWDER
  clam
    Boston, *162*
    Manhattan, *161*
  corn and fish, 245
CHRISTMAS, *346–353*
  cider, hot spiced, *352*
  eggnog, *349*
  fruitcake, *346*
  plum pudding, *350, 351*
Chutney, *157–158*
Cider, hot spiced, *352*
Cilantro, *see* Coriander
Ciolino, John, 98
Cioppino, 383, 397, 402
CLAM(S)
  general data on, 20, 23–24, 279–280
  chowder
    Boston, *162*
    Manhattan, *161*
  coctel, 258
  with mustard mayonnaise, 278
  Rockefeller, *37*
  spaghetti in red sauce, 20
  spaghetti in white sauce, 22
  for sushi, 146
Clambake, wash-boiler, *193*
Classic Italian Cook Book (Hazan), 261
Claustrophobic Cooking (McGinniss), 25
Coach House Restaurant, 281
COCONUT
  blanc mange, *57, 60*
  cabbage with mustard seeds and, *156*
  milk, *58*
COD, 45–49
  general data on, 45–46, 49
  fillets
    broiled, 48
    Florentine, 46
    with Mornay sauce and noodles, 47
  poached, 48
  salad with tarragon, *246*
  salt, 49
    fritters, *230, 232*
    mousse, 119
Colantro, *see* Coriander
Comme Chez Soi, 343
Concord grape aspic, 323
Confit d'oie, 385, 386, 389
Confit de porc, *48*
Coocoo, 85
CORDIAL PIE, 263
  variations, 264
CORIANDER, 59, 232–233, 236
  general data on, 232–233, 236

carrot soup with, 143
chicken with, 233
hot and sour fish soup with, 232, 234
meat balls with, 233, 235
yogurt soup with, 233, 236
CORN, 243–248
  on the cob, 243, 248
    seasoned butter for, 248
  curried
    and cheese soufflé, 245
    with green peppers, 246
  and fish chowder, 245
  gazpacho with zucchini and, *180*
  pudding, 246
  salad with zucchini and tomatoes, 247
  and zucchini au gratin, 247
  See also Hominy; Samp
CORN BREAD
  Southern, *322*
  stuffing, *307, 321*
Corned beef, home-cured, *211, 219, 220*
Côte d'Azur lentils, *136*
Cotechini, *133, 135*
Cotriade, 331
Coupe Normande, 156
COURT BOUILLON
  for garlic sausages, 391
  for poaching fish, 48
  for striped bass, *89, 243*
Cousins, Ivan R., 244
CRAB MEAT
  general data on, *281, 283*
  avocado with, 319
  fritters, *282*
  Maryland crab cakes, *281, 283*
  mushrooms stuffed with, *122*
  salad with tarragon, *246*
  and shrimp, *58*
  soup
    curried, *281*
    she-crab, 320
Crab roe, 59
CRABS
  deep-fried, *242*
  sautéed soft shell, 319
  tempura, *305*
Cranberry beans with prosciutto in tomato
    sauce, 171, 173
Cream sauce, 237
Crème fraîche, 81, *229*
CREOLE-STYLE
  fish, 273
  shrimp au Pernod, *68*
CRÊPES
  Belvedere, *146, 149*
  omelette, 403

(All page numbers in italics refer to Volume I)

Crespelle Belvedere, *146, 149*
Crostata de marmellata, *148*
Crostini alla provatura, 172
Crostini dello chef, *168*
CROUTONS, *242*
    French-style, 332
    garlic, 191, 250
    with liver paste, 346
Crumb potatoes, 42
Crumpets, 251, 256
CUCUMBER(S)
    mayonnaise, *10, 11*
    parsleyed ovals, 86
    soup with tomato and avocado, *180*
    and yogurt salad, 290
CUISINART FOOD PROCESSOR, 69, 70, 72
    recipes for, 117–122, 187
Cuisine of Hungary, The (Lang), 202
CUISINE MINCEUR, 333–340
    carrot cake, 336, 339
    sea bass with tomato sauce, 338
Cuisines of Mexico, The (Kennedy), 72, 117,
        213, 251
Cuisses de volaille aux herbes, *263*
Culantro, *see* Coriander
CURRIED
    chicken, *270*
    chicken wings, 157
    corn
        and cheese soufflé, 245
        with green peppers, 246
    crab meat soup, *281*
    fish soup, 67
    lamb, *271*
    shrimp, *269*
Curry powder, *153–154*
CURRY SAUCE, 238
    mushroom, 238
Custard, 26, 231

D

Dashi, 217, *306*
Dass, Ram, *267, 268*
Davern, Jeremy, 40
De Boerderij, *188–189*
DeMarco, Hazel, 108
Denis, M., *342–343,* 351–355
DESSERTS
    Bavarian cream, mirabelle-flavored, 363
    blanc mange, *57, 60*
    brownies, 39
    cake
        almond, 171, 174
        chocolate, *96*

    chocolate, Black Forest, 75
    chocolate, honey, 38
    chocolate, spongecake, 76
    fruitcake, *346*
    hazelnut cheesecake, 255
    honey-chocolate, 38
    pepper poundcake, 285
    prune-pecan, 287
    spongecake, 97
    spongecake, chocolate, 76
    spongecake, Italian-style, *50*
    zuccotto alla Michelangelo, *29, 46, 49*
cheesecake, 255
coconut, 57, 60
flan, tropical, *286*
fritters in syrup, *273*
fruit
    and berry compote, 136
    cherries with liqueurs, 279
    grape aspic, *323*
    mango slices with champagne, *237*
    melange, *130*
    pears in caramel syrup, *54*
    prune compote, *61*
fruitcake, *346*
gingerbread, *322*
hazelnut cheesecake, 255
ices and ice cream
    grapefruit ice, 16
    grapefruit and lemon ice, 131
    rum ice cream, *109*
    strawberry ice cream, *163*
    vanilla ice cream with apples and Cal-
        vados, 156
Indian pudding, 25–29
    baked, 27
    Durgin Park's, 28
    Kathleen and Sam Scranton's, 25
lemon soufflé, frozen, *291*
Napoleons, *199,* 205
pie
    cordial, *263*
    cordial, variations, *264*
    honey-pumpkin, 39
    marmalade, *148*
    mirabelle meringue, *99, 183*
    nut, 119
    pumpkin, 374
    sweet pastry for, 120, 374
poundcake, pepper, 285
pudding
    Indian, 25–29
    plum, *350, 351*
    Sussex Pond, 379
tarts
    apple, *142, 144*

(All page numbers in italics refer to Volume I)

DESSERTS (*Continued*)
  pastry for, *54*, 142
  pear, with ginger, *53*
  strawberry, *163*
  sweet cheese, Indian-style, *272*
  torta cavour, *29*, *182*
  trifle, 227, 230
  Laura Benson's, *321*
Devine, Fred, 212
Diana Kennedy, 251–259
Diat, Louis, *179*, 249
Dijon mustard, *44*, *45*
DILL
  lamb stew with, 125
  -mustard sauce
    for salmon, 106
    for shrimp, *168*, *169*
  rice with, 86
Djon-djon, *230*, *233*
Doan Thi Hon, Mrs., *340*–*343*
Dobbe, *191*
Dodd, Mrs. Ivy, 28
Dorgan, Tad, 41
Drechsler, Christina, 132–136, *196*
DUCK, 179–181
  condensed stock, 80
  with ginger root, 301
  with green peppercorns, 80
  grilled lemon, *249*
  hickory smoked, 66
  and meat balls in walnut sauce, *125*, *127*
  in red wine, 179
  roast, 180
Dulberg, Lee, 383
Dumplings, meat filled, *182*, *185*
Durgin Park Restaurant, 28
Düsseldorf mustard, *44*, *45*

E

EASTER, *106*–*109*
  fresh ham baked with herbs, *106*
  leftover eggs, 129
    stuffed eggs Princess Chimay, 130
EGG(s), 312–314
  general data on, 312
  anchovy and mushroom, 377
  leftover, 129
    stuffed, Princess Chimay, 130
  omelettes
    crêpe, 403
    spinach, 85
  pickled, 313

and salmon salad, 278
Scotch, 313, 314
scrambled
  with caviar, 334
  chicken stuffed with, 265
  veal stuffed with tarragon and, 266
and seafood canapé, 314
sorrel soup with egg yolks, 284
Egg bread, 322
Eggnog, Mississippi Delta, *349*
EGGPLANT
  general data on, *150*
  with almonds, *150*
  caviar, *182*, *183*
  au gratin, *152*
  rollatine, *151*
  spaghetti with, *150*
  spaghetti sauce, 399
  spiced, *271*
  stuffed, 89
  tempura, *305*
  and yogurt appetizer, 85
  and yogurt salad, 288
Elman, Dorotea, *55*–*57*
Eloges de la Cuisine Française (Nignon), *141*
Embury, David A., 40
Emison, Mrs. Sam S., *350*–*352*
Endive, *see* Belgian endive
English Food (Grigson), 377
English muffins, 253
ENGLISH-STYLE, 139–143, 375–380
  bread sauce for game, 347
  brioche with mushrooms, 378
  carrot soup with coriander, 143
  custard, 26, 231
  eggs with anchovies and mushrooms, 377
  pork chops in mustard-cream sauce, 142
  pudding, Sussex Pond, 379
  savory pastry, 141
  shrimp and almond quiche, 140
  spiced salt beef, 378
  sweet pastry for fruit tarts, 142
  tarragon cream sauce for vegetables, 141
  venison cutlets, 380
Epazote, *214*, *215*
Equipment, *69*–*73*
ESCABÈCHE
  of chicken, *231*, *232*
  of fish, *235*
Escalope de veau à la moutarde, 76
Escoffier, Georges Auguste, *141*, 303
Espadon à la crème, 79
Esterhazy, Count, *187*
Excelsior Restaurant, *187*

(All page numbers in italics refer to Volume I)

F

Fagiolo freschi in umido, 171, 173
Faicco, Ann and Edward, 160–161
Fales, Josephine Premice, *230–234*, 275, 276
Famularo, Joseph, *99, 116–121, 182–183*
Farmhouse pastry, 142
Fau, 182, 184
FENNEL, 366–371
  general data on, 366–367
  and avocado vinaigrette, 370
  and Belgian endive vinaigrette, 369
  breaded and fried, 370
  au gratin, 368
  with meat sauce, 368
  sea bass with, 371
  soup, creamed, 368
Field, Mrs. Margaret, 407, 409
Filé powder, 193
FILLET OF SOLE
  general data on, 168
  stuffed, with sauce Newburg, 168
  en timbales, 328
  in white wine with shrimp, 169
Fine Art of Mixing Drinks (Embury), 40
Finley, Blanch, 158
FIREPLACE COOKERY, *23–24*
  potée Bourguignonne, *23*
  preparing a fireplace, *24*
FISH
  Andalouse-style, 273
  broth, 318
  chowder, with corn, 245
  court bouillon for, 48
  creole-style, 273
  escabèche of, *235*
  gefilte, *95*
  glaze, 155
  and mushroom soup, 217
  raw, with green peppercorns, *240, 241*
  salad, 240, *246*
  sauerkraut stuffed, 127
  soup, 51, 65–67, 272
    bouillabaisse with vinegar, 331
    Chino's chavela, 310
    cioppino, 383, 397, 402
    corn and, *245*
    curried, 67
    hot and sour, 232, 234
    with mushrooms, 217
    Nags Head fisherman's, 317
    -onion, 66
    with potatoes, 66
    with shrimp and lobster, 65
    tart-flavored, *327, 329*
  stew
    Andalouse-style, 273
    channel bass or red drum, 318
    creole-style, 273
  stock, 67, 156, 274
  for sushi, 146
  tempura, *303, 304*
  velouté sauce, *14*, 295
  See also Channel bass; Cod; Fillet of sole;
    Herring; Salmon; Sea bass; Striped
    bass; Sushi
Fisher, M. F. K., *34*
Flageolets, leg of lamb with, *27*
Flan, tropical, *286*
Flanner, Janet, 157–158
Flatfish, *see* Fillet of sole
Flor Danica Grill, *176*
FOIE GRAS
  rice with mushrooms and, 64
  salad, 334, 337
Fondant icing, quick, *347*
Fonds d'artichauts Vieux Carré, *35, 36, 38*
Fong Lie, *190–191*
Food presses, *69–70, 71*
Formisano, Ralph, 366–367
Forum of the Twelve Caesars, The, 190, 238
Fosenjohn, *125, 127–128*
Four Seasons, The, *35*, 190, *199, 238*
"Francs and Beans" (Baker), 357–359
Franey, Pierre, 219, 275, 341, 353
French, Mrs. G. Warren, *10*
FRENCH BREAD, *80–84*
  baking, *84*
  Clyde Brooks's, *82*
  sourdough, *82, 83*
FRENCH MUSTARD, *44–45*
  de Meaux, *44*
FRITTERS
  batter for, *230, 232*
  cornmeal, with leftovers, 95
  crab meat, *282*
  salt cod, *230, 232*
  sourdough in syrup, 273
FRUIT
  and berry compote, 136
  lamb with, *125, 129*
  melange, *130*
  See also Desserts, fruit; *names of fruit*
Fruitcake, *346*
"Fruit-Flavored Yogurt and More. . . ."
  (booklet), 38

(All page numbers in italics refer to Volume I)

Frutta di mare, 199
Fukki-zushi Restaurant, 137, 144
Fultz, Mrs. H. F., 26–27

G

Gadgets, 70–71
Game, *see* Duck; Goose; Grouse; Pheasant;
    Quail; Squab; Venison
Garam assam, *327, 329*
Garam masala, *154, 156*
GARLIC
    and anchovy sauce for cold vegetables,
        146, 147
    croutons, 191, 250
    roast pork with, *33*
    sausage, *133, 135,* 390
    soup, 249, 250
    toast, 52
Gault, Henri, 116, 352
Gaylord Restaurant, 233, *267, 268*
GAZPACHO
    with corn and zucchini, *180*
    Mexican-style, 190, 191
Gefilte fish, *95*
Genghis Khan grill, *250, 251*
GERMAN-STYLE, 132–136
    fruit and berry compote, 136
    herring salad, 135
    meat balls in caper sauce, 197
    meat rolls, *133*
    spaetzle, 135
Getoff, Mary Mooney, 91
Giblet gravy, *322*
Gift for Young Housewives (Molokhovetz),
    183
Gigot au pastis, 209
Giles, José, 259
GINGER
    barbecued spareribs with, *237*
    beef with, 96
    duck with, 301
    pear tart with, *53*
Gingerbread, *322*
Ginsaryo Restaurant, *300–301*
Glasse, Hannah, *350*
Gleichenhaus, Pauline, 293–294
Golden Lion Restaurant, *333–334*
Golden Phoenix Restaurant, *335–336*
Good Things (Grigson), 375, 376
Goode, William (Sy), *221–224*
Goodman of Paris, The, 372
GOOSE
    fat, 387
    preserved, 385–387, 389

Gorman, Ed, *193*
Goto, Kaneyoshi, *302, 303*
GOULASH, 202–204
    general data on, 202
    soup, 203
    veal, 202
Grape aspic, 323
GRAPEFRUIT ICE, *16*
    with lemon, 131
Gravlax, 106
Great Cooking for the Gods (Zane), 105
GREEK-STYLE, 281, 288–290
    carp-roe spread, 290
    cucumber and yogurt salad, 290
    eggplant and yogurt salad, 288
    shrimp salad, *244*
    spinach pie, 106
    stuffed cabbage with egg and lemon
        sauce, 289
    taramosalata, *133, 136,* 281, 290
Green beans with cumin and shallots vin-
    aigrette, 201
GREEN PEPPERCORNS
    duck with, 80
    raw fish with, *240, 241*
GREEN PEPPERS
    and anchovies, *236*
    curried corn with, 246
    hot pepper jelly, 96
    pork and tarragon stuffed, 88
Gribiche sauce, 240
Grigson, Jane and Geoffery, 187, *375–380*
Gross, Sidney and Sue, *35–38, 82–84,* 364
GROUSE
    à l'anglaise, 347
    hickory smoked, 66
Guacamole, 117
Guadeloupe-style okra, *231, 234*
Guérard, Michel, 333–340
Guide Michelin, 342, 352
GUMBO
    general data on, 193
    chicken, 52
    Louisiana-style, 97
    seafood, with okra, 193

H

Hagman, Heidi, 101–105
HAITIAN-STYLE, 230–234
    chicken, *231, 232*
    fritter batter, *230, 232*
    rice with black mushrooms, *230, 233*
    rum punch, *230, 231*

(All page numbers in italics refer to Volume I)

salt cod fritters, *230, 232*
smoked herring salad, 276
Ham, fresh, baked with herbs, *106*
Hamburgers, *288–289*
Hansen, Ken, 123–125
Hard sauce, *352*
Harijou, *311*
Haussa rice, *57, 59*
Hazan, Marcella, *261,* 370
Hazelnut cheesecake, 255
Heatter, Maida, 279, *284–287*
Heptameron des Gourmets (Nignon), 141
HERB(S)
  baked fresh ham with, *106*
  butter, 201
  chicken legs baked with, *263*
  chicken and tomato broth with sour cream
    and, 129
  pork chops stuffed with, 303
  skewered beef with, *235*
  tomato sauce with, *283*
  See also Basil; Caraway seeds; Coriander;
    Dill; Fennel; Rosemary; Sage; Sor-
    rel; Tarragon
Herbs, Spices and Flavorings (Stobart), 232,
  366
HERRING
  salad, 135
    smoked, 276
  schmaltz, 182, 184
Hige-no-Tenpei, *299*
Hillman, Libby, 159
"Holiday Baking" (booklet), 38
HOLLANDAISE SAUCE, BASIC, 241
  variations, 241
Hominy and pork stew, 254, 260
HONEY, 35–41
  Bee's Knees cocktail, 40, 41
  bee-sting liqueur, 39
  brownies, 39
  chicken wings oven-baked with, 158
  -chocolate cake, 38
  frosting, 38
  -pumpkin pie, 39
Hoon, Jati, 267
Horseradish sauce with walnuts, *167*
Hot pepper jelly, 96
Hot and sour fish soup, 232, 234
Hotel de L'abbaye St-Germain, *171*
Hotel de la Côte d'Or, *141*
Hotel Equatorial, *335–336*
Hotel de l'Europe, *187*
Hugo's Restaurant, *334*
Hunam Restaurant, 54, 55
HUNAM-STYLE
  hot and sour fish soup, 232, 234

lamb, 57
Hundred Glories of French Cooking, The
  (Courtine), *34*
HUNGARIAN-STYLE
  beef broth, 204
  goulash soup, 203
  pork chops Esterhazy, 305
  spaetzli, 203
  veal broth, 204
  veal goulash, 202
Hush puppies, *319*

I

Iacono, Salvadore, *262–263*
ICE, GRAPEFRUIT, *16*
  with lemon, 131
ICE CREAM
  rum, *109*
  strawberry, *163*
  vanilla with apples and Calvados, 156
Icing, quick fondant, 347
Il Valletto, 171
Imperial Hotel, *331*
Inagiku, *299*
INDIAN PUDDING, 25–29
  baked, 27
  Durgin Park's, 28
  Kathleen and Sam Scranton's, 25
INDIAN-STYLE, *153–158,* 267–273
  general data on, *153–154, 157–158,* 267
  cabbage with mustard seeds and coconut,
    156
  chicken
    chat, 233
    curried, *270*
    skewered, *268*
  chutney, *157–158*
  curry powder, *153–154*
  eggplant, spiced, *271*
  garam masala, *154, 156*
  lamb
    curried, *271*
    grilled boneless leg of, *154, 155*
    ground, on skewers, *267, 269*
  prawn curry, *269*
  sourdough fritters in syrup, *273*
  sweet cheese dessert, *272*
Indonesia Restaurant, *190*
Indonesian-style chicken ketjap, 73
Innocenti, Gino, *46, 52, 185*
Invitation to Indian Cooking, An (Jaffrey),
  153
Italian Regional Cooking (Boni), *171*

(All page numbers in italics refer to Volume I)

ITALIAN-STYLE
  appetizers
    anchovy and garlic sauce for cold vege-
      tables, *146, 147*
    beef and mayonnaise, 32, *170*
    mozzarella toast with anchovy sauce,
      171, 172
    peppers and anchovies, *236*
    shrimp, oranges, and anchovies, 165,
      167
  chicken
    roast, 268
    sauté with prosciutto and mushrooms,
      175
  crêpes Belvedere, *146, 149*
  dessert
    almond cake, 171, 174
    marmalade pie, *148*
    spongecake, *50*
    sweet pastry, *148*
  octopus in wine and anchovy sauce, 198
  pasta
    orecchiette cinque terre, 349
    spaghetti à la fettucelle, 349
    spaghetti in red clam sauce, 20
    spaghetti in white clam sauce, 22
    tagliarini with four cheeses, 33
    tagliarini verdi ghiottona, 350
  pizza rustica, 164
  pork
    and bean soup, *147*
    breaded cutlets, 163
    Parmigiana cutlets, 163
    stew, 162
  salad, mozzarella cheese with tomatoes
    and anchovies, 33
  sauce
    meat with fennel, 369
    meat and tomato for pasta, 171, 174
    spaghetti, 162
  seafood, deep-fried, 199
  veal
    rolls, with tomato sauce, 165, 166
    scallops with prosciutto, 33
    scaloppine, breaded, *208*
  vegetables
    asparagus, *108*
    beans with prosciutto in tomato sauce,
      171, 173
Italy, water cure in, *195–198*
Izuma Soba House, *309*

J

Jade Room, *336*
Jaffrey, Madhur, *153–157*

Jalabi, *273*
JAPANESE-STYLE
  barbecue, 214–218
    general data on, 214–215
    grilled fowl, 215
    grilled fowl, sauce for, 215
    salmon, salt grilled, 216
  soup stock, 217, *306*
  sushi, 137, 144–148, *298*
  tempura, *298–299, 302–306*
*Jeanette's Secrets of Everyday Good
  Cooking* (Seaver), 207
Jelly, hot pepper, 96
Jensen, Rick, 275
Jerez de la Frontera, 189
Jingha tarhi, *269*
Johnson, Jennifer, 392
Joinville sauce for shrimp, 121
José Giles's pozole, 260

K

Karnig Tashjian, *127*
Kassos Brothers, *133–134*
Kasteel "De Hooge Vuursche," *192*
Kaye, Danny, 101, 110–112, 295
Kennedy, Diana, *72*, 117, *213–217*, 251–259
Kitchen Primer, The (Claiborne), 243
Kitcho Restaurant, *310*
Knives, *73*
Knob celery, purée of, *315*
Koenigsberger klopse, 196, 197
Komarek, Jerry, end-of-summer relish, *260*
Kopald, Susan, 292–293
Korea, *250*
Kovi, Paul, *238, 239*
Kumin, Albert, *3*, 75, *199*, 275
Kushihachi yakitori house, *298*
Kyubei Restaurant, *298*

L

La Côte Basque, *141, 142*
La Falcatule, *173*
La Ganke, Florence, *26*
La Maison du Caviar, 340
La Marée, *174*
La Pace, *46, 168, 185, 195–198*
La P'tite Tonkinoise, *177*
La Pyramide, *87–88*
Lahanodolmathes avgolemono, 289
LAMB, 207–211
  breast of, *114*
  curried, *271*

(All page numbers in italics refer to Volume I)

with fruit, *125, 129*
grilled, *154, 155, 250, 251*
Hunam-style, 57
leftover, and vegetables in brioche, 207,
   210
leg of
   with flageolets, *27*
   grilled, *154, 155*
   with Pernod or Ricard, 207, *209*
   Persian-style, 86
   roast, 99, *225–227*
with lemons, scallions, and walnuts, 207,
   210
with scallions, 300
shank, bean soup with, 108
on skewers, *267, 269*
stew, 389
   with beans, *114*
   with dill, 125
zucchini stuffed with pignoli and, *139*
Laverne, Pierre, *141–145*
Le Bec Fin, 87, 89
Le Cirque, *3*
Le Colisée, 219
Le Duc, *175*, 238, *240–242*
Le Français, *152–154*, 199
Le Mistral, *177–178*
Le Pavillon, *63, 293*
Le Petit Chevreau, *176*
Le Pot au Feu, 333–336
Lee, Dr. Calvin, 159
Lee, Virginia, *250*, 280, 316
Lee Chin Koon, Mrs., *326–330*
LEMON
   chicken with, *92*
   duck with, grilled, *249*
   and egg, stuffed cabbage with, 289
   and grapefruit ice, 131
   lamb with scallions, walnuts and, 207, 210
   soufflé, frozen, *291*
   soup, *125, 128*
   veal scaloppine with, *208*
   vodka with peel of, *182, 186*
LENTIL(S)
   Côte d'Azur, *136*
   purée of, *32*
   soup, 50, 196, 197
Les Prés et Les Sources d'Eugénie, *333*,
   336–337
Lewis, Sarah, 275, 277, 279, 280
Liederman, David, 77–79, 201
Life of Escoffier, The (Tauji), *302*
Lion's head (Chinese meatballs), 114
LIQUEUR
   bee-sting, 39
   Bing cherries with, 279
   See also Cordial pie

LIVER
   calf's, with vinegar glaze, 192
   chicken
      mousseline of, 122
      pâté, 362
Liver paste, croutons with, 346
Liverwurst, 187
LOBSTER
   baked with vegetables, 221
   chiffonade of, 359
   cooked on seaweed, *240*
   fish soup with shrimp and, 65
   with herb butter, 201
   salad with tarragon, *245*
Louis dressing, 240
Louisiana-style gumbo, 97
Lox, *165–167*
Lucas, Dione, 316
Lutèce Restaurant, 187
Luu Dinh, 177

M

Mabuhay, *134*
Macaroni casserole with beef, *43*
*McClane's New Standard Fishing Ency-
   clopedia*, 45–46
McCormick, James, 407–408
McGinniss, Barbara, *25–28*
Mackerel au vin blanc, 227, 229
Madras-style mussels, *240, 241*
Maine Cookery—Then and Now, 28
Maison du Danemark, *175–176*
Maison Glass, 190, 255
Majestic Restaurant, 335
Major Grey's chutney, *157, 158*
Maltaise sauce, 241
Mandolins, 44
Manganaro's, *134*
Mango slices with champagne, 237
Manhattan clam chowder, *161*
MANICOTTI
   with chicken and almonds, *117, 120*
   pancakes, *121*
Manila Hotel, *331*
Manocherian, Fred and Jennifer, 83–84
Manuel, Phenas, 316, 317, 322
Margaritas, 307
Margittai, Tom, *238, 239*
MARMALADE
   Florence La Ganke's three-day, 28
   pie, *148*
Maryland crab cakes, *281, 283*
Marzapane, 171, 174
Mastering the Art of French Cooking (Beck,
   Bertholle, and Child), 228

(All page numbers in italics refer to Volume I)

Masto badenjohn, 85
Masto khiar, 86
Matzoh balls, 95
MAYONNAISE, 9, 239–241, 279
  basic, 239
    variations, 240–241
  cucumber, 10, 11
  mustard and tarragon, 32
  tarragon and anchovy, 361
MEAT BALLS
  in caper sauce, 197
  Chinese-style (lion's head), 114
  duck in walnut sauce with, 125, 127
  Mexican-style (albondigas), 235
  spaghetti with, 239
  in tomato and chili sauce, 233, 235
Meat loaves, 274–277
Meat pie, Alsatian, 344
Meat pounders, 71, 72
Meat rolls, see Beef, rolls
Meat salad, 240
Meat sauce, fennel with, 369
Meat grinders, 72
Melitzanes me yiaourti, 288
Mendelson, Morris, 98–99
MERINGUE, 182–184
  mirabelle pie, 99, 183
  torta cavour, 29, 182
Merrill, Mrs. Imogene, 28–29
MEXICAN-STYLE
  chicken breasts, 277
  clam coctel, 258
  green chili gordas, 217
  meatballs in tomato and chili sauce, 233,
    235
  pozole, 225, 251–253
    de Jalisco, 254
    José Giles's, 260
  salsa cruda, 309–310, 311
  soup
    fish, 310
    gazpacho, 190, 191
  tacos, mushroom, 214
  tortillas, 213–217
  tostadas of jellied pig's feet, 215
Middle Eastern Cookery (Zane), 233
Millau, Christian, 116, 352
Miller Howe Hotel, 139–140
Mincielli, Jean, 238–242
Mirabelle meringue pie, 99, 183
Mirabelle-flavored Bavarian cream, 363
Misoshiru, 218
Mississippi Delta eggnog, 349
Miveh Makhlout, 125, 130
Molasses, blackstrap, whole wheat bread
    with, 78
Molinari Brothers, 133

Moore, Peter, 78
More Recipes with a Jug of Wine (Wood),
    383
MORNAY SAUCE, 238
  for cod and noodles, 47
Moti Mahal Restaurant, 267
Mottola, Jo, 268
Moules Madras, 240, 241
MOUSSE
  salt cod, 119
  shrimp with sauce Joinville, 120
Mousseline of chicken livers, 122
Mousseline sauce, 241
MOZZARELLA CHEESE
  toast with anchovy sauce, 171, 172
  with tomatoes and anchovies, 33
Mozzarella fresca con pomodoro e acciughe,
    33
Mrs. Beeton's Book of Household Man-
    agement (Beeton), 346
Muffins, English, 253
Murghi massala, 270
Murghi tikka, 267, 268
Murray's Sturgeon Shop, 69, 166
MUSHROOM(S)
  general data on, 122
  black, rice with, 230, 233
  dried, with chicken, 175
  and noodle casserole, 124
  sauce
    and cream, 276
    and curry, 238
    and oyster, 230
  soup
    with fish, 217
    with watercress, 20
  stuffed, 329
    with crab meat, 122
    with spinach and anchovies, 123
  for stuffings and fillings
    for brioche, 378
    for chicken breasts, 266
    with eggs, 377
    for patty shells, 204
    for quiche, 153, 154
    for zucchini, 105
  tacos, 214
  tempura, 304
Mushroom Feast, The (Grigson), 375,
    376–377
MUSSELS
  Madras-style, 240, 241
  alla Romana, 221, 223
MUSTARD
  "ball-park," 44
  Colman, 45
  French, 44–45

(All page numbers in italics refer to Volume I)

de Meaux, *44*
homemade, *45*
roast loin of pork with, *31*
sauce, 240, 278
  cream, for deviled chicken breasts, 382
  -dill, for salmon, 106
  -dill, for shrimp, *168, 169*
  pork chops with cream and, 142
  with tarragon, 32
veal scallops with, 76
Mustard seeds, cabbage with coconut and, 156

N

Nanni, Luigi, 171–172, 198
Nannie Craig's fruitcake, *346*
Nanni's Restaurant, 171, 198
Napoleons, *199, 205*
Navarin de homards, 221
Neapolitan-style tomato sauce, 239
Nesi, Marco, *46, 47, 168*
Newburg sauce, 169, 170
Niçoise sauce, 240
Nignon, Edouard, *141, 142*
"Nitty Gritty of Smoke Cooking, The" (Stair), 66
NOODLE(S)
  casserole
    with beef, *42*
    cod and, with Mornay sauce, 47
    with mushrooms, *124*
  soup, -chicken, 261, 269
    with tortellini balls, *110, 112*
  tempura, *305*
Nova Scotia salmon, *165–166*
Nuevo Cocinero Mejicano: Diccionario de Cocina, 213
Nuoc mam sauce, 249, 261, 271
NUT(S)
  and basil sauce for pasta, 260
  pie, 110
  stuffing for capon, 372
  See also names of nuts

O

Octopus with wine and anchovies, 198
Oden restaurants, *299–300*
Oesterbar, *191*
Oeufs de poule au caviar, 334
OKRA
  Guadeloupe-style, *231, 234*
  seafood gumbo with, 193

Okura Hotel, *301*
Old Tale Carved Out of Stone, An (Linevski), 183
Omar Khayyam's Restaurant, *335*
OMELETTE
  crêpe, 403
  spinach, 85
ONION(S)
  soup, 394
    -fish, 66
  tempura, *304*
Operakelleren Restaurant, 123, 342
ORANGE(S)
  appetizer with shrimp and anchovies, 165, 167
  and whole wheat bread, 73
Orecchiette cinque terre, 349
Oriental Barbecues (Trent), *247–250*
Osaka, *309–312*
Otomi, *299*
Oxtail soup with paprika, 396
OYSTER(S), *34–39*
  general data on, *34–36*
  artichoke bottoms stuffed with, *35, 36, 38*
  Chauveron, *39*
  chicken wings with sauce, 159
  and mushroom sauce, 230
  Rockefeller, *35, 36*
  and shrimp, stir-fry, 112
  -stuffed potatoes, *35, 36, 37*

P

P. Carnevale & Sons, *133*
Paella, *101–105*
Pagano, Barbara A., 268
Pan broiling, *73*
PANAMANIAN-STYLE
  paella, *101–105*
  yucca turnovers, *102*
PANCAKES
  manicotti, *121*
  potato
    Gleichenhaus, 294
    Kopald, 293
    -zucchini, 294
PARIS, *171–178*
  dinner for two ($4,000 cost), 341–343, 351–355
Paris Bar and Grill, 238
Paris-Lyon Express, *177*
PARMESAN CHEESE
  pork cutlets with, 163
  toast, 130
  zucchini, *140*

(All page numbers in italics refer to Volume I)

Parrish, Dr. Louis, 92–94, 97, 98
Parsleyed cucumber ovals, 86
PASTA
    basil and nut sauce for, 260
    meat and tomato sauce for, 171, 174
    See also Italian-style, pasta; names of
        pasta
Pastrami, home-cured, 211, 218, 220
PASTRY
    Alsatian, 344
    farmhouse, 142
    pasta frolla, 164
    puff, 199–206
        Napoleons, 199, 205
        vol-au-vents, 199, 203
        vol-au-vents Toulousaine, 204
    savory, 141
    sweet
        for fruit tarts, 142
        for pies, 120, 148, 374
    for tarts, 54, 142
Pastry cream, 164
PÂTÉ, 404–406
    de campagne, 327
    chicken liver, 362
    country, 405
    pork rind, 405
Patty Pans (La Ganke), 26, 27
Patty shells, 199, 203
    with creamed filling, 204
Paupiettes de volaille Florentine, 263
PEAR(S)
    in caramel syrup, 54
    and ginger tart, 53
Pearl's Chinese Restaurant, 17
PECAN(S)
    -prune cake, 287
    roast capon with, 372
Peck, Paula, 275, 277
Peking Restaurant (Singapore), 335
Peking Restaurant (Washington, D.C.), 55
Pépin, Jacques, 219, 249, 275
PEPPER
    general data on, 61
    green peppercorns
        duck with, 80
        raw fish with, 240, 241
    poundcake, 285
Peppers, see Green peppers; Red peppers
PERIWINKLES
    à la Goode, 221, 223
    piquantes, 240, 242
PERNOD
    leg of lamb with, 207, 209
    shrimp with, 68
Perrier, Georges, 87–91

PERSIAN-STYLE, 83–87, 125–130
    duck and meat balls in walnut sauce, 125,
        127
    eggplant and yogurt appetizer, 85
    fruit melange, 130
    lamb
        with fruit, 125, 129
        leg of, 86
    lemon soup, 125, 128
    rice
        with dill, 86
        plain, 125, 126–127, 129
    spinach omelet, 85
    yogurt salad, 86
Pesto, 260
Phalen, Jane and Clifton, 227–228
PHEASANT, SMOKED, 227, 229
    hickory, 66
Pho ga, 261, 269
Piana, Quinto, 46
Piccinini's, 133
Pickled eggs, 313
Pickles, sherry peppers, 191
Picnics, 235–237, 275–279, 361–363
    See also Barbecue
PIE
    cordial, 263
        variations, 264
    honey-pumpkin, 39
    marmalade, 148
    mirabelle meringue, 99, 183
    nut, 119
    pumpkin, 374
        -honey, 39
    savory
        cheese and sausage, 164
        meat, 344
        spinach, 106
    sweet pastry for, 120, 148, 374
PIGNOLI
    and basil sauce for pasta, 260
    zucchini stuffed with meat and, 139
Pig's feet, jellied, 215
Pine nuts, see Pignoli
Pinto beans, 409
Piquant salad sauce, 242
Piroshki, 182, 185
Pisco, 159
Pissaladière, 72
PIZZA
    rustica, 164
    squash, 111, 113
Plaisirs de la Table (Nignon), 141
Plum pudding, 350
Point, Fernand, 199
Poisson cru Le Duc, 240, 241

(All page numbers in italics refer to Volume I)

Polish-style roast chicken, 267
Pollo alla Campagnola, 175
Polpi moscardini, 198
Pommery mustard, 44
Pon pon chicken, 56
Pong tauhu, 327
PORK
  and bean soup, 147
  chops
    Esterhazy, 305
    herb-stuffed, 303
    in mustard-cream sauce, 142
  cutlets
    breaded, 163
    Parmigiana, 163
  fresh ham baked with herbs, 106
  ground
    meat balls in tomato sauce, 233, 235
    patties grilled in lettuce leaves, 247
    rolls in lettuce leaves, 339, 341
  hocks, ragout of, 135
  pig's feet, tostadas of, 215
  quiche Alsace, 344
  rind, pâté of, 405
  roast, 31, 32, 388
    with garlic, 33
    loin, with mustard, 32
    loin, with prunes, 313, 314
    loin, with spices, 46, 48
  sausage
    cakes, 212
    casings, 68
    casings, preparing, 74
    Chablis-style, 74
    and cheese pie, 164
    chicken casserole with, 92
    cotechini, 133, 135
    garlic, 133, 135, 390
    rosemary and sage, 212
    smoked Southern, 67
    and tortilla soup, 257
  and shrimp balls in soup, 327
  spareribs, barbecued with ginger, 237
  stew
    with hominy, 254, 260
    Signor Faicco's, 162
  for stuffing
    for green peppers, 88
    for zucchini, 139
Portofino Restaurant, 31
Poseidon, 134
Potage de cresson, 21
Potage Germiny, 283, 284
POTATO(ES)
  caraway, 42
  Château Chinon, 291, 292

crumb, 42
  gratinéed, 323
  Mont d'Or, 108
  -oyster stuffed, 35, 36, 37
  pancakes
    Gleichenhaus, 294
    Kopald, 293
    -zucchini, 294
  puréed, 314
  salad, warm, 391
  salad dressing with, 190, 192
  sautéed, 43
  straw, 44
  See also Sweet potatoes
Potée Bourguignonne, 23
Poulet roti au cresson, 21
Poulet sauté au vinaigre, 222, 224
Poundcake, pepper, 285
POZOLE, 225, 251–253
  de Jalisco, 254
  José Giles's, 260
Prawn curry, 269
Premice, Josephine, 230–234, 275, 276
PROSCIUTTO
  beans in tomato sauce with, 171, 173
  chicken sauté with mushrooms and, 175
  veal scallops with, 33
PRUNE(S)
  compote, 61
  -pecan cake, 287
  roast loin of pork with, 314
PUDDING
  corn, 246
  Indian, 25–29
    baked, 27
    Durgin Park's, 28
    Kathleen and Sam Scranton's, 25
  plum, 350, 351
  Sussex Pond, 379
  See also Custard
PUFF PASTRY, 199–206
  Napoleons, 199, 205
  vol-au-vents, 199, 203
    Toulousaine, 204
PUMPKIN PIE, 374
  -honey, 39
Purée mongole, 75

Q

QUAIL
  à l'anglaise, 345, 347
  braised, with scuppernongs, 320
  hickory smoked, 66

(All page numbers in italics refer to Volume I)

QUENELLES
  chicken, *204*
  shrimp, *293*
    shrimp sauce for, *294*
QUICHE
  Alsace, *344*
  Lorraine, quick, *221, 224*
  shrimp and almond, 140
  sweetbreads and mushrooms, 153, 154

R

Raffles Hotel, *331–332*
Ragout of pork hocks, *135*
Ragu Abruzzese, 171, 174
Rainbow Room, *46*
Ras malahyee, *272*
Ravigote sauce, 242, *244*
Red beans and rice, 95
Red cabbage braised with chestnuts, *325*
Red drum stew, 318
RED PEPPERS
  and anchovies, *236*
  hot pepper jelly, 96
  sherry pickled, 191
Red snapper, baked, 401
Regional Dishes of France, The (de Croze),
    291
Relish, *260*
Rémoulade sauce, 240
Renoir, Susan, 294
Restaurant Copenhagen, *175–176*
RESTAURANTS
  Amalfi, 19
  Amsterdam, *187–192*
  Bali, *316–318*
  Boston, 28
  Brussels, 342, 343
  Chicago, 152–154
  Eugénie-les-Bains, 333–336
  Hollywood, *123–125*
  London, 347
  Los Angeles, 398
  Lyons, 219
  Miami, *39*
  Montecatini Terme (Italy), *195–198*
  New York, 17, 30, 31, 54–56, 171, 219, 233,
    267–268, 281, 295
  Osaka, 137–138, 144, *309–312*
  Paris, *171–178*, 205, 340, 359
    dinner for two ($4,000 cost), 341–343,
    351–355
  Philadelphia, 89
  Roanne (France), 77, 116–117, 152, 284

  Singapore, *331–336*
  Stockholm, 342
  Tokyo, *296–301*
  Washington, D.C., 55
  Wheeling (Illinois), 199
  Whitman (Massachusetts), 27
  See also names of restaurants
Ribs, deviled, 381
RICE
  baked, *15*
  with black mushrooms, *230, 233*
  with dill, 86
  haussa, *57, 59*
  with mushrooms and foie gras, 64
  -noodle soup with chicken, 261, 269
  plain, Persian-style, *125, 126–127, 129*
  red beans and, 95
  seasoned yellow, *105*
  sushi, 145
  See also Wild rice
Rijsttafel, *189–190*
Rivel, Cecile, 69–71
Riz au djon-djon, *230, 233*
Robbins, Ken and Maria, 177, 182–183
Robles, Mrs. Marco A., *101–105*
Robot Coupe, 116
Rochelle, Carter, 407–408
Roe, crab, 59
Roe, Mary Willard, 27
Roll Basket, The (Gross), 364
Rollatini di vitello al pomodoro, 165, 166
Root, Waverly, 352
Roquefort cheese timbales, *228*
ROSEMARY
  roast chicken with, 361
  sausage with sage and, 212
  vinaigrette sauce with, 166
Rote grütze, 136
Rotor, *70*
Rouladen, 133
RUM
  caipirinha, *55, 57, 61*
  ice cream, *109*
  punch, *230, 231*
RUSSIAN-STYLE, 182–186
  bean purée, 182, 184
  beef broth, 185
  dumplings, meat filled, 182, 185
  eggplant caviar, 182, 183
  hamburgers, *289*
  sauerkraut and beef soup, 182, 184
  schmaltz herring, 182, 184
  vodka with lemon peel, 182, 186
RUTABAGA
  steamed, 320
  and sweet potato casserole, 43

(All page numbers in italics refer to Volume I)

S

SAGE
bean soup with, 109
sausage with rosemary and, 212
SALAD
avocado with crab meat, 319
black bean, 277
chicken, 240
cod with tarragon, *246*
corn, zucchini, and tomatoes, 247
crab meat with tarragon, *246*
cucumber and yogurt, 290
fish, 240, *246*
foie gras, 334, 337
herring, 135
smoked, 276
lobster with tarragon, *245*
meat, 240
potato, warm, 391
salmon and egg, 278
seafood, 240
shrimp à la Grecque, *244*
spin-drier for, *70–72*
striped bass with tarragon, *246*
yogurt, 86
eggplant and, 288
SALAD DRESSING, 241–242
basic, 242
variations, 242
with potato, 190, 192
Salade gourmande, 334, 337
SALMON
general data on, *165–166*
and egg salad, 278
lox, *165–167*
mustard-dill sauce for, 106
Nova Scotia, *165–166*
raw, with green peppercorns, *240, 241*
salt grilled, 216
salt and sugar-cured, 106
smoked, *165–166*
with sorrel, 153, 155
Salsa cruda, 309–310, 311
SALT COD, 49
fritters, *230, 232*
mousse, 119
Salt-rising bread, 392
Sama Sebo, *189–190*
Sambal soto, *320*
SAMP
general data on, 91
chicken and tomato, 91
"Samp" (Getoff), 91
Sashimi, *298*

SAUCES, 237–242
acaraje (hot pepper), *60*
Alexandre, *276*
anchovy
for cold vegetables, *146, 147*
for mozzarella toast, 171, 172
basil and nut, for pasta, *260*
béarnaise, 241
for beef
brown, *118*
deviled, 381
raw, *32*
beurre blanc, *89*
brown
for beef, *118*
for fowl, *15*
for game, 346
veal, *143*
champagne, 65
for chicken
deviled, 382
grilled, Japanese-style, 215
salad, 240
tomato, 326
cognac, 240
cream, 237
aux crevettes, *294*
curry, 238
-mushroom, 238
Delmonico, 26
fish velouté, *14, 295*
for game, 347
gribiche, 240
hard, 352
Hollandaise, basic, 241
variations, 241
horseradish with walnuts, *167*
hot pepper (acaraje), *60*
for lamb, 207, 209
Louis dressing, 240
Maltaise, 241
mayonnaise, *9*, 239–241, 279
basic, 239
basic, variations, 240–241
cucumber, *10, 11*
mustard and tarragon, *32*
tarragon and anchovy, 361
meat, 369
Mornay, 238
for cod and noodles, 47
mousseline, 241
mushroom
and cream, *276*
and curry, 238
and oyster, 230
mustard, 240, 278

(All page numbers in italics refer to Volume I)

SAUCES (*Continued*)
    deviled, 382
    -dill, for salmon, 106
    -dill, for shrimp, *168, 169*
    and tarragon, 32
Newburg, 169, 170
Niçoise, 240
nuoc mam, *249,* 261, 271
for pasta
    Ann Faicco's, 162
    eggplant, 399
    red clam, 20
    white clam, 22
pesto, *260*
piquant, 242
for quail, 345, 347
ravigote, 242, *244*
for red snapper, 401
rémoulade, 240
for salmon, mustard-dill, 106
salsa cruda, 309–310, 311
for scallops, sweet and sour, 113
for sea bass, 338
for shrimp
    Joinville, 121
    mustard-dill, *168, 169*
    tarragon and anchovy, 361
for sole, Newburg, 169
soy, 58, *249, 250*
for squab, *15*
tartare, 240
tomato, 238–239
    for all-American chili, 410
    basic, 238
    basic, variations, 239
    for chicken, 326
    for eggplant, *152*
    with herbs, *283*
    for jellied pig's feet, *216*
    for lamb, 207, 209
    Neopolitan-style, 239
    for pasta, 171, 174
    quick, *8*
    for Scotch eggs, 313, 314
    for sea bass, 338
    for spaghetti with clams, 20, 22
    for spaghetti with meat balls, 239
    for spaghetti alla puttanesca, 239
    vinaigrette, 82, *244*
veal, *143*
for vegetables
    cold, anchovy with garlic, *146, 147*
    tarragon cream, 141
vierge, 338
vinaigrette, 242, 277
    with rosemary, 166

    with tomato, 82, *244*
    watercress, *276*
    white, basic, 237
        variations, 237–238
    See also Salad dressing
Saucisses Chablisienne, *74*
SAUERKRAUT
    and beef soup, 182, 184
    with caraway seeds, *135*
    fish stuffed with, 127
    homemade, *259*
    preserving fresh, *260*
    soup, *110, 111*
Saumon à l'oseille, 153, 155
SAUSAGE
    cakes, 212
    casings, 68
        preparing, *74*
    Chablis-style, *74*
    and cheese pie, 164
    chicken casserole with, *92*
    cotechini, *133, 135*
    garlic, *133, 135,* 390
    rosemary and sage, 212
    smoked Southern, 67
    and tortilla soup, 257
Savory pastry, 141
Savoy Cocktail Book, 40
SCALLIONS, LAMB WITH, 300
    with lemons and walnuts, 207, 210
Scalloping procedure, 5–7
SCALLOPS, *5–11*
    general data on, *5–7*
    batter-fried, 113
    breaded, *9*
    ceviche with striped bass and, *221, 223*
    opening, *7*
    raw, with green peppercorns, *240, 241*
    in the shell with snail butter, *8*
    and shrimp mayonnaise, *8*
    tempura, *305*
    with tomato and paprika, *7*
Scaloppine bentivoglio, 33
Scandia Restaurant, 123–125
SCANDINAVIAN-STYLE, 123–128
    fish stuffed with sauerkraut, 127
    lamb and dill stew, 125
    stuffed cabbage, 126
Scherer, Barbara, 41
Schmaltz herring, 182, 184
Schoonmaker, Frank, *63,* 389
Scotch eggs, 313, 314
Scranton, Kathleen and Sam, 25
Scuppernongs, quail braised with, 320
SEA BASS
    with fennel, 371

(All page numbers in italics refer to Volume I)

with tomato sauce, 338
Sea View Hotel, *334*
SEAFOOD
    Andalouse-style, 273
    deep-fried, 199
    and egg canapé, 314
    gumbo with okra, 193
    salad, 240
    and wild rice casserole, 230
    See also names of seafood
Seaver, Dick and Jeanette, 207–209
SEAWEED
    dried (laver or nori) for sushi, 148
    lobster cooked on, *240*
    -wrapped sushi (dote), 147
Seder feast, *94–97*
Seranne, Ann, 97–98, 243
SHAD, *63, 85–86*
    fillets Doria, 85
Shangri-La Hotel, *336*
Sharma, Daulat Ram, *267, 268*
Shchi, 182, 184
She-crab soup, 320
Sheekh-Kabab, *267, 269*
SHERRY WINE VINEGAR, 189–192
    calf's liver with vinegar glaze, 192
    gazpacho, 190, 191
    pickled peppers, 191
    salad dressing, 190, 192
Shioyaki, 216
Shopping, Ninth Avenue, New York,
    131–137
Shore, Dinah, 397–403
SHRIMP
    balls, deep-fried, 75
    and bean sprout soup, 94
    and crab meat, 58
    curried, *269*
    fish soup with lobster and, 65
    to garnish soups, 217
    grilled chopped, *343*
    mousse, with sauce Joinville, 120
    à la moutarde de Meaux, *44*
    with mustard and dill sauce, *168, 169*
    with oranges and anchovies, 165, 167
    and oysters, stir-fry, 112
    paste, 76
    patties grilled in lettuce leaves, *248*
    au Pernod, *68*
    and pork balls in soup, *327*
    quenelles, *293*
        shrimp sauce for, *294*
    quiche with almonds, 140
    salad à la Grecque, *244*
    and scallop mayonnaise, 8
    sole in white wine with, 169

with sorrel, 286
for sushi, 147
tangy spicy, 57
with tarragon and anchovy mayonnaise,
    361
tempura, *304*
Uncle Tai's, 298
vatapá jodo, 57
xin xin, *57, 59*
Shun Lee Dynasty, 54, 55
Shun Lee Palace Restaurant, 17, 54, 55, 56
Sicilian-style eggplant, stuffed, 89
Singapore, *326–336*
Singapore Hyatt Hotel, *334*
Sklar, David, *165–167*
Slattery, Bill, 99
Slotnik, Joseph, 364
SMOKE COOKERY, 66–68
    chicken, 66
    game, 66
    Southern sausage, 67
Smoked salmon, *165–166*
Snail butter, scallops in the shell with, 8
Sole, *see* Fillet of sole
Someone's in the Kitchen With Dinah
    (Shore), 399
SORREL, 283–287
    general data on, 283–284
    chicken sautéed with, 286
    salmon with, 153, 155
    shrimp with, 286
    soup with egg yolks, 284
    striped bass with, 285
    substitution for, 287
Soto ajam, *316–318, 319*
SOUFFLÉ
    curried corn and cheese, 245
    frozen lemon, *291*
Soulé, Henri, *293*
SOUP
    avocado with cucumber and tomato, *180*
    bean, Japanese-style, 218
    bean sprouts and shrimp, 94
    borscht, 50
    broccoli, cream of, 400
    carrot
        with coriander, 143
        cream of, *181*
        and tomato, cream of, *106*
    chicken
        -noodle, with tortellini balls, *110, 112*
        rice-noodle, 261, 269
        soto ajam, *316–318, 319*
    clam chowder
        Boston, *162*
        Manhattan, *161*

(All page numbers in italics refer to Volume I)

SOUP (*Continued*)
cold, *179–181*, 249–250
crab meat, curried, *281*
cucumber with tomato and avocado, *180*
dried bean
and lamb shank, 108
and pork, *147*
with sage, 109
fennel, creamed, 368
fish, 51, *65–67*, 272
bouillabaisse with vinegar, 331
Chino's chavela, 310
cioppino, 383, 397, 402
corn and, 245
curried, *67*
hot and sour, 232, 234
with mushrooms, 217
Nags Head fisherman's, 317
-onion, *66*
with potatoes, *66*
with shrimp and lobster, *65*
tart-flavored, *327*, *329*
garlic, 249, 250
gazpacho
with corn and zucchini, *180*
Mexican-style, 190, 191
goulash, 203
lemon, *125*, *128*
lentil, 50, 196, 197
mushroom with watercress, *20*
onion, 394
-fish, *66*
oxtail with paprika, 396
pork and shrimp balls in, *327*
rice-noodle, with chicken, 261, 269
sauerkraut, *110*, *111*
and beef, 182, 184
she-crab, 320
sorrel, with egg yolks, 284
split pea, purée of, 75
tomato
cream of, 400
cream of, and carrots, *106*
with cucumber and avocado, *180*
with yogurt, 249
tortilla and chorizo, 257
truffle, 223
vegetable, 395
watercress, *21*
and mushrooms, *20*
yogurt with coriander, 233, 236
zucchini, 249
with yogurt, *221*, *222*
See also Stock
Soupe aux truffes Elysée, 223
Sour cream, chicken and tomato broth with
herbs and, 129

SOURDOUGH
French bread, *82*, *83*
fritters in syrup, 273
starter, *83*
"Sourdough Rye and Other Good Breads"
(Gross), 38, *82*
SOUTHERN-STYLE, 315–323
channel bass stew, 318
corn bread, *322*
crab meat
avocado with, 319
she-crab soup, 320
crabs, sautéed softshell, 319
egg bread, 322
fish broth, 318
fisherman's soup, 317
gingerbread, 322
grape aspic, 323
hush puppies, 319
quail braised with scuppernongs, 320
red drum stew, 318
rutabaga, steamed, 320
smoked sausage, 67
trifle, 321
Soy sauce, 58, *249*, *250*
Soyer, Nicolas, 19
Soyer's Paper-Bag Cookery (Soyer), 19
Spaetzle, 135
Spaetzli, 203
SPAGHETTI
Ann Faicco's sauce, 162
with chicken, 149
with eggplant, *150*
eggplant sauce, 399
à la fettucelle, 349
in foil, *19–23*
red clam sauce, *20*
white clam sauce, *22*
with meat balls, 239
alla puttanesca, 239
See also Pasta
Spanakopitta, 106
Spanish-style fish salad, *246*
Spareribs, barbecued with ginger sauce,
237
Spice Box, The, 203
SPINACH
chicken rolls stuffed with, *263*
meat loaf with, *274*
mushrooms stuffed with anchovies and,
123
omelet, 85
pie, 106
Spin-driers, *70–72*
Split pea soup, purée of, 75
SPONGECAKE, 97
chocolate, 76

(All page numbers in italics refer to Volume I)

Italian-style, 50
Spun sugar, 50
Squab, stuffed Derby, 13, 14, 15
Squash pizza, 111, 113
Squid tempura, 304
Stachowicz, Mrs. Wilhelmina, 267
Stafford, Jean, 177
Stair, Dan, 66
Staub, Rusty, 295
Steamers, 71
STEW
  fish
    Andalouse-style, 273
    channel bass or red drum, 318
    creole-style, 273
  lamb, 389
    with beans, 114
    with dill, 125
  pork
    with hominy, 254, 260
    Signor Faicco's, 162
Stewart's Fish Market, 11, 220
Stigliano-style roast chicken, 268
Stobart, Tom, 232, 366
STOCK
  duck, condensed, 80
  fish, 67, 156, 274
  Japanese-style, 217, 306
Stockli Company, 70
Strait of Malacca, 326–330
Straw potatoes, 44
STRAWBERRY
  ice cream, 163
  pisco, 159
  tart, 163
STRIPED BASS
  ceviche with scallops and, 221, 223
  with champagne, 13
  court bouillon for, 89, 243
  fermière, 142
  poached, 87, 88, 89
    cold, 243
  raw, with green peppercorns, 240, 241
  salad with tarragon, 246
  with sorrel, 285
  with tomato vinaigrette sauce, 81
Stuffing, corn bread, 307, 321
Sukiyaki, 311
Sushi, 137, 144–148, 298
Sussex Pond pudding, 379
SWEDISH-STYLE
  lamb and dill stew, 125
  loin of pork with prunes, 313
Sweet potatoes and rutabaga casserole, 43
Sweet and sour sauce for batter-fried scallops, 113

SWEETBREADS
  patty shells filled with, 204
  quiche with mushrooms and, 153, 154
Swordfish sautéed in cream sauce, 79
SYRUP
  caramel, pears in, 54
  for sourdough fritters, 273
Szechuan-style shrimp and crab meat, 58

T

Tacos, mushroom, 214
Taeuber, Richard C., 263–264
TAGLIARINI, GREEN
  with four cheeses, 33
  verdi ghiottona, 350
Tai, Wen Dah, 295–302
Taillevent, 173–174, 337
Takoume, 311–312
Tandjung Sari, 316, 318
Tandoors, 267
Taramosalata, 133, 136, 281, 290
TARRAGON
  and anchovy mayonnaise, 361
  chicken with
    and champagne, 64
    and cream, 93
  cold salad with, 246
  crab meat salad with, 246
  cream sauce for vegetables, 141
  green peppers stuffed with pork and, 88
  lobster salad with, 245
  and mustard mayonnaise, 32
  striped bass salad with, 246
  veal stuffed with scrambled eggs and, 266
Tartare sauce, 240
Tarte de friande, 142, 144
TARTS
  apple, 142, 144
  pastry for, 54, 142
  pear, with ginger, 53
  strawberry, 163
Tauji, Shizuo, 302–303
Tavola Calda da Alfredo, 30
Tempura, 298–299, 302–306
Terrail, Claude, 293
THANKSGIVING, 307, 321–325
  Brussels sprouts in cream, 324
  chestnuts, buttered whole, 324
  corn bread stuffing, 307, 321
  giblet gravy, 322
  potatoes, gratinéed, 323
  red cabbage braised with chestnuts, 325
  roast turkey, 321
Therapeutic cooking, 92–94
Timbales au Roquefort, 228

(All page numbers in italics refer to Volume I)

TOAST
  garlic, 52
  mozzarella, with anchovy sauce, 171, 172
  Parmesan, 130
  rounds, 287
Todeschini, Jean-Louis, 275
Tofeja, *147*
Tokyo, *296–301*
Toll House Restaurant, 27
TOMATO(ES)
  and anchovies vinaigrette, 278
  chicken and
    broth with sour cream and herbs, 129
    samp, 91
    sauce for, 326
    sautéed, 222, 224
  corn and zucchini salad with, 247
  dried beans with prosciutto and, 171, 173
  meat balls with chili sauce and, 233, 235
  mozzarella cheese with anchovies and, 33
  processing, *257–259*
  sauce, 238–239
    for all-American chili, 410
    basic, 238
    basic, variations, 239
    for chicken, 326
    for eggplant, *152*
    with herbs, 283
    for jellied pig's feet, *216*
    for lamb, 207, 209
    Neopolitan-style, 239
    for pasta, 171, 174
    quick, *8*
    for Scotch eggs, 313, 314
    for sea bass, 338
    for spaghetti with clams, 20, 22
    for spaghetti with meat balls, 239
    for spaghetti alla puttanesca, 239
    vinaigrette, 82, *244*
  soup
    cream of, 400
    cream of, and carrots, *106*
    with cucumber and avocado, *180*
    with yogurt, 249
  vinaigrette sauce with, *244*
  zucchini with, *138*
Tomkins, Calvin, 317
Tony's meat market, *116*
Torigin Restaurant, 297
Torta cavour, *29, 182*
Tortellini balls, chicken noodle soup with,
    110, 112
Tortilla Book, The (Kennedy), *213–217*, 251
TORTILLAS, *213–217*
  and chorizo soup, 257
Tostadas of jellied pig's feet, 215
Tour d'Argent, *293*

Tovey, John, 137–141
Trans-European-Express, *177–178*
Trattoria da Alfredo, 30
Trattoria di Ciccio, 19
Trent, May Wong, *247–250*
TRIFLE, 227, 230
  Laura Benson's, *321*
Trillin, Calvin, 407
Troisgros, Jean, 77, 78, 111, 152, 153
Troisgros, Pierre, 78, 152, 153
Troigros Restaurant, 77–78, 116–117, 152,
    284
Tropical flan, *286*
Trout stuffed in the style of Fernand Point,
    199
TRUFFLE(S)
  general data on, 205
  soup, 223
Truites farcis Fernand Point, 199
Tung, Harrington, 55
Turkey, roast, *321*
Turnovers, yucca, *102*

U

Uncle Tai's beef, 297
Uncle Tai's Hunan Yuan Restaurant, 17,
    233, 295
Uncle Tai's shrimp, 298
United Supermarket, *250*

V

Vanderhoops, Adrian, 259
Vanilla ice cream, with apples and Cal-
    vados, 156
Vatapá jodo, *57*
VEAL
  general data on, *207–209*
  brezolles à la maurette, *142, 143*
  broth, 204
  brown sauce, *143*
  calf's liver with vinegar glaze, 192
  chops with Belgian endive, *40*
  goulash, 202
  and mushroom meat loaf, 275
  patties with cognac and cream sauce, *289*
  quiche Alsace, *344*
  rolls with tomato sauce, 165, 166
  sauté, in tomato sauce, *41*
  scallops
    with mustard sauce, 76
    with prosciutto, 33
  scaloppine
    breaded, *208*

with lemon, *208*
with marsala, *209*
for two, *207*
stuffed with tarragon-flavored scrambled eggs, 266
VEGETABLE(S)
  bâtonnet-style, 222
  cold, anchovy and garlic sauce for, *146, 147*
  leftover lamb in brioche with, *207, 210*
  lobster baked with, 221
  soup, 395
  steamed, tarragon cream sauce for, 141
  See also names of vegetables
Velouté sauce, fish, *14, 295*
Venison cutlets, 380
Verdun, Pierre, 116–117
Vergé, Roger, 111
Vergnes, Jean, *3, 275*
Vermont pumpkin pie, 374
Viazzi, Alfredo, 17, *30–34, 275, 348*
Vichy carrots, 121
Vierge sauce, 338
Viet Nam Center, Inc., 270
Vietnam, *247, 252, 261, 337, 339–341*
VIETNAMESE-STYLE, *247–250, 339–343*
  barbecue, *247–250*
    lemon duck, *249*
    nuoc mam sauce, *249*
    pork patties grilled in lettuce leaves, *247*
    shrimp patties grilled in lettuce leaves, *248*
  grilled chopped shrimp, *343*
  meat rolls deep-fried in lettuce leaves, *339, 341*
  nuọc mam sauce, *249, 261, 271*
  rice-noodle soup with chicken, *261, 269*
Villa Lorraine, *342, 343*
VINAIGRETTE
  avocado and fennel, 370
  Belgian endive and fennel, 369
  green beans with cumin and shallots, 201
  tomato and anchovies, 278
VINAIGRETTE SAUCE, 242, 277
  with rosemary, 166
  with tomato, 82, *244*
VINEGAR, 330–332
  bouillabaisse with, 331
  chicken in cream with, 331
  chicken sauté with, 332
    and tomatoes, 222, 224
  sherry wine, 189–192
    calf's liver with vinegar glaze, 192
    gazpacho, 190, 191
    pickled peppers, 191
    salad dressing, 190, 192

sushi, 146
Vithaldas, Yogi, 316
Vizzotto, Mariano, *29, 46, 47, 168*
Vodka with lemon peel, 182, 186
VOL-AU-VENTS, *199, 203*
  Toulousaine, *204*
Volhynian-style roast chicken, 267
VonGlahn, John, *11, 238*

W

Wagener, Mrs. Winfield G., 383
Wagner, Susan, 189–190
WALNUTS
  duck with meat balls and, *125, 127*
  horseradish sauce with, *167*
  lamb with lemons, scallions and, 207, 210
  roast capon with, 372
Wang, Tsung Ting, 17, *54–56*
Warnock, Lorena, 40
Wash-broiler clambake, *193*
Water cure in Italy, *195–198*
WATERCRESS, *18–22*
  general data on, *18–20*
  roast chicken with, *21*
  sauce, chicken meat loaf with, 276
  soup, *21*
    with mushrooms, *20*
Wawo-Runtu, Wija, *316–320*
Wenburg, Gus, 170
White, Jane, 17, *30–32, 275*
White, Walter, 31
WHITE SAUCE, BASIC, 237
  variations, 237–238
WHOLE WHEAT BREAD
  with blackstrap molasses, 78
  orange, 73
WILD RICE
  buttered, 180
  and seafood casserole, 230
Wing Fat Company, *250*
WNET (Channel 13), 341, *351*
Wolf, Sandra, 407, 409, 411
Wood, Morrison, 383

X

Xin xin, *57, 59*

Y

Yakitori, 215, *297–298*
Yakitori-no-tare, 215
Yick, Robert, 111–112

(All page numbers in italics refer to Volume I)

YOGURT
 and eggplant appetizer, 85
 salad, 86
  and cucumber, 290
  and eggplant, 288
 soup
  and coriander, 233, 236
  and tomatoes, 249
  and zucchini, *221, 222*
Yucca turnovers, *102*
Yuet Hing Market, *250*

Z

Zane, Eva, 105, 233, 235
Zeger, Mrs. Baruch, *94–97*

ZUCCHINI
 and corn au gratin, 247
 gazpacho with corn and, *180*
 green, fried, *139*
 Parmesan, *140*
 -potato pancakes, 294
 salad with corn and tomatoes, 247
 soup, 249
  with yogurt, *221, 222*
 stuffed
  meat and pignoli, *139*
  mushroom and cheese, 105
 in a style of Provence, *28, 138*
 with tomatoes, *138*
Zuccotto alla Michelangelo, *29, 46, 49*